SECOND LIFE®

THE OFFICIAL GUIDE

SECOND EDITION

Michael Rymaszewski

Wagner James Au

Cory Ondrejka

Richard Platel

Sara Van Gorden

Jeannette Cézanne

Paul Cézanne

Ben Batstone-Cunningham

Aleks Krotoski

Celebrity Trollop

Jim Rossignol

Wiley Publishing, Inc.

ACQUISITIONS EDITOR: WILLEM KNIBBE

DEVELOPMENT EDITOR: CANDACE ENGLISH

PRODUCTION EDITOR: PATRICK CUNNINGHAM

COPY EDITOR: CANDACE ENGLISH

PRODUCTION MANAGER: TIM TATE

VICE PRESIDENT AND EXECUTIVE GROUP PUBLISHER: RICHARD SWADLEY

VICE PRESIDENT AND EXECUTIVE PUBLISHER: JOSEPH B. WIKERT

VICE PRESIDENT AND PUBLISHER: NEIL EDDE

MEDIA ASSOCIATE PROJECT MANAGER: LAURA ATKINSON

MEDIA ASSISTANT PRODUCER: ANGIE DENNY

MEDIA QUALITY ASSURANCE: KIT MALONE

BOOK DESIGNER AND COMPOSITOR: PATRICK CUNNINGHAM

PROOFREADER: ASHA JOHNSON

INDEXER: TED LAUX

COVER DESIGNER: RYAN SNEED

COVER ILLUSTRATION: JANE HA

Published by Wiley Publishing, Inc., Indianapolis, Indiana

Published simultaneously in Canada

ISBN: 978-0-470-22775-6

10 9 8 7 6 5 4 3 2 1

When *Second Life* launched in 2003, running on just 16 servers with barely 1,000 dedicated users, it was the culmination of a kind of dream for me. One of the things I'd always been interested in, ever since I was a young boy, was how we manipulate the world around us. The world had so much *stuff* in it; there was always something I wanted to change, something I wanted to add, something I wanted to build out of the things I saw around me. That, to me, was magical: seeing the world change shape in response to the ideas in my head. One of the things I wanted to do when we started developing *Second Life* almost a decade ago was to give anyone a chance to work that same magic.

That's exactly what we have. *Second Life* now runs on more than 3,000 servers and has close to two million registered users, but the fundamental idea of the world hasn't changed: it's a place where you can turn the pictures in your head into a kind of pixelated reality. It's a venue for self-expression that's among the richest and most satisfying out there. In *Second Life*, if you see something you want to build or change, the ability to do so is at your fingertips. The world is a place you experience, but more importantly, it's a place you create.

And those users—you—have created quite a world. You add millions of objects to *Second Life*—in the form of cars, clothes, castles, and every other kind of thing you can imagine—every day. You spend close to $5 million there every month; and that's money you spend not on the things Linden Lab creates, but on the things that other users have created and added to the world. To me, that's the beauty of *Second Life*: all we've created is a platform, an almost empty world; where we got lucky is in the fact that you came along and breathed life into it. If *Second Life* is a world at all, it's because you've created it.

When Wiley approached us about this book, it seemed like a great opportunity to let even more people be involved in that process of creation. Like *Second Life* itself, the book developed as a collaboration. Michael Rymaszewski and the other authors have been helped by any number of residents who've contributed their thoughts and experiences throughout the text. Here you'll find information, tips, stories, profiles, and even some secrets that should make a great offline resource for everyone, but especially for new residents. If you're looking for a way to get on your feet quickly in *Second Life*, this book is a great choice.

For those brand-new to virtual worlds, you need not fear. *Second Life*'s geography, society, culture, and technology are all laid out here in easy-to-understand terms. There's a wealth of information and practical advice about creating and customizing your avatar, building objects, earning money, becoming part of a community, and more. In various chapters, profiles of *Second Life* residents give a look at how various people have found their place in the world, be it socially, through business ventures, as game developers, or simply as visitors to the fascinating society that's emerging as a result of their efforts.

The main purpose of this book is to allow you to more easily become part of that society yourself. *Second Life* is growing every day; all it takes to get in on the action is a computer, an Internet connection, and an open mind. There's a lot of stuff in *Second Life*, but there's always room for more. I look forward to seeing what you add to the world you find there.

—Philip Rosedale
CEO and Founder, Linden Lab

Dedication

To Olga, who inspired me to get a second life

—Michael Rymaszewski

Acknowledgments

It's not easy to write a guide to a virtual world, a place that exists in cyberspace. There were voices raised that said it's just impossible—and without many extra voices, that might have well been true. Just like *Second Life*, this book has been created thanks to many people contributing to its content.

So, a very big thank-you to everyone who worked on the book. Willem Knibbe at Wiley was the person who actually conceived this book and made sure it became reality. Candace English edited it so that it reads as well as it does, and Patrick Cunningham made it look as good as it does. At Linden Lab, Catherine Smith exhibited a saint-like patience in dealing with numerous requests for help and extra information. Last but not least, many *SL* residents contributed quotes on selected topics—little pearls of wisdom that will improve the quality of your virtual life.

Thank you, guys. You're the kind of people one hopes to meet when starting another life.

—Michael Rymaszewski

Michael Rymaszewski is a veteran writer who has authored more than 20 strategy guides. His *Age of Empires III: Sybex Official Strategies and Secrets* was named a Best Computer & Internet Book of 2005 by Amazon.com. Michael wrote Chapters 5, 6, 7, and 13, and compiled the appendices.

Wagner James Au writes New World Notes (`http://nwn.blogs.com`) and covers the culture and business of high technology and gaming for GigaOM.com, Kotaku.com, Salon.com, and *Wired*. He's also written for the *Los Angeles Times*, *Smart Business*, and *Game Developer*, among other publications and websites. From 2003 to 2006 he served as the embedded journalist for *Second Life, and he's currently an SL* partner with the metaverse development company Millions of Us. You can contact him at `wjamesau@well.com`. James wrote Chapters 4 and 14, and updated Chapters 1 and 2.

Cory Ondrejka is chief technical officer at Linden Lab. He leads the *Second Life* development team in creating and leveraging such technologies as distributed physical simulation, 3D streaming, and real-time, in-world editors. He also spearheaded the decision to allow users to retain IP rights to their creations, helped craft Linden's virtual real-estate policy, and created the Linden Scripting Language. Cory coauthored Chapter 9.

Richard Platel, aka Wednesday Grimm, has been a resident of *Second Life* and an LSL scripter since before the public beta, and has been a professional software developer for over seven years. Richard organized and help create the very first *Second Life* group build and community, Lindenberg. He has created many popular builds and scripts, and recently scripted the marine life in sim Meteora. Richard coauthored Chapter 9.

Sara van Gorden is a lead graphic designer and builder at The Electric Sheep Company. There she builds custom textures, avatars, buildings, and animations. She has been with The Electric Sheep Company since 2006. Sara wrote Chapter 8.

Jeannette Cézanne (aka Sherpa Voyager) writes reviews for Second Seeker, is a published author of both novels and nonfiction, has had her work translated into 15 languages, and does freelance gigs for publications ranging from industry-specific magazines to literary e-zines. She provides copywriting and search engine optimization services through her company, Customline Wordware, writes a weekly column for *7-Plus*, a Romanian newspaper, and is a frequent and popular speaker at international conferences. Jeannette co-authored Chapter 3.

Paul Cézanne (aka Seeker Gray) is the founder of Second Seeker (`www.secondseeker.com`), a blog that provides ongoing reviews of interesting non-sleazy places and activities residents can try out in *Second Life*. While still a student at MIT he once had the opportunity to restart the Internet. He's a real-life software engineer working on user interface projects and is a *Second Life* artist working with glass and political statements (as PleaseWakeMeUpIdler, with a gallery at Artropolis). Paul co-authored Chapter 3.

Ben Batstone-Cunningham helped start the *Second Life* machinima community when he was still creating new *SL* scripts at Linden Lab. He soon realized it was more fun to be part of the community full time, and left to start Alt-Zoom Studios, a development agency in *SL*. Ben wrote Chapter 10.

Aleks Krotoski has written about interactivity professionally since 1999. She writes about the social dimensions of interactive entertainment, emerging community experiences in virtual worlds, and other aspects of social software. She also writes policy, government, and industry reports covering media regulation, technological forecasting, demographics, game-industry regulation and more; she regularly speaks about interpersonal processes in online communities. Aleks is currently working toward a PhD in social psychology mapping the social relationships and following social influence through the communities of *Second Life*. Aleks wrote Chapter 11.

Celebrity Trollop is the owner, publisher, and editor in chief of Second Style Media, producer of *Second Life*'s original fashion magazine, *Second Style*. Active in *Second Life* since January 2006 and born to shop, Celebrity has become a well-known fashion reviewer and journalist. Behind the keyboard, Celebrity's typist is 33, married, and lives in Minneapolis, Minnesota. Celebrity wrote Chapter 12.

Jim Rossignol is a British author and journalist specializing in writing about video games. He has written for The BBC, *The London Times*, *Wired*, and *PC Gamer UK*. He lives in the historic city of Bath with two cats and an Amazonian crab. Jim wrote Chapter 15.

When you visit a new place—city, country, continent—a good guide comes in really handy. You need a guide that will go beyond advice on which sights are worth seeing and where to stay; a guide that will tell you about the people who inhabit your new destination, the local laws, best places to pick up bargains, and whether it's OK to drink the tap water.

Second Life is a virtual world. A whole world, virtual or not, definitely merits a guide. But how can one give advice and provide guidance about a world that's changing constantly, and much faster than what we call the real world? It's difficult enough when dealing with a land that consists of soil and rock; how does one handle a land made out of bytes? In *Second Life*, changes that would take millennia of groaning and straining in the real world can be completed within a few hours. If real life is all about evolution, *Second Life* is evolution squared. How do you write a guide to a place like that?

Well, to begin with, you focus on things that are there to stay. *Second Life* is and always will be a representation of the world as we know it. It has been conceived by and is being created by humans, and people tend to do things in a certain way. It doesn't matter whether the world they're in is virtual or "real." Real is what exists in the mind. We may live in an enlightened age, but emotions and fantasies rule just like they always did (if you disagree, watch the evening news). And while we may be vastly different from each other on the outside, inside we're all the same: blood, guts, and plenty of dreams. Even the dreams are the same: everyone wants love, success, happiness. The people who don't are either dead or ready to die.

All these banal truths become even more true in *Second Life*. It lets you concentrate single-mindedly on the pursuit of your own, private happiness. You don't need to deal with all the mundane stuff that eats up a lot of time on planet Earth, and you're free to do what you want. The few restrictions that do apply in *SL* are nonintrusive, and simply represent common sense applied to a social situation. In fact, the only thing that may obstruct you in your virtual pursuit of real happiness is real life. Well, what do you expect? It's not easy to live two lives in the same timeframe.

We hope this new, second edition of the Official Guide to *Second Life* will make it easier. Here's what you'll find inside:

Chapter 1 introduces *Second Life*: what it is about, how it came into being, and how it has evolved since its beginning. It discusses basic *SL* concepts and rules, including types of *SL* memberships and their benefits.

Chapter 2 guides you through the process of getting acquainted with *Second Life*. It discusses the *SL* interface, views, and movement within the virtual world, as well as virtual land ownership. It also covers *SL* resident groups and communities.

Chapter 3 takes you on a tour of the virtual world. It lists a number of must-sees for the *SL* tourist—places that represent what might be called the culture of *Second Life*.

Chapter 4 features portraits of interesting *SL* people—residents whose presence in the virtual world has had a lasting impact of one kind or another.

Chapter 5 deals with a pretty delicate subject: your appearance in *Second Life*. It discusses the myriad considerations involved in choosing a good *SL* name for yourself, and the complex task of making your *SL* avatar look the way you want it to look.

Chapter 6 reviews the hundreds of gifts you receive when you enter the virtual world for the first time. These are contained in a special folder called the Library, and they are often overlooked by new *SL* residents.

Chapter 7 advises you on how to manage and tame the *SL* monster known as the Inventory. Your avatar's Inventory is where you keep all your belongings in *Second Life*, including readymade houses, spaceships, and hundreds of cool things to wear. The number of your Inventory items reaches four figures even before you arrive on the *SL* mainland, and getting a good grip on your Inventory is very important—otherwise, you're likely to spend many hours of online time just looking for stuff.

Chapter 8 expertly guides you through the process of creating new objects in the virtual world. It reveals the intricacies of the mysterious prim, explains the *SL* building and object-editing tools, and lets you gain an understanding of the almost-infinite possibilities for creating new stuff in *Second Life*.

Chapter 9 focuses on LSL (the Linden Scripting Language), which is used to write scripts that animate objects in *Second Life*. It explains how LSL works, and what you should know to make it work for you. Together with Chapter 8, it provides all the basic info you need to join in one of the most rewarding activities in *Second Life*: creating new content.

Chapter 10 discusses machinima—the art of making movies in a virtual world. You'll learn about the history of machinima, and about how to create your own machinima, from preproduction through postproduction and screening.

Chapter 11 discusses the process of creating a virtual identity—your *SL* persona. What impact does your real-world self have on your virtual persona? And how do you go about expressing yourself in the virtual world?

Chapter 12 is the shopper's guide to the virtual world. It covers the myriad types of in-world goods, and where you can acquire them.

Chapter 13 talks about making money in *Second Life*. Yes, it's possible to make real money in a virtual setting, and this chapter tells you what's involved. It reviews *SL*'s most popular paying jobs and the considerations involved in running a virtual business.

Chapter 14 describes noteworthy developments and events in *SL* history, such as the famous prim tax revolt.

Finally, **Chapter 15** examines the real-life lessons and real-world value of *Second Life*'s virtual world. There's real life in cyberspace, and this chapter explores the implications.

Eight appendices round out this guide. Appendix A is addressed to real-world educators interested in taking advantage of a virtual environment. Appendix B reviews the presence of media in *SL*—both real-world media companies and their virtual counterparts. Appendix C deals with real-world brands and retail outlets in *Second Life*, and Appendix D contains a glossary of in-world and technical terms. Appendix E directs you to sites that contain valuable *SL* info. Appendix F explains *SL*'s pull-down menu functions. Appendix G covers the *Second Life* community standards, and Appendix H covers what you'll find on the CD that accompanies this book.

We hope you'll find this book as enjoyable as it is useful. See you in *Second Life*.

CONTENTS

⬇ CHAPTER 9: USING THE LINDEN SCRIPTING LANGUAGE — 178

⬇ CHAPTER 13: BUSINESS AND MONEY — 272

⬇ CHAPTER 14: A CULTURAL TIMELINE — 310

CHAPTER 1

WHAT IS SECOND LIFE?

Second Life is a virtual world. No, *Second Life* is a 3D online digital world imagined, created, and owned by its residents. But hang on—there's more: analysts often describe *Second Life* as a metaverse, like the one in the classic cyberpunk novel *Snow Crash*. And here's the coolest thing: all the statements above are true. *Second Life* is basically anything you want it to be. It's your virtual life, after all, and what you do with it is up to you.

Second Life is a virtual environment in which almost all of the content is created by users—people like you. You are the one who determines what *Second Life* means to you. Do you enjoy meeting people online, talking to them, and doing things together in real time? Welcome to *Second Life*. Do you enjoy creating stuff and making it come alive? Welcome to *Second Life*. Do you enjoy running a business and making money—real money? Welcome to *Second Life*. The list of possible *Second Life* activities is as long as you can imagine.

This chapter discusses basic *Second Life* concepts, rules, and activities. Some of these—for example, benefits linked to given types of *SL* memberships—are subject to frequent changes. However, certain basic principles remain constant and are covered here.

CONTENTS

CHAPTER 1

A BRIEF HISTORY
OF *SECOND LIFE*

HOW DOES IT
WORK?

MEMBERSHIP
TYPES

A BRIEF HISTORY OF *SECOND LIFE*

Second Life was originally conceived by Philip Rosedale. Like all artists, he'd always wanted to create a masterpiece that represents the world in a microcosm. Instead of paint, words, marble, or clay, he used bytes. Philip started working on the concept that would become *Second Life* (initially it was called *Linden World*) in 1991. At first it looked like a video game, with flying robots, exploding grenades, and rock-eating snakes, but Rosedale and his early team of developers quickly realized that their users should create their *own* experiences in it. Their job, instead, was to give them—and you—the tools to do so.

FROM LINDEN LAB
SECOND LIFE IS ...

Here's what some Lindens said when we invited them to complete the sentence "*Second Life* is...."

"... a constantly evolving expressive medium." —Morpheus Linden

"... a positive supplement to a first life." —Torley Linden

"... the next frontier." —Prospero Linden

"... all about augmenting your real life. This means doing things you can't do in real life, meeting people you'd never meet in real life, and fully exploring your creative potential. *Second Life* doesn't replace your real life. It makes it better." —Pathfinder Linden

Beta testing began in November 2002, and it was opened to the public just six months later. The beta version included a teleporting fee, as well as a tax on prims (short for *primitives*) on top of land-maintenance costs; fees were charged for rezzing and maintaining all resident-created objects in the virtual world. On the surface, this step seemed very sensible, as every extra prim places a tiny extra burden on the hardware that runs *Second Life*'s virtual world. However, taxing residents' creations wasn't a wise move in a political sense, and it led to big consequences down the line.

On June 23rd, 2003, *Second Life* went live. In October of that year, a major update introduced a host of new features: improved search functions and world map, new land-management options, a new copyright/permission system for resident creations, and many graphic improvements. The update also included tools to minimize tax evasion, but that was counterbalanced by a new stipend called *dwell*, which essentially rewarded people for socializing. Many creative *SL* residents were appalled, believing that pointless gatherings were being rewarded, while creators of new *SL* content were still penalized through prim tax.

The crackdown on prim-tax evaders brought drama and dissent; some *SL* resident groups fell apart, and themed communities were hit particularly hard: making an area reflect a certain theme requires plenty of new prims. The stage was set for a very real-life development; a grass-roots social movement began to form in the virtual world. Within a few weeks, a revolution was underway.

In December 2003, the revolutionaries won: an entirely new tax system based on land ownership *sans* the prim tax was introduced. This update also introduced the concept of *SL* time (same as Pacific Standard Time) and a number of new scripting and interface features.

More updates and improvements followed, and landmark updates introduced custom animations and gestures (June 2004), the LindeX currency exchange (October 2005), and an end to stipends for Basic membership plans (May 2006).

ADDITIONAL INFO
MORE *SL* HISTORY

If you're interested in *SL* history, refer to Chapter 14 and visit the *Second Life* Historical Museum. You'll find the museum's landmark in the *SL* Guidebook that you can obtain on Help Island; you can also use the *SL* Search function to find it. The museum exhibits are updated as *Second Life* evolves, and include many resident creations as well as illustrated presentations of memorable events in *SL* history. Further info can be found at SL Wikia (`http://secondlife.wikia. com/wiki/Main _ Page`). Like the museum exhibits, the history info at SL Wikia is updated constantly with fresh entries and articles as *Second Life* continues to grow and evolve.

HOW DOES IT WORK?

From your point of view, *SL* works as if you were a god. Not an almighty god, perhaps—more like one of those mythological minor gods, who tended to specialize in certain areas, get drunk, have sex, fight, and (most important) cast spells at will. (Figure 1.1). And just like a mythological god, you're also able to fly, and teleport wherever you like in an instant.

You can also change your appearance whenever you want to, and into pretty much whatever you like. In case you've ever dreamed of pulling a Zeus number and wooing someone as a swan, say, *Second Life* offers you the opportunity.

The *SL* virtual world physically resembles the real world. It consists of interlinked regions that contain land, water, *and* air (*SL* lets you build castles in the sky), with gravity, weather, and a sun and moon that regularly cut across the horizon. Each region has an area of 65,536 *Second Life* square meters.

CHAPTER 1

CHAPTER 2

CHAPTER 3

CHAPTER 4

CHAPTER 5

CHAPTER 6

CHAPTER 7

CHAPTER 8

CHAPTER 9

CHAPTER 10

CHAPTER 11

CHAPTER 12

CHAPTER 13

CHAPTER 14

CHAPTER 15

APPENDICES

CHAPTER 1
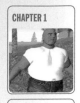

A BRIEF HISTORY
OF *SECOND LIFE*

**HOW DOES IT
WORK?**

MEMBERSHIP
TYPES

Figure 1.1: Abracadabra, one, two, three—pow!

SL regions are both geographical and administrative units: they are governed by rules and regulations that may change from region to region. The entire *Second Life* world is divided into areas that can include any number of regions governed by a given set of rules. For example, a separate area called the Teen grid is reserved for *SL* members between the ages of 13 and 17. Members in that age group are not allowed into the main adult area, and vice versa. You'll find more info on *SL* mores, customs, and social etiquette later in this chapter, and in Chapter 2.

ADDITIONAL INFO
REGIONS AS SIMS

SL residents often refer to regions as *sims*—short for simulators. This is because originally, one server or simulator held one entire region. Now there are two regions per server, but the old name has stuck.

Second Life is populated by avatars: virtual representations of *SL* members, known as residents. The *SL* world also contains a great variety of objects. Ranging from palaces to pebbles, almost all the objects in *Second Life* have been created by *SL* citizens. Creating new objects—clothes, guns, spaceships—is one of the most popular *SL* activities, and the driving force behind *SL* commerce. *Second Life* keeps track of everything that's happening in its virtual world by assigning unique identifiers not only to in-world objects and avatars, but also to anything that has significance (see the "How *Second Life* Keeps Track of Things" sidebar).

FROM LINDEN LAB
HOW *SECOND LIFE* KEEPS TRACK OF THINGS

"A UUID (Universally Unique Identifier) is a 16-byte string that looks like this: 987fc1b0-bd3b-47fb-8506-2b1ffbec8984—it's 8 characters, 4 characters, 4 characters, 4 characters, 12 characters, all separated with hyphens.

"Across the *Second Life* platform, we use UUIDs in a variety of places where we want to represent a complex bundle of data with a smaller, simpler reference—a UUID is only 16 bytes long. Some of the data that have a UUID 'name' include the following:

- Avatar agents.
- Land parcels. As you create, subdivide, merge, or otherwise modify parcels, they get a new UUID every time.
- Groups. Every group that is made gets a UUID.
- Regions. They not only have a unique name, but they also have unique UUIDs.
- Simulator states, which are snapshots of a region. These are periodically saved and given a UUID.
- Money transactions and inventory transactions.
- Your login sessions.
- Folders in your inventory.
- Any snapshot you take.
- Every event or classified ad you create.
- Assets, which are sharable resources including textures, objects, landmarks, clothing, and almost anything that goes in your inventory.

"What does this mean? Well, any of the data above is guaranteed to be unique across space and time—that is to say, if you have a texture and you know its UUID, you can be confident that no other texture had, has, or will have the same UUID.

"Many LSL functions take a UUID and operate on the texture/sound/inventory item with that UUID. For example, you must give `llSetTexture()` the UUID of the texture you want to set your object to."

—Jeff Luan, Linden Lab

⬇ THE MAGIC PRIM

Almost all the objects you see in *Second Life* are created or built from solids (3D geometric shapes) called prims. Each region can support 15,000 prims (plus a reserve of around 10 percent over that number so the system can account for moving objects).

Figure 1.2: Your ability to create and manipulate prims is probably the most godlike feature of *Second Life*.

Prims can assume any shape you want, but they begin in a variety of shapes to make transformations easier. You can also make prims look any way you want by applying selected textures to their surfaces (Figure 1.2). They can be given certain qualities and features (such as transparency or the ability to flex/bend with the wind), they can be linked together, and they can be made to *do* things by a script written in LSL—*Second Life*'s scripting language. For example, a *Second Life* dog that runs and barks is an animated object made of linked prims, scripted to move in a certain way and play custom sound effects. In mid 2007, Linden Lab introduced "sculpted" prims, which enable residents to import graphic tiles that change a prim's topography, for even more detail and variety. You'll find a detailed discussion of prim- and scripting-related issues in Chapters 8 and 9.

You don't have to be a building and scripting guru to acquire and enjoy all the objects you'd like to have in *Second Life*. Like in real life, you can buy them with the local currency, in this case Linden dollars. But unlike in real life, you can also count on being given tons of cool freebies the moment your avatar enters the *SL* world. The Library folder in your Inventory is packed with stuff—follow the advice in Chapter 6 of this guide, and check it out. Many new *SL* citizens don't, and some of them subsequently spend a lot of Linden dollars to buy items they already have in their Libraries from a smiling con man (or con woman). Yes, those exist in *Second Life*, too.

FROM LINDEN LAB
LINDEN PLANTS

Linden plants from the Library are special objects with unique properties. Although they appear to be much more complex than prims, each plant counts as a single prim—something to keep in mind when you become a proud property owner and want to do some landscaping.

⬇ *SL* Money

As you know by now, *Second Life* has its own currency: the Linden dollar. Linden dollars are exchangeable for real-life dollars. The exchange rate fluctuates; like most real currencies, its market value is determined by supply and demand (while supply, in turn, is influenced by ongoing tweaks to *SL* stipends and bonuses, as well as the ratio between new Premium and Basic accounts started by fresh *SL* residents—the differences between these two account types are discussed in the section at the end of this chapter).

At this writing, US$1 is worth nearly 270 Linden dollars. Historical highs had the exchange rate hovering in the low 200s per US$1, while a relatively recent low saw an exchange rate of well over L$300 to US$1. Inside *Second Life*, a Linden dollar has much more purchasing power than real-life money, of course. (A glamorous wardrobe or a luxury car can run you the L$ equivalent of a few bucks, for example.)

You can obtain Linden dollars in a variety of ways (which are described in Chapter 13). Your means of earning income are as numerous as in the real world, if not more so, You may opt to take a virtual job—the *SL* Classifieds always feature many job ads—or you may want to try turning a profit by running your own business. If you're a gamer, you can make money playing games of skill; if you're talented, you can design and create saleable items; you can even earn some L$ by visiting the many regions where land owners actually pay residents to hang out as a way of promoting their events and activities. (They usually don't pay a lot, though—around L$3 every 15 minutes. Then again, while L$3 is roughly worth one US cent, it can buy you a lot of nice items in *Second Life*.) You can also buy Linden dollars with *SL*'s LindeX exchange, and at a number of third-party currency exchanges, paying in US dollars or euros. This is often a wise course of action since it lets you spend your *SL* time on activities other than on making money.

Depending on the membership plan you choose, you may also receive Linden dollars when you begin your *SL* membership. This is discussed in more detail later in this chapter.

CHAPTER 1
CHAPTER 2
CHAPTER 3
CHAPTER 4
CHAPTER 5
CHAPTER 6
CHAPTER 7
CHAPTER 8
CHAPTER 9
CHAPTER 10
CHAPTER 11
CHAPTER 12
CHAPTER 13
CHAPTER 14
CHAPTER 15
APPENDICES

CHAPTER 1

A BRIEF HISTORY
OF *SECOND LIFE*

**HOW DOES IT
WORK?**

MEMBERSHIP
TYPES

👁 ADDITIONAL INFO
THE BEST THINGS IN *SECOND LIFE* ARE FREE

You don't have to have money to enjoy the best *Second Life* has to offer. Making new friends is free of charge, and so is having a fun time doing something you like with people you like. Yes, owning a few things that bring private joy is nice, but you'll find out that in *Second Life* you can get lots of very nice stuff for free, or, of course, create your own objects in the many "free build" sandboxes. Check the *SL* Classifieds for offers by *SL* merchants, and once you log into www. secondlife.com, check Resident Resources for a full list of third-party *SL* retail websites. And as mentioned earlier, in *SL* you can make Linden dollars by just hanging around in specific locales for a while.

⬇ YOU AND YOUR AVATAR

In *Second Life*'s virtual world, your avatar represents you. You can change your avatar's appearance as often as you like. *SL*'s interface includes a powerful avatar-appearance editor, and on top of that every avatar comes with a Library full of modification goodies, including a number of complete alternate avatars. Very broadly, an avatar consists of shape (the body) and outfit (what's worn on the body, plus any body attachments). You'll find a discussion of avatar-appearance editing options in Chapter 5, and more details about the Library in Chapter 6.

Figure 1.3: I wonder if that's really me....

The vast majority of *SL* citizens opt to stay human in *Second Life*. But some choose avatars inspired by fictional characters from real-life movies, comic strips, or books. There are more vampires in *Second Life* than in all of Transylvania (they are very friendly vampires, for the most part). The Furries—*SL* residents who choose to role play furry animal avatars—are another large group. Interestingly, some groups have grown so big and have become so highly organized that they're referred to as *micronations*.

Your avatar choices say a lot about who you are; to the people you encounter in the *SL* world, your avatar *is* who you are. It's true, too—your avatar choices reflect your personality and mentality. It's good to keep that in mind (Figure 1.3).

Avatar choices do not affect your access to *Second Life* options and privileges *except* when they breach community standards. So you may want to think twice before you attach a potentially offensive appendage to your avatar prior to a stroll through the streets of *Second Life*. Of course, you are free to be just about as radical as you want on land that you own, or on any privately owned or group-owned land whose owners allow anything and everything. This and other aspects of land ownership are discussed in Chapter 2.

⬇ What to Do with Your New Life

As you know by now, *Second Life* gives you the freedom to pursue your dreams and interests. For some residents, this means having as much virtual sex as possible; for others, it may mean attending a religious service or playing combat games in spaceships they helped build. You'll find examples of various *SL* lifestyles in Chapters 4 and 11.

Virtual hedonism is fun, of course, but do not let it blind you to other possible *SL* activities. For many residents, *Second Life* primarily represents a great opportunity to develop their talents as creators and artists. In addition to building and scripting, *Second Life* lets you take photographs (i.e., screenshots) and make movies. If you feel talented in one of these areas, you could gain more than just applause. Because residents retain the underlying intellectual property rights to their *SL*-based creations, they can shop them in the real world; some top creators have sold the rights to their *SL* games, movies, and artwork to outside companies. Chapter 3 discusses these activities in more detail.

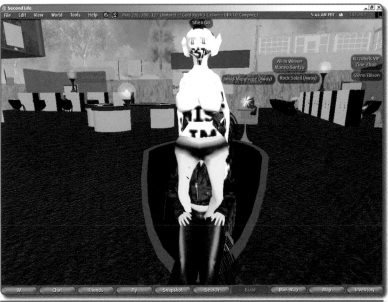

Figure 1.4: You'll see plenty of interesting new faces in *Second Life*.

For a lot of *SL* citizens, however, the virtual world is simply a great place to meet other people (Figure 1.4). It is also a great place to play with others—as explained earlier, *Second Life* allows all kinds of virtual social interaction. Whatever takes place in *Second Life* happens by mutual consent: anyone who does not like what's going on can leave the world with two mouse clicks. It's also a great place to interact with people not just one-on-one, but via group instant messaging, where dozens or even hundreds can participate in live conversation—an important communication platform that's become more important in recent years as the population has grown.

CHAPTER 1

CHAPTER 2

CHAPTER 3

CHAPTER 4

CHAPTER 5

CHAPTER 6

CHAPTER 7

CHAPTER 8

CHAPTER 9

CHAPTER 10

CHAPTER 11

CHAPTER 12

CHAPTER 13

CHAPTER 14

CHAPTER 15

APPENDICES

CHAPTER 1

A BRIEF HISTORY
OF *SECOND LIFE*

HOW DOES IT
WORK?

MEMBERSHIP
TYPES

The right thing to do, of course, is not to leave the world, but simply to find something that you *do* like. There's no shortage of choices—shopping, visiting art galleries, skydiving, bowling, and attending live dance recitals and concerts are just some of the options available. Note also that not all the people you meet in *SL* are there just to have fun. Increasingly, *Second Life* is the venue for real-world companies, study, and research programs—a place where scientists, businesspeople, teachers, programmers, and students can meet even though they're thousands of miles apart in the real world.

ADDITIONAL INFO
SECOND LIFE EVENTS

Second Life is rich in events of all kinds—from movie festivals and shows by major real-life artists to local events organized by individual residents. Locations of current and upcoming events are marked by a pink or purple star on the world map, and advertised both in the *SL* Classifieds and at `http://secondlife.com/events/`. For a full list of *SL* events, click the Search button and select the Events tab on the Search panel.

Second Life does contain rules and regulations that limit resident activities: different areas allow different types of activity. Areas listed as Mature allow activities that you would see in a movie rated for adults, while PG areas impose stricter rules. Many areas are dedicated to pursuing a specific kind of activity within a specific environment.

However, a general principle applies to all activities: no matter what they are, there is a place for nearly all of them somewhere in *Second Life*. If you're exceptionally hard to satisfy, then you'll want to acquire private land and set your own rules. Many *SL* residents form groups to purchase land and set their own rules to pursue shared interests. However, land ownership is permitted only with Premium *SL* membership; see the relevant section further on in this chapter for more details.

ADDITIONAL INFO
ROLE PLAYING

Role playing is very popular among *SL* residents, and areas are specially themed to enhance the role-playing experience. If you've always dreamed of living in the Victorian era or in the Wild West, you can—see Chapters 2 and 3 for more info. Interestingly, one of the most popular forms of individual roleplay in *Second Life* is real-life males appearing as virtual females and vice versa—in one online poll, 18.6% of male members confessed to living their *Second Life* as the opposite sex.

⬇ *SL* Rules and Etiquette

Second Life's community standards are listed on a notecard in your Library (Notecards folder). There are six cardinal sins (called "the Big Six"):

- 🔷 **Intolerance.** As in real life, being derogatory or demeaning another person's race, ethnicity, gender, religion, or sexual orientation is a big no-no.

- 🔷 **Harassment.** Harassment can take very many forms, but the common denominator is that someone is intruded upon. If your actions or words are upsetting someone and they make that plain more than once, stop.

- 🔷 **Assault.** This includes pushing, shooting, and shoving another *SL* resident in an area marked as Safe (Safe status is displayed as an icon on the top info bar). Making fellow residents miserable by attacking them with scripted objects is forbidden, too.

- 🔷 **Disclosure.** Information about another resident can be freely shared only if it is displayed in the resident's profile, or if you have their consent to share this information. This includes residents' real-life data as well as their conversations in-world and on other official Linden Lab sites (forums, blogs, etc.)—posting or otherwise sharing conversation logs requires prior consent of the people affected.

- 🔷 **Indecency.** It's simple: if what you want to do can be offensive to other people, do it on private land in Mature areas.

- 🔷 **Disturbing the peace.** Briefly, don't be a pest. Every resident is entitled to an enjoyable, peaceful *Second Life*.

Figure 1.5: You may find a new friend among the dragons, vampires, and gangstas of *Second Life*.

As you can see, *SL* community standards are pretty reasonable and straightforward, and they amount to this: don't interfere with other people's enjoyment of their virtual experience. If what you want to do constitutes a threat to other people's enjoyment, do it at home—that means on land owned by yourself or by a group of *SL* citizens who share your special interests. Otherwise, just employ the same common sense you use in real life to decide what sort of behavior is acceptable. This will leave you with a comfortable safety margin—*Second Life* is a more relaxed social environment than the real world, and the people inhabiting its world are markedly friendlier than you're used to in real life (Figure 1.5). It's interesting to note *Second Life* is particularly appreciated by women; see the "Being a Woman in *Second Life*" sidebar.

CHAPTER 1

CHAPTER 2

CHAPTER 3

CHAPTER 4

CHAPTER 5

CHAPTER 6

CHAPTER 7

CHAPTER 8

CHAPTER 9

CHAPTER 10

CHAPTER 11

CHAPTER 12

CHAPTER 13

CHAPTER 14

CHAPTER 15

APPENDICES

CHAPTER 1

A BRIEF HISTORY
OF *SECOND LIFE*

HOW DOES IT
WORK?

MEMBERSHIP
TYPES

RESIDENTS SPEAK
BEING A WOMAN IN *SECOND LIFE*

RESIDENTS

"*SL* is a world where women have equality to a much greater extent than in RL [real life]. The primary advantage men have over women in RL, which influences many things, is physical strength. Here I am just as strong as any man. I don't need him to move or lift something. I can truly do anything men can do. So I have an equal opportunity to do anything I want to try.

"Also, the good-old-boy networks do not exist. Men aren't given advantages just because they are men.

"I don't have to split my time between a man, children, and doing what I want to do. I don't have to feel guilty if I chose work over children. If a woman wants to devote full time to making money, she can easily do so and not feel guilty.

"The second advantage is harder to explain. It has to do with a sense of security. Here, I can get all the attention and positive affirmation without the downside. I don't have to worry about unwanted attention. I do not have to fear the male's greater physical strength.

"The last thing that comes to mind is that the little girl inside can be as beautiful as she likes. All the wishes 'if only I…' can come true. We can be as glamorous, sexy, trampish, or whatever as we wish. We are not judged by men on looks we can't do anything about."

—Jennifer McLuhan

"Personally, I enjoy *SL* for a lot of reasons… this world has opportunities for everybody; where you go and how well you do is based on your imagination and your talent, not your connections or your gender or any other thing that influences RL opportunities.

"I enjoy it because I love being able to do so many things that aren't possible in the real world… and because I love having the tools to turn anything from my imagination into reality. I love being able to meet so many people who I'd never have a chance to meet in RL.

"And yes, I enjoy *SL* because I love being able to look as good as I want, being able to change my look in an instant, being able to look completely different from my RL self.

"And I totally understand the security thing… it's great to have control here, to not have to worry about my personal safety. That's equally true for anyone here, male or female, but it's particularly significant for women, I think."

—Ilianexsi Sojourner

CHAPTER 1

CHAPTER 2

CHAPTER 3

CHAPTER 4

CHAPTER 5

CHAPTER 6

CHAPTER 7

CHAPTER 8

CHAPTER 9

CHAPTER 10

CHAPTER 11

CHAPTER 12

CHAPTER 13

CHAPTER 14

CHAPTER 15

APPENDICES

"I wanted to see what it would be like to play a male, so here's how it went:

"Went shopping. Limited choices! Men have limited choices in *Second Life* and real life. I guess it would be difficult making male lingerie or something sexy for men. The clothes were as pricey as female, but there wasn't much to buy. No wonder why there are so many female avatars.

"Went to a few clubs and found that men get catty like women, especially over other women. A guy wanted to kick my ass just for talking to his virtual girlfriend.

"I told people that I am a scripter and no questions were asked, but when I was a female avatar questions were asked, including 'Are you a male in RL?'

"I thought it would be easier to be a male, but not really. Women have more choices of clothing, hair, shoes, etc."

—Damien Ferris

ADDITIONAL INFO
COMMUNITY RULES

Make sure you read the Community Standards notecard! Taking out an *SL* membership means you automatically agree to respect *SL* rules. Penalties include suspension and banishment from *Second Life*.

MEMBERSHIP TYPES

As *Second Life* marches on, it evolves. Accordingly, membership plans can and do change. However, it's a safe bet that future variations will include the two membership types that are available at the time of writing. These are Basic membership and Premium membership, and both let you have lots of fun (see the "Membership Type Choices" sidebar).

A BRIEF HISTORY
OF *SECOND LIFE*

HOW DOES IT
WORK?

**MEMBERSHIP
TYPES**

RESIDENTS SPEAK
MEMBERSHIP TYPE CHOICES

"Well, I am a free [Basic] member and can honestly say I'm having a ball here. Sure, if you want to own land you have to pay for a Premium account, but if your goal is simply to meet people and have fun at events you can easily do that for free. If you want extra L$ to buy clothes or whatever, you could use the camping chairs or dance pads. You can also attend games like trivia contests and bingo and maybe win some L$. I won L$100 last night at an '80s trivia event.

"There are so many cool things to see at *SL* that I never get bored just looking around. If you want a home you can always rent land and get a free house at a yard sale (I'm doing this right now).

"Have fun, because that is the best part of *SL*!"

—Hedgie Till

"[Until recently I] still wore freebie jeans. I have a Premium account and spent very few L$, yet I still manage to have fun and create and feel that I am getting all of the game.

"It all depends on your perception of 'all of the game.' Do you want to spend money on all sorts of gadgets, or do you want to create, explore, and try all sorts of different things?

"I don't see why a free account member cannot have the same experience that a Premium account member does, aside from owning land. Do you really need a house? Are you actually going to sleep in *SL*?

"Get out, explore the world, experiment with building and scripting; most of all, enjoy yourself!!! Welcome to *Second Life*."

—Artemis Cain

ADDITIONAL INFO
A DUAL-ACCOUNT LIFE

For current information about *Second Life* membership plans, visit `http://secondlife.com/whatis/plans.php`. Consider establishing a free Basic membership right away to get a taste of what *Second Life* is like, and when you're ready to put down roots, create a second, Premium account that lets you own land. It is always worth your while to have two *Second Life* accounts, as it lets you easily back up your Inventory.

⬇ Basic Membership

CHAPTER 1

CHAPTER 2

CHAPTER 3

CHAPTER 4

CHAPTER 5

CHAPTER 6

CHAPTER 7

CHAPTER 8

CHAPTER 9

CHAPTER 10

CHAPTER 11

CHAPTER 12

CHAPTER 13

CHAPTER 14

CHAPTER 15

APPENDICES

A Basic membership plan entitles you to enter *Second Life* completely free of charge. It lets you enjoy all of *Second Life*'s activities and privileges except for one: you cannot own land in the *SL* world. (The consequences of this are explained later in this chapter.)

You may open additional Basic membership accounts; at the time of writing, each extra Basic account costs a one-time fee of US$9.95. In spite of the cost, this might be a wise step if you have many Inventory items that you'd hate to lose. Creating a second account lets you create an alternate resident name and identity. Many residents like to maintain two or more accounts so they can freely explore different aspects of *Second Life*: one avatar for casual fun, for example, with another for taking care of in-world business. Furthermore, having an alternate avatar lets you back up your Inventory. This might not sound like a big deal if you've just started out as an *SL* resident. But after you've spent some time in-world, your Inventory is likely to contain many thousands of items, and at least a few one-off specimens that cannot be copied. The process of backing up your Inventory is described in Chapter 7.

⬇ Premium Membership

Premium membership lets you own land. (Many residents prefer to sublet a parcel from landowning residents, rather than upgrade to Premium, however.) The advantages and disadvantages of land ownership are discussed in Chapters 2 and 13; however, be aware that having space of your own in *Second Life* is important. It lets you store items outside an avatar's Inventory (see Chapter 7 for details).

Premium membership costs vary depending on how you choose to pay. At the time of writing, the base rate of $9.95 per month shrinks to $6 when paid in an annual lump sum. Regardless of payment plan, you receive the coveted land-ownership rights plus a L$1,000 signup bonus and a weekly stipend of L$300. Note that all the quoted numbers are subject to change; please visit `http://secondlife.com/whatis/plans.php` for updated info.

There is no limit on how much land you can own in *SL*. However, the cost of owning land increases with the size of your real-estate holdings. This and other practical issues are discussed in the next chapter.

ADDITIONAL INFO
JOINING *SECOND LIFE* THROUGH ALTERNATE SITES

It's now possible to create an *SL* account and begin your orientation through alternate website portals run by third-party organizations. Some of them are operated by established companies, others by educational or nonprofit groups; all of them are aimed at creating an initial experience in *Second Life* that's customized for their version of the *SL* experience. Many of them are designed for non–English speakers, others are associated with popular TV shows and brands. Take a look at the official *Second Life* blog (`http://blog.secondlife.com/`) to check announcements of one that might be the best starting point for your own *Second Life*.

CHAPTER 2

GETTING STARTED

Living a life means making choices, and you'll be making plenty from the moment you log into *Second Life* for the first time.

There is a third-person view and a first-person view. There are pull-down menus at the top of the screen and a button menu at the bottom. Should you stay on Help Island for a while, or dive into the action on the mainland right away? And once you've arrived on the mainland, what should you do next?

This chapter will help you sort out those and other issues that appear the moment you begin your virtual existence. It is intended mainly for new *SL* denizens, but it can also be very helpful to anyone who impatiently dived headfirst into *Second Life*. If you've ever wished you could return to Help Island, if only to grab some of the new freebies that have become available there, this chapter's for you, too.

CONTENTS

CHAPTER 2

TAKING CONTROL
OF YOUR *SECOND
LIFE*

LEARNING ABOUT
SECOND LIFE

TAKING CONTROL OF YOUR *SECOND LIFE*

Being familiar with the *Second Life* interface enriches your virtual experience: almost every button, menu, and options panel is a doorway to new possibilities. The following sections synthesize the main interface info for your convenience. You'll find some extra information and how-to instructions in the *Second Life* Knowledge Base (`http://secondlife.com/knowledgebase`).

ADDITIONAL INFO
KEYBOARD SHORTCUTS

To obtain a list of *SL* keyboard shortcuts, visit `http://wiki.secondlife.com/wiki/ Help:Keyboard _ shortcut _ keys`. It's a good idea to print the list and keep it handy until you've memorized the shortcuts you use. The camera-control shortcuts are particularly helpful.

⬇ FIRST STEPS

If you intend to become a new *SL* resident, begin by checking whether your system allows you run the viewer software. At the time of writing, the system requirements are as follows. (Please note that this book is written with the assumption that you're using a PC as the portal to your second life. If you're using a Mac, please refer to `http://secondlife.com/corporate/sysreqs.php`.)

- **High-speed Internet connection:** DSL, cable, wireless, etc.

- **Operating system:** Windows Vista, Windows XP (Service Pack 2), *or* Windows 2000 (Service Pack 4)

- **Computer Processor:** 800MHz Pentium III or better

- **Memory:** 256MB or better

- **Video/graphics card:** NVIDIA GeForce 2, GeForce 4mx, or better *or* ATI Radeon 8500, 9250, or better

ADDITIONAL INFO
VISTA COMPATIBILITY

Note that while *SL* has been upgraded to support Windows Vista, there are unique system requirements for Vista users. See the system-requirements URL on the next page for details.

To view the very latest system requirements, please visit `http://secondlife.com/corporate/sysreqs.php`.

CHAPTER 1

CHAPTER 2

CHAPTER 3

CHAPTER 4

CHAPTER 5

CHAPTER 6

CHAPTER 7

CHAPTER 8

CHAPTER 9

CHAPTER 10

CHAPTER 11

CHAPTER 12

CHAPTER 13

CHAPTER 14

CHAPTER 15

APPENDICES

Figure 2.1: Adjusting the settings on the Preferences panel can optimize *SL* performance on your computer.

If you're running a firewall, note that *Second Life* needs to connect to ports 443/TCP, 12035/UDP, 12036/UDP, and 13000-13050/UDP. You should configure your firewall to allow outbound traffic on those ports, and related inbound traffic.

Upon launching the *Second Life* software, you're presented with a login screen that contains an important button: Preferences (Figure 2.1). Many new *SL* citizens are so eager to enter the virtual world that they never check it out. If you're one of them, click it the next time you log in. It opens the Preferences panel, which contains 12 tabs:

ADDITIONAL INFO
THE AGE OF VERIFICATION

As of this writing, Linden Lab is implementing and beta-testing a voluntary age/identify verification from a third-party company called Integrity. By early 2008, this system will likely be in active use—it's an opt-in system for landowners who want to protect themselves from liability by blocking unauthorized under-age users from their Mature content, or to check other real-world information. When visiting a private island, you may be asked to go through this process, and you may choose to do so, or not to.

- **General** offers basic *SL* options such as avatar name and title display, notifications of friends online and of money spent or received, etc.

- **Input and Camera** lets you adjust mouse sensitivity in mouselook (first-person view) and a quality called camera springiness. If you're after precision, use the sliders to reduce mouse sensitivity and camera springiness to 0.

- **Network** is where you configure settings if you're logging onto *Second Life* from inside a LAN. You can also lower maximum bandwidth if you have a slow connection (the default of 500 kbps is comfortably in excess of actual available bandwidth). Disk Cache Size determines how much

CHAPTER 2

TAKING CONTROL
OF YOUR *SECOND
LIFE*

LEARNING ABOUT
SECOND LIFE

of the *Second Life* world is streamed and stored in your computer's temporary memory; people with computers several years old might improve their performance by lowering this, and also clicking Clear Cache.

Web determines performance of the web browser that appears in your avatar profile (more on that later) and elsewhere in your viewer.

Graphics presents basic graphic settings such as screen resolution and draw distance. Draw distance determines how far you can see in the virtual world. If you have a relatively slow system or an old video card, lowering draw distance and screen resolution can improve performance.

Graphics Detail. This lets you adjust the amount of detail visible in the virtual world. Lower settings improve performance on slow systems/old video cards. Note that some options, such as Enable Ripple Water, may be disabled if your system or video card is not up to par.

Adv. Graphics presents more graphic-detail choices; their effects are explained in the submenu. Generally, lowering the displayed default values improves performance on your PC but decreases graphic vividness and realism.

Audio and Video contains options you'll definitely want to review. They include audio muting, playing streaming music and videos, SFX volume, etc.

Text Chat lets you switch chat bubbles on and off, change the color and size of displayed text, and adjust miscellaneous chat settings.

Voice Chat configures and adjusts your voice-communication feature.

Communication adjusts the way you interact in the world. Go here to determine whether you'd like your online status to be publicly known, how you want your chat and IM logs saved, and more.

Popups lets you choose which messages you want to see displayed in the world.

Take the time to review the default settings in the Preferences panel, and adjust them as appropriate for your system and Internet connection. If you'd like more info on what individual options can do for you, visit the Knowledge Base in the support area of the *Second Life* website.

ADDITIONAL INFO
THE STATISTIC BAR

To get detailed info on how well *Second Life* is running on your computer, activate the Statistic Bar by pressing Control-Shift-1. Visit the *Second Life* Knowledge Base to find out more.

⬇ What's on the Menu

CHAPTER 1

CHAPTER 2

CHAPTER 3

CHAPTER 4

CHAPTER 5

CHAPTER 6

CHAPTER 7

CHAPTER 8

CHAPTER 9

CHAPTER 10

CHAPTER 11

CHAPTER 12

CHAPTER 13

CHAPTER 14

CHAPTER 15

APPENDICES

Figure 2.2: The pull-down menus contain commands and helpful shortcuts, such as the one to the LSL scripting guide.

Second Life's main screen features a top bar and a bottom bar. Both are packed fairly tightly with features. Many of these, though not all, are discussed in the *SL* Knowledge Base in the Support area of the *Second Life* website. The following sections review what is what.

The top bar includes a set of Windows-style pull-down menus (Figure 2.2). Some of the commands available through the pull-down menus are *not* accessible through any other menu or shortcut. You'll find a full list of pull-down menu commands and an explanation of their functions in Appendix F.

To the right of the pull-down menus, you'll see icons showing whether any activities are disallowed in your avatar's present location. If you are unsure what an icon means, hover your mouse cursor over it to bring up a tooltip. Your avatar's location—name of region, map coordinates, area rating, etc.—is shown right next to the icons.

Moving farther right, you'll see a clock displaying Pacific Standard Time. Residents call it "*SL* time." Money comes next: the little round Linden-dollar icon lets you buy *SL* currency through the LindeX (Basic members should note this requires credit card info). Your current L$ balance is next: it's updated instantly following every financial transaction. Finally, at the extreme right of the top bar, you'll see packet-loss and bandwidth indicators, represented by two vertical bars. Pay attention to these; high packet loss and low bandwidth may mean it's wise to cancel that planned visit to a busy nightclub.

THE BOTTOM LINE

The bottom bar features a row of buttons. From left to right, here's what is what:

💠 **Communicate** opens a panel listing all the *SL* residents who've agreed to be your friend and tells you which of them are currently online. It acts as a small administrative center for common *SL* actions, such as sending IMs, paying residents, offering teleports to your current location, etc.

23

CHAPTER 2

TAKING CONTROL
OF YOUR *SECOND
LIFE*

LEARNING ABOUT
SECOND LIFE

Chat opens the Chat box for typing text to residents in your vicinity. Pressing the Enter key is much simpler and has the same effect.

Fly toggles the Fly mode and is quite useful despite the convenient keyboard shortcuts (Page Up/Page Down is the default). Clicking it while in midair makes you stop flying; your avatar flails and falls into a semihard landing (depending on how high you've been soaring around).

Snapshot opens the Snapshot Preview panel for taking snaps of the virtual world. Set all the options, such as snapshot size, resolution, image quality, emailing screenshots, etc. here.

Search brings up a panel where you search for upcoming events, popular places, land sales, people, groups, and more. Enter a keyword in the Find slot and click Search.

FROM LINDEN LAB
SUPER SEARCH

"Just as this book was heading to the printer, we were extending our in-world search mechanism to improve the search experience and results for all *Second Life* residents. The primary goals are to make it easier to find places to go in-world and to make it simpler to find interesting and relevant things to do and make it easier to locate objects to purchase. The Search All dialog box has been dramatically changed and improved, and search results have been greatly expanded to now include land parcels, resident profiles, groups, *Second Life* wiki articles, events, and even objects present on public parcels.

"The search results will be available both in-world and from the *Second Life* website (and may eventually be picked up by external search engines, such as Google and Yahoo!). While search-result information isn't tied to residents' real-life identity (it's the same info anyone with a free *Second Life* account could see), residents have the ability to exclude their land, profiles, groups, and objects if they so desire.

"To find out more details, please visit the official *Second Life* website (https:// secondlife.com/support)."

—Jeska Linden

Build opens the Build panel, which is active only if the land you're on allows building, such as a sandbox area or your own land.

CHAPTER 1

CHAPTER 2

CHAPTER 3

CHAPTER 4

CHAPTER 5

CHAPTER 6

CHAPTER 7

CHAPTER 8

CHAPTER 9

CHAPTER 10

CHAPTER 11

CHAPTER 12

CHAPTER 13

CHAPTER 14

CHAPTER 15

APPENDICES

Mini-Map opens a small, directional map in the upper-right corner of the screen. It can be useful when trying to orient yourself by the compass, or when finding your way somewhere, especially in crowded areas such as malls and entertainment complexes.

Map is, hands down, the most powerful button of them all. It opens a resizeable, rescaleable map of the *SL* world that's much more than a map. It includes search functions and is also an interface for instant travel: double-clicking on any spot teleports your avatar to that location. In the virtual world, activities such as walking or driving a vehicle are entertainment choices, not necessities. Now you know why most of the roads and streets in *Second Life* are empty!

Inventory opens the Inventory panel (Control-I is the shortcut).

ADDITIONAL INFO
INACCESSIBLE MENU?

This button menu may be inaccessible if you've set your Windows taskbar to stay on top of other application windows; in that case, right-click the Windows taskbar and select Properties to make the necessary changes.

ADDITIONAL INFO
THE PIE MENU

Right-clicking on almost anything in the virtual world brings up a pie menu. The menu's options are context-sensitive and depend on the properties of what you clicked on. To find out more about *SL* pie menus, visit the *Second Life* Knowledge Base.

VIEWS AND MOVEMENT

The standard *SL* view is the "follow" mode, with the camera behind and slightly above your avatar. However, some people find the mouselook or first-person view more convenient when moving around. If walking down a street and keeping to the pavement proves a comically difficult exercise using the standard view, switch to mouselook. Mouselook is also great for flying: you'll fly in the direction indicated by your mouse cursor. Thus, you can turn, ascend, and descend by moving your mouse—it looks and feels as if you were flying a plane.

CHAPTER 2

**TAKING CONTROL
OF YOUR** *SECOND
LIFE*

LEARNING ABOUT
SECOND LIFE

FROM LINDEN LAB
MASTERING THE CAMERA

"I'm very fond of Natural Selection Studios' 'Noob Be Gone' camera tutorial: `http://
naturalselectionstudios.com/?cat=59`."

—Prospero Linden

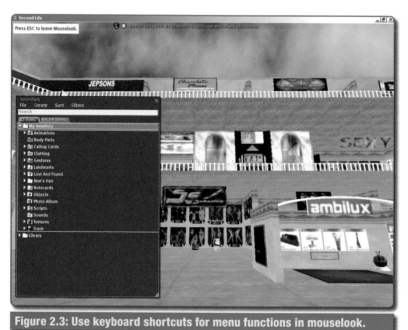

Figure 2.3: Use keyboard shortcuts for menu functions in mouselook.

You cannot access the onscreen menus in mouselook, but you can still use shortcut keys to execute commands: for example, open your Inventory by pressing Control-I (Figure 2.3). Keeping the Alt key depressed lets you move the mouse cursor without changing the view; when the cursor is over a panel, you can let go of the key and proceed to do what you wanted to do (for example, rearrange Inventory items). The Alt key also lets you move the camera around and zoom in and out while in the standard "follow" view.

ADDITIONAL INFO
FLIGHT PACKS

The *SL* marketplace features all types of aircraft as well as many models of "flight packs." These can be very sophisticated and very affordable—see the "Flying High in *Second Life*" sidebar for a few examples of aircraft for sale. Chapter 3 discusses Abbott's Aerodrome, a popular place to purchase aircraft.

ADDITIONAL INFO
FLYING HIGH IN *SECOND LIFE*

CHAPTER 1

CHAPTER 2

CHAPTER 3

CHAPTER 4

CHAPTER 5

CHAPTER 6

CHAPTER 7

CHAPTER 8

CHAPTER 9

CHAPTER 10

CHAPTER 11

CHAPTER 12

CHAPTER 13

CHAPTER 14

CHAPTER 15

APPENDICES

DefCon 1 Aerospace Vehicles (free demo flights)

Sponsored by Marlin Engineering. Some of the best flying vehicles in *Second Life*, smooth and responsive flight model … sleek stylish looks, low prim for low lag. Nice features and reasonable price, one- and two-person fighters L$500, five-person shuttle L$600.

Intelligent flight assist / jetpack @ Aodhan's Forge

It's no ordinary jetpack. The Scarab was designed with your convenience in mind. Making a flight pack go fast is easy, but what really matters is making a flight pack do what you want it to do … automatically. The Scarab almost completely takes away the fumbling with typed commands while giving you the flight assist you need, when you need it. Details at `SL.AodhansForge.com`.

DreamTech Aeronautics

Specializing in airships of various kinds, historic, futuristic, and fantastic. Visit us for a test flight today!

Zeppelins, airships, flying ships, aircraft, blimps, sailboats, sailing, yachts, teleporters, teleportation system.

CRYSTALTECH *Vehicles*

Home of the unbeaten most realistic vehicle models in *SL*!

Vehicles store. Get spaceships, choppers/helicopters, and jetfighters. All featuring physical smooth flight.

As mentioned earlier, "ordinary" movement—walking, flying, driving a vehicle, or taking the streetcar—is a source of entertainment and an opportunity to socialize; it's not a practical necessity. The introduction of instant teleporting, free of charge, any time and to nearly anywhere, has made all other modes of movement unnecessary except when inside small, confined spaces. But a drive in a virtual car, a stroll around a shopping mall, or a visit to a nightclub can be entertaining. Walking and flying are definitely the preferred movement modes when you're sightseeing. The *SL* world contains more interesting places to visit than most tourist hotspots in the real world; you'll find more details in Chapter 3.

Set landmarks on the *SL* map to move quickly between your favorite places, or to arrive in specific spots, such as a venue for an event you want to attend. Visit the *Second Life* Knowledge Base for detailed info on navigation and movement in *Second Life*.

LEARNING ABOUT *SECOND LIFE*

Second Life offers you almost as many choices as real life does, and many more that the real world doesn't. Visit the *Second Life* Knowledge Base `http://secondlife.com/knowledgebase` at the start of your new existence, if only to review the topics covered—it will help you get an idea of what's possible. The Knowledge Base is updated constantly as new features become available, so it's a good idea to revisit it on a regular basis. The guides and how-to articles featured there are a great way to find out more about how things work in the virtual world. It's complemented by the *Second Life* Wiki `https://wiki.secondlife.com/wiki/Main _ Page`. These two sources contain invaluable information, regardless of whether your interest is in running a virtual business, making movies, or socializing and role playing.

Puzzled about something? Enter the appropriate keyword into the *SL* Knowledge Base search box. Chances are you'll find a whole series of articles, guides, and tutorials related to your chosen subject.

If you need a little personal guidance, acquire a mentor. Mentors are volunteers who are longtime *SL* residents. Most often, they specialize in a particular skill or knowledge area—for example, creating new virtual objects with prims. You'll encounter some mentors on Help Island. And if you don't come across one in the arrival area on the *SL* mainland, use the search function: enter "mentor" and pick the Groups tab on the Search panel. You can refine your search further to find a mentor who is knowledgeable about a topic you're interested in.

CHAPTER 1

CHAPTER 2

CHAPTER 3

CHAPTER 4

CHAPTER 5

CHAPTER 6

CHAPTER 7

CHAPTER 8

CHAPTER 9

CHAPTER 10

CHAPTER 11

CHAPTER 12

CHAPTER 13

CHAPTER 14

CHAPTER 15

APPENDICES

FROM LINDEN LAB
BE A SHUTTERBUG

"Learn how to take snapshots early on and capture memories of your second life. Your in-world 'firsts' will not just be remembered fondly, you'll always have something precious to look back on as you continue living your second life. This is especially true when making new friends during those seminal early days and weeks."

—Torley Linden

⬇ ORIENTATION ISLAND AND HELP ISLAND

Figure 2.4: Make sure you explore all of Help Island.

Your virtual existence begins on Orientation Island. The short tutorial offered there will teach you a few basics, but not more than that. Your next stop is Help Island (Figure 2.4), and this is where you should stay awhile. In addition to snapping up the freebies from the Freebie Shop, you should definitely visit the tutorials and demo areas. If you don't understand something clearly, ask the mentors on duty in the Help Island arrival area.

ADDITIONAL INFO
RETURNING TO YOUR ROOTS

Your avatar cannot return to Orientation or Help Island once it has arrived on the mainland, but **you** can. There is now an "Orientation Island (Public)" and "Help Island (Public)" on the mainland—exact copies of the two islands you go through when you enter the world. Just use the Search > Places function to find them. So you can always revisit those when you want. You can also start a new Basic account and revisit the two original islands. In any case, creating a second or alternate avatar is a wise step, since it lets you back up your Inventory (see Chapter 7).

Make sure you collect and keep all the notecards from Help Island; you'll be seeing and experiencing too many new things to remember everything. In particular, the Explorer Guidebook (which tells you where to go on the mainland if you want to repeat Orientation Island tutorials) and Real Life Education Places notecards are worth keeping when you're doing your first big Inventory cleanup prior to departing for the mainland.

Once you've arrived on the mainland, use the Search function to find out where you can learn more about various aspects of *Second Life*. Choices range from attending classes and courses at one of the many schools and universities to learning how to be a good servant to an *SL* master. The classes and courses available aren't limited to *Second Life* subjects; you may pick up valuable real-life skills!

⬇ Mainland Choices

Once you're on the mainland, your priorities are shaped by the kind of virtual life you want to live. A big part of that will be choosing to become part of specific communities (or if you prefer, none). It's generally a good idea to at least consider where you might fit into the wide variety of social networks out there, because you're bound to feel at home in at least some.

FORMING AND JOINING GROUPS

Any two *SL* residents, regardless of membership plan type, can form a group (right-click on your avatar and choose Groups from the pie menu, then Create). The resident who initiated this process becomes the group's founder and enjoys special privileges. The creator can designate different members with various levels of power and access, and choose to run the group as a democracy (there is a feature for conducting group votes) or as a benevolent dictator. You'll find more details at `http://secondlife.com/app/help/new/groups.php`. The robust group structure promises to be helpful to the long-term survival of many organized *SL* communities who want more control over their land and experiences.

FROM LINDEN LAB
PEOPLE ARE THE KEY

"It's easy to get lost in the vastness and think 'There's nothing here.' And yet, there's almost certainly something here that will engage you in ways you hadn't even thought about before. Try seeking like-minded people rather than places."

—Morpheus Linden

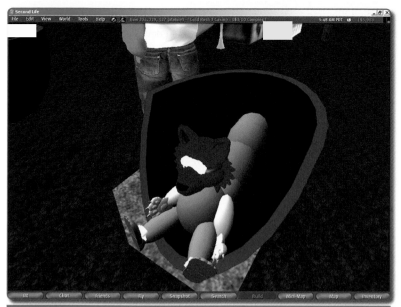

Figure 2.5: There is a place for everyone and everything in the virtual world.

Organized communities greatly enrich the virtual world (Figure 2.5). There are no restrictions on community size or the degree of their organizational development, and some even resemble micronations. However, many communities—and estate owners—have goals other than expansion (see the "Groups and Communities" sidebar). If you look around, you're sure to find many groups whose goals or activities appeal to you. You can belong to as many as 25 different groups, including those that you started yourself.

CHAPTER 1
CHAPTER 2
CHAPTER 3
CHAPTER 4
CHAPTER 5
CHAPTER 6
CHAPTER 7
CHAPTER 8
CHAPTER 9
CHAPTER 10
CHAPTER 11
CHAPTER 12
CHAPTER 13
CHAPTER 14
CHAPTER 15
APPENDICES

ADDITIONAL INFO
GROUPS AND COMMUNITIES

"The Neualtenburg Projekt is a private land cooperative formed in 2004, and once occupied one entire simulator or 'sim' of 64 virtual acres in *Second Life* acquired directly from Linden Lab in May 2005. It attempts to simulate the look and feel of a functioning Bavarian city with residential, commercial, and public spaces. The cooperative has a democratic republican government with three branches and a constitution. The simulated city is open to the public, but participation in the government requires the acquisition of virtual land in the city. Acquisition of land constitutes agreement to abide by various specific standards of building and activity in the city.

"Title to the entire sim is actually 'owned' (licensed from Linden Lab) by an avatar known as 'Estate Owner.' This status allows the treasurer to deed land to ownership groups and to reclaim land from those groups. For its convenience, Neualtenburg has chosen to appoint the 'alt' of its treasurer to accept title to the land as estate owner on behalf of the municipality.

"In return for a one-time payment, resident's ownership groups receive grant deeds to particular parcels, allowing them rights to use specific parcels of virtual land as long as they conform to the city's land use regulations and payment of monthly land use fees in the nature of

CHAPTER 2

TAKING CONTROL
OF YOUR *SECOND
LIFE*

**LEARNING ABOUT
*SECOND LIFE***

property tax. Residents' rights may be terminated and their virtual property reclaimed by the city for breach of the various covenants and agreements. Residents in good standing may sell their virtual land rights to third parties approved by the city."

—from "The Neualtenburg Projekt Summary" by Frank Lardner

[Editor's note: In late 2007, the Neualtenberg group profile reads: "After a coup in the city on 1 June 2006, the project forked, and the private sim changed its name and theme. The Projekt continues its experimentation, participating in the drafting of founding documents for external groups and forging ahead with the next phase of the Projekt."]

"Earlier today I have formed the *Second Life* chapter of the Socialist Party. In doing this, I hope to provide an alternative way for individuals to commune, interact, and produce. I also hope to utilize Party membership to launch some in-world political activism. Our goal isn't to overthrow the free market of *Second Life* or anything like that, as most people seem to enjoy virtual capitalism, we just want there to be options. If anybody is interested in helping out with SP*SL*, then instant message Lenin Camus.

"Also, for members in need, I'm offering some free rent homes."

—Lenin Camus

"Caledon is a small, windswept forested country at a temperate latitude. Wild creatures, country estate life, sights and sounds that were common well over 100 years ago are the hallmark of the land.

"Technology is approximately that of the 19th century, though some astonishing breakthroughs have provided for incredible wonders. Ground vehicles, airships, and even a device known as a Telehub are made possible through the power of exotic material properties and the wonders of steam technology. (The Steampunk community has a strong presence in Caledon, including The Manor, headquarters of the Steampunks group.)

"The government is an expansionist monarchy, supported by a strong aristocracy (i.e., residents). Caledon offers the opportunity for residents to take their turn at 'Stewardship,' a post which can involve answering questions, restarting sims, banning obvious griefers, etc."

—from *SL* History Wiki: The Independent State of Caledon

Community Land

A group is an association of two or more residents sharing common aims and/or interests. However, groups may and frequently do own land that is purchased from Linden Lab by the estate owner, or donated by individual group members.

CHAPTER 1

CHAPTER 2

CHAPTER 3

CHAPTER 4

CHAPTER 5

CHAPTER 6

CHAPTER 7

CHAPTER 8

CHAPTER 9

CHAPTER 10

CHAPTER 11

CHAPTER 12

CHAPTER 13

CHAPTER 14

CHAPTER 15

APPENDICES

ADDITIONAL INFO
THE BENEFITS OF COMMUNITY LAND

The land-ownership structure in *SL* rewards residents who form organized communities: member land-tier donations to group estates receive a 10% bonus to their land allowance. Thus, donating 512 square meters of tier results in the group being able to hold 563 square meters. (And only if that donation is made.)

Land ownership in *Second Life* does not require a Premium membership plan when the land in question is purchased from an estate owner. The intricacies involved are explained in detail in the *Second Life* Knowledge Base: just keep in mind that becoming an estate owner—purchasing land from Linden Lab—does require Premium membership and can carry significant extra costs.

OWNING VIRTUAL LAND

Owning land in *Second Life* carries land-use costs too. Your Premium membership includes land-use costs for up to 512 square meters of real estate. If you want to own more, the costs increase. Table 2.1 displays land area/associated land-use costs at the time of writing.

Table 2.1: Land-Use Costs

ADDITIONAL LAND (OVER 512 SQUARE METERS)	MAXIMUM AREA (IN SQUARE METERS)	MONTHLY LAND-USE FEE
1/128 Region	512 sq. meters	US$5
1/64 Region	1,024 sq. meters	US$8
1/32 Region	2,048 sq. meters	US$15
1/16 Region	4,096 sq. meters	US$25
1/8 Region	8,192 sq. meters	US$40
1/4 Region	16,384 sq. meters	US$75
1/2 Region	32,768 sq. meters	US$125
Entire Region	65,536 sq. meters	US$195

Land Use Fees are always charged monthly and are determined by peak land ownership within the period for which they apply. So, for example, if you're a real-estate speculator beginning and ending the month with 512 square meters but hitting a peak 10,000 square meters midway through the month, you'll pay Land Use Fees for 1/4 Region (US$75). Note that donating land to a group does not absolve you of carrying its Land Use Fees. However, a Basic membership plan holder who buys land from an estate owner does not have to pay land-upkeep fees *unless* this is specified in the land covenant. Owners of land in organized communities often make periodical payments such as land "taxes" that defray Land Use Fees to the estate owner or administrator.

CHAPTER 2

TAKING CONTROL
OF YOUR *SECOND
LIFE*

**LEARNING ABOUT
*SECOND LIFE***

If you look at the table data carefully, you should notice a pattern: the more land you own, the less it costs per square meter. This is unlikely to change even if the fees do. This can have important implications on trading for profit in the land market. Chapter 13 discusses more ways to make money in *Second Life*.

ADDITIONAL INFO
REAL-ESTATE RICHES

At the time of writing, the richest *SL* resident is Anshe Chung—a real-estate tycoon whose virtual land holdings are valued in excess of US$1 million.

There is no limit on your virtual land holdings. If you like, you can order and purchase your very own made-to-order island from Linden Lab. *Second Life* islands cannot be smaller than a single region (65,536 square meters). At the time of writing, the two island sizes on offer are one and four regions. Note that regardless of the island's starting size, extra land in the form of additional islands may be added to the island at a later date (if there is room around the island on the map). Additionally, recent changes to the land ownership/management system (including group covenants, powers associated with land managers versus land owners, and so on) are important to consider; check the official site for the latest details on these.

Unsurprisingly, owning a little personal empire is not cheap. At the time of writing, island-setup fees are US$1,675 for a one-region island and around $5,000 for the four-region model. In addition, island owners pay standard Land Use Fees. Visit `http://secondlife.com/community/land-islands.php` for up-to-date island-ownership info, and `http://secondlife.com/whatis/landpricing.php` to check on current Land Use Fees.

Before you commit to joining any groups or buying real estate, it's wise to get an idea of the lay of the land (so to speak) and have a comprehensive picture of what goes on where. Accordingly, the next chapter takes you on a tour of the *SL* mainland.

ADDITIONAL INFO
THE ABOUT LAND PANEL

Right-click on land you own and select About Land to open a panel with many land-management options (Figure 2.6). These include restricting access, issuing permission to run scripts, playing music, banning specific residents, etc. Note that when you buy land from an estate owner, land-management options may be modified in accordance with the land covenant.

Figure 2.6: You rule your land through the About Land panel.

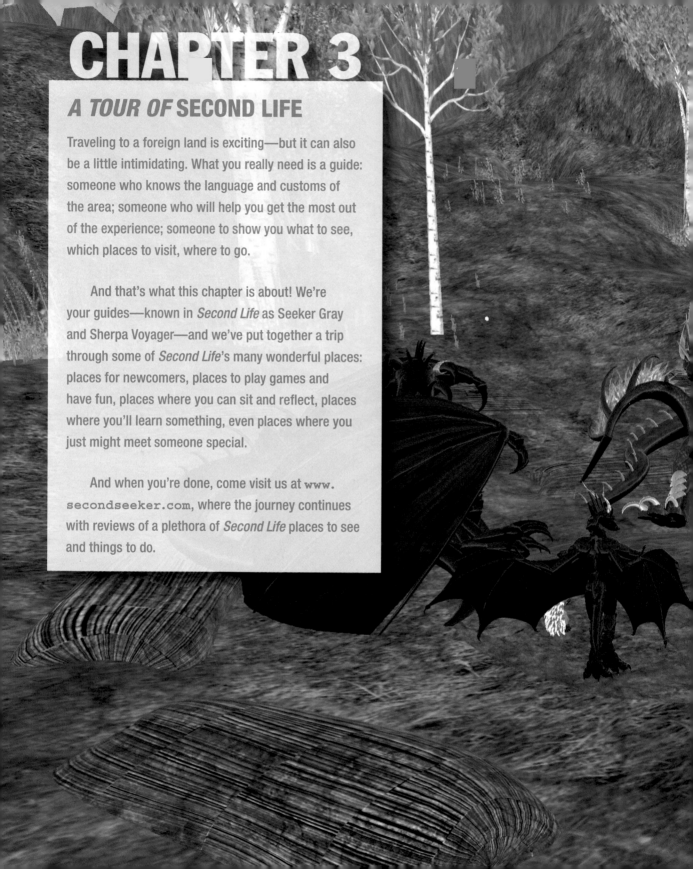

CHAPTER 3

A *TOUR OF* SECOND LIFE

Traveling to a foreign land is exciting—but it can also be a little intimidating. What you really need is a guide: someone who knows the language and customs of the area; someone who will help you get the most out of the experience; someone to show you what to see, which places to visit, where to go.

And that's what this chapter is about! We're your guides—known in *Second Life* as Seeker Gray and Sherpa Voyager—and we've put together a trip through some of *Second Life*'s many wonderful places: places for newcomers, places to play games and have fun, places where you can sit and reflect, places where you'll learn something, even places where you just might meet someone special.

And when you're done, come visit us at www. secondseeker.com, where the journey continues with reviews of a plethora of *Second Life* places to see and things to do.

CONTENTS

HEY! I'M NEW HERE!

So you're new to *Second Life*—what now? Where do you go?

We're going to start at the very beginning: There are destinations designed especially with newcomers in mind, where you can learn to find your way around, practice walking, talking, building … just about anything you'll need to know to navigate around in-world.

⬇ NEW CITIZENS INCORPORATED: KUULA (53, 175, 28) AND HAMNIDA (237, 82, 113)

This may be one of the most useful places you'll visit. The plaza offers classrooms teaching everything from *Second Life* social skills to the proper handling of weapons to building and scripting classes, and there are a lot of people around who are willing (delighted, even!) to answer any of your questions about *Second Life*. Be sure to check out the free publications at the newsstand, the landmarks to areas that will teach you something, and the New Citizens Incorporated (NCI) Homeowner's Association. Note the two locations: Hamnida is New Citizens' Plaza South, and less crowded than the original (also in Kuula).

⬇ THE SHELTER: ISABEL (59, 230, 81)

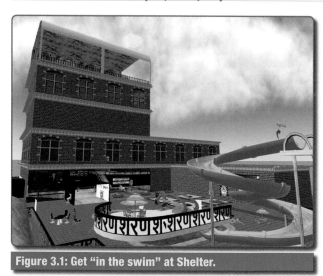

Figure 3.1: Get "in the swim" at Shelter.

Owner Travis Lambert calls the Shelter "the friendliest spot in *Second Life*," and he may well be right (Figure 3.1). It's where you can go to have fun without pressure: you can dance at the disco, take a dip in the pool, and participate in games, contests, lotteries, and other fun activities, all of which will help you get more comfortable in and oriented to *Second Life*.

⬇ YADNI'S JUNKYARD: LEDA (201, 27, 54)

YadNi Monde calls his space a "newbie paradise," and indeed it is! Come here for sculptie textures, expressions and gestures to experiment with, even statues and swords of your very own. No politics, no shooting, and there's a Spanish version available.

⬇ The FreeDove: Gallii (113, 53, 33)

Clothes, clothes, clothes, and all of them free! The FreeDove looks like a hundred other shops you'll find in *Second Life*, but with a twist: you won't need to spend any of your precious Lindens here. Stop by to get rid of that "newbie" look, and explore what you'll eventually want your avatar to wear.

⬇ Ivory Tower Library of Primitives: Natoma (209, 164, 28)

Prims (short for "primitives") are the building-blocks of *Second Life*, and the Ivory Tower is where you'll want to go to learn about them. Here you'll find a plethora of self-paced tutorials and space in which to experiment with what you're learning.

⬇ WHAT ARE SOME MUST-VISIT DESTINATIONS?

CHAPTER 1
CHAPTER 2
CHAPTER 3

CHAPTER 4
CHAPTER 5
CHAPTER 6
CHAPTER 7
CHAPTER 8
CHAPTER 9
CHAPTER 10
CHAPTER 11
CHAPTER 12
CHAPTER 13
CHAPTER 14
CHAPTER 15
APPENDICES

Now you're all dressed up with no place to go! Never fear; we've put together a group of locations that should provide something for everyone, showing the wide range of places you can visit in *Second Life*. From the delicate beauty of Mont St. Michel to the eerie shadows of Atrocity, if you can think of it, you can probably find it here! We'll travel the world, travel back in time, and travel through the imagination, starting now.

⬇ *S.S. Galaxy*: Galaxy AFT (58, 44, 21)

The era of the great cruise ships may be over, but the *Galaxy* (Figure 3.2) is here to remind us of it: architect and owner Bill Stirling's creation is true, wonderful, sumptuous style and luxury, a place to go when you need a sense of elegance and taste. Visit the skating rink, the restaurants, and the ballroom in particular. Captain Skolnick and his staff are ready and available to give tours, answer questions, or just make your visit enjoyable. "The *Galaxy* takes details from some of the world's great ocean liners," he remarks. Take an hour to tour the *Galaxy* and relive a time that is no more.

Figure 3.2: A city afloat

39

⬇ ATROCITY: ESOTERICA (200, 65, 27)

Figure 3.3: Catch the midnight bus at Atrocity

From beauty to … well, something different! Violet Morellet has created a dark, grungy area full of fairly creepy places to explore. Use whatever lighting suits you, but take it from us: the playground itself (complete with razor wire; Figure 3.3) really needs to be seen at night! Atrocity includes the indie/alternative music nightclub Umbra Penumbra, where all the cool kids hang out, with live music most nights after 9 PM eastern time—as well as more-sedate facilities such as a bowling alley, a movie theater, and a video arcade. There's even a submarine to explore!

⬇ TABLEAU: TABLEAU (198, 179, 18)

Drift along with the tumbling tumbleweeds at Tableau, a bit of the American Southwest right in *Second Life*. You can take the recreation route (it's a great place to go horseback riding) or the spiritual path, (by entering the small trailer that will start you on a life-changing vision quest). Or just sit in a café and enjoy the dry desert night air! Whatever activity you choose, Tableau will provide a dramatic backdrop for it.

FROM LINDEN LAB

OUR FAVORITE PLACES

"I really like the environment that Kriss Lehmann has created with sculpty trees at 'Botanical'—http://slurl.com/secondlife/Straylight/197/14/37."

—Morpheus Linden

"I have so many favorite places, I post pictures of them regularly at http://www.flickr.com/photos/torley/ with SLURLs inside."

—Torley Linden

"Dinosaurs Park: http://slurl.com/secondlife/Dinosaurs%20Park/222/138/25. Nargus Asturias makes a great line of dinosaur avatars. However, the park itself is a really neat build. While it's focused around the avatar shop, it has a lot of character and atmosphere, from the warning sounds that you get when you open the door, to the reinforced geodesic domes designed to keep the scary dinosaurs out, to the very design of his vending devices. Outside the dome is a nice landscape with amusing dinosaur-related signs, and even a 'live' dinosaur or two."

—Prospero Linden

CHAPTER 1

CHAPTER 2

CHAPTER 3

CHAPTER 4

CHAPTER 5

CHAPTER 6

CHAPTER 7

CHAPTER 8

CHAPTER 9

CHAPTER 10

CHAPTER 11

CHAPTER 12

CHAPTER 13

CHAPTER 14

CHAPTER 15

APPENDICES

⬇ NEO KOWLOON CITY: KOWLOON (146, 12, 24)

There was once a real Kowloon Walled City: China's enclave in Hong Kong, a city that grew organically, with fluorescent lighting providing illumination to the narrow winding streets and small squares. Walk around, have something to eat at a noodle shop, explore streets and catwalks alike; you'll definitely feel that you've been in a foreign country after this stop!

⬇ STEELHEAD CITY: STEELHEAD (115, 124, 30)

Oregon in the 1880s is what you'll find in Kattrynn Severine's Steelhead City (Figure 3.4), with a vibrant urban community supporting it. Don't miss the Steelhead Grand Hotel and Ballroom, offering ballroom dancing on Saturday nights (in period costume if at all possible)—what could be more charming than that?

Figure 3.4: Nightfall at Steelhead City

CHAPTER 3

HEY! I'M NEW
HERE!

**WHAT ARE SOME
MUST-VISIT
LOCATIONS?**

WHERE CAN I
PARTICIPATE IN
SOMETHING?

WHERE CAN I FIND
A MOMENT OF
PERFECT BEAUTY?

WHAT CAN I LEARN
IN *SECOND LIFE*?

WHERE CAN I
FEED MY SOUL?

WHERE CAN I
MEET SOMEONE?

WHAT CAN I BUY?

⬇ BEDROCK: DRYMONIA (171, 37, 251)

Figure 3.5: A yabba-dabba-doo time at Bedrock

Yabba dabba doo! It's time to meet the Flintstones at Tigey Honey's skybox re-creation of the fictional Bedrock (Figure 3.5). One refreshing aspect of this build is that the visitor is not expected to take it too seriously! Bring a date (there are cuddle pose balls) and ride the dinosaur-powered Ferris wheel, get a burger (or brontosaurus ribs!) and watch a movie at the drive-in; you can even relax in the mud spa. Have a yabba-dabba-doo time!

⬇ MONT ST. MICHEL (AU PÉRIL DE LA MER): SHIVAR (125, 175, 21)

YadNi Monde has re-created the beautiful tidal island and walled city from France's Normandy coast. Very much like its real-life counterpart, it has stone buildings and streets clinging desperately to the hill that is the *mont*; the quicksand that surrounds it has trapped many an unwary visitor. In *Second Life*, you can walk around the narrow winding cobblestone streets, enjoy a coffee, then climb or fly up to the ramparts for some spectacular views.

⬇ THE FIRST *SECOND LIFE* CHURCH OF ELVIS: IRON FIST (176, 28, 350)

Figure 3.6: Greeting the King

The Reverend Elvis Faust is your host and spiritual advisor at the First *Second Life* Church of Elvis (Figure 3.6), whose commandments include rules such "thou shalt not build thine dreams on suspicious minds," "thou shalt not step on my blue suede shoes," and "thou shalt not take us seriously." Stop by on Sunday at noon (*Second Life* time, or *SL*T) for the service, which is well attended and curiously moving.

⬇ Midnight City: Midnight City (121, 136, 26)

Figure 3.7: Sunset at Midnight City

Midnight City (Figure 3.7) is *Second Life*'s oldest continuously operating shopping mall; but there's much more to do there than just shop. There's a fabulous Exploratorium with a number of science exhibits and eclipse-related art. Consider stopping by the Yak Shack and purchasing your very own yak; proceeds go to *Save the Children*. "This gritty urban build," explains owner Aimee Weber, "is currently the home of many events and activities, including a radio show, a vampire role-playing game, and the occasional rousing game of soccer."

⬇ Nexus Prime: Cyberpunk City of the Future: Bonificio (213, 108, 31)

Authors William Gibson and Bruce Sterling are well known for writing in the "cyberpunk" subgenre of science fiction, a genre where things are either dark and dirty and wet, or else corporate squeaky-clean (which can be even scarier!). Nexus Prime is the embodiment of this culture in *Second Life*. It's old; construction started in early 2003 as a Linden-subsidized, community-built themed project by the Tyrell Corporation Group.

ADDITIONAL INFO
SECOND LIFE COMMUNITIES

If you want a sense of belonging, of connecting with others who share your interests, beliefs, identity, or sense of adventure, then explore some of the *Second Life* communities. This list highlights a few of them; you can find pretty much whatever you're looking for in-world.

(Continued)   **43**

FANTASY CREATURES COMMUNITIES

- Isle of Wyrms: Limbo (169, 182, 26)—A dragon group "organizing a community, which is what the islands are really all about," as Onix Harbinger notes.
- Tol Eressea: Tol Eressea (98, 222, 35)—An elven community.
- Eryn Lasgalen: Tol Lasgalen (208, 171, 22)—An elven and medieval sim.
- Faedwer: Maculata (208, 125, 21)—Merfolk and faeries.

GAY, LESBIAN, BISEXUAL, AND TRANSGENDER (GLBT) COMMUNITIES

- Welcome Pavilion: Monty (56, 74, 43)—Pick up your welcome kit here.
- Provincetown: Provincetown (112, 137, 29)—A collection of GLBT sims.
- Mysteria: Mysteria (89, 128, 24)—For lesbian and bisexual women only.
- Transgender Resource Center: Pavonia (24, 34, 101)—Lots of resource material.

FURRY COMMUNITIES

- Alchera: Alchera (32, 90, 23)—Furry, feral, elf, and vampire roleplay.
- FurNation: FurNation Prime (127, 144, 39)—Furry roleplay.
- Luskwood: Lusk (193, 104, 52)—Most famous furry haunt, and very PG (no sexual content or pressure).

INTERNATIONAL COMMUNITIES

- Wonderful Denmark: Wonderful Denmark (133, 131, 22)—A Danish-speaking sim where people greet each other by name.
- Second House of Sweden: Swedish Institute (70, 212, 29)—Two sims sponsored by the Swedish government showing cultural, historical, and artistic aspects of Sweden; there's also a Swedish orientation island for newcomers.
- Cooperation française: Area 51 (135, 119, 28)—A lobby and exhibit in French showing various aspects of *Second Life.*
- Paris 1900: Paris 1900 (8, 171, 16)—A re-creation of Paris in 1900, complete with a Moulin Rouge, its elephant, and an Eiffel Tower from which you can parachute.
- Calamaro Planet: Mignon (180, 234, 24)—Beach-themed Portuguese-speaking area with a dance club.
- New Berlin: New Berlin (130, 118, 201)—Includes a replica of the famous Fernsehturm television tower, as well as references to cultural events.
- Psychedelic Poland by Cezary Fish: De Lodi (83, 55, 22)—A re-creation of Poland's industrial roots coupled with a vision of an artistic future. (See top of next page.)

CHAPTER 1
CHAPTER 2
CHAPTER 3
CHAPTER 4
CHAPTER 5
CHAPTER 6
CHAPTER 7
CHAPTER 8
CHAPTER 9
CHAPTER 10
CHAPTER 11
CHAPTER 12
CHAPTER 13
CHAPTER 14
CHAPTER 15
APPENDICES

RELIGIOUS COMMUNITIES:

- *Second Life* Catholic Church: PalmVegas Region (172, 174, 23)—Provides liturgies including Mass and the Sacrament of Reconciliation. Collections are sent to the Vatican.

- Ir Shalom: Ir Shalom (249, 137, 22)—An active Jewish community covering one sim.

- Vedic Cultural Center: Cool (16, 244, 21)—A gorgeous temple with some information kiosks.

- Hare Krishna Community Welcome Area: Grimes (185, 100, 50)—A welcome area not just for community members; some notecards.

- Thai Buddhist Temple: Golden Green (133, 111, 30)—A well-marked *wat*.

WHERE CAN I PARTICIPATE IN SOMETHING?

Now that you've had a chance to look around, we're going to take you to places where you won't be just an idle bystander—you'll want to *participate*. Some of these stops are role-playing sites, where there may be rules about how you can interact with others and with the environment. There's something here for everyone, so look around and enjoy! You're sure to find something that suits you.

WIZARD'S ALLEY & HOGWARTS: SUNSET HARBOR (147, 140, 26)

Teleport into Wizard's Alley and you can purchase just about everything you'll need to step into your very own *Harry Potter* adventure. If you go to a pub called The Leak, you'll be able to get directions to Hogwarts itself, where you can start the roleplay (you can be a character from the Harry Potter world, or even just yourself!).

⬇ Suffugium: Suffugium (102, 116, 34)

This is the way roleplaying *should* be: smart, intense, and with an amazingly realistic backdrop. The product of the Squidsoft Collective, Suffugium is a futuristic decaying city; you may pass by a crashed burning vehicle or have to submit to a "routine biological scan" to ensure "your future security within our jurisdiction." Remember Suffugium's mandate—"Keep silent, keep safe"—and enjoy one of the richest role-playing opportunities in *Second Life*.

⬇ Dark Life: Navora (19, 43, 22)

Dark Life is a fantasy MMORPG (massively multiplayer online role-playing game) with a traditional leveling-up routine: you start by killing rats, you recover from the wounds they inflicted, and you move up a level. There are different areas to *Dark Life*—some traditional quasi-medieval villages along with "adventure areas" where you're most likely to meet the monsters that you will need to vanquish to move on. More often than not, people help each other and work quite cooperatively.

⬇ The Forest of Kahruvel: Rodeo (28, 37, 49)

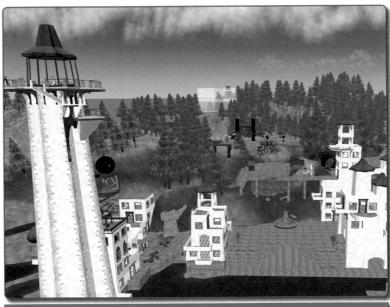

Figure 3.8: Solve the mystery.

If you like beauty and mystery, then the Forest of Kahruvel (Figure 3.8)—the work of the officers of the Phineas Jack Memorial Trust Group and Salazar Jack—is for you. It has spectacularly beautiful scenery (an amazing forest of old-growth trees) as well as a detailed and interesting backstory. If you continue on to the seaside village, you'll find a tower containing the clues that will set you toward solving the mystery.

⬇ The Pot Healer Adventure, Numbakulla Island Project: Numbakulla (214, 17, 22)

Numbakulla is the work of Caliandras Pendragon and her Pot Healer team, who built and developed the sim as what they call "an immersive game of exploration and puzzles." It is, frankly, one of our favorite places in *Second Life*. This game is about finding pieces of a broken pot and reassembling it. What do you do *after*? Well, that's part of the game, and you'll have to find out for yourself! This is not an area in which you will spend a single evening; it can take months to get through all of Numbakulla. As the notecard tells you, "Stranger stop and stranger see / Listen, stranger, carefully / My song is sung, my race is run / But yours is barely now begun…"

⬇ Samurai Island: Samurai Island (154, 98, 23)

If what you'd really like to try is a good, old-fashioned Japanese swordfight, complete with a free ceremonial bokken, then Samurai Island is for you. The major rule? This is for sword fighting: not for tricks, or *Second Life* magic, or guns, or spells—just sword fighting. You can purchase a more elaborate sword at one of the nearby shops. Some of the athletes here are very impressive: it's well worth a stop just to watch them in action.

⬇ Hollywood: Hollywood (142, 53, 25)

Figure 3.9: All Aboard at Hollywood!

If sailing, golf, and movies sound like a great combination to you, then head on over to Hollywood (Figure 3.9), where MarkTwain White and Nber Medici offer the oldest and biggest yacht club in *Second Life*, complete with exciting one-design races and regattas. Hollywood is also a premier golf destination and, true to its name, screens films. The owners are very nice and will show you the ropes of whatever activity you choose. "The builds and activities," says MarkTwain White, "represent the highest quality of workmanship, game design, and solid event scripting."

CHAPTER 1
CHAPTER 2
CHAPTER 3

CHAPTER 4
CHAPTER 5
CHAPTER 6
CHAPTER 7
CHAPTER 8
CHAPTER 9
CHAPTER 10
CHAPTER 11
CHAPTER 12
CHAPTER 13
CHAPTER 14
CHAPTER 15
APPENDICES

HEY! I'M NEW
HERE!

WHAT ARE SOME
MUST-VISIT
LOCATIONS?

**WHERE CAN I
PARTICIPATE IN
SOMETHING?**

WHERE CAN I FIND
A MOMENT OF
PERFECT BEAUTY?

WHAT CAN I LEARN
IN *SECOND LIFE*?

WHERE CAN I
FEED MY SOUL?

WHERE CAN I
MEET SOMEONE?

WHAT CAN I BUY?

MOTORATI ISLAND: MOTORATI (238, 153, 23)

Motorati Island (Figure 3.10) is a collection of six connected sims that celebrate the automobile: Pontiac, Velocity, Ride, Drive In, Garage, and, of course, Motorati. You'll find roads and cars everywhere, and you can stop by the Pontiac dealer: they'll put you in a new Solstice in no time at all. There are a number of different racetracks and styles of racing, from

Figure 3.10: Gentlemen, start your engines!

go-karts to oval and drift tracks, and they'll all put you in the driver's seat! There's even a monster-truck course. Cool off afterward with a malt at the diner.

ADDITIONAL INFO
ROLEPLAYING

If role-playing interests you, there are plenty of places to do it in *Second Life*! Some of the roleplaying sims are listed here.

SCIENCE FICTION

- *SL* Starfleet Welcome Center: Starfleet Sector 001 (224, 183, 22)—A vibrant roleplaying community.
- Star Trek Museum of Science: TovaDok II (25, 211, 36)—Science from a Star Trek perspective.
- Dantooine: The Outer Rim (64, 203, 53)—An active Star Wars community.
- Telos IV: Telos IV (162, 161, 496)—Very alive and active Star Wars roleplay in Atticus Jetaime's community; some combat. (See top-left of next page.)
- Dune Roleplay on Arrakis: Dune Imperium (187, 133, 298)—A bit of a hard landing, but Disraeli Calderwood assures us that it's well worth it! (See top-right of next page.)

CHAPTER 1
CHAPTER 2
CHAPTER 3

CHAPTER 4
CHAPTER 5
CHAPTER 6
CHAPTER 7
CHAPTER 8
CHAPTER 9
CHAPTER 10
CHAPTER 11
CHAPTER 12
CHAPTER 13
CHAPTER 14
CHAPTER 15
APPENDICES

MEDIEVAL

In *Second Life*, medieval role playing is the world of Tolkien, inhabited by elves, dragons, and even vampires—it doesn't have much to do with actual history.

- Avilion Mist: Avilion (4, 128, 41)—Serenity Sieyes's magical roleplay (see left).

- Tamerthon Village: Tamerthon (114, 34, 346)—This sim blends medieval role playing with fantasy and some sex; it's not for everyone.

DARK FANTASY

A word of warning: much of the dark fantasy role playing in *Second Life* is violent, sexual, or both. Knowing that, if you still want to pursue it, you might begin here:

- City of Lost Angels: Satellite (17, 171, 331)—One of the oldest role-playing communities in *Second Life*, and still extremely active.

- Midian City: Midian City (139, 45, 30)—A dark dystopic role-playing sim: another world war has come and gone, and its survivors now face an uncertain future.

- Toxian City: Toxia (247, 136, 23)—A dark, urban live-action role-playing game, with players united against a variety of monsters.

CHAPTER 3

HEY! I'M NEW
HERE!

WHAT ARE SOME
MUST-VISIT
LOCATIONS?

WHERE CAN I
PARTICIPATE IN
SOMETHING?

WHERE CAN I FIND
A MOMENT OF
PERFECT BEAUTY?

WHAT CAN I LEARN
IN SECOND LIFE?

WHERE CAN I FEED
MY SOUL?

WHERE CAN I MEET
SOMEONE?

WHAT CAN I BUY?

HISTORICAL

■ Independent State of Caledon: Caledon (190, 190, 23)—A tremendous area (25 sims!) of steampunk, life in a slightly altered Victorian setting. Very popular.

■ Tombstone, Arizona: Broken Rose (113, 182, 703)—Madminxmag Vanderperck's accurate re-creation of the scene of the famous gunfight at the OK Corral (see left).

■ Ancient Rome: ROMA (214, 25, 22)—Role playing is optional in this re-creation of ancient Rome, and note: combat is restricted to the arena!

WHERE CAN I FIND ONE MOMENT OF PERFECT BEAUTY?

After you've had some fun role playing, you might want to take some time to slow down and drink in some of the wonders of *Second Life*. Here are some of the destinations that (with a nod to *Babylon 5*), we call "one moment of perfect beauty."

Take a deep breath, and enjoy.

⬇ OYSTER BAY SCULPTURE GARDEN: OYSTER BAY (20, 176, 82)

Figure 3.11: Soak in some art.

Oyster Bay (Figure 3.11) is an art gallery/museum with a constantly shifting array of sculpture artists. Whatever is there when you visit, you can be assured that owner and curator Morris Vig will be offering the very best of what *Second Life* has to offer. "Oyster Bay is a portal for people to expose themselves to the innovation and creativity that comes from art that uses *Second Life* as a medium in itself … and to have a fun time doing it," says Vig. There is an aquarium associated with the art, and live music is also often on offer.

⬇ Second Louvre: Thompson (152, 97, 99)

The Second Louvre, while not affiliated with the Musée du Louvre in Paris, does give one the sense of visiting a real museum—someplace weighty and important. The tall stone galleries lend themselves to that sense of awe; curator Kharis Forti has developed and watches over an impressive place, to be sure.

⬇ Artropolis: Artropolis (17, 122, 22)

Don't be deterred by Filthy Fluno's name: he's a talented artist (in both worlds) and at Artropolis (Figure 3.12) he has put together a true artists' colony, where creativity flourishes. About a dozen artists have space here, including Filthy himself, painter Esch Snoats, glass artist PleaseWakeMeUp Idler, and many others. There are also spaces for events, and regular art talks and presentations are scheduled.

Figure 3.12: The artists' colony at Artropolis

⬇ Museum of Contemporary Art at Neufreistadt: Neufreistadt (189, 135, 180)

The museum has two floors and a rooftop area containing sculpture, paintings, and videos of some of the best *Second Life* artists. Some of the sculptures are interactive in ways that real-life art simply cannot be, which can be really exciting to explore. As with most museums, the exhibits here change from time to time. Tour the lovely surrounding walled city of Neufreistadt while you're visiting the museum!

⬇ Lascaux Caves: Modesta (94, 46, 55)

The *Second Life* Lascaux Caves are the work of Bizarre Berry, and are not meant to duplicate the real caves in France, but rather to provide a feel for them. There are candles and torches to light your way; but you must be comfortable walking around tight *Second Life* spaces.

CHAPTER 1
CHAPTER 2
CHAPTER 3

CHAPTER 4
CHAPTER 5
CHAPTER 6
CHAPTER 7
CHAPTER 8
CHAPTER 9
CHAPTER 10
CHAPTER 11
CHAPTER 12
CHAPTER 13
CHAPTER 14
CHAPTER 15
APPENDICES

⬇ ZERO POINT: KELHAM (170, 97, 99)

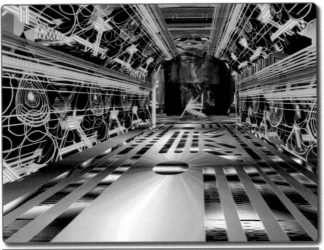

Figure 3.13: Watch your step at Zero Point!

Zero Point (Figure 3.13) is an immersive art installation created by *Second Life* artist Sabine Stonebender and consisting of a traditional sculpture garden on the ground floor and two immersive areas (art that's meant to be walked through, stood inside of, and even ridden) in the sky. Use the "Bunnyporter" to teleport to the first level, where you'll be surrounded by a dazzling array of brightly colored shapes and mists, most of them in motion. "I love illusions," says Stonebender, "and *Second Life* is well suited to making them."

⬇ ETHEREAL TEAL: TEAL (196, 65, 21)

Ethereal Teal is the creation of Jopsy Pendragon, one of the magician scripters of *Second Life*, and is filled with things to see and places to explore. Take the balloon ride and visit any of a number of places: St. Mark's Plaza, the Firework Show, Ethereal Beach, the Floating Citadel, Jopsy's Workshop, the Caves, Cloud Chateau, or—if you want to see through the illusionist's illusions—the Particle Lab. Be sure to explore underwater and see the corals and the sunken ruins.

⬇ GREENHOUSE: GREENHOUSE (63, 113, 22)

Figure 3.14: Greenhouse on a perfect day

If there is any place in *Second Life* that epitomizes "one moment of perfect beauty," it is Transparent Banshee's Greenhouse (Figure 3.14). These are rich builds—rich in content and rich in design of how the content is displayed. There is a flow, a pattern to the design, and it is gorgeous. "Greenhouse is meant to be a secluded spot," notes Banshee, "where nature hopefully will help calm the stress in overstimulated minds ..." Some areas are designed for living, and others are designed for display.

WHAT CAN I LEARN IN *SECOND LIFE*?

CHAPTER 1

CHAPTER 2

CHAPTER 3

CHAPTER 4

CHAPTER 5

CHAPTER 6

CHAPTER 7

CHAPTER 8

CHAPTER 9

CHAPTER 10

CHAPTER 11

CHAPTER 12

CHAPTER 13

CHAPTER 14

CHAPTER 15

APPENDICES

It's not all fun and games in *Second Life*. How about learning something while you're here? With many educational institutions going online—even National Public Radio's *Science Friday* is here!— it's no surprise that teachers and learners are finding each other in *Second Life*. Whether you're eager to complete a real-life degree or you just want to learn about a new topic or nourish a new interest, there's something here for you!

⬇ VIRTUAL HALLUCINATIONS PROJECT: SEDIG (21, 28, 22)

The Virtual Hallucinations Project from UC Davis is modeled to look like a psychiatric unit, a place not unknown to many schizophrenics; and it's schizophrenia that you're here to learn about. As you wander through various rooms, hallucinations are demonstrated—and explained. A poster's words morph into a derogatory message, with only those words becoming legible. At the exit, you're allowed to stop the voices. Although a visit does not give the *full* sense of what a person experiencing hallucinations is going through, it's a frighteningly good introduction.

⬇ FREETHINKING CENTRAL: SAENEUL (23, 35, 103)

Don't visit Kidney Bean's Freethinking Central looking for sights to see, for they are few. But it's a veritable feast for the intellect. You can read and contemplate a number of notecards, or you may sign a petition at `http://firstfreedomfirst.org`. There's also a portal to `http://humanlight.org`. We liked the globe suspended in the space, affirming that we have more in common than we have differences.

⬇ THE HOLOCAUST MUSEUM: IR SHALOM (139, 66, 24)

This isn't a visit for the faint of heart. It's one thing to know that this evil thing happened, and quite another to see its photographic evidence. The museum is a frightening place, and perhaps even more so for its very starkness. There is nothing to see but photographs of death, nothing to read but words of death. It's not uplifting, but it's a valuable experience.

⬇ BETTER WORLD: BETTER WORLD (54, 211, 21)

The island's creators had the wisdom, in showing visitors places where things are very wrong in the world, to make it clear that we can change that darkness; and the beauties of the island give testament to the possibilities that we all carry inside ourselves. The Peace Tiles project and the Garden of Hope

contrast with Camp Darfur and the Baghdad Streets. Leave the Center for Water Studies for the end of your visit and enjoy the flora and fauna there.

 SHINAGAWA: KAWAII (54, 205, 21)

Dithean and Modhuine Ringo have constructed a faithful reproduction of a *shinden-zukuri*, a style of architecture from Heian-era Japan; and if you've ever been curious about Japan's past, this is a good place to learn. When you teleport in, you'll be able to pick up a notecard welcoming you in English and Japanese and explaining the few rules. The shinden-zukuri is based on the tales of Genji Monogatari. The Ringos enjoy showing off Shinagawa and would love to walk you through it.

LITERATURE ALIVE!: EDUISLAND II (185, 240, 21)

Beth Ritter-Guth, an English professor, runs Community Colleges Without Borders, which hosts *Second Life*'s Literature Alive!—with avatars and a virtual classroom, you can almost smell the chalk. But Literature Alive! also takes advantage of the ability to build: classes on Gothic literature are taught in a castle, engaging multiple senses and making learning more powerful.

> ### ADDITIONAL INFO
> ## ARTIFICIAL LIFE
>
> Artificial life (aka A-life) is a field of study and associated art forms that examines systems related to life, its processes, and its evolution, using simulations based on computer models, robotics, and biochemistry. It's a fascinating field of study and is happening right now in *Second Life*:
>
> - Svarga: Svarga (7, 122, 22)—Simply a beautiful place.
> - Terminus: Terminus (147, 105, 26)—Stark scenery but the species are clear.

WHERE CAN I FEED MY SOUL?

A poet, when asked what he would do with a coin, noted that he would buy hyacinths—something completely ephemeral and useless from a practical standpoint—"to feed my soul." This section serves as a starting point for feeding your own soul in *Second Life*. Whether your spiritual life leans toward the Tao or the Tarot, there is something for you here!

⬇ Support for Healing: Support for Healing (148, 41, 36)

Zafu Diamond's Support for Healing is a place to go when you feel overwhelmed, shattered, raw. A number of notecards will inform you about suicide; but even if that issue does not speak to you directly, the place will draw you in. There truly is something here for everyone, from calming beauty to a dance area that feels dizzyingly like you're a mermaid dancing with the fish, and from Zafu's own spiritual retreat to the numerous support groups that you can join.

⬇ St. Paul's Cathedral: Grace (71, 226, 130)

The *Second Life* St. Paul's Cathedral is an almost-faithful reproduction of the real-life church. You really need to fly all around the interior and exterior to fully appreciate the architecture. Inside you see the famous black-and-white floor along with colorful mosaics, installed (in the real-life church) in the mid 19th century at Queen Victoria's insistence that the interior was "most dreary, dingy, and undevotional."

⬇ Asagao Memorial Park: Asagao (83, 167, 24)

Figure 3.15: Time and space to reflect

After spending some time at Support for Healing (or, perhaps, *before* spending time there), you may wish to visit Peter Gretsky's Asagao Memorial Park (Figure 3.15); there you can reflect on those you love who have "lost their lives to suicide," as the plaque at the start of the park phrases it. The park also offers a place for healing and support for people affected by suicide. You have the opportunity to leave something to remember a loved one.

⬇ First Unitarian Universalist Church in *Second Life*: Lovelace (49, 48, 23)

When you arrive, follow the path before you to reach the meeting place. You'll be rewarded at the end of the walk with a lovely open space, perfect for services and meetings alike; the tenets of the UU church (all of which should be read) are on a bulletin board nearby. Interesting quirk: here, the stained glass is *above* you!

CHAPTER 1
CHAPTER 2
CHAPTER 3

CHAPTER 4
CHAPTER 5
CHAPTER 6
CHAPTER 7
CHAPTER 8
CHAPTER 9
CHAPTER 10
CHAPTER 11
CHAPTER 12
CHAPTER 13
CHAPTER 14
CHAPTER 15
APPENDICES

⬇ GLBT Memorial: Provincetown (127, 193, 27)

This is a memorial for *all* Holocaust victims, with special attention to the GLBT community. On one wall are the first few stanzas of George Eliot's "O May I Join the Choir Invisible." The specific experiences of gay people in the concentration camps are not documented, but it is not asking much to remember them, so that thoughts of their suffering might, as the poem says, "pierce the night like stars."

⬇ Jewish Temple in Jerusalem: Holy City (8, 4, 28)

At one level, this build is historical: it provides a reconstruction of the second temple of Jerusalem that was destroyed in 70 CE. But don't let the historical details derail you: this is a truly spiritual place, filled with wandering, sometimes mournful music and more opportunities for reflection than you can imagine. For those who want an additional challenge, the lost ark with the ten commandments is here, too: try to find it! Modest dress, please.

⬇ Medicine Buddha Stupa: Support For Healing (171, 96, 67)

A *stupa* is traditionally a simple structure or object (originally just a mound) that creates a space and place for meditation, recollection, etc. This one is dedicated to the Medicine Buddha. A notecard on the main painting will give you information on the different manifestations of the Medicine Buddha; it's a good read.

⬇ Chebi Mosque: Chebi (151, 212, 84)

Figure 3.16: Chebi Mosque

Marino Nuvorali's Chebi Mosque (Figure 3.16) offers a notecard that explains many of the aspects of the mosque and gives pointers for further study. Female avatars need to attach a free veil before entering. Sunbeams come in through the windows and play among the arches. It's airy and beautiful and peaceful, and well worth a visit.

⬇ Skeptical Buddhists' Sangha: Toowoomba (128, 24, 87)

"Skeptical Buddhism" is essentially Buddhism without beliefs, adopting the basic tenets of Buddhism while leaving behind all the artifacts of other religions that it has picked up through the centuries. There are regular meetings in the sky *sangha*: see the notice board there for details. You'll be invited to stay for a meal, and you'll be given an exquisite Mala meditation: "There is an end," it promises, "to the path of suffering."

⬇ Pagan Learning Grove: Samhain (21, 163, 27)

Anam Turas ("soul journey" in Irish) offers a beautiful and peaceful experience at the Pagan Learning Grove, where Gaia the earth mother is the teacher, assisted by others who frequent the area. It is filled with the lush sounds of running water and bird calls and crackling fires. There are myriad circular areas embellished with Celtic symbols where you can stop and think, or perhaps converse with those you meet here. Each area hides a delightful surprise: splashing water, beautiful flowers, a sudden flurry of butterfly wings.

⬇ WHERE CAN I MEET SOMEONE?

We, your tour guides, do not run a dating service, but we can introduce you to just a few places where you might meet that temporary (or even permanent!) special someone.

⬇ The Club Scene

There probably are more clubs in *Second Life* than there are in your real-life haunts, so we're just scratching the surface here, showing you some that we like or that we feel are particularly noteworthy. Start with these, and find where you feel the most comfortable!

The Black Sun Nightclub: Hayek (59, 193, 31)

The Black Sun is a re-creation of the club of the same name in Neal Stephenson's *Snow Crash.* Come here for gorgeous lights and glitter, and a chance to step into a "novel" environment!

Cirque Mystique: Oceanus (205, 95, 25)

Okay, so it's a little weird to have a techno nightclub inside a pirate ship, but hey, why not? All the requisite undulating purple lights are here, along with a bar and a truly international crowd.

CHAPTER 1
CHAPTER 2
CHAPTER 3

CHAPTER 4
CHAPTER 5
CHAPTER 6
CHAPTER 7
CHAPTER 8
CHAPTER 9
CHAPTER 10
CHAPTER 11
CHAPTER 12
CHAPTER 13
CHAPTER 14
CHAPTER 15
APPENDICES

CHAPTER 3

HEY! I'M NEW HERE!

WHAT ARE SOME MUST-VISIT LOCATIONS?

WHERE CAN I PARTICIPATE IN SOMETHING?

WHERE CAN I FIND A MOMENT OF PERFECT BEAUTY?

WHAT CAN I LEARN IN *SECOND LIFE*?

WHERE CAN I FEED MY SOUL?

WHERE CAN I MEET SOMEONE?

WHAT CAN I BUY?

THE WITCH'S BREW PUB: EVALUA (222, 228, 28)

Trinity Cole's Witch's Brew Pub is one of the nicest places we've found in *Second Life* to meet and hang out. Be sure that you read the pub rules, which include no discussion of lovers' spats or dramas (thank goodness!), no cyber sex, no gay bashing, no role playing, and respect for all.

THE ELBOW ROOM: MARE (95, 40, 56)

Elbow room is about all the space you'll have in this intimate little bar, undoubtedly the smallest in *Second Life*, but oddly appealing. Chatting is encouraged.

CLUB KANDOR: KANDOR (80, 101, 21)

At the site of the old Dazzle Dance Factory, Club Kandor offers 35 possible dances to use on the disco-lighted floor, surely more than anybody would need. A nice touch: the airplane parked just outside for quick getaways!

NITRO NIGHTCLUB: NORTH HALSTED (99, 81, 25)

Nitro proclaims itself to be *Second Life's* "hottest gay nightclub," and there are flames just inside the door in case you're not persuaded. Lots of contests, and a runway for hot young things to strut their stuff.

⬇ INTERNATIONAL HANGOUTS

Here we feature some places where you can go to meet people from your country or culture of origin—or people from other cultures and countries of origin! Think of it as a way to tour the world—at night.

HOLLAND'S GLORIE: HOLLAND (93, 168, 23)

This is a small, intimate club complete with fireplace, dance floor, and a nice bar. Come to sit and chat or dance the night away … but be sure that you speak Dutch, because everyone else here does!

ILHA BRASIL: BRASIL (169, 184, 26)

"Dance Explosion!" shouts the sign on the wall of this Brazilian dance club, with the requisite disco ball, neon-blue dance floor, and dance balls for your own exercising pleasure. Polish up your Portuguese and head on over!

FRANCE PITTORESQUE: SEYCHELLES (152, 145, 21)

While not technically a club, there is dancing near the beach at this lovely French hangout. Welcome is in French or English; but be sure to remove any group identifiers when you arrive, upon request of the owners.

SALSAS Y BOLEROS: APOLLO (131, 31, 38)

Care for some Latin dancing? Who wouldn't? Salsas y Boleros is part of Dane Zander's excellent Apollo sim, and will give you the opportunity to try out some of those sexy—albeit not sexual—moves.

⬇ Jazz Clubs

Smoky, elegant, intense, groovin'—those are just a few words that come to mind when describing jazz and the clubs where it's played. Here are a few of the places where you can hear some amazing music in *Second Life*.

BLUE NOTE JAZZ LOUNGE: THE BLUE NOTE (239, 185, 21)

A very cool venue for some very hot jazz. There's a piano on the stage and great dance balls ("the "dip" and "swept away" are our favorites); the music runs the gamut from big bands to swing to oldies—and, of course, some outstanding jazz. There are cuddle balls in the garden outside if you'd like to spend some quiet time with a friend.

JADE'S JAZZ LOUNGE: HAEOREUM (190, 21, 69)

This is a lovely club, with a wide, panoramic view of the ocean on one side, and space for live performances opposite. There's plenty of room for dancing, and there are cozy overstuffed sofas and cuddle balls near the fireplace. It's a great place to meet someone.

ADDITIONAL INFO
ONCE YOU'VE MET SOMEONE...

Now that you've met that special someone, here are some romantic getaway places for you to visit together:

- 🎁 Casablanca Society Lounge: Iladil (162, 216, 71)—Go here for a touch of elegance in your nightlife.

(Continued)

CHAPTER 1
CHAPTER 2
CHAPTER 3

CHAPTER 4
CHAPTER 5
CHAPTER 6
CHAPTER 7
CHAPTER 8
CHAPTER 9
CHAPTER 10
CHAPTER 11
CHAPTER 12
CHAPTER 13
CHAPTER 14
CHAPTER 15
APPENDICES

CHAPTER 3

HEY! I'M NEW
HERE!

WHAT ARE SOME
MUST-VISIT
LOCATIONS?

WHERE CAN I
PARTICIPATE IN
SOMETHING?

WHERE CAN I FIND
A MOMENT OF
PERFECT BEAUTY?

WHAT CAN I LEARN
IN *SECOND LIFE*?

WHERE CAN I FEED
MY SOUL?

WHERE CAN I MEET
SOMEONE?

WHAT CAN I BUY?

- Midsomer Isle: Midsomer Isle (149, 123, 27)—Charming, with lovely privacy if you want it. Check out the tower and the chess terrace.
- Dragon Moon Resort: Dragon Moon (128, 198, 26)—Typical couple area but with lots of dragons; some activities like scuba diving as well.
- Serenite Gardens: Serenite (57, 218, 24)—Free cuttings garden, lots of beauty to explore, some Wiccan activities and items.
- Lost Gardens of Apollo: Apollo (21, 62, 72)—Gay-friendly couples place; no nudity and no sex.
- Des Les: Msitu (89, 129, 28)—Not only for lesbians; a women-friendly hangout.

WHAT CAN I BUY?

If you like to shop, it's your lucky day, because if there's one thing that's ubiquitous in *Second Life*, it's the shopping! Most items are outrageously inexpensive, so you can shop 'til you drop and still have something left over for a restorative cappuccino. Here we've assembled a list of what we think are among the most interesting things to buy, and where you can buy them.

MALLS AND SHOPPING AREAS

They're all over *Second Life*, so we're going to highlight just two.

METAMART HUD MARKETPLACE: SOBAEKSAN (199, 201, 65)

Here you're invited to wear a heads-up display (HUD), which enables you to have the marketplace with you, as it were. Go to the Items tab and enter what you wish to buy in the search field. It's like using a search engine to shop online.

FOREST PLAZA: GYEONGJI (45, 155, 81)

What can we say—it's an outdoor mall with separate shops, and you can buy just about anything here. It's a good place to start.

⬇ Specialty Shops

Many locations you'll visit have specialty shops attached to them. For example, Midsomer Isle has a lovely gift shop. So when you visit new places, look around and see if you'd like to do any shopping there.

CHAPTER 1
CHAPTER 2
CHAPTER 3

CHAPTER 4
CHAPTER 5
CHAPTER 6
CHAPTER 7
CHAPTER 8
CHAPTER 9
CHAPTER 10
CHAPTER 11
CHAPTER 12
CHAPTER 13
CHAPTER 14
CHAPTER 15
APPENDICES

HOUSE OF BLADE MALL: SAMURAI ISLAND (129, 234, 23)

Part of Samurai Island, these shops allow you to outfit yourself in whatever *sharp* apparel you choose: knives, swords, scimitars, and—of course—the proper Japanese clothing to go with your choice of blades. The area is quite lovely, with tinkling wind chimes, shoji screens, and cherry blossoms throughout.

SERENITE: SERENITE (57, 218, 24)

Go shopping in a village-like atmosphere, complete with a beribboned maypole. Here you'll find Wiccan supplies—crystals, candles, very practical magic—but also the opportunity to take cuttings from the garden and to teleport to a meditation spot and teaching altar.

GAY WORLD: GAY WORLD (226, 97, 26)

Gay World offers—not surprisingly—gay-friendly clothes shopping, plus some specialty items with mature content.

⬇ Avatars

Ever wanted to be a puffin? A potted plant? If you can dream it, you can find it in *Second Life*. Be creative—you don't actually *have to* look like a Barbie doll. Here are a few places to start searching for your ideal avatar look.

DWEIA'S DREAMS: LASPARA (103, 137, 102)

Dweia undoubtedly has some of the best avatar looks in-world: unusual, distinctive, and far from run-of-the-mill. Her shop's a great destination; once you've secured your avatar look, head downstairs to Dweia's Bar and dance the night away. Even if you *are* a potted plant!

ABSTRACT AVATARS: CRIMSON (220, 44, 28)

As the sign says, "Haven't you heard? Chicks dig robots!" There's lots to dig in this shop that allows you to be limited only by your imagination.

FURIOUS STAR WAR AVATARS: ROTHENBURG (95, 23, 451)

This place is worth a visit even if you don't end up buying anything, just to relive the movies that we all watched and loved. Your shopping experience is accompanied by random Star Wars sound effects, and who knows—you could end up looking like R2D2. It's a lot of fun!

⬇ FASHION

Expressing your creativity through your avatar and what she or he wears is a lot of fun. Here are our tips for picking up some of the coolest threads in *Second Life*.

CERES CLOTHIERS: PICASSO (120, 162, 24)

Visit this women's shop for the elegance of the venue: marble pillars, floors, and staircases, Regency-style furniture and accessories, heavy velvet draperies, and more. The merchandise is like much of women's clothing in *Second Life*: it reveals far more than it hides.

HOUSE OF RFYRE: ISLE OF RFYRE (68, 132, 42)

If all shopping were like this, we'd be more enthusiastic shoppers! The House of RFyre is what one might call Elegant Goth; where else could one find the ordinary *Second Life* fare (eyes, skin, hair) mixed in with items such as a carriage hearse … complete with coffin. Downstairs there are fabulous gowns, all velvet and brocade … yum!

N. ESCHER FASHIONS: NOYO (115, 71, 24)

All the best in bellydancing and harem wear. Instead of the usual flat pictures on the walls, here there are interesting cut-out figures doing the modeling.

LITTLE REBEL DESIGNS: GALLINAS (144, 101, 58)

Buy everything here from skins to fashions to houses; there are lots of styles and there's something for everyone.

⬇ MISCELLANEOUS

There are some shops that simply defy categorization. So here's the section to turn to when you need those miscellaneous everyday household items such as a new airplane, a weapon, some interior design help, or your own virtual reality.

SECOND SKIES: DOGFIGHT ATOLL (77, 18, 23)

If you've ever wanted to fly, want no longer: at Second Skies you can fly anything from a dirigible to a helicopter, and just about everything in between. The third floor allows you to mix and match pieces to manufacture your own plane.

CHAPTER 1
CHAPTER 2
CHAPTER 3

CHAPTER 4
CHAPTER 5
CHAPTER 6
CHAPTER 7
CHAPTER 8
CHAPTER 9
CHAPTER 10
CHAPTER 11
CHAPTER 12
CHAPTER 13
CHAPTER 14
CHAPTER 15
APPENDICES

ARMORY ISLAND: ARMORY ISLAND (127, 235, 80)

From handguns to nuclear missiles, if it kills, you'll find it here—and it's all for sale. Creepy in a high-tech kind of way.

ELEMENTS IN DESIGN: ELEMENTS IN DESIGN (209, 171, 26)

From the moment you arrive and are greeted by owner Gwen Carillon with the traditional "merry meet," you know that this will be a different sort of experience. And it is. This is seriously cool furniture and design—the most eclectic that we've found in-world. If you have your own place in *Second Life*, this is where you should come to furnish it.

VIRTUAL REALITY ROOM & SHOP: SOLARIAM (218, 162, 431)

We saved the best for last. Remember the Star Trek holodeck? You'll want to make a virtual-reality purchase here only if you own space that will permit its installation. (You should have an area somewhere between 20 and 50 meters on one side, because you're really creating a space within a space.) No property? Not enough room on your property? You can still visit and experience the remarkable and dazzling virtual room here. Choose from a plethora of scenes—nature, urban, fictional—and find yourself, suddenly, a part of them! You can walk around inside the scene and feel that you're really there. As Seeker Gray said, it's a jolly good time!

ADDITIONAL INFO
A STATE OF FLUX

Please note that the sites presented in this chapter might not be around forever (or might move), since much of *Second Life* is in a constant state of flux.

If you'd like to locate other places to visit, play, or shop, take advantage of the "newbie" areas like those covered at the start of this chapter, where people are eager to help you get around. You can also use the Search function to look for places, people, and communities.

And don't forget to check our blog at `http://www.secondseeker.com` for ongoing reviews of great *Second Life* places to visit and experience!

CHAPTER 4

REAL RESIDENTS

Toward the end of 2006, as *Second Life* reached the critical mass of several hundred thousand active monthly users, the population diversified even further. This chapter is but a very small sampling of that populace, with special attention on residents who were born relatively recently, or whose *SL* identity is merged with their real-life activity.

CONTENTS

BETH ODETS

Before joining *Second Life* in 2005, she was a former social worker, a mother of two, and a fiddler in a locally popular Southern band. A couple years after becoming Beth Odets, she had several unlikely titles on her resume: virtual artist, professional metaverse builder, and founder of a popular Jewish community.

Though she had no previous experience with online games, a fellow artist convinced her to try *SL*. "I've never worked in a graphic computer environment at all," she says. "I know surprisingly little about using computers." So she taught herself in-world, even creating a technique for uploading textures. "I still have no idea how to use Photoshop (I can't believe I am admitting that)," she says. These talents intersected with her real-life spirituality when a friend showed her an *SL* version of the Torah.

"When she pulled it out, I said, 'that isn't what it really looks like … let me show you,'" she recalls. Within hours, she had not only created a Torah, but an ark to house it, and the main structure for the temple to contain that. Then something wonderful happened.

"Three days later people were already coming to see it … I had no idea it was the first complete synagogue in *Second Life*," she says. "It wasn't till I understood that there was a lack of Jewish community in *SL* that I realized how important it was to people that I keep moving forward with that project. It became a huge passion for me, and it changed my life." Jewish residents from around the world began congregating around the temple, even enacting important traditions of their faith; Beth built a sukkah, for example, a temporary structure representing the tents Israelis used during their Biblical exodus.

"Someone in the sukkah told me that while being Jewish, they weren't raised with any Jewish education, and had never actually been in a sukkah because they were embarrassed that they didn't know about it," she remembers. Here in *Second Life*, they finally had the chance to do so. Beth cried for a week afterward.

And now she had a mission: "It inspired me to start making educational events surrounding our holidays … being able to give that to people has been the most rewarding and inspiring thing about *Second Life* Synagogue." Many people have told her that enacting the *SL* version of Jewish traditions, like their weekly Sabbath candle-lighting ceremony, has carried over to their first lives. "In my opinion, that is what it's all about."

CHAPTER 1

CHAPTER 2

CHAPTER 3

CHAPTER 4

CHAPTER 5

CHAPTER 6

CHAPTER 7

CHAPTER 8

CHAPTER 9

CHAPTER 10

CHAPTER 11

CHAPTER 12

CHAPTER 13

CHAPTER 14

CHAPTER 15

APPENDICES

FROM LINDEN LAB
A NOTEWORTHY RESIDENT

"Beth Odets has a dual role in *Second Life*. [In addition to having become the center of a Jewish community within *Second Life*], she's one of our live musicians—she performs weekly at her own venue called The Ark. In the past, she's done a mishmash of classical music, Broadway tunes, bluegrass, and her own compositions mostly on her violin. More recently, she's been performing with a partner from her real-life band, Fish Fry Bingo."

—Prospero Linden

Her temple has since evolved into an entire neighborhood, including the editorial offices of *2life*, the Jewish magazine in *SL*, a Passover Pavilion, and a music venue that resembles Noah's ark, where Beth performs violin for a live audience. Her day job in-world is in the same space.

"After the success of the synagogue and lots of media attention in early 2007," she explains, "I was offered my first building job in *Second Life*. Now I work in *SL* full-time doing builds."

ANSHE CHUNG

No list of the rich and famous is complete without mentioning Ms. Chung, owner of Dreamland, an entire continent, and thousands of dollars worth of oceanfront property across the world. In *SL*-related media, US$150,000 is the dollar figure you'll read most—it's the amount Linden Lab estimates Anshe makes per year from her in-world real-estate business, with her *SL*/RL partner Guni Greenstein through their company, Anshe Chung Studios. Ms. Chung has arguably become *Second Life*'s most prominent avatar in the outside world, appearing on a May 2006 cover of *BusinessWeek* beside the appropriate title, "Virtual World, Real Money." The story launched the explosion of interest in outside corporations and organizations in this quirky online world, and as such, the face of Anshe launched millions of real-world dollars into *Second Life*.

SUZANNA SOYINKA

Darkly beautiful if decidedly Mature, *City of Lost Angels* (*CoLA*) is currently the most popular role-playing game created within *Second Life*, combining post-apocalyptic cyberpunk with supernatural Goth flavor. There's nothing quite like it in *Second Life*, or, for that matter, in other online worlds. "Seeing angels hang out with nekos [humanoid cats] on street corners is one thing," *SL* game reviewer Onder Skall wrote on my blog New World Notes (`http://nwn.blogs.com`), "but it all gets more interesting when a few demons get into an argument with vampires over which one of them gets to feast on the human up the alley and then some lycans jump them both just for fun. Oh, and let's not forget the guy with the supernatural powers that dives into the mix for the hell of it." Famed MMORPG designer Scott "Lum the Mad" Jennings, once a harsh critic of *Second Life*, was so impressed by *CoLA* and other *SL* communities, he reconsidered his initial skepticism. ("If you're looking for me when I'm in *SL*," he wrote on his own blog, "I'm an insane angel from the future in the *City of Lost Angels*.)

Both its lead creator and owner, Suzanne was inspired to develop *CoLA* when she grew bored with a vampire-themed region she usually hung out in after she joined *Second Life* from another MMORPG.

"I had around two-thirds of the Satellite sim," she remembers, "and I figured, well, the worst that can happen is I'll have a nice build for my shop to be in, at least. So I decided to try something different. Something that wasn't a mall, wasn't a club, but something outside the norm for *SL* at the time." Her development partner Jora Welesa helped create a new RPG/combat system called Community Combat System, which tracks and updates player stats. "I basically applied the same mode of thinking I applied when I made my vampire fangs," she says. "Nobody was making the kind of fangs I wanted, so I made the set I wanted. Turned out a lot of people wanted them—same with *City of Lost Angels*."

She now makes a living from being the mistress of the City. "I'm not making rockstar money from it," she allows, "but I am making ends meet."

Her advice to other RPG developers who'd like to try *Second Life* as a development platform? "Don't do it for the money. A pure concept takes care of itself financially and doesn't need to be ridden like a pony to fill your bank account. Make the game you always wanted to play … and then realize you won't have much time to play it because you'll be very busy maintaining it. And most of all, remember to be open and friendly to the people who enjoy your content."

CHAPTER 1

CHAPTER 2

CHAPTER 3

CHAPTER 4

CHAPTER 5

CHAPTER 6

CHAPTER 7

CHAPTER 8

CHAPTER 9

CHAPTER 10

CHAPTER 11

CHAPTER 12

CHAPTER 13

CHAPTER 14

CHAPTER 15

APPENDICES

HACKSHAVEN HARFORD

In mid 2006, a unique client became a landowner on the *Second Life* grid: the United States government, through the auspices of its National Oceanic and Atmospheric Administration (NOAA), which entered at the behest of Hackshaven Harford. In real life, Hackshaven's worked for NOAA since high school, remaining with the agency while he earned a degree in electrical and computer engineering. At first he joined *SL* for personal reasons—his father was already a resident and told him about *SL*, and his sister, wife, and brother-in-law are also active members—but Linden Lab education evangelist Pathfinder Linden loaned him some land to experiment with visualizing real-world data in-world.

Satisfied with the early results, Hackshaven tentatively approached his bosses at NOAA. The result was Meteroa, an island where residents can experience a tsunami hitting the shore and ride an airplane through a hurricane.

And that's just the start: "NOAA is testing the *Second Life* platform for use in educational outreach and data visualization," says Hackshaven. "*Second Life* caters to a worldwide audience and as such we have access to people that could never visit our 'real life' offices. Ideally, our growing land mass could be used in a classroom setting to show students parts of our world they would otherwise be unable to see. For example, very few people will ever be able to ride in a submarine or see the northern lights. Also, much of the data that NOAA produces is inherently 3D and *Second Life* provides unique opportunities for visualization not currently found on the traditional 2D web."

This means expanding: "In addition to our original island," he says, "we will shortly be opening an expansion to our oceanic content. Work is also under way on a nine-sim beast called 'Second Earth' that hopes to blend the capabilities of tools like Google Earth or Microsoft Visual Earth with the collaborative capabilities of *Second Life*."

Hackshaven also founded the Real Life Government in *Second Life* group. "At last count, there were 10–15 agencies from three or four countries participating with the next real-life meeting scheduled for November 2007." His advice for fellow government employees who want to move their work in-world? "Start small, focusing on a topic that is of interest to your local management. Linden Lab is keen on seeing serious applications inside *Second Life* and has a history of supporting the individual effort required to jump-start an organization's virtual-world awareness. Baby steps are the key, as managers can have 30-second attention spans. If you don't wow a manager with an easily understandable and relatively cheap application, you may lose your chance to prove *Second Life* and virtual worlds in general are more than a 'video game.'"

Then again, those concerns don't weigh on the real-life man behind Hackshaven. In his personal time, he launched Maya Realities, an *SL*-based business that tracks and analyzes visitor patterns for virtual land owners and content creators. "Recently I've taken a back seat to my much handsomer avatar Hackshaven Harford," he muses. "In fact, as time progresses and I see an increasingly large ratio of Google hits for my avatar as compared to myself, I have to wonder, down the line who will be controlling who."

KEYSTONE BOUCHARD

In May 2006, the real-life person behind Keystone was reading *Wired* magazine when he came across a single-paragraph mention of *Second Life*. "When I read that there was actually a place where users created their own content, I literally dropped the magazine," he says. He had recently finished his master's thesis project in architecture school, and it explored ways in which virtual reality would eventually influence real-world architecture. Shortly after *Wired* hit the floor, Keystone Bouchard was born.

"At this time, my wife Kandy and I were operating our own design practice, Crescendo Design, specializing in environmentally friendly or green design." Shortly after joining *Second Life*, he began building a neighborhood of homes, "and was amazed to watch avatars cluster around the houses, and walking around inside. Someone even started decorating the interior of the home with furniture and appliances. That's when I understood that *Second Life* wasn't just another modeling tool, but was a living community of people. That afternoon, someone invited me to attend a Society for Virtual Architecture meeting, where I was introduced to other architects and designers from all over the world, and I knew *Second Life* was something very unique—something I really wanted to be a part of." He created a virtual studio for Crescendo, and began bringing his real-life clients into *SL* to experience design concepts. "They could test paint colors, material types and finishes, furniture layouts, and even landscaping options." During an open-house tour, someone from Berkeley, California–based Internet marketing company Clear Ink met him in *SL* and invited him to visit their real-world office.

That's how Keystone and his family left the Midwest, where their studio was based, to become the company's "3D Experience Architect" in *Second Life*. One of his first Clear Ink projects was for US Congressman George Miller, who wanted to create an *SL* presence built to resemble Capitol Hill. "It wouldn't have been appropriate (or even feasible) to build an exact copy of the real House in *Second Life*," says Keystone, "so the challenge was to include enough familiar elements while at the same time highlighting its virtuality."

So to say *Second Life* influenced Keystone's real life would be an understatement. "It has been completely transformed," he says. "In my new career in virtual architecture, I have had the opportunity to work with such real-life architecture luminaries as Cameron Sinclair, Chris Luebkeman, Sergio Palleroni, and Phil Bernstein, that I would have never had access to in my traditional career path." He founded the Architecture in *Second Life* group, and lately he finds his professional course becoming even more *SL*-based. "I have started to become more interested in designing virtual spaces than real-life spaces," he explains. "I'm also interested in the ways virtual architecture could become the 'ultimate green' insofar as certain functions can transcend physical presence altogether. After all, what could be more green than not building anything at all?"

His advice for other architects interested in *Second Life*? "Don't think of *Second Life* as a replacement for your detailed 3D modeling software. Think of it as you would a cardboard or clay study model. *Second Life* is a perfect environment for modeling schematic design concepts, and for collaborating with your clients and members of the community who will help make your design ideas stronger. *Second Life* is first and foremost a community."

CHAPTER 1
CHAPTER 2
CHAPTER 3
CHAPTER 4

CHAPTER 5
CHAPTER 6
CHAPTER 7
CHAPTER 8
CHAPTER 9
CHAPTER 10
CHAPTER 11
CHAPTER 12
CHAPTER 13
CHAPTER 14
CHAPTER 15
APPENDICES

KATT KONGO

Although there have been numerous attempts to create an in-world newspaper, it was Katt Kongo who succeeded where so many had failed. (Unsurprisingly, she had nearly a decade of professional experience as a real-world journalist to draw from.) Launched in fall of 2005, within a year her biweekly *Metaverse Messenger* was reportedly attracting a monthly circulation of nearly 50,000, evolving into the grid's leading voice for information, advertising, and community.

I first glimpsed China on YouTube's *Second Life* machinima stream; she was a startlingly vivid avatar introducing herself in a video clip with Chinese subtitles. In subsequent months, I learned she was an accomplished multimedia artist, creator of "i.Mirror," a beautiful, three-part machinima of the *Second Life* experience—and as such, perhaps the most world-renowned artist thus far to use *SL* as a medium. This is because China Tracy is Cao Fei, a Guangzhou artist who's "a key member of the vibrant new generation of Chinese artists emerging in the early twenty-first century," according to *Art Forum*'s description, and has been featured by the New York MOMA, among many other galleries, museums, and biennial exhibitions across the globe.

In early 2007, Cao discovered *Second Life* and embarked on a six-month tour of *Second Life* as China Tracy. She experienced all the usual activities: "Fly, chat, build, teleport, buy, sex, add friends, snapshot…" (Yes, she even tried virtual sex, though a prospective lover misplaced his equipment at the worst possible moment.) All the while, she captured video of her experiences documentary-style, which went into "i.Mirror," a sad, dreamy, but ultimately optimistic 30-minute epic in three parts that first screened in a silvery, inflatable tent at the prestigious Venice Biennial art exhibition. The installation was such a hit, a major Italian fashion company purchased a high-res version of the movie for exclusive showing in the owner's gallery.

In "i.Mirror," China falls in love with a handsome young man who turns out to be much older in real life. Throughout, she explores a place of great beauty—but often overwhelmed by commercialism. "For me," says China, "*SL* is a new world, but it's still surrounded by an old-world system—it parallels and mirrors our RL." She continues, "[Residents are] not what they originally are, and yet they remain unchanged. I'm not criticizing the *Second Life* world, because this world is created by us (international citizens.) Whether RL or *SL*, everywhere is full of consumerism/expansionism. *SL* is an artificial/digital landscape, but totally human nature is behind that, so you can see how real we are. But on the reality end of this combined ultra-space, there is still love for simplicity and the pursuit of freedom, creativity, and imagination, and only these possibilities made me treasure this *SL* world."

China Tracy has remained an active resident, and is planning a new *Second Life*–based art project, launched on Creative Commons' island Kula: RMB City (named after the renminbi, China's currency), a fantastic, funhouse rendition of modern Beijing, with Tiananmen Square turned into a swimming pool and a giant panda dangling from a crane.

CHAPTER 1
CHAPTER 2
CHAPTER 3
CHAPTER 4

CHAPTER 5
CHAPTER 6
CHAPTER 7
CHAPTER 8
CHAPTER 9
CHAPTER 10
CHAPTER 11
CHAPTER 12
CHAPTER 13
CHAPTER 14
CHAPTER 15
APPENDICES

ADDITIONAL INFO
AVATAR MASTERS AND PERSONALITIES

BIZARRE BERRY

At various times, Bizarre has been a prehistoric man showing off cave paintings in Modesta, a magic tree Ent in the forest (pictured), and an old bag lady pushing a shopping cart. A world-traveled real-estate broker with a degree in international relations, Bizarre has played with many personae in *Second Life*. He also spends much of his time wandering the virtual world, meeting residents from nearly every country on the globe. "I like people and other cultures, which is part of the attraction of *SL*," he says. But it was during those wanderings that he noticed something missing.

"I saw people had created church buildings for what I presume were merely atmospheric purposes," he says. "I wondered how a real church community might function in *SL* and I am an avid Unitarian Universalist in real life. I had a real Kevin Costner *Field of Dreams* moment where I thought, 'Build it, and see if they will come!' Well, they sure did, in droves! It was awesome!" His open church sits in a forest glade and has become "a real, self-sustaining community." That includes a genuine ordained Unitarian minister. "At least several of the members are disabled in real life and unable to attend a real-life church. The church in *SL* has allowed them to reconnect to a spiritual community, and that is immensely gratifying and humbling."

KAZUHIRO ARIDIAN

To look at Kazuhiro's avatars, breathtakingly detailed humans fused to robot exoskeletons, you'd think she's already a professional 3D artist. (Spotting her in the Wastelands, a post-nuclear role-playing area, cult writer Warren Ellis was suitably impressed and promptly featured her in one of his Reuters *Second Life* columns.) In fact, Kazuhiro is still an art student in college, who joined *SL* when another artist friend showed off his own fantastic creations. Applying her illustration skills, she's shaping her avatars into 3D art samples as a way to break into computer animation. "I'd like to apply at Pixar at some point [and] my current project will be portfolio-worthy," she says. "Hopefully more avatars of this caliber to come." They also serve a role-playing purpose and a kind of embodied art.

(Continued) 73

"Everything I create I relate to my sense of feel," says Kazuhiro. "So when I look at things of metal, it feels sharp, painful. I created this avatar as a response to that, as reflected in the original drawings I made. It is painful, skeletal, ethereal, and almost human, but things like the inverted knees and elongated hands make it not human at all. Even with all this painful metal, it retains a human face, almost as a mockery of humanity."

TASRILL SIEYES

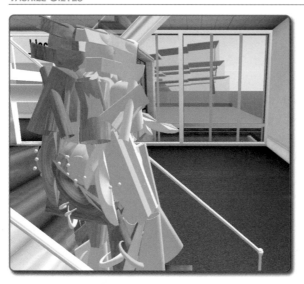

When I first met Tasrill, he looked to me like a work of art—literally. He had created his avatar to resemble Marcel Duchamp's classic "Nude Descending a Staircase." Already known as a master of abstract avatars, some spiky, some coiled like a stack of chrome disks, Tasrill was commissioned by a resident to re-create one of the 20th century's greatest artworks. "[S]he loves the painting and after seeing my other work she wanted to see what it would look like transformed into *SL* form," shares Tasrill.

A college student majoring in architecture, he sees *SL* as a new medium. "What intrigued me was that you could build and share what you build with others," he says. "Just like a giant art gallery mixed with Wikipedia—everyone working together to make something beautiful." Simply expressing himself through his avatar is enough for him; he enjoys "[w]atching people think about avatars [as] walking art and sculpture, not just a pretend human.... When I am abstract, I don't have to worry about the preconceived notions of gender, race, or anything else but someone's view on abstract art. I can just be pure intellect."

KATHARINE BERRY

One summer day in 2007, a 15-year-old member of *Teen Second Life*, admittedly motivated by little more than "boredom, wanting to talk to people," went to her computer, and changed *SL* forever. Since she couldn't access *Second Life* from her school, she tinkered with *SL*'s open-source code and created AjaxLife, a way of accessing selected *Second Life* functions from the Web, including *SL*'s instant messaging/ chat, map, and teleport features.

Within a couple days of announcing AjaxLife on her blog (`http://blog.katharineberry. co.uk/`), the project was swamped by attention, including a prominent mention on Boing Boing, one of the Net's most popular blogs. She didn't let this sudden attention go to her head. "Mostly I just ignored it. The fame's gone now," she concluded after her site's spiking traffic went back to normal, "and I'm not complaining."

More likely, it's only just beginning. Before AjaxLife, accessing *SL* required a separate client download and a powerful graphics card—two high hurdles for many people on the Internet. A number of would-be *Second Life* competitors had been targeting this very weakness, aiming to create a Web-based user-created world without such an awkward, time-consuming barrier to entry. Using protocols from libsecondlife, the open-source *SL* project, Katharine removed that prerequisite. (Nothing like disrupting the entire online-world industry just for fun.) Because of all this, it's not an exaggeration to say that Katharine helped Linden Lab take *Second Life* into its next generation.

Katharine explains, "I joined *SL*, rather dully, because Apple happened to have it as a 'featured game' on the default Safari homepage. And it looked fun, so I signed up. I started with Web development stuff when I was about nine (having learnt some dialect of BASIC when I was 8, unintentionally), and started on actually vaguely interesting stuff when I was 13. I actually learnt how to do the sort of thing involved with AjaxLife (e.g., a useful implementation of AJAX) while making it—that's my general approach to learning things." That last part bears repeating: she created AjaxLife as she figured out how to program in AJAX.

As a result, Linden Lab flew her out to *SL* Views, a regular user-feedback session held in the company's San Francisco headquarters. After she's finished with her education, Katharine hopes to turn *Second Life* into her career. Right now, she continues improving AjaxLife, including features like "[I]nventory management, texture/sound uploads, list of people near you, etc. I also intend to work on stability, so it can run without constantly crashing. I also need to get it working with the latest libsecondlife, which has made certain things harder … but not impossible." She sees this like other open-source projects as essential to *Second Life*'s growth. "Linden Lab lacks the time to do many semi-trivial but useful tasks that people will eventually get annoyed enough by to do themselves. For example, Sleek [another open-source client] is great for getting on *SL* when you lack the resources. AjaxLife serves its purpose when running programs isn't an option at all—e.g., at my school."

EPREDATOR POTATO

In 2006, one of the world's biggest and most renowned high-tech companies joined *Second Life* in a huge way, and it's due in large part to a resident who looks like the movie *Predator*'s alien.

"I had heard about *SL* years before I joined, but ignored it," admits Epredator, a staffer with IBM's Hursley division in Britain, "but had looked at it as a gamer. I was doing a customer pitch on the future of games and my brain realized *SL* was something very different, a 3D wiki using game technology. So I dived in, then realized what I had missed. Socially and technically it was the right time. Being an emerging-technology person, and being part of the social media revolution (blogs, user-created content etc.), I was not going let this opportunity slip. I set about persuading people around me and in the company to take notice."

Epredator donned a new mantle in IBM: metaverse evangelist. "This grew from being the crackpot [in the company] to being known for this and asked to help others." He helped launch a blog called Eightbar (www.eightbar.com) devoted to covering projects he and IBM colleagues were doing in online worlds, primarily in *Second Life*. While most mainstream attention on *SL* fixated on big companies using the world as a marketing platform, Epredator and team were busy on a private *SL* island, prototyping metaverse-based applications. The first one I noticed was an incredibly useful and powerful translator HUD, created by Eightbar member Yossarian Seattle, which sends text messages by XML to several on-queue web translation services like Babel Fish, then back into the world, in 10 languages. An Epredator application models Wimbledon tennis data, so you can follow a match in real time and in 3D. "Hursley has been a hub of people that were the start of a movement. This spread across the company at a global level and many other people are part of this." As a result, IBM now has a massive presence in *SL*, a corporate campus/marketing/sandbox continent which is also one of the most popular company sites in-world, in terms of foot traffic.

Epredator continues his work in *Second Life*, striving to merge it with IBM's vision of the Internet's near future. "IBM, like many companies, has a need to use virtual worlds like *SL* inside their own organizations," he says. "Moving to open-source servers, allowing self-hosting and inter-metaverse operability, I believe will lead to some amazing discoveries and exciting projects."

CHAPTER 1

CHAPTER 2

CHAPTER 3

CHAPTER 4

CHAPTER 5

CHAPTER 6

CHAPTER 7

CHAPTER 8

CHAPTER 9

CHAPTER 10

CHAPTER 11

CHAPTER 12

CHAPTER 13

CHAPTER 14

CHAPTER 15

APPENDICES

ADDITIONAL INFO
AUTHORS, ARTISTS, AND INNOVATORS

LILLIE YIFU

While many websites and blogs are devoted to *SL* sex, Lillie garnered a wide readership with 2nd Sex (`http://sexsecond.blogspot.com/`), which merges her experiences playing a top escort in *SL* with insights that reveal a keen literary eye. (Unsurprisingly, she's incorporating these into an upcoming novel.) "Working in the adult entertainment business in *SL* has taught me about the inner lives of people," she explains. "*SL* is like *A Midsummer Night's Dream*, where what we wish, fear, hope, long for is all visible. Avatars, even venues and builds, in the end, become a reflection of the inner person, the one that screams to get out in what we call real life. I want to write about that, what we are inside." In this way, she provides deeper context to what people often dismiss as "just virtual sex." For example, Linden Lab has reported that only 18 percent of *SL*'s landmass is designated as having Mature activity, but Lillie provides the story behind that figure. "The 'direct sex' industry, to which I belong, is smaller than, and subsidiary, to the indirect sex industry," she once wrote on her blog, explaining why a romantic, PG-rated nightclub called Phat Cats became more popular than most adult-themed clubs. "Romance and sex make people happy, and while the direct sex industry brings people momentary touches of joy and bliss, the hope of most people is to have not a moment of passion, but a life of love."

ORDINAL MALAPROP

One of *Second Life*'s best scripters seems to be the oldest, for Miss Malaprop looks, acts, and writes as if she's from a fictional 19th century London. "Ordinal really grew organically within the world," she explains. "I think that I picked up the mannered and fussy Victorian style as a reaction to the rude and chaotic Mainland that I lived in at the time. I then discovered Steampunk and Victorian Retrotech groups, where

(Continued)

CHAPTER 4

BETH ODETS
ANSHE CHUNG
SUZANNA SOYINKA
HACKSHAVEN
HARFORD
KEYSTONE
BOUCHARD
KATT KONGO
CHINA TRACY
KATHERINE BERRY
**EPREDATOR
POTATO**

so many others seemed to have naturally come to that same position." Her blog, *An Engine Fit for My Proceeding* (`http://ordinalmalaprop.com/engine/`), is a treasure trove of scripting information and fabulous devices she has built (like the Caledon tram and balloon tour, a Confucian Oracle, and ornate weaponry worthy of Jules Verne) all described in a writing style that resembles an Ada Lovelace journal. She's dabbled in 2.0 technology too, creating a Twitter interface so residents can send messages to the popular social-network system from directly in *SL*.

Formerly a real-life programmer, Ordinal is now a freelance scripter in *SL*. "Which," she notes, "is definitely a very positive outcome, or at least it seems that way so far. It can be a bit tricky explaining to people what I do, though."

Iris Ophelia

A somewhat reclusive, extremely busy art major, Iris joined *SL* in 2006 as a way to occupy herself outside schoolwork. After developing a knack for virtual fashion, she began writing for various *SL* publications to pay for her shopping excursions, but her heart wasn't in those assignments. Then Katt Kongo of the popular *Metaverse Messenger* offered her a new gig covering fashion. "I thought that would be perfect for me, since that was the whole reason I was writing in *SL* at all. My motivations for staying in *SL* fashion journalism have changed dramatically since that first month, however, and it means a lot more to me in both lives now." That's because she's become one of the world's most renowned fashion writers, spotting trends and energetically exploring the vast oceans of new designs to find the best in *SL*'s biggest industry.

"*SL* pays for a good chunk of my life now.... I have reporters calling me a couple times a month, not just trying to get quotes but actually listening to what I'm trying to say." She now has a large readership on the several blogs she writes for (including, I'm proud to say, mine), and fields employment offers from people who want to hire her as an *SL* fashion consultant. "I don't know if it's completely changed my career plans," she says, "but it's certainly affected them."

Christophe Hugo

The Matrix was partly inspired by French philosopher Jean Baudrillard (Morpheus's words to Neo, "Welcome to the desert of the real," are actually Baudrillard's) so it's not surprising he inspired Christophe Hugo to join *Second Life*, too. An academic from Paris now teaching in Canada, Christophe created his *SL* avatar as part of his research into "the layerization of simulacra."

Obscure maybe, but everyone recognizes Christophe's avatars: using the appearance-customization tools, he creates 3D caricatures of real-life celebrities and politicians that are instantly identifiable if cruelly hilarious. George W. Bush, Hillary Clinton, Conan O'Brien—they're widely seen across the Web as screenshots and videos— and, when the mood strikes Christophe, in *SL* itself. (Immediately after France elected Nicolas Sarkozy as president, Christophe was seen strutting around in-world as Sarkozy, shooting a bazooka.)

Christophe believes his talent comes from a mild autism that makes it difficult to recognize and remember faces. "My guess is that my brain compensates for that by naturally and automatically 'caricaturing' the faces of the people I meet." His *Second Life* profile once read, "Caricatures are to me what Reality is to you." ("And that," he adds, "was no joke.")

When he was younger, Christophe haughtily rejected the chance to go commercial with his caricature drawings. "I have regretted my move since then, and now that I am experiencing my middle-age crisis, I am trying to leverage *SL* to finally do something with my caricatures." He's won some prominent fans, including a *Le Monde* editor who was in-world during the 2007 election. (Two of France's top candidates had *SL* headquarters.) "One more good example of the democratic aspect of *SL*: even from the Canadian prairies, one can meet some influential people!"

Madcow Cosmos

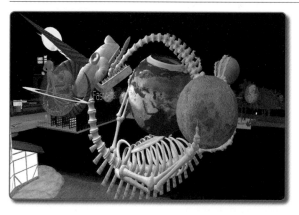

Aptly named, Madcow is a master of skeletal sculptures, creating incredibly complex, gigantic, fantastic skeletons of creatures that never existed (except maybe in a previous, unknown epoch of *SL*). In real life, he's actually a young chef based in the northwest U.S., and has no experience with 3D creation platforms. ("I'd been too intimidated to try any of the high-end programs," he says.) *Second Life* seemed less daunting, so he jumped in, and quietly earned a reputation for himself, to the point where the curators at Oyster Bay, a leading *SL* gallery/content showcase site, offered to house his works. "I build for the pure pleasure of building," he says. "A thousand fantasy novels, science journals, and images are always floating around in my head and I try to release some of them through the creation of art. I really couldn't stop creating even if I wanted to."

CHAPTER 1
CHAPTER 2
CHAPTER 3
CHAPTER 4

CHAPTER 5
CHAPTER 6
CHAPTER 7
CHAPTER 8
CHAPTER 9
CHAPTER 10
CHAPTER 11
CHAPTER 12
CHAPTER 13
CHAPTER 14
CHAPTER 15
APPENDICES

CHAPTER 5

YOUR APPEARANCE

As you know from Chapter 1, *Second Life* offers you the opportunity to be reborn in many ways. This is especially true of your avatar's appearance. You can change it as often as you like, and you can be as crazy as you like. You can enter the world as a fire-breathing dragon, turn into a vampire halfway through your online session, and eventually log out as a middle-aged, bald, beer-bellied male construction worker with a long, furry tail.

The importance of avatar appearance becomes obvious the moment you enter *Second Life*: the arrival lot on Orientation Island is often packed with freshly born avatars whose appearance is being edited by their owners. Every resident begins *Second Life* as an attractive young male or female in jeans and T-shirt, and almost every resident immediately begins working to make their avatar their own. This chapter discusses this process, explains the options available, and offers practical hints and notes. All this advice is only advice: feel free to choose your own path through *Second Life*. But whatever you do, remember that your presence in the virtual world—your virtual identity—is defined by your appearance.

CONTENTS

FIRST CHOICES

Figure 5.1: Your avatar is officially born the moment you give it a name.

Your first big "avatar appearance" choice is made even before you enter *Second Life*. You make it when you choose your *SL* name (Figure 5.1). Your avatar's name is displayed for all to see, and it always has a major impact on how others perceive you. A seven-foot-tall hunk called Daisy Pony is definitely perceived differently than a seven-foot-tall hunk called Rocky Balboa! As this demonstrates, avatar appearance is a sum of many parts. Generally speaking, these are as follows:

Avatar name. Your avatar's name is very important: you get to choose it only once (it cannot be changed). Choose a name that fits your *SL* image, and make sure you can live with it for a long, long time. It's not easy, especially for first-time users, who choose a name with very little advance knowledge of what avatars can look like. A safe way out is to pick a name you'd be comfortable with in real life—however, at the same time you want an avatar name that's attractive and memorable.

Avatar shape. This goes beyond silhouette: basically, avatar shape includes all body parts and body features (body thickness, height, shape of head, eyes, nose, etc.).

Avatar skin. Avatar skin is what you see covering avatar shape in the absence of any clothing. Its appearance may be changed with *SL* tools. However, to get realistic-looking human skin, you'll have to acquire a custom skin—skins that are created using an external application such as Adobe Photoshop, then imported/uploaded into *Second Life* at a nominal fee. Luckily, you don't have to make one to own one; there are lots of very sharp custom skins for sale, and you can also get a good freebie skin if you look around.

Avatar hair and eyes. Avatar hair and eyes constitute a separate category because although they're body features, they can also be worn as attachments (prim hair, eyes worn as attachments that cover the default eyes). You'll find more hair and eye details later in this chapter.

CHAPTER 1

CHAPTER 2

CHAPTER 3

CHAPTER 4

CHAPTER 5

CHAPTER 6

CHAPTER 7

CHAPTER 8

CHAPTER 9

CHAPTER 10

CHAPTER 11

CHAPTER 12

CHAPTER 13

CHAPTER 14

CHAPTER 15

APPENDICES

FROM LINDEN LAB
AVATARS FOR SALE

"Flea Bussy (of the store Grendel's Children) has created some of the most creative and expressive avs around: `http://slurl.com/secondlife/Avaria%20Tor/206/235/251`."

—Morpheus Linden

Avatar attachments. This, predictably, includes clothes and any other objects that can be attached to an avatar's shape (a hat, a gun, hair).

Avatar animations. Each avatar comes with a set of animations. However, longtime *SL* citizens view the standard animations with disdain. You can buy custom animations that will make your avatar move with extra grace. Creating custom animations involves using an external application (many *SL* citizens use Poser) and writing an override script in LSL (*Second Life*'s scripting language) so that custom animations are played instead of the defaults. You can acquire freebie animations too if you look around. As you might have guessed, if you're interested in virtual sex, custom animations (and attachments too) are a must.

Your own voice. Enabling voice in *Second Life* has greatly increased the impact of your virtual image on other people. It also forges a new, strong link between the real-life you and your avatar. It makes sense to consider what you sound like when you're deciding what you want to look like. For example, let's say you're a male with a smoky basso. Will your avatar be a whiskered, cigar-smoking gent in a Victorian suit and top hat, or will it be Mickey Mouse? Add the fact that switching avatar appearance is as easy as dragging an icon from your Inventory and onto yourself, and you can see how speech capability has added a new dimension to avatar appearance.

ADDITIONAL INFO
CHANGING YOUR SKIN

Your Library contains a number of avatar skins—you'll find some nice ones in the More Outfits subfolder inside the Library's Clothing folder. Open an outfit folder (GI Joe, Little Red Riding Hood, etc.), and drag the skin icon onto your avatar to check out what it looks like.

CHOOSING YOUR NAME

At the time of writing, the options here aren't unlimited—you have to choose a last name from those available at the time. However, the list (which changes periodically) always features plenty of choices, and of course you can give yourself any first name you like—as long as someone else isn't already using

85

the same first-name/last-name combination. If you encounter this problem, a small tweak can put things right: popular solutions include changing the spelling of the first name to get a unique combination—for example, "Oskar Peterson" instead of "Oscar Peterson." Other widely used solutions are to make the first letter of your first name lowercase, (as in "sandy" instead of "Sandy") or to add a letter (for example, your middle initial: "John A. Smith" becomes "JohnA Smith").

Remember that the name you've chosen won't appear in isolation; it will be viewed in combination with your avatar. Therefore, you should consider how it will fit the appearance of the avatar(s) you intend to use in *Second Life*. Are you going to switch between sexes? If so, you might want to consider a "unisex" name: for example, Sandy Sprocket or RobertA Hansen. Is your avatar's appearance going to be outrageous, beautiful, dangerous, friendly—or maybe all four at once? It *is* possible with the right combination of name, avatar appearance, and animation/gesture set.

> **FROM LINDEN LAB**
> ## YOUR NAME SET IN STONE
>
> While you can change your avatar's appearance as many times as you like, you cannot change your avatar's name. The name you choose to set up an account *is* the account, and the only way to reappear in *SL* under a new name is to open a new account.

Choosing Your Sex

First of all, remember this: in *Second Life*, you can change your sex every 10 minutes if you so desire. It doesn't involve any painful operations—just a few mouse clicks. You can be male, you can be female, you can be neither (by creating or choosing an avatar that's gender-neutral, such as the ready-made White Wolf from your Library). It's interesting to note that given all this freedom, most *SL* denizens choose to stay true to their real-life gender. Here are some numbers from an *SL* forum poll:

Male playing male—41.95%

Female playing female—40.05%

Male playing female—14.45%

Female playing male—3.55%

These numbers are very telling even when you assume the poll isn't very accurate. They show clearly that the majority of *SL* denizens make a conservative choice and stick to their real-life gender. At the same time, many *SL* people state that they treat their *SL* existence as the perfect opportunity for role play, that they switch sexes at the drop of a hat, and that everyone is free to choose whichever sex they fancy at any given moment (see the sidebar "Gender-Bending"). So, where's the truth?

The truth, as always, lies in the middle. No one will mind if your avatar's of a different gender than *you* really are as long as they do not have a close personal relationship with you. As a certain disappointed

Figure 5.2: Let people know what you want them to know about the real-life you.

CHAPTER 1

CHAPTER 2

CHAPTER 3

CHAPTER 4

CHAPTER 5

CHAPTER 6

CHAPTER 7

CHAPTER 8

CHAPTER 9

CHAPTER 10

CHAPTER 11

CHAPTER 12

CHAPTER 13

CHAPTER 14

CHAPTER 15

APPENDICES

female avatar said, "I wouldn't have minded if he told me he's really a guy within the first few weeks. But when he told me after six months, wow, it just blew me away. I just find him impossible to trust after that."

Do not let this stop you from switching gender when you feel like it. But if you want to form a virtual friendship with someone, it's important that they know who you *really* are. The best way to handle this is simply to include some info about the real-life you in your *SL* Profile (Figure 5.2).

ADDITIONAL INFO
GENDER-BENDING

If you choose an avatar of the opposite gender from yours in real life, be prepared for unexpected twists and turns in your virtual friendships. The rules that apply there are the same as the rules in real life: friends don't like to be deceived.

LOVE ME, PLEASE LOVE ME

All of us want to be loved and admired, and an appealing avatar goes a long way toward satisfying that need. However, there is no love and admiration without trust. You have to be trusted to be liked—hardly a revelation, is it?

The plot thickens if you're serious about *Second Life*, and use the virtual world to form real-life friendships and make real-life money. As more and more real-life companies and organizations establish a virtual presence, being trustworthy becomes increasingly important. And no, you don't have to be boring to be trustworthy—but frankly, a bit of plainness helps. For example, let's say you're interviewing for an important real-life job in *Second Life*—a practice that's becoming more and more common as, um, life goes on. Attending a job interview as an octopus wearing purple sunglasses and a straw sombrero might *not* be the best way to get that nice job.

This is because when it comes to trust, humans are somewhat boring: they tend to trust whatever looks most like them. The philosopher Arthur Schopenhauer defined attraction and hostility as degrees of self-identification: when a human meets another human, old Arthur said, the first reaction is one of those two thoughts: "It's me!" or "It's not me!" The first thought breeds attraction, the second—hostility.

Now that we've established that we're all self-centered, navel-gazing jerks, let's turn to how this trait affects avatar appearance in *Second Life*. There have been a number of scientific studies done already—those scientists, always busy poking their noses into everything! The results are in, and guess what—humans tend to trust other humans, and human avatars rule in the trust game, trouncing even the lovable Furries (Disney-like animal avatars). In fact, it seems old Schopenhauer was right, and that the more someone resembles us, the more we trust that person.

It's a little sad somehow, given that *Second Life* lets you be whatever you want to be. So, it makes sense to own a number of avatar skins complete with outfits. This way, you can be the respectable gent or lady when and as needed, and change back into your sweet natural vampire self as wanted (see the "Switching Avatars" sidebar). Just like real life, eh?

RESIDENTS SPEAK
SWITCHING AVATARS

"It's hard to say what motivates me to look the way I do in *SL*, I have so many looks to choose from. I have a firm belief in tasting everything on the buffet, and being picky like I am, I went for the best of the best. It is hard to tell what I'm going to be from one day to the next: a magnificent dragon, a bipedal wolf, a vampire, or a really good-looking human. That's the beauty of *SL*; you're not stuck in any single stereotypical role unless you choose to do that to yourself."

—Lupus Delacroix

"As Lupus noted, you can create as many avatars as you like. Save them as 'outfits' and include the gender and all body parts—then just wear the entire folder. There is no limit to what you can be; you can be Neo one minute and slip into your Donna Dominatrix avatar the next. If you do a search on [OnRez] or SL Exchange for avatars, you will see the amazing range of what is out there and what you can make yourself.

"What motivates people to look a certain way is something I wouldn't even begin to speculate on. Ultimately, your avatar is your representative in-world and can run the entire range of your personality. It's your second life; be whomever and whatever you want to be."

—Isablan Neva

"I actually have several different avs; some I used for fun, others are utilitarian. Most of the time, I run around in a Luskwood Red Dragon av. Although, I also use a Ninja Weasel Studios Red

Eastern Dragon av, and a mu Kingyo Gold av (giant fishy). I do have my old 'generic' av for times when I need to attach something, and a furry av won't do the job. All of my avs are modded, some of them heavily. Generally on my usual av, I wear a Maximillion in Plum suit from Silver Rose, a custom-made top hat (which sits at an angle and is oversized), and a pair of round-rim glasses with purple lenses."

—Khashai Steinbeck

CHAPTER 1
CHAPTER 2
CHAPTER 3
CHAPTER 4
CHAPTER 5

CHAPTER 6
CHAPTER 7
CHAPTER 8
CHAPTER 9
CHAPTER 10
CHAPTER 11
CHAPTER 12
CHAPTER 13
CHAPTER 14
CHAPTER 15
APPENDICES

CHANGING YOUR APPEARANCE

Figure 5.3: The number-one priority of almost every new *SL* denizen: changing their avatar's appearance

You'll most likely be struck by an overwhelming urge to work on your avatar's appearance the moment you enter *Second Life* (Figure 5.3). Be strong, and resist the temptation to begin tinkering with your looks right away.

There are several good reasons for postponing your avatar's appearance improvements for a little while. To begin with, you won't be guilty of crowding Orientation Island's arrival area.

Next, just a few steps into Orientation Island, you'll have the first of many chances to acquire freebie avatars complete with clothes. And soon enough, you'll be leaving Orientation Island for Help Island, where you'll undoubtedly hit the freebie store for a selection of outfits and hair types. And after *that*, you'll hit the mainland, where hundreds and hundreds of stores offer avatar appearance enhancements of outstanding quality. You can acquire them for free or nearly free if you periodically check out *Second Life*'s Classifieds, SL Exchange, and OnRez.

ADDITIONAL INFO
FREE DOWNLOADS

There's a range of free downloads that include avatar mannequins and animation files; templates for creating new avatar skin, hair, clothes, and eyes; and a selection of high-quality textures at `http://secondlife.com/community/downloads.php`. The downloads are accompanied by a concise manual. In addition, many *SL* creators offer free templates—you'll find numerous links to free template downloads in forum posts at `http://forums.secondlife.com/index.php`. Use the Search function to locate the templates you're interested in; for example, type "skin template" in the Search box.

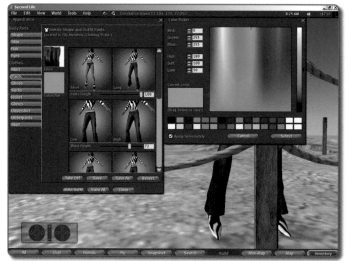

Figure 5.4: Switching the tint and texture of the default shirt and jeans takes just a couple of mouse clicks.

If you absolutely cannot bear the default avatar look, limit avatar appearance editing on Orientation Island to a few quick, simple changes (Figure 5.4). Doing anything more is a waste of time given the extra options that soon become available.

By now, you've probably gotten the idea that avatar appearance is a sum of several parts, and that these include more than the body parts from *SL*'s Appearance menu. The sections that follow discuss each of these parts and offer polite suggestions of what to do with the parts you don't like. Naturally, we'll start with the body-part choices: Shape, Skin, Hair, and Eyes.

ADDITIONAL INFO
APPEARANCES COUNT

Opening the Appearance menu loads your avatar's current shape and outfit. Your Library contains several ready-made shape/outfit combinations, and you'll be adding many more to your Inventory during your new existence. Switching avatar shape and outfit is as simple as dragging the appropriate folder from your Library or Inventory and onto the avatar. Don't forget to save your own unique shape/outfit combinations into your Inventory—and don't forget to delete the oldest/least used as your second life goes on.

RESIDENTS SPEAK
AVATAR APPEARANCE

"I'm on the short side and trim. Always wanted to be bigger but genetics and metabolism declared otherwise (a few hundred people I know wish they had my metabolism). So my avatar is a bit tall and on the heavy side (but neither pudgy nor muscle-bound). He's Irish even if I'm not because I decided to port over my ID (Aodhan) from the last MMOG I was in. Irish name goes best with Irish surname.

"The cybernetic right arm was something I started fooling around with when I was new. I liked it and I just kept evolving it. It rarely fails to catch the attention of people I meet. I was initially planning to make a product version of it because it was attracting attention, but I decided not to because people liked that it gave me a unique look. In a world where any look can be made but where some looks are mass-produced, it's nice to know that one has something that is unique.

"I'm a techie-geek and proud of it. My look reflects that in all original equipment from the arm to the visor to the gadgety-looking belt."

—Aodhan McDunnough

"Here's a breakdown of what to consider:

"Skin: This is probably the most important aspect. A good skin can make or break an avatar's appearance. Demos are usually dirt-cheap, so stock up and experiment. Once you find a good design, then you'll have to decide skin tone and facial hair, as that overrides the default controls.

"Hair: Prim hair is a must. Finding good prim hair for men is hard. Women's hair outnumbers men's by about 1,000 to 1, it seems. And even when you do find men's hair, very often it's the same style. Nothing against long hair, mind you, but this far I've not been able to find hair that gives the *GQ* look, although the prim hair I have now is pretty close.

"Shape: Your shape will radically change how your skin looks, especially on the face. Professional shapes are usually better than what you can do yourself, but even then, its tough to find a shape that is everything you want.

"Eyes: Good eyes can add a nice touch.

"Animation override: The best avatar in the world will still look clunky if you use the default animation set.

"Clothing: As in real life, clothes mean a lot. There's a lot of garbage out there and some really nice things too. Don't be afraid to ask where people got their stuff. More often than not, other people are willing to help, and once in a while, you meet some cool people who turn into friends."

—Cannae Brentano

SHAPE

Shape (found under the Body Parts option) is the default option when you open the Appearance menu. Shape options are applied to nine categories, from Body to Eyes and Ears to Legs. Each category opens up a series of second-life-changing options, easily adjustable on a scale of 0 to 100 via a slider. You can save any combination of options as a separate male or female shape (with or without clothes/outfit) to your Inventory, then switch shape types at a moment's notice. If only changing this stuff in your first life were so easy!

The following sections discuss the options available in the order in which they appear in *Second Life*. This is done for ease of reference only and does not imply you should edit your avatar's appearance in the same order. On the contrary, editing avatar appearance is easier if you follow a different order. You should edit Body, then jump to Torso and Legs at the very bottom of the menu list, and only then proceed to edit Head options (second from the top). All such irregularities are highlighted in the sections below.

ADDITIONAL INFO
RANDOM INSPIRATION

Make a point of clicking the Randomize button (at the bottom of the Appearance menu) a few times before you begin editing individual avatar body parts. It's very entertaining, and lets you see clearly how changing proportions between body parts can result in a completely new look. What's more, many random avatars are very nicely put together, and you may want to use one of the randomly generated avatars as the base model when attempting to create your first unique shape.

Figure 5.5: Exactly what I was looking for! Hmmm ... well, almost, anyway.

The most powerful avatar appearance options are found under Body and Head. Adjustments to the values found there have a strong effect on your avatar's appearance; often, changing a single value results in a number of changes. Alterations to other appearance options are more predictable, affecting only a single body part or facial feature.

Finally, keep in mind that the suggestions below are just one take on what's involved in creating the most difficult avatar form you can possibly aim for: a natural-looking human being. Don't let that stop you from creating whatever avatar you fancy—remember that they can be switched in a wink of an eye! You have unlimited choice, so of course making a choice is really difficult (Figure 5.5).

CHAPTER 1

CHAPTER 2

CHAPTER 3

CHAPTER 4

CHAPTER 5

CHAPTER 6

CHAPTER 7

CHAPTER 8

CHAPTER 9

CHAPTER 10

CHAPTER 11

CHAPTER 12

CHAPTER 13

CHAPTER 14

CHAPTER 15

APPENDICES

BODY

Under Body, you'll find the following slider-adjustable options:

Height. The default is 80, and this translates roughly into six feet or 180 centimeters in real life. This is a safe middle-of-the-road value. Changing your height affects overall body shape, and you'll want to fiddle with the slider after you've done all the other adjustments and your avatar's shape still seems not quite right. Sometimes a shape that's just a bit off-kilter at 80 snaps into exactly the right proportions at 75.

Body Thickness. The default value is a waif-like 20. While most *SL* denizens are unbelievably lithe and slender, rather the way we'd all like to be in real life, you might want to nudge the slider up a little—a value of 35 to 40 results in a more realistic body shape. Don't worry—your avatar will still appear attractively slim given all the other options.

Body Fat. The default here's set at 0. Many *SL* denizens are more than happy to leave it at that. However, if you want to inject just a small dose of realism into your new existence, go for a value of 25 to 30—your avatar acquires a nice, solid aura, so to speak, that can make it a little more convincing.

The Shape options open by default when you enter the Appearance menu, and it's a safe bet you'll adjust them first. Make a point of returning to adjust them at least once before you finalize all the shapes that make up your new avatar. Adjusting the shape of your avatar's body often puts the final touch on its appearance.

ADDITIONAL INFO
KNOW WHAT YOU WANT

Editing avatar appearance becomes much easier if you have a precise idea of what you want, and you refer to an existing image (photograph, drawing, illustration) while working. Also, it's a good idea to strip your avatar naked when editing selected Shape options (Body, Torso, and Legs) as well as Skin.

HEAD

Here things get noticeably more complicated, as they should. Upon selecting Head, you'll face the following options:

Head Size. The default here is 70. The default is a meaningless, inoffensive choice, because the size of your head should harmonize with your Body Shape choices. If you're really tall, the default is too small; if you're short, it's too large. What's more, head size has to harmonize with the facial features you'll choose. It's necessary to perform at least two head-size adjustments: one after setting Body Shape and another after you've gone through all Head submenu choices. Just like with Body Shape, quite often a final, slight adjustment of head size makes all other Head adjustments fit perfectly.

CAMERA CONTROLS
ADDITIONAL INFO

Figure 5.6: Use camera controls to view your avatar from different angles while editing its appearance.

Don't forget to activate and use camera controls (View menu) while editing your avatar's appearance! It's impossible to get things right otherwise (Figure 5.6). If you enjoy editing avatar appearance, consider getting a pose stand: standing on it freezes the avatar in a certain pose. If you'd like to get one, begin by using the in-world search to find who is offering free pose stands next time you log in.

Head Stretch. This is a very powerful option: adjustments here affect head shape, size, and a lot of facial features (for example, chin and nose shape). The default value is 20, and it's smart to leave it at that while working on your first avatar appearance. Once everything's done, use this option to fine-tune facial features and head shape. Of course, if you've always dreamed of having a head that resembles an eggplant stood on one end, go for it and slam the slider up to 100 right away.

Head Shape. The default here's a neutral 50. Making your avatar's head more square gives it a masculine air, more round—feminine. Note that any movement of the slider, up or down, results in perceived increase of head size. This is yet another powerful option that strongly affects facial features, especially lower jaw and chin shape.

Egg Head. This option dramatically affects head shape. The term "Egg Head" illustrates this option's two extremes: a head shaped like an egg standing on its pointy end, or like an egg standing on its blunt end. However, this describes only the straight-on view of your avatar's head; when you use the camera controls to view it from the side, you'll see that any movement of the slider results in big changes to your avatar's profile. Areas particularly affected are the back of the head, the forehead, and the chin/jaw. The default value of 75 is best suited for female avatars; if you're going for a classic male look, 50 to 60 is a good choice.

Head Length. Sweeping adjustments to the default 55 value are definitely not recommended—*unless* you want an avatar that looks like a character in a fantasy cartoon. Head Length makes a strong impact on facial features, too! Slight adjustments upward result in a more feminine appearance, and moving the slider down a few notches creates a more masculine look.

Face Shear. Moving the slider either way rotates one side of your face up and the other down: extremes make your avatar look, (when viewed straight on) as if it had been struck with partial face palsy. This is good for outlandish characters; otherwise, settle for small tweaks of three to six points on either side of the default 50 value. The default results in a face that is perfectly symmetrical, and thus a little bland; a slight skew to the features adds a certain attractive *je ne sais quoi* that injects extra character into a face.

Forehead Angle. This option is best left alone until you've chosen a hair type/style that you're going to wear for a while. The default value of 37 is perhaps a little on the low side; adding a few points often results in a more natural look. Radical adjustments work great if you're after a fantasy look— for example, definitely go the Vertical Forehead route when re-creating Frankenstein.

Brow Size. Big, bony, protective protuberances above the eyes are usually associated with lower rungs of evolutionary development; probably that's why the default here is set at a highly civilized value of 13. Once again, this is an appearance option that's best left alone until you've got the hair (and eyes) you like and are likely to stick with for a while. Setting Brow Size at 0 gives your avatar's head a slightly ethereal air.

Upper Cheeks. This is another option with a relatively low default. At 37, it lends your avatar's face a very civilized, sophisticated look; making the cheeks puffier results in a certain roughness. Increasing cheek puffiness by just a few points will give your avatar's face a more natural air, whereas decreasing it to 0 results in fashion-model sleekness.

Lower Cheeks. This option is best left at the default 45 until you've completed work on your avatar's facial features. It tends to work best when applied as the final, finishing touch to the jaw and jowls.

Cheek Bones. The default 38 value is a little low; adding up to a dozen points gives your avatar's face more character without a meaningful change in facial features.

CHAPTER 1

CHAPTER 2

CHAPTER 3

CHAPTER 4

CHAPTER 5

CHAPTER 6

CHAPTER 7

CHAPTER 8

CHAPTER 9

CHAPTER 10

CHAPTER 11

CHAPTER 12

CHAPTER 13

CHAPTER 14

CHAPTER 15

APPENDICES

ADDITIONAL INFO
SHAPE-SHIFTING

Don't spend too much time perfecting your avatar's features at the outset of your new existence. You'll be messing with them again the moment you acquire a custom avatar skin, as discussed later in this chapter. After a while, you're likely to have a number of different physical profiles saved in your Inventory. *Second Life* offers you great freedom: for example, if you like a certain hairstyle but it doesn't suit you, you can make yourself suit the hairstyle.

EYES

Eye-editing options pop up twice on the Appearance panel:

- In the Shape submenu, the Eyes button lets you adjust eye-detail options for your current avatar. These are the options discussed in this section.

- In the main Body Parts menu, choosing the Eyes tab opens a submenu that lets you adjust the eye template, such as size of pupil, iris width and texture, and pupil/iris size. These options are discussed later on in this chapter.

Adjusting eye-detail options is much more straightforward than messing around with Body and Head, because the changes you make here affect the eye area only. However, they do impact your avatar's facial profile—use the camera controls to check it out.

The eye-detail options have no hidden implications or complex consequences like the ones encountered when editing Head options. Nevertheless, there are a few things you should keep in mind:

- Eye Size and Eye Opening complement each other, so work those two sliders together. The relatively low default setting of 40 for Eye Size still has a strong *anime* feeling; try lowering it to 35 and increasing Eye Opening to 65 from the default 60.

- Review Eye Depth after you've completed work on your avatar's nose and cheekbones, since these three facial features work together straight on as well as in profile.

- If you're after a natural-looking face, use the Eye Bags and Puffy Lids sliders to make your avatar's face more convincing; add a handful of points to the default values in each case.

- The rather wild-looking Pop Eye option yields great results when used in moderation. Perfect symmetry is bland, so moving the slider either way by just a few points makes your avatar's face more interesting.

Figure 5.7: The Eyes tab submenu lets you change your avatar's eye color as well as use alternate eye templates.

CHAPTER 1

CHAPTER 2

CHAPTER 3

CHAPTER 4

CHAPTER 5

CHAPTER 6

CHAPTER 7

CHAPTER 8

CHAPTER 9

CHAPTER 10

CHAPTER 11

CHAPTER 12

CHAPTER 13

CHAPTER 14

CHAPTER 15

APPENDICES

Remember that your Library contains extra eyes, so to speak. You'll find a pair of base (brown, blue) eye-color models in the Body Parts folder, and extra eye-color variations as part of the ready-made Shape/Outfit combinations in the Clothing folder. However, note that editing eye color and depth (darkness) is done through the *other* Eyes submenu—the one that opens when you click the Eyes tab under Body Parts (Figure 5.7). You'll find more details later in this chapter.

EARS

Editing your avatar's ears is even more straightforward than working on eye detail. Most of the time, you'll adjust ear options while viewing your avatar's profile; use camera controls to check on the effect of your changes straight on as well as from a three-quarters-front view. Also, note that although the Attached Earlobe images are correct, the Unattached and Attached labels are reversed.

NOSE

Editing your avatar's nose so that it combines character with a natural appearance is a complicated job. The editing options available here are straightforward and self-explanatory; however, adjusting one option almost invariably necessitates adjusting one or more other options. You'll certainly gain a new appreciation for real-life nose-job artists once you've attempted to edit your avatar's nose! Here are some suggestions that should make nose editing easier:

- The nose is a prominent facial feature that must work well with other facial features. So edit other facial features first, including your avatar's mouth and chin—it makes determining the right nose shape and size much easier.

- It's easier to work on a bigger nose. The default Nose Size is a cute, button-like 11 whose appearance straddles the line between fantasy and real life. You can safely increase nose size to 25 right away—that's the natural size for the default head, but it might be more if you've already edited head shape and size. In any case, it truly is much easier to work on a bigger nose, even if what you want is a small nose (see the "Nose Jobs" note).

ADDITIONAL INFO
NOSE JOBS

Try increasing the nose size for shape-editing purposes, then size the shaped nose down—it will necessitate extra tweaks to some options, but should ensure a much easier time overall. Just remember to keep the size difference to no more than 10 points or so!

- Nose and Nostril width as well as Nose Thickness and Nose Tip shape are very closely linked to mouth shape and size; tweak Mouth options as appropriate.

- When adjusting Upper and Lower Bridge, pay attention to how your changes work with the appearance of your avatar's brows and forehead.

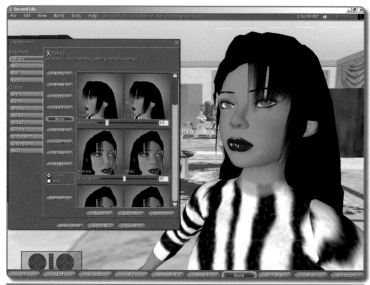

- Using the camera controls often is key to doing the job right: all nose changes greatly impact your avatar's appearance from any viewing angle between two-thirds-back and full frontal.

You'll be spared a lot of effort if you go the fantasy-avatar route. A Pinocchio-like schnozzle is much easier to model than a natural-looking nose (Figure 5.8).

Figure 5.8: Performing a good nose job will test your avatar-editing abilities.

MOUTH

Shape your avatar's jaw and chin before starting to edit its mouth; you'll have a much easier time. The Mouth editing options are very straightforward, but focus almost exclusively on the lips, and there's more to the mouth than lips alone—the lips are just the final touch. As mentioned earlier, you'll also want to tweak Mouth options once you've finished working on your avatar's nose.

CHAPTER 1
CHAPTER 2
CHAPTER 3
CHAPTER 4
CHAPTER 5

CHAPTER 6
CHAPTER 7
CHAPTER 8
CHAPTER 9
CHAPTER 10
CHAPTER 11
CHAPTER 12
CHAPTER 13
CHAPTER 14
CHAPTER 15
APPENDICES

Chin-editing options are powerful—changes there can necessitate a rethink of your avatar's head shape and size. Here's what you'll be dealing with:

Chin Angle. On one end of the scale we have Mr. Lantern Jaw; on the other, the Chinless Wonder. The default setting of 52 is a little on the Chinless Wonder side, which isn't bad for female avatars. However, natural-looking male avatars require you to nudge the slider lower.

ADDITIONAL INFO
MOLDING YOUR CHIN

Although Chin Angle is the topmost option in the Chin submenu, editing Chin Angle is easiest when you've already finished shaping your avatar's jaw.

Jaw Shape. This is one of the jaw-shaping adjustments that should precede finalizing Chin Angle. The default value of 55 results in a decidedly feminine chin and jaw, and you should add at least 20 points for a masculine look. However, note that this is true only if the other jaw-shaping settings are left at default. Changes in Chin Depth, Jaw Angle, Jowls, and Chin-Neck settings have a big impact on the Jaw Shape setting. You'll find yourself tweaking some of the options again and again after making changes elsewhere.

Chin Depth and Jaw Angle. These two options are grouped together because any adjustments to Chin Depth should be done in tandem with adjustments to Jaw Angle. A lower Jaw Angle naturally fits a deeper chin. The changes you make to these two settings have a strong impact on your avatar's appearance! Make sure you view your avatar's face from several angles following each setting change. The default settings of 42 for Chin Depth and 76 for Jaw Angle are on the feminine side; increase Chin Depth and decrease Jaw Angle for a more-masculine shape. Expect to readjust settings after any changes to Jowls and Chin-Neck.

Jaw Jut. This option should be handled very delicately unless you're after a comic effect. Slight deviations (literally a couple of points) from the default 50 value work fine—a tiny underbite can look good on a female avatar, and a similarly small overbite can be flattering on a male.

Jowls. The default value of 17 results in a model-like, jowl-less look. Add points here for a more natural appearance, readjusting other Chin options as necessary.

Chin Cleft and Upper Chin Cleft. Adjustments here put the final touches on your avatar's chin; leave them till the very end. Making changes may necessitate rethinking your Mouth settings, particularly Lip Cleft and Lip Cleft Depth.

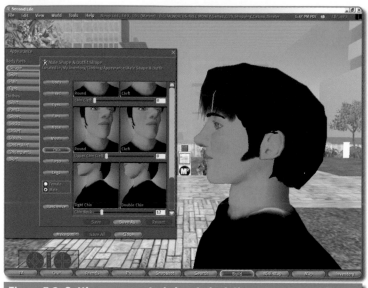

Figure 5.9: Getting your avatar's jaw to look the way you want it requires skill and patience.

Chin-Neck. Any changes here are likely to impact Jaw Shape, Jaw Angle, and Jowls settings, and vice versa. Treat this option as part of the jaw-shaping package (Figure 5.9).

In summary, your avatar's chin has a powerful influence on your avatar's appearance. In real life, eyes and jaw shape are very important in projecting a personality type; in *Second Life*, jaw shape is extra important because of technical considerations that, at the time of writing, limit eye-appearance impact.

TORSO

You should edit your avatar's torso right after you've finished adjusting Body options. The Torso options are very straightforward and do not require extra explanations. However, there are a few things to remember:

- Adjusting torso muscles also changes arm muscles—high settings have unfortunate visual effects.

- Neck Thickness and Neck Length should be finalized only once you've finished messing with your avatar's head.

- Torso-editing options collectively default to create the ideal torso: knockout busts for the females, broad shoulders and rippling muscles for men, etc. You may want to nudge the appropriate sliders a few points away from their default settings for a more realistic look.

- Arm Length and Hand Size are the two options you should start with. They are linked to Body choices as well as Leg Length and Foot Size. Torso Length should be proportionate to Leg Length.

- Love Handles and Belly Size are obviously best adjusted in tandem, and any adjustments here should be considered together with Body Thickness and Body Fat settings.

CHAPTER 1

CHAPTER 2

CHAPTER 3

CHAPTER 4

CHAPTER 5

CHAPTER 6

CHAPTER 7

CHAPTER 8

CHAPTER 9

CHAPTER 10

CHAPTER 11

CHAPTER 12

CHAPTER 13

CHAPTER 14

CHAPTER 15

APPENDICES

ADDITIONAL INFO

CANNIBALIZING AVATARS

Remember than any avatar can be cannibalized for body parts. You can switch body parts between avatars with ease or add custom body parts of your own.

LEGS

Editing your avatar's legs includes setting their length and their shape. If you go to the trouble to take off your avatar's pants, you'll have an easier job. Note that Leg Length has a marked effect on Leg Shape, and that you can change leg appearance by adjusting Body Height, Body Fat, and Body Thickness values.

Leg-editing options include adjusting the size and shape of your avatar's hips, crotch, and buttocks. Adjustments in these three areas influence one another and may require quite a lot of tweaking following any significant change. Note that Body settings play a big part here, too.

Appropriately, at the very bottom of the Legs submenu you'll see a Foot Size option. Many *SL* people claim they get on very happily with a foot size of 0, and it's true that a scaled-down foot makes footwear look better. It's up to you to strike the right balance between realism and beauty here. In real life, foot size corresponds to hand size, but this is *Second Life*, where most custom shoes are made to fit size-0 feet.

⬇ SKIN

Figure 5.10: Born into a virtual world a day ago and already showing age? Must be the pace of your second life.

Clicking on the Skin tab on the Appearance panel brings up a list of options that are very straightforward and limited. They allow you to make basic changes to avatar skin appearance, such as change skin color (and not much more). The Face Detail and Body Detail submenus can be successfully used to create an older-looking avatar, but they won't make the skin more convincing (Figure 5.10).

FROM LINDEN LAB
HOW THE LINDENS LOOK

"Why does it look like this? Well, as for the body shape, hairdo, and goatee, I decided not to try to make this avatar look too much like me. My original avatar from my pre-Linden days was designed to look like a trimmer version of myself. I did go for the black curly hair look for this avatar in emulation of a Shakespearean actor in California named Julian Lopez-Morillas. The summer before 7th grade, I got involved with the Berkeley Shakespeare Festival, and among other things ushered for productions of *The Tempest* in which Lopez-Morillas played Prospero. For outfits, I try to find something that looks vaguely like it comes from the Reniassance, and could plausibly belong on a Shakespearean duke of Milan who has aspirations of being a wizard."

—Prospero Linden

"I saw someone wearing this skin in the welcome area and had to have it. I was previously human, but think this avatar pulls off the 'tough but nice' look better than my prior avatar did. I love that so many people can have a same element (in this case a skin) and still never look anything alike."

—Jill Linden

"Initially, I simply wanted to look somewhat 'abstract' and mysterious instead of appearing in a basic human form. I thought it would be fun. Over time my avatar began to resonate deeply with my identity, which is why is hasn't really changed in almost three years. I enjoy changing avatars now and then for special events or presentations, but I always come back to this form."

—Pathfinder Linden

CHAPTER 1
CHAPTER 2
CHAPTER 3
CHAPTER 4
CHAPTER 5

CHAPTER 6
CHAPTER 7
CHAPTER 8
CHAPTER 9
CHAPTER 10
CHAPTER 11
CHAPTER 12
CHAPTER 13
CHAPTER 14
CHAPTER 15
APPENDICES

"What do my avatars look like? Like this and more! I presently have over 50 avatars, almost all of them watermelon-colored: `http://torley.com/a-guide-to-torleys/`."

—Torley Linden

Most *Second Life* residents agree that a custom avatar skin is a priority because of the dramatic effect it has on your avatar's appearance. Nice-looking skins can be obtained free of charge (you'll find a couple in your Library), and let's-have-virtual-sex-right-now skins can be had for the low four figures in Linden dollars. At the time of writing, Linden Lab recommends Flea Bussy (of the store Grendel's Children) for some of the most creative and expressive avatars around: `http://slurl.com/secondlife/Avaria%20 Tor/206/235/251`. However, that's just one of many sources you should check out when looking to improve your avatar's appearance. You may also attempt to create your own custom skin if you have the bent and the external application needed. You can download free skin templates, and *SL*-related forums are full of good, clear advice on what's involved in creating a new skin. Of course, you'll find that being nice to other *SL* residents in-world pays dividends that go beyond good advice (see the "Advice for the N00b" sidebar).

RESIDENTS SPEAK
ADVICE FOR THE NOOB

"I have a box of quality free stuff for newbies. Whenever someone I don't recognize, or someone who just stands out as a newbie, strolls into the area, I immediately check their profile so see how new they are. If they have a blank profile and/or a birthday less than two weeks ago … I try to help guide them in *SL*. If you're nice, polite, don't beg, don't act like the 'typical noob' … you will probably get a box from me that will help you get started with your new *SL* experience. I've been known to take newbies to the good free places. Several businesses have low-cost high-quality items just for newbies to help introduce them [the places' products]. I'll take you to a few of them. If you're nice, polite, etc.… and willing to spend 30 minutes with me, I'll take you shopping so you can get good stuff at low or no cost. Thirty minutes with me and at least you won't *look* like a noob."

—Lolita Pro

"The stuff you find you use the most won't be the things that you spent the most on. If you're a guy, for example, look for the Prince Charming skin in the Library folder. Prim hair isn't compulsory, either."

—Cannae Brentano

"Pose stands are useful because they lock you into a fixed pose. Otherwise, if you're trying to edit an earring or nosering whatever, your avatar has the habit of looking at where your mouse pointer is … which can make it *very* tricky to grab attachments."

—Jopsy Pendragon

"Ways to check yourself out:

- Stand on a posing stand. This lets you see your avatar from the front, with arms out. You can't edit appearance while on the stand, but you can always get back on after making your changes. Help Island has posing stands to use in the freebie store, and you can get your own for free in various places.

- Hold down the Alt key and click on yourself. You can zoom in and back, and circle around. It takes some practice, and you may quickly wear out that key on your keyboard if you do it enough.

- Use the dial thingy on your mouse to zoom in and out.

- Pull down your View menu and click on Camera Control. This lets you adjust your view with the most precision."

—Sanjame Baroque

⬇ Hair and Eyes

Avatar hair and eyes can alter your avatar's appearance. Unfortunately, most *SL* denizens seem to agree that trying to customize either through the Hair and Eyes tabs under Body Parts yields average-quality results at best. Yes, you can easily achieve a meaningful appearance change by adjusting basic values such as Color for both eyes and hair. However, any further attempts to mess with your hair are likely to end with much frustration, and taking eye changes beyond color and depth isn't possible without acquiring a new eye template, or an eye attachment that your avatar will wear over its default eyes. Some eye attachments come with scripts that add features such as simple animation (for example, blinking). If you want to have a stab at creating your own custom eyes, download the free eye template from `http://secondlife.com/community/templates.php`.

If you want your avatar to have good-looking hair, you'll definitely have to get a custom job. As mentioned earlier, the best-looking custom hair is built of individual prims and is worn as a head attachment. As you know by now, you can easily acquire decent prim hair for free, and great-looking custom hair is affordable, with prices ranging from a few hundred Linden dollars to the low four figures for hot new styles.

ADDITIONAL INFO
HAIRY CHOICES

When shopping for new hair, the three things to consider are the look, the price, and the number of prims involved. A hairstyle created using a large number of prims can have a negative effect on *SL*'s performance on your computer because of increased lag whenever your new hair appears in the view. A master *SL* hairstylist always uses the minimum number of prims required to provide the intended effect.

⬇ Clothes and Other Attachments

If you like clothes, *Second Life* will feel like heaven. You'll arrive with your Library containing several wardrobes' worth of clothing, and you'll add new outfits and individual clothing items while exploring Orientation and Help Islands. Within minutes of arriving on the mainland, your options to acquire good-looking clothes for free multiply like rabbits. You'll also see plenty of clothes (and other attractive things) offered at the symbolic price of L$1 (Figure 5.11). As pointed out elsewhere in this guide, even if you have zero Linden dollars and absolutely refuse to buy any, you can make a few Linden bucks instantly by engaging in such activities as sitting in a chair for L$3 per 15 minutes. In other words, *SL* lets you acquire a huge wardrobe for next to nothing in record time.

Making a few basic alterations to the ready-made Library clothes is relatively easy. The tabs under Clothes in the Appearance panel list standard clothing-item classes—Shirt, Pants, etc. The items your avatar is wearing at the time automatically become available for editing. In addition to sliders adjusting

CHAPTER 1
CHAPTER 2
CHAPTER 3
CHAPTER 4
CHAPTER 5
CHAPTER 6
CHAPTER 7
CHAPTER 8
CHAPTER 9
CHAPTER 10
CHAPTER 11
CHAPTER 12
CHAPTER 13
CHAPTER 14
CHAPTER 15
APPENDICES

clothing details such as Sleeve Length or Pants Crotch, you can change the color/tint and texture of the selected clothing item:

- Clicking on the Fabric square opens a panel featuring the Library folder, which contains a special subfolder of fabric textures. Clicking a texture activates it.

- Clicking on the Color/Tint square opens a Color Picker panel. This lets you quickly pick a color by clicking a square, or create a custom color.

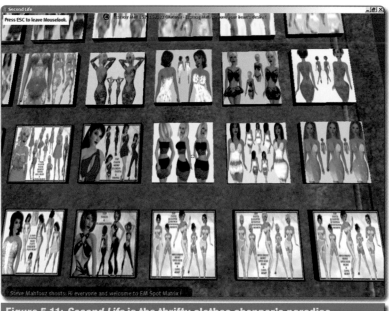

Figure 5.11: *Second Life* is the thrifty clothes shopper's paradise.

The clothing-editing options on the Appearance panel are great for simple alterations. However, if you want to design a clothing item from scratch, the plot thickens. As the *SL* template manual points out, it's not easy to design something in an external 2D application and subsequently make it fit a 3D object (your avatar).

You may also create clothing out of prims. However, even a relatively small and simple item such as a flexi miniskirt needs a number of carefully shaped prims. If you're interested in pursuing clothes design as a serious hobby or as a source of income, begin by signing up for at least a few of the tutorials and classes offered in *Second Life*. To see a list of the tutorials and classes currently on offer, open the Search panel and type "classes" or "tutorials" into the Search box.

ADDITIONAL INFO
TATTOOS AS CLOTHING

In *Second Life*, tattoos fall into the clothing category. Tattoos can be worn as clothing items that are fully transparent except for the area covered by the tattoo. They also may be created in an external application and imported into *Second Life* as textures.

Clothes have decisive impact on your avatar's appearance—the old saying that clothes make the man has never been more true than in the virtual world. Most likely, over half of the many thousands of items in your Inventory will consist of clothing, and 90% of that clothing won't ever be worn. There's a doctorate in sociology waiting for whoever draws the right conclusions.

CHAPTER 1
CHAPTER 2
CHAPTER 3
CHAPTER 4
CHAPTER 5
CHAPTER 6
CHAPTER 7
CHAPTER 8
CHAPTER 9
CHAPTER 10
CHAPTER 11
CHAPTER 12
CHAPTER 13
CHAPTER 14
CHAPTER 15
APPENDICES

Figure 5.12: Armed and dangerous? Not quite.

Earlier in this chapter, Aodhan McDunnough described how he outfitted his avatar with a mechanical arm. While this is a somewhat extreme example, it illustrates the wide range of options you have for enhancing your avatar's appearance with an extra attachment. Appearance-enhancing attachments can include almost anything: you can wear a hat or a cap, lead a dog on a leash, or have a flying fish hovering over your head and attached by an invisible (i.e., fully transparent) thread. It's up to you to choose whatever you think suits your image (Figure 5.12).

Jewelry is another type of appearance-enhancing attachment. There's plenty of jewelry available, and it ranges from very simple to very elaborate: while everyone is talented enough to create a simple ring out of a single prim, few people are capable of making a multistone necklace whose jewels are scripted to display dazzling light effects. Note that jewelry can take many forms: animated, sparkling boot buckles and shoe laces are good examples.

⬇ AVATAR ANIMATIONS AND GESTURES

Avatar animations include every single move your avatar makes: ordinary walking, a gesture, dancing. Gestures are animations with extra content, such as sounds and/or special effects. Animations may be very simple (a hand wave, a nod) or very complex (a fencing system). They may be innocent or naughty, and some of the naughty ones are truly complicated.

Figure 5.13: I burn with shame.

Most *SL* residents who have been around for a while recognize the value of quality animations; a custom walk animation is high up on the list of avatar-appearance enhancements. However, you do not need to acquire a custom animation right away to inject a little more life and charm into your avatar. You enter *Second Life* with a vast Library of gestures waiting to be used. All you need to do is activate the ones you like most by assigning them hotkeys, and display a sense of humor and good timing when you use them (Figure 5.13).

Avatar animations are most often created using an external application called Poser (there's also a free application called Avimator, though it isn't as sophisticated); they are much more complex than the simple animations you can apply to objects while remaining within the world. Subsequently, they are imported into *Second Life* and, if meant to replace a default animation, given an override script. Like most *SL* creations, custom animations can be obtained for free or for a symbolic price, but the flashiest animations can cost many thousands of Linden dollars.

ADDITIONAL INFO
BECOMING AN ANIMATOR

Creating custom animations isn't easy, which is why animators in *SL* are both rare and well-paid. If you're interested, check out the Animation Guide within the *Second Life* Knowledge Base. Log in with your *SL* name and password at `https://secure-web0.secondlife.com/community/support.php`, and type "Animation Guide" into the Knowledge Base's search box.

Custom animations greatly enrich your virtual life because they enable your avatar to behave in a new way through custom moves or to participate in a new activity. However, you can greatly enhance your avatar's ability to socialize simply by using the animations or gestures from the Library. Accordingly, the next chapter takes a look at Library contents.

CHAPTER 6

USING YOUR LIBRARY

You already know that Library items and choices are a great help while working on your avatar's appearance. However, the Library is much more than that: its contents are your starting kit for creating a fulfilling second life, and many of the items it contains remain very useful throughout your *SL* existence.

The Library does not have its own onscreen button. It's just a folder in your Inventory, and it's accessed by clicking the Inventory button. That is why many new players, eager to get on with their new lives, fail to check out its contents. But you won't make that mistake, will you?

In this chapter, we'll discuss the Library in detail. You'll find out how it can get your new life off to a flying start, and which items remain uniquely useful no matter how long you've inhabited the *SL* metaverse.

CONTENTS

WHAT IS THE LIBRARY?

You can look at it this way: the Library is your starting Inventory, courtesy of Linden Lab. Every new *Second Life* resident receives the same set of items: a comprehensive starting kit that contains much more than clothing. Library contents include a livable house (Atoll Hut) with an extra-small footprint for small land lots, a driveable vehicle (Kart), a popgun, and a wide range of landscaping items. New items may appear following periodical *SL* updates, so make sure to review your Library's contents regularly! It really pays—if you find it hard to believe, check out what some experienced *Second Life*rs have to say on the subject.

RESIDENTS SPEAK
THE LIBRARY

"The Library is great—I use it more and more the longer I play. They occasionally add new things to it (for example, there are a number of full avatars there now which are much more interesting than the default Orientation Island avies), and it's a convenient place to find textures and other items useful in quickie landscaping and other kinds of builds.

"I've also made frequent use of the furniture; it's nice to be able to toss down some chairs or a bed for some role-playing without having to go shopping while in the middle of a scene."

—Wildefire Waldcott

"I use the Library quite a bit. The trees, of course, are the top item I use out of there. I'm a terraformer and landscaper and prefer the Linden trees over resident-made trees for their interaction with the wind and fewer prims. Even my waterfalls are made from Library parts."

—Ghoti Nyak

"I use a lot of the Linden plants for my terraforming and landscaping jobs. It's fantastic to have big, good-looking plants like the Plumeria bush and some of the trees, that fill a lot of space yet take up only one prim.

"I also use several of the Library textures in my building work, and the scripts and stuff for waterfalls in the Library have been very useful of late."

—Ceera Murakami

As mentioned in the previous chapter, you could have paid a few quick visits to the Library while editing your avatar's appearance—choosing a new texture or color automatically takes you to the Library folder, and the textures and colors contained therein. Later in this chapter, we'll look at the Library subfolders one by one, following the same order in which they're displayed in *Second Life*. This should make in-game reference easier and encourage you to use the Library often.

And use it often you should, right from the start. If you do, you'll feel like a veteran *SL* citizen even before you leave Help Island. Countless newbies will gape with slack-jawed amazement as you conjure up weapons, vehicles, and houses with effortless flicks of your wrist. The air shall ring with excited cries such as "Where did you get that gun?" and "How do you build this stuff so fast?" To which you'll reply, "I got it from the Library."

CHAPTER 1
CHAPTER 2
CHAPTER 3
CHAPTER 4
CHAPTER 5
CHAPTER 6
CHAPTER 7
CHAPTER 8
CHAPTER 9
CHAPTER 10
CHAPTER 11
CHAPTER 12
CHAPTER 13
CHAPTER 14
CHAPTER 15
APPENDICES

ADDITIONAL INFO
MOVING ITEMS

You can move items between the Library and the Inventory. Open the folders, then just select and drag items from one location to the other. You can also give any item from either the Inventory or the Library to another *SL* denizen; to do so, select and drag the folder onto the recipient's avatar. However, some items are not transferable—find out by right-clicking on an item and selecting Properties.

LIBRARY CONTENTS

As you must have gathered by now, there's more to the Library than meets the eye, especially at the hurried first glance thrown by a new, impatient resident of *Second Life*. The sections below list Library folders and comment on their contents (Figure 6.1). The folders and items you'll find in your Library give a good idea of the range of activities that are available in your new virtual life.

Figure 6.1: There are many nice surprises waiting for you inside the Library folders.

⬇ ANIMATIONS

This folder contains a handful of animations, including a couple of dance animations. Dancing to streamed-in music is very popular in *SL*, but a lot of the time you'll be using dance animations embedded in nightclub dance pads/balls. Stepping on one of these loads the dance animation contained within. Other animations in this folder include Fuego!, which has your avatar burst into flames following a typed command, and Kung Fu, which makes your avatar execute martial moves. Note that most *SL* denizens end up investing in custom animations—not only new moves, but also new takes on existing *SL* animations. For example, many people regard the default "walk" animation as clunky and jerky, and acquire or create custom jobs that make their avatars move more gracefully.

⬇ BODY PARTS

You'll most likely access this folder while editing the appearance of your avatar, as described in Chapter 5. Its contents reflect a certain obsession with hair among *SL* citizens (there are many parallels between the virtual and real worlds; this is one of them). At the time of writing, the Body Parts folder contains these items and subfolders:

Hair—Men's. This subfolder contains a number of hairstyle choices, including a rather wild afro. If you decide to use them, treat them as a starting point for creating your final stunning hairdo. Remember that you'll acquire new, better-looking hair shortly after starting your new existence. The Freebie Shop on Help Island will yield some, and soon after you move to the mainland you'll most likely get high-quality prim hair. As you'll discover, looking for the perfect hairstyle can be as important as it is in your real life!

Hair—Women's. This subfolder contains hairstyles for female avatars. Keep in mind that you can and indeed should try applying male hairstyles to female avatars and vice versa—the results can be surprisingly good.

Creating Avatar Hair Textures. This short document, discussed in the previous chapter, is a must-read if you're going to mess with your hair. Don't go that route unless you're prepared to put in some real time and effort! Doing your own hair is as difficult in *Second Life* as it is in real life—maybe even more so.

Eyes—Dark Brown. This is an instant eye-color choice that should be treated as a starting point for determining your avatar's eye color.

Eyes—Gray. Another starting point for determining your avatar's eye color.

Green Hair. The right choice if you're celebrating St. Patrick's Day in *Second Life*.

Hair. This item should probably be called "No Hair"—dragging it onto your avatar's skull turns your avatar into a baldie. That's the thing to do if you want your avatar to sport new prim hair that's worn as an attachment.

Hair—Medium Brown. This is probably the most natural-looking instant hairstyle choice at the time of writing, if you don't mind looking a little like a small-town lounge lizard. However, if your ambition is to become a virtual hairdresser, it makes a good starting point for creating male and female hairstyles alike.

Shape—Thin. This treasured Library item immediately endows your avatar with the svelte figure we all want to have in real life. It looks good, too, but remember that a cookie-cutter body is a cookie-cutter body, no matter how beautiful. As someone clever once put it, there's nothing as boring as perfection.

Skin—Lightly Tanned. This choice gives your avatar the bronze skin tone favored by many movie stars. If you find it a little on the dark side, adjust it as described in Chapter 5.

The Body Parts folder is, predictably, most useful right at the start of your new life. As you spend more time in the *SL* metaverse, you'll inevitably acquire many more interesting options, starting with the Help Island freebies discussed in Chapter 3. The moment you move to the mainland, you'll have even more custom hair, skin, and body-shape choices, including plenty of freebies.

⬇ CLOTHING

Your avatar is born wearing a rather proletarian outfit: T-shirt, jeans, fire-sale flip-flops, plus standard underwear and socks. And as you know from the preceding chapters, the *Second Life* metaverse is a very fashion-oriented world, because literally everyone is a clothing—scratch that—a *costume* designer. It's never been as easy as it is in *Second Life*.

The Library comes with a thick Clothing subfolder, its size silently confirming the importance of looking good in *Second Life*. Inside the Clothing subfolder, you'll find enough stuff to fill several big real-life wardrobes, with new items added following almost every *SL* update:

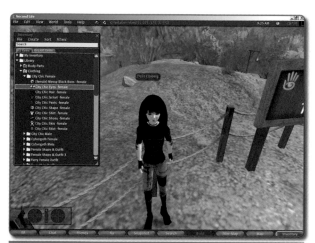

Figure 6.2: Customizing a complete outfit from the Library is the quickest way to look original.

Complete Outfits. You'll see a long column of subfolders containing complete male and female outfits (City Chic, Goth, Harajuku, etc.). Hint: you can mix and match various items from different outfits, and save the results as a new outfit in your Inventory. Treat most of the complete outfits you'll find in the Clothing subfolder as the equivalent of real-life off-the-rack suits: you need to apply a little personal touch to make things look good (Figure 6.2). Note that the More Outfits folder includes uniforms.

CHAPTER 1
CHAPTER 2
CHAPTER 3
CHAPTER 4
CHAPTER 5
CHAPTER 6

CHAPTER 7
CHAPTER 8
CHAPTER 9
CHAPTER 10
CHAPTER 11
CHAPTER 12
CHAPTER 13
CHAPTER 14
CHAPTER 15
APPENDICES

Individual Clothing Items. These include everything down to a spare set of underpants. This is important, since your carefree existence in *Second Life* means you don't really *have* to wear underpants, and with a little customization and imagination they may become an attractive trade item. Few people can resist entering a business dialogue when you open with, "Hey, I'm new and I'm poor. This stuff you make is so amazing I'd be willing to trade in my last set of underwear to have some of that."

The Clothing folder contains a lot of stuff, and upon examining its contents you should do what you'd do if you were suddenly given trunkloads of new clothes. Choose what you're likely to wear, and move it into your Inventory: select and drag items between the Library and Inventory folders, and save complete outfits as new Inventory subfolders.

⬇ GESTURES

This Library folder usually draws little interest from new *SL* residents. This is a big oversight: entertaining gestures can do more for your avatar's memorability than a top-of-the-line designer outfit purchased for many Linden dollars. It's been noted in Chapter 5, but to drive it home let's have it again: the impression you make on people you meet in *Second Life* depends on what you do, not only by what you look and sound like. Creating and activating a personal Gesture folder is among your priorities.

There is also a Gesture subfolder in your Inventory; however, it contains just two subfolders—Common Gestures and Male Gestures if your avatar is male, Female Gestures if it is female. There are five Gesture subfolders in the Library: Common, Female, Male, and Other Gestures. Regardless of your sexual preferences, do not let yourself be limited by your avatar's sex when selecting gestures. A female making a male gesture can be very entertaining and memorable, and the same applies to a male making a female gesture. So if you want *SL* people to remember you, it's truly worth your while to assemble your very own gesture set from the Library choices right at the start of your existence. Here's what you'll find in the Library's Gestures subfolders:

Common Gestures. This subfolder contains a set of gestures meant for avatars of either sex. There are some very nice animations in there, in spite of the "Common" moniker, so take the time to look through them all. As explained in Chapter 5, the timing of a gesture gives it a new meaning: for example, the "count" gesture works great when you want to emphasize a point in conversation. This folder also contains the three gestures needed for playing the popular "rock, paper, scissors" game.

Female Gestures. This set of "standard" gestures includes a female voice where appropriate. Again, the gestures within seem slightly bland when employed by an avatar of the intended sex, but gain in originality when used by males. You'll crack people up if you are a big, well-muscled guy who unexpectedly says "Get lost" in a high-pitched female voice.

Male Gestures. This set of "standard" and slightly bland gestures includes a male voice where appropriate. Some of the animations are identical to those in the Female Gestures subfolder. This is perhaps the least exciting gesture subfolder in the Library, at least if you use them for the intended gender.

Other Gestures. Make sure you check out this subfolder in detail: some of the animations within are very entertaining. "Embarrassed," "nya," and "shrug" are good examples of gestures that work equally well for avatars of both sexes.

Speech Gestures. This folder contains many gestures that are designed to work with *SL*'s voice capability. If there's something more staid than the traditional "typing" animation that switches on while typing chat text, it's an avatar that stands still while its creator is speaking. Use the gestures in that folder to put some color into your conversations.

ADDITIONAL INFO
UTILIZING YOUR LIBRARY EARLY ON

Remember that when you begin your new life, the Library has much more to offer than the Inventory does. The little folder at the end of the Inventory list looks unimportant to many fresh *SL* inhabitants, so making use of its contents can instantly make you stand out from the crowd of newborn *SL* citizens.

CHAPTER 1
CHAPTER 2
CHAPTER 3
CHAPTER 4
CHAPTER 5
CHAPTER 6
CHAPTER 7
CHAPTER 8
CHAPTER 9
CHAPTER 10
CHAPTER 11
CHAPTER 12
CHAPTER 13
CHAPTER 14
CHAPTER 15
APPENDICES

⬇ LANDMARKS AND NOTECARDS

Figure 6.3: Some people will go to great lengths (and heights) to make sure they're noticed.

These two Library subfolders are most useful at the start of your new existence. The Landmark folder contains just a single landmark: the Welcome Area on the *SL* mainland. The Welcome Area is where you should go upon leaving Help Island; it is the right spot to pick up information on ongoing *SL* events. It is also a very good spot to pick up, er, make new friends. Many new *SL* denizens hang around there for a while, eager to show off their new selves (Figure 6.3).

The Library's Notecard folder contains just four notecards, but three of these are pretty important, and you would be wise to keep them:

HELP! This notecard contains answers to many of the questions new denizens have about *Second Life*. It's worth your while to check out the contents even if you don't want to read it (there's a lot of stuff in there!). The topics covered in this notecard will instantly make you aware of the multitude of options available to you in your new existence. Read the titles of the featured Beginner's Guides to various aspects of *Second Life* (such as owning land), and check out the step-by-step instructions for selected *SL* activities. Purchasing and owning land, removing items from a box, and making movies in *Second Life*—these are just some of the issues covered in the Library's HELP! notecard. Obviously, this notecard's a keeper.

Community Standards. This notecard explains what you can and cannot do in *Second Life*. The *Second Life* metaverse can continue to exist only if its inhabitants follow certain rules. These are explained in the Community Standards notecard. They are very reasonable; the only denizens likely to find them oppressive are those who are consumed by hunger for sex and violence. If you happen to be one of them, remember that mutual consensus rules in *SL*. Join or assemble a group of like-minded people in a defined area who play by your kind of rules.

Media Player Help. This notecard discusses activating streaming media so that you can play music and movies on your land. Music and movies draw people, which can be useful. It most likely will be a while before you turn into a media mogul, so keep this card for future reference.

Welcome Note. This ultra-short note tells you how to obtain extra notecards discussing selected aspects of *Second Life*. These extra notecards will appear in the Notecard subfolder in your Inventory.

You may drag the three keeper notecards into your Inventory's Notecard folder so you have all your notecards collected in one place.

⬇ Objects

This is one of the most interesting among the Library folders. It contains plenty of subfolders and individual items that you'll find useful and entertaining throughout your *Second Life* existence. Its contents may change following an *SL* update, so check them now and then! Here's a descriptive list of the goodies that are available at the time of writing:

Atoll Continent Stuff. This modestly titled subfolder contains an Atoll Hut–style home complete with accessories (footbridge, walkway, etc.). As you know from Chapter 3, you can pick up a free house on Help Island—a design much classier than the modest Atoll Hut. But one thing about the Atoll Hut is unbeatable: it has a tiny footprint, making it a very good choice on the small, pay-no-upkeep building lots, aka First Land. When you have only 512 square meters to play with, and are determined to have a house that stands on virtual land instead of floating in the sky, the Atoll Hut's small space requirements can make it a good choice. Of course, you can customize the hut—change the default textures here and there, put in a bigger window, etc.

Business. This subfolder contains a Resident Store Kit. You can set up your own store in a blink of an eye—the kit comes with a notecard containing what's probably the simplest set of instructions ever written for erecting a small commercial building.

Dominos. This subfolder contains a single, large domino block that can be copied endlessly. See the "What Can You Do with Library Objects?" sidebar to find out how other users play with dominos.

Household. Here you'll find another freebie starter home—a small, single-room cabin—plus a builder's tape measure and the basic furnishings for your new home (bed, lamp, coffee table, rug, etc.). Other interesting items in this folder include a dead parrot waiting for a script to bring her to life … or to face whatever fate you devise. Some *SL* denizens seem to like parrot soup.

CHAPTER 1
CHAPTER 2
CHAPTER 3
CHAPTER 4
CHAPTER 5
CHAPTER 6

CHAPTER 7
CHAPTER 8
CHAPTER 9
CHAPTER 10
CHAPTER 11
CHAPTER 12
CHAPTER 13
CHAPTER 14
CHAPTER 15
APPENDICES

Figure 6.4: Some of the plants included in the Library's Landscaping folder are little works of art.

Landscaping. This is yet another very useful folder. Contents include quite pretty freestanding and potted plants (Figure 6.4), an assortment of ornamental rocks, and decorative items such as latticework.

Orientation stations with notecards. This folder contains the interactive signs and orientation stations you pass by right after you start your second life. These signs and stations are demo pieces; treat them as starting points for your own interactive signs. Note that you can right-click on a sign and choose Open from the pop-up pie menu—this will reveal object contents, such as attached sound effects and scripts. If you've missed your chance to obtain Male or Female Outfit #3 at the start, right-click the Outfit #3 signs and choose Open from the pie menu. You'll be given the option to wear each sign's clothing content, and/or copy it to your Inventory.

Telehubs. Telehubs can be used as arrival points for teleporting *SL* denizens. This folder offers three models: the Invisible Telehub, the Small Telehub, and the big Linden Telehub (which has sentimental value for long-term *SL* citizens—a long, long time ago, residents could not teleport at will, and were forced to use Telehubs). Telehubs are useful when you want to direct traffic on land you own; most commercial landmarks are set on Telehubs. Use Invisible and Small Telehubs for low-volume traffic (home, small business) and the big model for high-volume traffic (large commercial establishments, events).

Trees, plants, and grasses. This Library folder is extremely useful throughout your second life. A lot of the flora it contains looks superior to most user-made items; as mentioned earlier, it's even used by professional *SL* landscapers. You'll really appreciate the contents of this folder when you acquire virtual land and are in a hurry to make it look good.

Walkways. There are five types of walkways on offer here. Click and drag the icon for the selected type repeatedly to lay down the walkway of your choice, piece by piece.

119

ADDITIONAL INFO
LIBRARY OBJECTS AND SCRIPTING

Library objects are extremely useful if you're planning to create items. Editing Library objects is a great exercise in building and texturing. The scripts in the scripted items can be copied to newly created objects, and most can also be modified. Adding or deleting a couple of script lines is always easier than writing everything from scratch!

The Walkways subfolder is followed by a series of individual objects that provide tons of fun. You must check them out, even if you don't look at anything else! Many new denizens don't, and they are the ones who will be staring at you and asking, "Where did you get that gun?"

RESIDENTS SPEAK
WHAT CAN YOU DO WITH LIBRARY OBJECTS?

"The Library popgun is fun to shoot each other with. The popgun is good when you are learning scripting. It serves as an example of how to rez an object from another one.

"The beach ball is fun to play with. It has a good script for beginning scripters also. The basic chair is good to use as a model when you are learning to build. It has another good basic script, a sit script. The dice and fireworks have good beginner's scripts in them.

"The dominoes—who could forget the dominoes? Thousands of dominoes stacked in a delightfully tempting manner, and they set themselves back up automatically. For fun, make an object that pushes dominoes, so when you find a set of dominoes, turn on your domino pusher, plough into the dominoes, and watch them fly away at high velocity.

"There's some things in the Landscaping folder that a person might find useful setting up a small home. Everyone starting out needs a pink flamingo.

"The gesture folders are pretty nice to have. In case anyone doesn't know it, you can activate an entire folder of gestures such as the Common Gestures by dragging the folder onto your av.

"There's now some Linden Telehubs in there, quaint reminders of the days of yore. Whatever yore is.

"Some of the orientation stations are in there in case one gets nostalgic for Orientation Island and can't be bothered to go to Orientation Island Public [100, 171, 33]."

—SuezanneC Baskerville

Figure 6.5: A car! A gun! That's every real guy's get-rich-quick kit, no?

For many *SL* denizens, the standalone items in the Objects folder will be worth more than a freebie custom house complete with furniture (Figure 6.5). All of them come with operating instructions, which are accessed by right-clicking the chosen object and selecting Open from the pie menu. This will let you view the object's contents, which usually include a notecard with instructions.

The following is a descriptive list of the standalone items in the Library's Objects folder at the time of writing:

Kart 1.0. This is your freebie *SL* starter vehicle: a smart little go-cart in bright red. It goes pretty fast, too. To go for a drive, drag the Kart icon onto the ground, right-click on it to open the pie menu, and click on Drive. If you can't be bothered to read the Kart notecard, keep in mind that movement is activated by the arrow and WASD keys.

Media Player. This item contains the media player and its script. Drag the Media Player icon from your Library and onto building-permitted ground, then right-click the elegant oblong box that appears to view its contents. They consist of the media player proper—a nifty flat screen—and the script. There is *no* notecard with operating instructions; after rezzing the Media Player, right-click on it and choose Open from the pie menu, then double-click on the Media Controller script icon to find operating info.

Popgun. For many players, this is the best freebie Library item of them all. Drag the Popgun icon onto your avatar, and the gun will appear in your right hand.

ADDITIONAL INFO
FIRING A POPGUN

To fire your new gun, follow the onscreen instructions: first, switch to mouselook and zoom into first-person view. Moving the mouse aims the gun, and left-clicking fires sickly green orbs at your target. They're powerful enough to knock someone back, and a series of hits can move the targeted avatar a fair distance. There is no injury involved.

Basic Chair. This is a very useful item for more than the obvious reasons. The chair comes with a Sit Down script attached, and this script can be copied as is to furniture you make yourself.

Beach Ball. Big, colorful, and bouncy, the beach ball comes with a piece of script that features extensive comments: it's almost like a little script-writing tutorial. As usual, access the contents by dragging the object icon onto the ground, right-clicking on it, and choosing Open from the pop-up pie menu.

Celtic Sword. What do you know: Library offerings even include a wicked-looking hand-to-hand-combat weapon. However, there isn't much sense in walking around with a sword in your hand if you can't hit people with it, and hitting people involves making appropriate gestures and scripting appropriate, complicated effects. You may wait with bated breath for an update that includes all this stuff; you can try to buy appropriate scripts (of course, look first if there are any available for free), or—in a pinch—you can use appropriate Library gestures. For example, playing Pointme from the Common Gestures subfolder while holding the sword results in an animation that looks like a rather elegant, if unhurried, block against an enemy sword thrust.

Dice. Drag the Dice icon to the ground, then switch to mouselook and click on the dice to roll them.

Firework Launcher. The firework launcher comes with an inexhaustible supply of rockets and operating instructions. The launch animation and sound effects are very well done and deserve to be copied (hint, hint).

Hand Lamp, Party Hat. An old-fashioned hand lamp and a conical party hat round off the list of standalone Objects-folder items. The hand lamp doesn't have to be attached to your hand; it can be put anywhere to function as an ordinary lamp (and actually looks very appropriate in a cabin home). To put the hand lamp upright, right-click on it, choose Edit from the pie menu, and use the Rotate function.

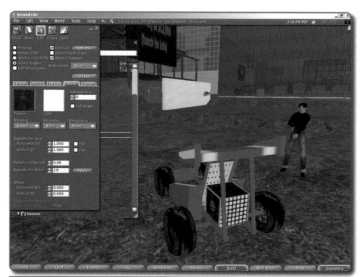

The standalone objects in the Objects folder are a great help when you begin creating your own items and building things. As mentioned earlier, it's always easiest to begin by modifying existing stuff instead of building from scratch, and the vast majority of the Library items can be modified and copied any way you like (Figure 6.6).

Figure 6.6: Modifying Library objects is a great way to learn building and scripting.

The Objects folder is followed by an empty Photo Album folder. It's up to you to fill it with snapshots. However, if you get serious about *SL* photography, you might want to invest in a virtual photo album or a TV set to display your art with all the glory it deserves.

⬇ THE BUILDING AND SCRIPTING STUFF

The last three Library folders are especially important to everyone who wants to get creative in *Second Life*. After you've explored a little, you're bound to try your hand at bringing new items into existence by modifying existing items, and building new ones from scratch. This involves making things look and sound the way you want them to, and eventually adding scripted animations.

The Library offers you plenty to work with:

Scripts. This folder contains three useful scripts. As you might guess, Anim Smooth smoothes out animations; HoverText Clock turns an object into a clock by making it display Pacific standard time; Rotation Script is extremely versatile and can be included in a wide variety of objects. For example, right-click on the hand lamp that you've just rotated upright with the Edit panel's Rotate function; then click on the New Script button and paste the Rotation Script contents inside the New Script file (delete any existing content; the New Script file always contains the code for creating a New Script file). Save, exit, and watch the hand lamp turn round and round. There—you've just scripted an object to behave in a certain way.

Sounds. This folder contains a subfolder titled Gestures. Its contents include male and female sounds, and sound bites designed to go with specific avatar gestures, but of course they have more uses than that. If you've ever wanted a dog that speaks with a human voice, for example, use some of the sound bites from the Gestures folder. Simply upload custom-made sound bites, and who knows—maybe you'll be the first *SL* citizen to breed talking police dogs? "Hands up!" he barked, and all that. The folder also contains Button Up and Button Down sounds that can be ruthlessly copied to and played by objects you create or edit.

Textures. The final folder in the Library is also its biggest: it contains an awesome number of textures, plus Avatar Body and Clothing templates. You'll use these templates and selected textures in Hair and Fabric folders frequently while editing your avatar's appearance. Take the time to review all the other choices, because there are quite a few, and new ones are added often. Naturally, many textures can be used for purposes other than the ones intended. For example, Atoll Wood Plank can be used whenever you want a nice wood plank texture, Sand or Mulch look good on carpets and rugs, and Asphalt (from the Building subfolder) may be used to imitate thick-grain leather texture. There are so many choices, and so many different tastes, that the best way to find what works for you is to experiment, and attend one of the many tutorials run in-world—check the Classifieds for listings.

CHAPTER 1
CHAPTER 2
CHAPTER 3
CHAPTER 4
CHAPTER 5
CHAPTER 6

CHAPTER 7
CHAPTER 8
CHAPTER 9
CHAPTER 10
CHAPTER 11
CHAPTER 12
CHAPTER 13
CHAPTER 14
CHAPTER 15
APPENDICES

ADDITIONAL INFO
DOWNLOADING FREE TEXTURES

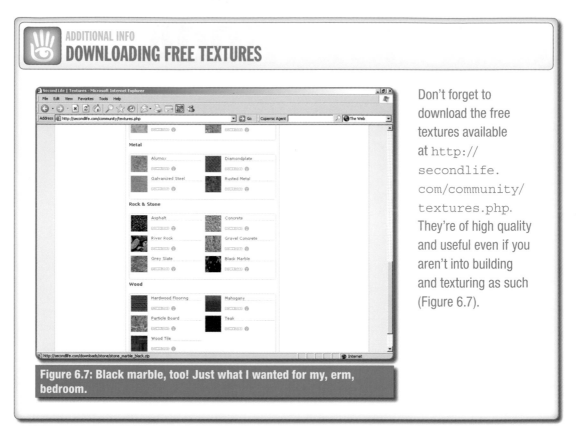

Don't forget to download the free textures available at `http://secondlife.com/community/textures.php`. They're of high quality and useful even if you aren't into building and texturing as such (Figure 6.7).

Figure 6.7: Black marble, too! Just what I wanted for my, erm, bedroom.

As you can see, the Library folders are a veritable treasure trove. Whether you're trying to get your *SL* existence off to a quick start or looking for ways and means of improving your building and scripting skills, the Library's invaluable. It provides a huge selection of ready-to-use items, as well as countless examples to emulate while learning to create exciting new stuff in *Second Life*. However, as you live your new life, the Library's importance and size will be eclipsed by your Inventory's.

The next chapter discusses the Inventory and its role in your virtual life. It also explains how it differs from the Library and provides advice on Inventory management.

CHAPTER 7

MANAGING YOUR INVENTORY

The Inventory is very many things. It is your own, unique collection of *Second Life* items ranging from complete houses and spaceships to socks and bubble gum. It is also a pet that grows into a monster. If anyone ever wanted clear proof that humans are insanely acquisitive by nature, the *SL* Inventory is that proof. A long time ago, when *Second Life* was in its infancy, there was a cap on the number of items you could have in your Inventory: 255. Now that there's no limit, most *SL* denizens quickly accumulate many thousands of objects. It's easy to let your Inventory get out of control, and once it does, more and more of your new life will be spent looking for stuff instead of enjoying yourself. Sound familiar?

If you're new to *Second Life* and are frowning with disbelief, consider this: *SL* is a world in which you carry everything you own—house, car, 50 wardrobes of clothing, and so on—on your person. And if you're also running a business, and/or constantly creating new unique items ... let's just say keeping track of all the items in your Inventory isn't easy. It's in your best interest to have as little as possible (for most *SL* denizens, "as little as possible" means fewer than 5,000 items).

In this chapter, I'll take a close look at the *SL* Inventory and discuss how to manage it effectively. You'll find out how to organize Inventory folders, and keep them under control even though they're multiplying like rabbits. You'll also learn how to store stuff outside your Inventory, and about ways to prevent and fix inventory loss. In short, this chapter is an Inventory master plan that should make your new existence more carefree and enjoyable.

CONTENTS

THE INVENTORY VS. THE LIBRARY

THE INVENTORY
VS. THE LIBRARY

ORGANIZING
YOUR INVENTORY

INVENTORY
TROUBLE-
SHOOTING

THE FIVE
GOLDEN RULES
OF INVENTORY
MANAGEMENT

When you begin *Second Life*, your Inventory seems to be an underdeveloped offspring of the Library. The few folders in the Inventory correspond to Library folders with the same names, but they are mostly empty, or at best have just part of their Library equivalents' content. There is no warning of your Inventory's imminent mutation into something resembling a garage sale thrown by a freshly bankrupted and slightly deranged millionaire. This moment of peace is ideal for taking a look at the important differences between the Inventory and the Library.

The Library, as you might guess, is public: it's shared by everyone. Your Inventory is your own, and no one else's. Of course, initially your Inventory is identical to everyone else's, but it quickly becomes as unique as the choices you make in *Second Life*.

You cannot delete or modify the contents of your Library, but you can do as you please with the Inventory (there are exceptions, discussed later in this chapter). Note that when you use a Library item, it is automatically copied into the appropriate folder in your Inventory. These copies are prime candidates for the trash can during your periodical Inventory cleanouts. Your number-one Inventory-management rule is to never keep two copies of an item in the same Inventory. Stick to this rule from the start, and you'll save yourself lots of time. Otherwise you might spend most of your new existence looking for stuff hidden among thousands of other items!

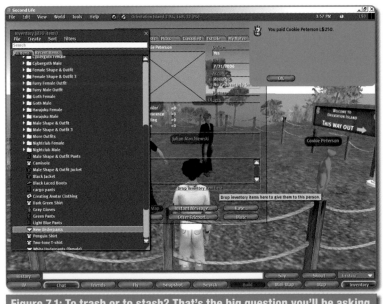

Of course, no matter how hard you try, you'll always have a ton of stuff in your Inventory. As you know from Chapter 3, your Inventory will start to grow almost as soon as you arrive on Orientation Island—that's even before you get to Help Island and begin filling your Inventory with all the cool freebie items available there. If you don't monitor your Inventory from the very start, you'll be overwhelmed before you know it. An important Inventory-management rule

Figure 7.1: To trash or to stash? That's the big question you'll be asking yourself again and again in *Second Life*.

is to organize Inventory contents right at the start of your new existence (Figure 7.1).

CHAPTER 1
CHAPTER 2
CHAPTER 3
CHAPTER 4
CHAPTER 5
CHAPTER 6
CHAPTER 7

CHAPTER 8
CHAPTER 9
CHAPTER 10
CHAPTER 11
CHAPTER 12
CHAPTER 13
CHAPTER 14
CHAPTER 15
APPENDICES

ADDITIONAL INFO
PARTING WITH YOUR CREATIONS

Don't get overly sentimental about your own creations. Don't keep everything you've made just because you made it. The very next object you make will be exclusively yours too, and most likely better than what you created earlier. If you want a private museum of your work, store it outside your Inventory.

ORGANIZING YOUR INVENTORY

One of the first things you should put into your Inventory is some order. Trash unwanted items and reorganize your Inventory before you depart Help Island for the *SL* mainland. It's best to get a handle on things right away! Most newborn *SL* denizens don't, and the *SL* forum features plenty of sob stories with this common denominator: my second life is screwed up because of Inventory problems. You don't want to go there, do you?

ADDITIONAL INFO
KEEPING YOUR INVENTORY UNDER CONTROL

When you open your Inventory, a line at the very top will tell you how many items it contains. If you do not work on keeping the Inventory under control with beady-eyed zeal, the number displayed will reach four figures before you leave Help Island and will grow to five figures soon after you arrive on the mainland.

GETTING THE RIGHT TOOLS

Opening the Inventory for the first time is a little like stepping into a treasure cave: all those freebies! But after you've rolled around in the coins and thrown a few fistfuls of jewels into the air, read the writing on the wall: examine the Inventory window menu and its commands. You'll discover Inventory-management tools that make keeping everything in order and finding stuff much, much easier. Here's what it all means:

The File menu features two very helpful commands: New Window and Show Filters. Use New Window to open extra Inventory windows—as many as you like! Extra Inventory windows make it easier to move stuff between folders—just drag whatever you want moved to the right folder in the new window. Show Filters is very helpful when you're looking for specific items or subfolders and when you're sorting Inventory contents by item class/type.

129

The Create menu lets you create new folders. You will *not* be able to get your Inventory under control without creating a new set of folders, and many sets of subfolders. You'll find some related comments and ideas later on in this chapter.

The Sort menu does not, sadly, contain a magic command that sorts everything out just the way you'd like with a single mouse click. Sorting folders by date can be helpful for *SL* businesspeople, of course, and sorting them by name is useful when you employ a special folder-naming convention—a prefix that will group related folders together. For example, names of folders that contain outfits you wear while nightclubbing in *SL* can be given an "nc" prefix: ncRed Suit, ncGreen shoes, and so on.

The Inventory window also features a search box that lets you look for folders and items whose names contain whatever you typed into the search box—be it one letter or ten numbers (Figure 7.2). This can be an invaluable tool when your Inventory is messed up for whatever reason, and works extra well if you use prefixes for folder and item names.

Figure 7.2: The Inventory search box lets you find stuff instantly—now, uh, what was that name?

ADDITIONAL INFO
USING FOLDER- AND ITEM-NAMING CONVENTIONS

Adding prefixes makes names look ugly and introduces a cold, down-to-earth note into your virtual existence. But it's a great system for helping you find whatever you want to find right away. Just type the prefix into the search box or use the Sort menu's Sort by Name function, and you've got what you want right in front of your face. There's a Nobel prize waiting for whoever invents a gizmo that works like this in real life.

If you regularly use the Inventory tools provided with your Inventory, you'll minimize your chance of having Inventory problems. You may also want to run a Search in *SL* for inventory-management tools such as DisQ Hern's Inventory Sorter, which makes keeping things in order almost completely painless. You'll find more specific, how-to advice on Inventory troubleshooting later on in this chapter.

Finally, remember to use the Recent Items tab in the Inventory window to keep track of what items you've used most recently. The item list displayed upon clicking that tab shows what you actually use in-world, and may prompt you to revise your Inventory setup.

⬇ THE NEW ORDER

Your Inventory comes with a set of folders that feature little icons. These Inventory folders cannot be moved, deleted, or even renamed; they're part of the default Inventory setup. As their names indicate, the default folders organize items by class or type, and it's best to leave them as is. Organizing your possessions by class/type looks great, but it doesn't work that well in life—real or second.

What works best is organizing stuff on the same principle you use in real life: frequency of use. Items you use often are kept handy, items you use seldom can be tucked away out of sight and out of reach, right? In real life, items are strictly organized by class only when you don't use them often (as in, "those cartons in the corner of the basement are all full of books I thought were full of wisdom"). In real life, your briefcase/handbag/backpack contains diverse stuff. So, it makes perfect sense to use the frequency-of-use principle while organizing your Inventory in *Second Life*. Whenever you use an item from one of the default, icon-marked folders, transfer it into one of your newly created folders that you set up on the frequency-of-use principle.

Begin organizing your Inventory by creating your own set of folders. Create a new folder for items used every time you visit *SL*, another for items used from time to time, yet another for items used rarely, and so on. Call them Every Day, Every Week, Monthly, Never—exact names don't matter, you get the idea. When you use an item for the first time, it should go into the Every Day folder. When you open that folder and see items you haven't used for a couple of weeks, move them into the Every Week folder, and so on—after a couple of months of non-use into Monthly, after another couple of months into Never. Once every few months. look through the Never folder and move the contents into Trash. Then examine the Trash folder contents before you log out, salvage whatever you love even though it doesn't make sense (maybe create a "Love Makes No Sense" folder), and empty the Trash. There. That's all it takes to keep your Inventory lean and mean.

ADDITIONAL INFO
MORE FOLDER- AND ITEM-NAMING CONVENTIONS

Another approach to organizing your Inventory is to copy the setup you have in real life. Whenever you use an item in *Second Life*, put it away where you'd put it in real life. Put clothes away in folders named Bedroom Wardrobe, Hall Wardrobe, etc. (or maybe bdWardrobe and hallWardrobe if you want to organize folders by imaginary location), put notecards and snapshots in a folder named Desk, put the outfit you wore last time you logged on into the Bedroom Floor folder— whatever feels right.

CHAPTER 1
CHAPTER 2
CHAPTER 3
CHAPTER 4
CHAPTER 5
CHAPTER 6
CHAPTER 7

CHAPTER 8
CHAPTER 9
CHAPTER 10
CHAPTER 11
CHAPTER 12
CHAPTER 13
CHAPTER 14
CHAPTER 15
APPENDICES

CHAPTER 7

THE INVENTORY
VS. THE LIBRARY

**ORGANIZING
YOUR INVENTORY**

INVENTORY
TROUBLE-
SHOOTING

THE FIVE
GOLDEN RULES
OF INVENTORY
MANAGEMENT

ADDITIONAL INFO
FOLDER-MANAGEMENT OPTIONS

Double-click to open and close folders. Right-click on a folder to open a menu that shows a list of folder-management options. If the menu that appears is blank, the selected folder is part of the Inventory setup and cannot be manipulated in any way.

Naturally, and no matter how often you trash items, your newly created folders will contain more and more stuff. When you have to scroll to view the full list of items in each frequency-of-use folder, it's high time you created a set of subfolders. This time around, it may be helpful to organize items by class or type, but do remember that some things just go together even though they belong to different classes. For example, outfits that you wear to entice other avatars into cybersex, and sexual act animations/related gestures belong to different classes but work well when sharing a folder—call it Good Times or whatever describes it for you.

Figure 7.3: Keep the number of items in your Inventory as low as possible.

To sum up, you should always strive to keep your Inventory lean and mean (Figure 7.3). In real life, he who travels light travels fast. In *Second Life*, he who travels light has more fun. And you can still own as much stuff as you like—no one is going to take away this basic right from you. However, if you're carrying around more than a few thousand items, you should consider storing some of your possessions somewhere else—outside your Inventory. The simplest way to do this is to create a storage prim (see the following section).

ADDITIONAL INFO
WHAT YOU OWN CAN HURT YOU

A big Inventory means longer download times and greater risk of inventory loss because of the *SL* equivalent of a real-life natural disaster: server malfunction. Don't forget to check out the Inventory-management advice from longtime *SL* residents in the sidebars!

RESIDENTS SPEAK
MANAGING INVENTORY CONTENTS

"Subfolders are your friend. Making your own folders to keep 'important' stuff and your 'single copy' objects really helps keep things organized."

—DolphPun Somme

"I think of it the same way I think of organizing my hard drive. General folder, more specific subfolder, specific subfolders … i.e., clothing, casual, shoes. Or building materials, textures, exterior textures, brick. I spend around 30 minutes of every session cleaning up, naming, and moving around Inventory items.

"Something I just discovered last night in terms of clothing: activate the debug menu (Control-Alt-D) and then go to the bottom of it and select Clothing. A list of everything you have that's defined by the system as clothing appears and can be put on/removed via the list. It's a good way to find the undershirt under the shirt under the jacket that you think you might have on."

—Rakkasa Lewellen

"Throw things out. There are a million freebies out there, and 90% of them suck. Keep what you like, and toss the rest or your Inventory will be a disaster."

—Watermelon Tokyo

CHAPTER 1

CHAPTER 2

CHAPTER 3

CHAPTER 4

CHAPTER 5

CHAPTER 6

CHAPTER 7

CHAPTER 8

CHAPTER 9

CHAPTER 10

CHAPTER 11

CHAPTER 12

CHAPTER 13

CHAPTER 14

CHAPTER 15

APPENDICES

CREATING AND USING STORAGE PRIMS

Figure 7.4: Twenty pairs of pants, ten pairs of shoes, a dozen shirts—all packed uncreased into a tiny metal cylinder! Only in *Second Life*.

You can put any number of Inventory items inside a storage prim (Figure 7.4). Storing stuff inside a prim lightens your Inventory, but it does have its drawbacks: you cannot store folders inside a prim. If you attempt to move a folder into a prim, you'll move the folder's contents but not the folder itself. Upon opening the storage prim, you'll see all of the folder's items in exactly the same order as they were in the folder.

Obviously, your very first storage prim should contain all the stuff from the Never Used or Almost Never Used folder (or whatever you've named it). This will be

133

CHAPTER 7

THE INVENTORY
VS. THE LIBRARY

**ORGANIZING
YOUR INVENTORY**

INVENTORY
TROUBLE-
SHOOTING

THE FIVE
GOLDEN RULES
OF INVENTORY
MANAGEMENT

your *Second Life* version of the basement, attic, or garden shed where you put all the stuff that should be thrown away—one day. Note that it makes sense to name the storage prims after the folders that originally contained the prim-stored stuff, or in another way that's descriptive of the prims' content. This is because you cannot see what a storage prim contains until you actually open it. The other drawback to storage prims is this: if they're not in your Inventory, they have to be stored somewhere, too. Proud Premium-account land owners won't have a problem, but if you have a free Basic account, you'll have to rent storage space.

ADDITIONAL INFO
THE 16-SQUARE-METER PLOT

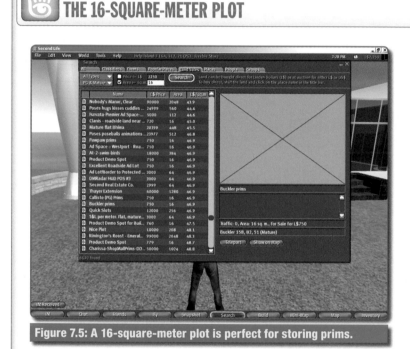

If you have a free account that doesn't allow you to own land, try renting! There are always plenty of tiny 16-square-meter plots available for sale or rental; they let you store up to three prims (Figure 7.5). How much stuff you store within those prims is, of course, your private business.

Figure 7.5: A 16-square-meter plot is perfect for storing prims.

Here's the procedure for creating and using a storage prim:

1. Make sure you're on land that allows building: the top menu bar will show the No Build icon if it's not allowed.

2. Create a prim—any prim. Size and shape don't matter; you're free to make it anything you like. My personal favorites are mysterious black cubes, and steel-plate cylinders. They simply look cool.

3. Name the prim right away (under the General tab in the Edit menu). As mentioned earlier, give it a name that's illustrative of its contents.

4. Open your Inventory, and right-click on the item or items you want to put inside the prim to check their properties. As a rule, don't mix items that can be copied with items that cannot. Create a separate storage prim for no-copy items.

5. Click and drag the folder/items from your Inventory and onto the storage prim. You'll see the cursor change to a little white folder marked with a plus sign; release the mouse button to drop the transferred item into the prim. Occasionally, you may run into trouble when transferring entire folders: you'll see the universal red circle with a slash through it to indicate your action is forbidden. Try opening the affected folder and transferring the items within one by one; that's how they'll be stored inside the prim, anyway.

6. Right-click on the prim to bring up the pie menu. You should see an active Open option. Click on it to view prim contents, and note the buttons at the bottom of the Contents menu that let you instantly copy all stored items into your Inventory (assuming they're replicable). You may also view the prim's contents by choosing Edit from the pie menu and selecting the Contents tab.

7. Decide whether you want to keep the storage prim's contents private: select the appropriate check boxes in the Edit menu (General tab).

CHAPTER 1
CHAPTER 2
CHAPTER 3
CHAPTER 4
CHAPTER 5
CHAPTER 6
CHAPTER 7
CHAPTER 8
CHAPTER 9
CHAPTER 10
CHAPTER 11
CHAPTER 12
CHAPTER 13
CHAPTER 14
CHAPTER 15
APPENDICES

Figure 7.6: Store your stuff in style in a special security box.

As you can see, storing items in prims is a simple process. However, there are also more-elegant solutions, such as special security boxes (Figure 7.6). If your building and scripting abilities don't allow for making one of those, you can purchase them at stores such as the THiNC store mentioned in the "Storing Inventory Contents" sidebar later in this chapter.

The THiNC store is just one of many that specialize in offering great Inventory-management aids. There is a wide variety on offer, and who wants to keep *SL* snapshots in a boring folder named Photo Album when they can be stored and viewed on a copyable TV set? Consider spending a few minutes and a few hundred Linden bucks to find and purchase specialized Inventory-management tools; you'll likely find they're your best *SL* investment.

FROM LINDEN LAB
INVENTORY MANAGEMENT

"Use the search box at the top of the Inventory panel to quickly locate Inventory items by associated keywords. For example, typing 'WORN' into the search box returns a list of all the items your avatar is currently wearing, along with their Inventory locations. The keyword you enter into the search box acts as a filter regardless of whether it's an item name or property. For instance, if you enter 'NO MODIFY' you'll see a list of all Inventory items that cannot be modified, while entering 'HAIR' will display a list of all the hair in your Inventory.

"To run a check on Inventory items acquired [since] your last online session, select the Recent Items tab on the Inventory panel. Note also that you can sort all Inventory folders and items by name or by date of acquisition.

"When you want to rearrange your Inventory, select New Window from the File menu to open a mirror Inventory panel—it's easier to keep track of what you're doing when you have two identical Inventory panels side by side. Drag the Inventory items and folders you want to move to their new locations in the mirror Inventory panel."

—Torley Linden

"It's never too early to organize. Create folders and set up a system that works for you. I also have created backups of everything I have created and placed them inside objects named for their contents. It never hurts to have extra copies hidden away."

—Jill Linden

"You can have multiple Inventory windows open at the same time for easier sorting. Open the Inventory window, and choose File > New Window.

I've also done video tutorials on this very topic:"

```
http://youtube.com/watch?v=AULw9Oa_1Bw
http://youtube.com/watch?v=C3P1JOz1ARA
```

—Torley Linden

CHAPTER 1

CHAPTER 2

CHAPTER 3

CHAPTER 4

CHAPTER 5

CHAPTER 6

CHAPTER 7

CHAPTER 8

CHAPTER 9

CHAPTER 10

CHAPTER 11

CHAPTER 12

CHAPTER 13

CHAPTER 14

CHAPTER 15

APPENDICES

FROM LINDEN LAB
TRANSFERRING FOLDERS TO AN OBJECT'S INVENTORY

When a folder is dropped into the inventory of an object, all of the folder's items are transferred individually to the object. Note that scripts transferred using this process are deactivated (each script must be dragged separately, or selected using Shift and/or Control-clicking and dragged as a mass selection). A UUID number is automatically attached to items without unique names (the *UUID*, or *Universal Unique Identifier*, is the 128-bit unique number assigned to every asset in *Second Life*).

INVENTORY TROUBLESHOOTING

Are you ready to face an awful truth? Your life—real or virtual—boils down to a bunch of data. It can be stored on corkscrewed slime (real life) and/or on computer hard drives (real life/*Second Life*), but wherever it is stored, there seems to be a cosmic law that all data gets corrupted or lost as time goes on. And so, your *SL* Inventory may become corrupted. At the very worst, you can lose everything you own in *Second Life* just because of a few rogue electrons somewhere. In spite of the tearful stories on the *SL* forum, it's not the end of the world—definitely less painful than your very own electrons going astray in real life. It still hurts, though, so you should know there are ways to prevent Inventory disasters in *Second Life*. An ounce of prevention is worth a pound of cure, so let's look first at what you can do to minimize risks to your precious Inventory.

INVENTORY INSURANCE

To make your Inventory safer, make it small; less data means less chance of data corruption. There have been no scientific studies on the subject, but *SL* forums reveal that the vast majority of inventory disasters befall big Inventories. At the time of writing, 5,000 items seem to be considered the safe limit, but this can change greatly depending on circumstances. To keep things as safe and secure as possible, follow these simple rules:

Small is beautiful. Yeah, it's been said a few times before, but it can't be repeated too often. If, starting tomorrow, there were a 5,000 item Inventory limit, you'd still manage—wouldn't you? You don't carry all your belongings around in real life, so don't do it in *Second Life*. Get rid of everything you don't actually use, and store everything you don't use often outside your Inventory.

Don't juggle electrons in an electron storm. If you want to fool around with your Inventory, find a quiet spot. Don't do it while at a party or inside any heavy-traffic area. As discussed later on, *SL* veterans recommend teleporting to uninhabited water regions to sort out Inventory problems.

137

CHAPTER 7

THE INVENTORY
VS. THE LIBRARY

ORGANIZING
YOUR INVENTORY

INVENTORY
TROUBLE-
SHOOTING

THE FIVE
GOLDEN RULES
OF INVENTORY
MANAGEMENT

Back up your Inventory. You can copy your entire Inventory (sans Library, which is common property, so there's no need) into one or more storage prims. To make things even safer, you can create an alternate avatar just for inventory-backup purposes, as explained later in this chapter. At the time of writing, creating a second avatar carries a one-time cost of US$9.95, a reasonable price to pay if you really value your *SL* possessions.

If you follow those rules, you'll sharply reduce the risk of running into Inventory problems. However, if and when they happen, don't get your virtual knickers in a twist—there are solutions that can help you restore Inventory contents even when you've lost everything you had.

⬇ DAMAGE CONTROL

Picture this: you wake up and everything you ever had is gone, except maybe for the clothes you wore when you last logged out … er, fell asleep. Or this: you walk into the kitchen to make your morning coffee and there is no kettle, no mugs, no nothing except for 87 frying pans. Or this: you dig into your pocket and come up with a small lump of grayish matter that explodes into 200 different objects, including 5 spaceships armed with cannon and 16 sets of vampire fangs. Can things ever be the same? Can you return to that peaceful, quiet virtual life you had and recover your collection of 128 custom guns and rocket launchers? Of course you can.

Second Life is a pioneer computer application that is being tested, improved, and otherwise stretched every which way even as you live your virtual life. Yes, mishaps can and will happen, but most can be corrected, just like your computer can be repaired after an idiot friend visited a *really* unsafe website behind your back. Here's what you can do if you've lost part or all of your Inventory:

1. Check whether the "lost" items haven't been moved to another location within your Inventory. Quite often, a bit of server stutter may result in them appearing in the Lost & Found or Trash folder. Yep, it's a good idea to look into your Trash before you empty it.

2. Log into *Second Life* again. The Internet's still young, and it isn't perfect. Move your arrival spot to a quiet sim—as mentioned earlier, a water-only region works well. Be patient; sometimes, it takes a while for your Inventory to load. Simplify things by logging into *SL* at a relatively quiet time; at the time of writing, traffic is lowest in the early morning hours, *SL* or Pacific Standard Time (GMT −8 hours).

3. Clear the network and browser caches and log in again. You can do that from within *Second Life*—select Preferences from the Edit menu to open the Preferences panel. You can also open the panel by clicking on the Preferences button on the login screen; in either case, click on the Network and Browser tabs, and on the Clear Now buttons that appear (Figure 7.7). You'll need to log in again if clearing the caches from within *SL* to see if it helped. You may need to repeat those steps several times before your Inventory returns to normal.

Figure 7.7: If you have Inventory problems, clear network and browser caches before logging into *Second Life* anew.

CHAPTER 1
CHAPTER 2
CHAPTER 3
CHAPTER 4
CHAPTER 5
CHAPTER 6
CHAPTER 7
CHAPTER 8
CHAPTER 9
CHAPTER 10
CHAPTER 11
CHAPTER 12
CHAPTER 13
CHAPTER 14
CHAPTER 15
APPENDICES

4. Wait a couple of days. Your Inventory may reappear of its own accord (rare, but documented). Well, what did you expect? It's cyberspace, humankind's new frontier.

5. Uninstall and reinstall *Second Life*. This may restore your Inventory when all other measures have failed.

If you've done everything you could and your Inventory's still screwed up, file a Bug Report (from the Help menu). Provide all the detail you can, including lost-object names, where they were in-world if they were out of your Inventory, and which folder they were in if they were inside your Inventory. It may take a while before you get a response, but *SL* residents *have* recovered lost Inventory items after filing a bug report.

ADDITIONAL INFO
RECOUPING LOST NO-COPY ITEMS

If your Inventory is backed up, you won't get hit hard, but you might get hit where it hurts most. If you lose the no-copy items you were carrying in your Inventory, contact the *SL* merchants who sold you the lost item; most of them should be kind enough to give you a replacement.

Remember it's good not to litter in *Second Life*! Here's why: all the objects you've strewn in your wake are returned to your Lost & Found folder as one object, albeit represented by a different icon that indicates it is a cluster of objects. Without getting too technical, *SL* software "glues" all your lost objects onto a single, chosen object before dropping the whole package into your Lost & Found folder. If you've lost a lot of objects containing a lot of prims, you may have to go to a sandbox area to untangle the knot: the number of prims in the 5 spaceships and 16 sets of vampire fangs you've left behind may exceed the maximum allowable number of prims on a private land plot.

THE INVENTORY
VS. THE LIBRARY

ORGANIZING
YOUR INVENTORY

**INVENTORY
TROUBLE-
SHOOTING**

THE FIVE
GOLDEN RULES
OF INVENTORY
MANAGEMENT

RESIDENTS SPEAK
FIXING CORRUPTED INVENTORIES

RESIDENTS

"Relog in a quiet sim. One of the Linden water sims that connect the two mainland masses is my favorite. Also, if you can log in before there are 35,000 people online, that helps too. More than that, and the database starts to pant and moan and sweat.

"Once you get back in, open your Inventory window, go to the Search field, and just hit Backspace. This sends a query to the database and loads your Inventory. The more you have, the longer this takes.

"Aside from the changing numbers, you can tell that you're still loading Inventory by the '...' after the number of items. So an Inventory in progress would look like (8,954...) while one that was complete would look like (15,452)."

—Jessica Elytis

"Set the Inventory to list in alphabetical order, not the default date—that way you can see all the 'Objects' together—that is my personal bugbear—thousands of anonymous items named 'Object'."

—Elgyfu Wishbringer

"If you are going to rez unfamiliar or improperly named articles in order to find out what they are, do so in a Script Disabled area. This is a simple safety precaution in case someone has slipped you a Grey Goo, or a self-replicating prim in the hope that you will accidentally start another Grid Attack."

—Angelique LaFollette

"I strongly advise keeping backup copies of all your products in a folder in your Inventory, and also in a box on your land in case your Inventory gets nuked.

"I also advise saving all important scripts you write as text documents on your computer."

—Cortex Draper

CHAPTER 1

CHAPTER 2

CHAPTER 3

CHAPTER 4

CHAPTER 5

CHAPTER 6

CHAPTER 7

CHAPTER 8

CHAPTER 9

CHAPTER 10

CHAPTER 11

CHAPTER 12

CHAPTER 13

CHAPTER 14

CHAPTER 15

APPENDICES

ADDITIONAL INFO
OBJECTS NAMED "OBJECTS"

Type "objects" into the Inventory window's Search box to uncover any unnamed, mysterious objects that may have sneaked into your Inventory. They may be there because of your own carelessness, and they may be there because of a sudden stutter in cyberspace. Rez them in a public sandbox to avoid unpleasant surprises such as self-replicating junk.

CREATING AN ALTER EGO FOR INVENTORY BACKUP

Copying your entire Inventory to another avatar is the ultimate in Inventory insurance. It involves opening a second *SL* account to create a mule that will carry the copies of your virtual possessions.

Having created an alter ego, move it to the mainland and transfer all the no-copy items you really, really don't want to lose to the mule's Inventory. Of course, you can do it via a storage prim—just make sure your alternate avatar has the rights to open the prim and to copy its contents into its own Inventory! However, you can also effect a direct Inventory-to-Inventory folder and item transfer using the Search function:

1. Click the Search button on the main game menu, and select the People tab.

2. Type in your alternate character's name.

3. Click the Search button next to the name you typed in. This opens your alternate character's Profile panel on its default *Second Life* tab. You'll see a Give Item slot near the bottom of the panel.

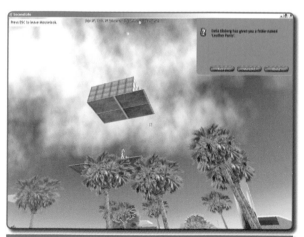

Figure 7.8: If another *SL* denizen gives you something while you're offline, you'll get a message as soon as you return to *Second Life*.

4. Drag and drop Inventory folders and/or items into the slot, one by one. A blue info panel will tell you about your alter ego's offline status and state that the items will be saved for delivery.

5. When you log on as your alter ego, you'll see a blue info panel asking whether you want to accept the items; and after you accept them, you'll find them in your Inventory (Figure 7.8). Note that, at the time of writing, transferring an Inventory item via the Profile panel to someone who is *online* isn't confirmed until the recipient accepts delivery.

RESIDENTS SPEAK
STORING INVENTORY CONTENTS

THE INVENTORY
VS. THE LIBRARY

ORGANIZING
YOUR INVENTORY

INVENTORY
TROUBLE-
SHOOTING

THE FIVE
GOLDEN RULES
OF INVENTORY
MANAGEMENT

"It is possible to put items in prim boxes to reduce Inventory clutter, and reduce the complexity of your Inventory.

"Once you have made one of these storage collections, you can store one copy of the box in-world, or you can give a copy to a friend (or an alt) to keep in their inventory in case yours gets corrupted. I highly advise doing that, as inventories are just collections of data records in the asset server database, and Linden Lab is *not* responsible for restoring lost content!

"The downside is, you can't search Inventory to *find* any of those items unless you look inside the contents of each box and see what's there! Ever open a box that's been stored for years? Ever been surprised that you even owned half the stuff in there? You can repeat this as much as needed. Have a prim called ZZZ—The Attic and store all the other boxes in that.

"Warning: If you want to store no-copy stuff this way, such as purchased clothes that you don't wear very often, make sure the storage box has been named *before* you put the first no-copy item into the box! I advise keeping the no-copy stored items separate from the copy-permitted ones, because while there is a no-copy item in a storage box, the entire box's contents can't be duplicated."

—Ceera Murakami

"I will tell you my secret to *my* perfect Inventory system. First of all, every matching outfit gets its own prim box, and is labeled according to what that outfit is. Then I put the prim boxes into the copyable, no-transfer organizer boxes from THiNC. Why are the THiNC boxes so wonderful? They have arrows on them that let you browse through the contents, and quickly retrieve what you want.

"My 4,500+ textures are organized by type. The THiNC copyable, no-transfer machines let me pull out a fresh one for, say, castle-type textures and store all my castle textures in there. All my tile textures go into another one, and so on.

"My entire Inventory is organized this way, and it is mainly because of the Library that my Inventory is at 2,000—yes, you read it right; my Inventory is at 2k and I grumble over it constantly. I try to keep it as low as possible so I do not get any Inventory lag."

—Tyci Kenzo

THE FIVE GOLDEN RULES OF INVENTORY MANAGEMENT

CHAPTER 1
CHAPTER 2
CHAPTER 3
CHAPTER 4
CHAPTER 5
CHAPTER 6
CHAPTER 7

CHAPTER 8
CHAPTER 9
CHAPTER 10
CHAPTER 11
CHAPTER 12
CHAPTER 13
CHAPTER 14
CHAPTER 15
APPENDICES

In summary, getting a firm grip on your Inventory right from the start is a major—some might say *the* major—factor in enjoying your new life to the max. It frees you from the drudgery afflicting real life, in which the tyranny of material things makes people go postal. To maximize your chances of freedom and eternal happiness in *Second Life*, here are the five main Inventory-management points:

1. Organize Inventory contents before you leave Help Island for the mainland, and don't keep two copies of the same, replicable item in your Inventory. This includes all the items in your Library folder.

2. Create your own folder system based on the frequency-of-use principle. Move items you don't use down the scale to the less-used folders, and eventually into Trash.

3. Don't carry stuff you aren't likely to use in the near future. Trash everything you probably won't use, and store seldom-used items inside storage prims. Store the storage prims outside your Inventory, except maybe for the single prim containing no-copy items. This is best stored in an alternate avatar's Inventory.

4. Make a backup copy of your Inventory. Put it in a storage prim outside your Inventory, or copy folders and items into an alternate character's Inventory.

5. Make a point of emptying the Trash at the conclusion of every *SL* session, because the items take up as much space as they did in their original folders. There always should be something to delete at the conclusion of a session; if there isn't, you're either an Inventory-management genius, or rather hopeless.

Accumulating enough of your own stuff to fill a large museum is easier than you may think. A large part of *SL* activity revolves around creating new in-world objects—not surprising, considering that the *SL* world as such has been mostly built by *SL* denizens. Accordingly, the next chapter discusses building new things.

CHAPTER 8

BUILDING

Unlike in other virtual environments, nearly everything you see within *Second Life* is actually created within *Second Life* itself—not by the company that runs the world, but by its users. You don't need a lot of special software or training to build things in *SL*; you only need a *Second Life* account. Building is fun and easy, like playing with Lego® bricks. In this chapter, we'll discuss how these simple building blocks can be used to construct everything from houses to vehicles.

CONTENTS

THE BASICS

The following sections will introduce you to the basic terminology behind building in *Second Life*.

PRIMS

In *Second Life*'s 3D graphics, a primitive, or *prim*, is a basic three-dimensional geometric object. The term "prim" refers to a single unit of the "matter" that makes up all *Second Life* objects. Prims are the irreducible building blocks of *Second Life*—the unsplittable atoms that make up the things of the world.

In *Second Life*, a prim is one of several 3D shapes: a box, a cylinder, a prism, a sphere, a torus, a tube, or a ring. In addition to these, there are two specialty object types that are not made up of primitives: grass and trees. These last two are obviously not basic shapes, but they're built into *Second Life*, and therefore are treated like ordinary prims.

OBJECTS

The term *object* refers to a single prim, or a group of prims that have been linked together to function as a single item, like a table, chair, or house. An object can contain anywhere from 1 to 255 prims. Yes, this means a single prim is an object in its own right.

PARAMETRIC MODELING

If you have previous 3D modeling experience, you may find it useful to know that *SL*'s building tools use parametric models. Parametric modeling reduces the amount of data traveling between your computer and the *Second Life* servers. This is what allows *Second Life* to display changes to you and others around you instantaneously, in real time. Parametric modeling uses a few simple parameters to describe prims and objects, rather than the detailed information that a traditional 3D modeling program uses.

Parametric modeling reduces the amount of data traveling between your computer and the *Second Life* server because it describes objects using a few simple parameters rather than explicitly describing every part of every object like other modeling techniques do.

MODELS

In the world of 3D graphics, a model is a 3D representation of an object, whether or not it represents something that exists in the real world. Models are constructed out of many two-dimensional polygons grouped together.

Prims in *Second Life* are models, though they're not very complex. However, their simplicity is what allows them to be so flexible for builders.

The grass and tree prim types are examples of more-complex 3D models. As mentioned earlier, they're not primitives in the classical 3D-graphics sense but are treated like other prims within *Second Life*. Another example is the avatar model, though you can't use it like you can a prim. These more-complex models have been added to fill out the sorts of builds that *Second Life* residents enjoy. Without them, the world would be a far blockier and less organic place.

⬇ MESHES

The term *mesh* comes from the pattern of triangles that typically comprise a 3D model. One way to think of this mesh is as a "skin" over the surface of the object. For example, the avatar object in *SL* is a mesh. (So, for that matter, are *SL* primitives, but within *SL* designers refer to prims simply as *prims*.)

⬇ REZZING OBJECTS

To create a prim or object is to *rez* it. It sounds like slang, but the term is actually also used officially within LSL scripting calls to create or reference the creation of new prims. When you make a new prim or pull an object from your inventory to bring it into the world, you're rezzing the item. Also, when you first enter an area of *Second Life* and the information for surrounding objects is streaming to your computer, it is said you're *rezzing* the area—waiting for it to come into existence around you.

This term refers to Disney's 1982 film *Tron*, in which the anthropomorphic inhabitants of a computer are forced to play video games until they "de-rez," or die.

GETTING STARTED

If you've used other 3D modeling software in the past, adjusting to *Second Life*'s system might take a minute or two. It's a little different. There's no mesh-import functionality. Everything within *Second Life* is made up of primitives, and they can't be deformed as freely as they can in professional 3D software like Maya or LightWave. The trade-off, as mentioned earlier, is that these limits allow object data to be streamed from the server very quickly—there simply isn't a lot of data to send.

If you've never used graphics or modeling software before, that's OK. Most residents pick up *Second Life*'s building tools fairly quickly, and many people find this platform a great introduction to the world of 3D modeling and building. Don't be discouraged if you don't get the hang of it right off, though. Some new builders need to try several approaches before they find one that works. If you feel you need more guidance after reading this chapter, try attending a building class.

CHAPTER 1
CHAPTER 2
CHAPTER 3
CHAPTER 4
CHAPTER 5
CHAPTER 6
CHAPTER 7
CHAPTER 8

CHAPTER 9
CHAPTER 10
CHAPTER 11
CHAPTER 12
CHAPTER 13
CHAPTER 14
CHAPTER 15
APPENDICES

REZZING YOUR FIRST PRIM

Figure 8.1: The pie menu when you're clicking on an object

Figure 8.2: The Build window's Create tab

Building in *Second Life* is restricted to land that you own, or land where you have permission to create new objects. As a new resident of *Second Life* you may not own land yet, but that's OK. Use Search and type in "Sandbox" to find a list of places where you can practice building.

First, right-click on the ground or on another object (but not the sky or an avatar!). Right-clicking will display a pie menu, from which you can select Create (Figure 8.1). This will open the Build tools window, which you'll use to create and edit objects. (You can also open it simply by pressing the Build button at the bottom of your screen, or the B key if you use WASD keyboard setup). It'll also put you into Create mode. Now all you have to do is choose which prim you want to create, click the position at which you'd like to create it, and voilà— you now have a prim (Figure 8.2).

EDITING YOUR PRIM

You can edit a prim right after creating it. Upon its creation, you'll automatically switch into Edit mode. You can tell when you have a prim/object selected thanks to a few visual keys—the object will have a highlighted outline, and small particles will stream from your avatar to the object. If you deselect your prim after creating it, just click it again while in Edit mode, and you'll be editing it again. If your Build window has closed altogether, right-click/Control-click your object and select Edit; you'll be back editing it once more.

⬇ Object Handles

The most basic and flexible way to manipulate your prims and objects is through the use of their object handles. These are just what they sound like: things you can grab to manipulate your objects. When editing your object, you'll notice several red, green, and blue cones and triangles attached to it. These are your object handles, color-coded according to the following axes and real-world directions:

X: east/west (red)

Y: north/south (green)

Z: up/down (blue)

When you hover your cursor over an object handle, the object handle will brighten. This tells you that you can select it. You can click and drag it around. Depending on which object handle it is, it will do different things.

⬇ Move Handles

In normal Edit mode, you'll see the Move handles. The three intersecting lines allow you to drag the object along a given axis. This axis can be relative to the rest of the world or to the object itself. The triangular planes allow you to move an object on two axes at once, treating the object as if its axes were three two-dimensional planes. There are ways to add more accuracy to your movements, which we'll cover shortly.

⬇ Rotate Handles

Holding down the Control key allows you to enter Rotate mode, which replaces the object handles with a sphere inside three circles. Clicking and dragging the sphere allows you to manipulate the object's rotation in all three dimensions at once, while clicking and dragging one of the circles rotates the object on that axis alone. When you hover over a circle it will brighten, letting you know which circle you're about to activate once you click it.

⬇ Stretch Handles

Holding down Control and Shift puts you into Stretch mode. This places a white object handle on the eight corners of your object, as well as a colored one on each of the six sides. (Remember—even if your object isn't a cube, the editing tools still treat it like a box.) By clicking and dragging the side handles, you'll stretch the entire object along the associated axis, making it wider or narrower, taller or shorter. By clicking and dragging the corner handles, you'll stretch the entire object proportionately (Figure 8.3).

CHAPTER 1
CHAPTER 2
CHAPTER 3
CHAPTER 4
CHAPTER 5
CHAPTER 6
CHAPTER 7
CHAPTER 8

CHAPTER 9
CHAPTER 10
CHAPTER 11
CHAPTER 12
CHAPTER 13
CHAPTER 14
CHAPTER 15
APPENDICES

CHAPTER 8

THE BASICS
GETTING STARTED
REZZING YOUR FIRST PRIM
EDITING YOUR PRIM
USING THE CAMERA
LINKING PRIMS
TAKING COPIES
USING THE GRID
COLLABORATING WITH OTHER RESIDENTS
ATTACHMENTS
LANDSCAPING
TEXTURING
CREATING TEXTURES
UPLOADING TEXTURES

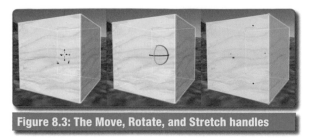

Figure 8.3: The Move, Rotate, and Stretch handles

If the Stretch Both Sides check box in the Build window's Edit mode is checked, your object will remain in one location; dragging a handle will just scale the object as if it were pulled from both the handle you're clicking on and the one on the opposite side or corner, keeping the center of the object in the original position.

In the case of linked objects, you won't be able to stretch the object along one axis, but you will be able to scale it and to stretch individual prims in the object.

⬇ BUILD WINDOW

Now that you're editing your prim, you'll want to extend the Build window by clicking the More button to access the other editing options. These are the heart of the building tools.

GENERAL TAB

Figure 8.4: The Build window's General tab

The General tab (Figure 8.4) contains the following options:

Name: It's a good idea to name your unique objects according to what they are. That way, you can easily identify them in your inventory. "Front Door" and "Roof" are acceptable names, but you can be more descriptive: "My Brick House - Red Door" will let you know both what the object is and what project you used it in. Either way, an inventory full of things named "Object" is not fun to search through!

Description: You can store extra information about your objects in this field. You can't search your inventory for objects' descriptions, but the Description field lets you and others know more specific information about an object.

Creator: This is the account that created the prim. No matter how much you modify the prim, it will still have the original creator's name in this field. In a linked object, only the root prim's creator will show up as the creator. (More on root prims when we discuss linking prims.)

Owner: Who currently owns this object? Remember, an object's current owner is frequently different than its creator.

Group: This doesn't have to do with linked objects, but rather with the resident group to which an object is set. By default, the group is the one the object's owner belonged to when the object was rezzed. To change the group, click the Set button and pick one of your groups. This is a useful way to filter objects on your land. If only members of a certain group can keep prims there, you won't need to worry about other people leaving their prims on your land.

OBJECT TAB

The left side of the Object tab is always the same. The right half of the tab changes, depending on the type of prim being edited. Different primitives use different parameters.

Locked: You can lock your objects in place within the region, stopping yourself or anyone who has modify permissions from repositioning or editing them. The Select Only Movable Objects option under the Tools menu allows you to select a group of prims without selecting locked objects. This can be useful for ensuring you don't link the wrong prims together. Locking objects once they're in place can help prevent you from accidentally moving or deleting them once you're done building. You can always unlock them again by unchecking the Locked check box.

Physical: This toggles how your object will interact with *Second Life*'s physics engine. Making an object physical will allow it to be kicked (like a ball), dropped off buildings, and so on. Physical objects mostly come into play when they are also scripted, such as cars or boats. They can be fun to play with, though!

Temporary: Setting this and then re-rezzing the object will cause that object to disappear after about 60 seconds. This isn't very useful for building, but it's a good feature for scripters.

Phantom: This setting allows you to designate whether physical objects or avatars will penetrate the prim. A phantom object can be walked through or driven through or have a ball tossed through it. When you link phantom prims together, the resulting linked object will take on the property of the root prim. If the root prim is phantom, the whole object will be phantom as well.

Position: These values tell you where in relation to the sim the object is located. All space within a sim can be defined with those three X, Y and Z coordinates, which goes from 0 to 256m on the X and Y axes, and 0 to infinity on the Z axis.

Size: Prims in *Second Life* can be as large as 10m and small as 0.01m (1cm) on any axis. Though many builders find it restrictive, the 10m limit helps prevent problems with the server code and accidentally building into areas that don't belong to you.

Rotation: Objects can be rotated between 0 and 360 degrees on any of their three axes. Prims can be rotated along multiple axes and will retain their rotation when re-rezzed from your inventory.

Material: The Material setting allows you to swap between the preset collision particles and sounds you hear when your avatar hits an object. You can choose between several settings—Stone, Metal,

CHAPTER 1
CHAPTER 2
CHAPTER 3
CHAPTER 4
CHAPTER 5
CHAPTER 6
CHAPTER 7
CHAPTER 8

CHAPTER 9
CHAPTER 10
CHAPTER 11
CHAPTER 12
CHAPTER 13
CHAPTER 14
CHAPTER 15
APPENDICES

CHAPTER 8

THE BASICS
GETTING
STARTED
REZZING YOUR
FIRST PRIM
EDITING
YOUR PRIM
USING THE
CAMERA
LINKING PRIMS
TAKING COPIES
USING THE GRID
COLLABORATING
WITH OTHER
RESIDENTS
ATTACHMENTS
LANDSCAPING
TEXTURING
CREATING
TEXTURES
UPLOADING
TEXTURES

Glass, Wood, Flesh, Plastic, and Rubber—each with its own collision properties. Material settings are, again, used mostly by scripters when using them in conjunction with Physics settings, and most builders never find reason to change the default Material setting.

The right side of the Object tab allows you to make various modifications to the type, cut, and hollow of the prim you're working with. The options available depend on the prim type, which you can change on the fly using the Building Block Type drop-down box. Common modification options include the following:

Path Cut: "Slices away" a portion of the prim from a preset starting point

Hollow: Removes the interior of the prim while leaving the exterior intact

Hollow Shape: Determines the shape of the hollow area inside the prim

Twist: Twists the prim

Taper: Tapers the top or bottom of the prim along the specified axis

Top Shear: Angles the prim without rotating the prim—leaves the top and bottom faces parallel to the ground, for example

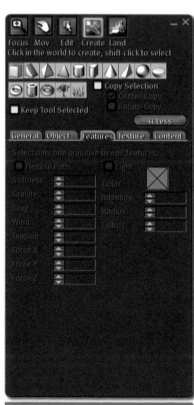

Figure 8.5: The Features tab

In the Building Block Type drop-down box, among the standard prim types, you can also choose Sculpted. This turns your basic prim into a special type of prim that you create in an external, traditional 3D program and then import into *SL*. For more info on this type of prim, turn to the "Sculpted Prims" section.

FEATURES TAB

The Features tab (Figure 8.5) combines the control for two special editing features: Flexible Path and Lighting. These allow you to achieve some of the most realistic and stunning effects in *Second Life*.

Flexible Path

Flexible prims, popularly known as *flexiprims*, are a purely client-side effect. This means that they don't appear to be flexible from the server's perspective, because they don't interact with anything on the server. Of course, everyone viewing flexiprims will see them as flexible, though not necessarily flexing in the exact same position (Figure 8.6).

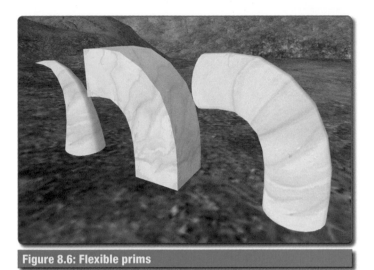

Figure 8.6: Flexible prims

Flexible prims have eight setting types that will modify the flexible effect. Using these you can create the appearance of soft flowing fabric, a flag whipping violently in the wind, or anything in between.

Softness: Determines how stiff or flexible a flexiprim is. This setting adds "joints" to the flexiprim that determine where it can bend. Goes from 3 (very flexible) to 0 (very stiff).

CHAPTER 1

CHAPTER 2

CHAPTER 3

CHAPTER 4

CHAPTER 5

CHAPTER 6

CHAPTER 7

CHAPTER 8

CHAPTER 9

CHAPTER 10

CHAPTER 11

CHAPTER 12

CHAPTER 13

CHAPTER 14

CHAPTER 15

APPENDICES

Gravity: Sets the push force along the Z-axis on the flexiprim. You can create effects similar to gravity, weight, and wind using this setting. Goes from 10 (very heavy/strong wind pushing down) to –10 (very heavy/strong wind pushing up from the ground, like antigravity).

Drag: Simulates air resistance on the flexiprim. Goes from 0 (violently whips back and forth) to 10 (heavy drag with slow movement).

Wind: Sets the amount of effect *SL* wind has on the flexiprim. Wind in *Second Life* isn't often seen, but it is a universal setting that certain scripts, and now flexiprims, can interact with. The user has no control over the speed and direction of *SL* wind, but the flexiprim Wind setting allows you to fine-tune how much impact it has on your flexiprim's movement. Goes from 0 (no effect) to 10 (very strong wind effect).

Tension: Sets the apparent tensile strength of the flexiprim. This setting acts much like the Softness setting combined with the Drag setting. However, at a setting of Tension 0, you will see the flexiprim does not move back into its original shape after being moved, acting instead like a piece of bent metal.

Force X/Y/Z: Sets the external force on the flexiprim along any of the three axes. Like Wind, the external force will bend your flexiprim. Unlike Wind, you can adjust these settings specifically to your preference and there is no "fluttering" effect from *SL* wind. Goes from 0 (no external force) to 10 (strong external force).

RESIDENTS SPEAK
USING FLEXIPRIMS

"Flexiprims have allowed me to take digital clothing to a whole other level from both a creative standpoint and an experiential standpoint for my customers. They allow hems to float and with their various physical settings, I can simulate both heavier materials and more diaphanous materials like chiffon and silk.

"I have used flexiprims for everything from ribbons on cuffs or dress bows to the ruffles on a blouse; they're staples in every skirt and dress I make. I've even made flexi cowls and draped fabric on outfits. I use them wherever the RL counterpart components to an outfit would have loose, hanging, draped, or skirted material."

—Ginny Talamasca

Lighting

Figure 8.7: A prim set as a light source casting light onto the ground and an avatar

Second Life supports emissive OpenGL lighting. What does this mean? Simple: you can set a prim as a light source and illuminate other objects around it (Figure 8.7).

While you can use as many light sources in your build as you like, *Second Life* will show you or others only the closest six sources at a time. Use light sources sparingly, as lights will flicker when they come into and out of view. Lighted prims are another client-side effect, and you can turn the ability to see them on or off in your preferences. People with older graphics cards may not be able to see them at all. Lighting effects can be controlled with the following options:

Color: The color of the light emitted by your prim

Intensity: Your light's brightness, anywhere from 0.0 to 1.0

Radius: The radius of your light source's effects

Falloff: How sharply the edge of your light source stops

TEXTURE TAB

The Texture tab allows you to set the color, texture, and shininess of an object. We'll discuss advanced texturing techniques later in this chapter.

CONTENT TAB

In the previous chapter you learned about your avatar's inventory. Like avatars, objects have inventories where you can place any inventory items. Putting things in an object's inventory is most useful when you're dealing with scripts or selling/giving away numerous objects in a set, but we'll talk about that more in Chapter 9.

⬇ SCULPTED PRIMS

A brand-new type of prim in *Second Life* is the sculpted prim. Sculpted prims are the only type of prim whose shape you cannot fully modify from within *Second Life*.

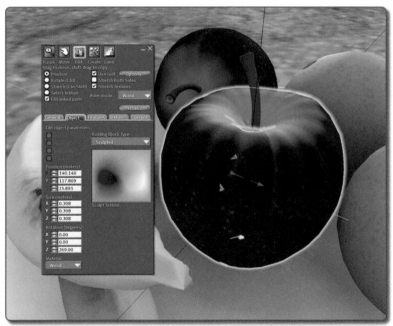

Figure 8.8: The Build menu's Object tab with Sculpted Prim type selected, and the Sculpt Texture window

Sculpted prims are created using any of a variety of 3D programs, such as Maya or new free programs created by *Second Life* residents, to model the shape. Then, using the program-appropriate script or option, the shape is exported in the form of an image file. When the image is uploaded into *Second Life* and applied to the Sculpt Texture area in the Build menu, the prim will take the shape of the shape you created in the 3D program (Figure 8.8)!

Sculpted prims open new doors to making realistic, organic creations in *Second Life*. However, some practice and understanding about how sculpted prims are created and function is required, as is a 3D program that supports the export of the sculpted prim textures. Going into depth on how to create sculpted prim textures is outside the scope of this book—however, there is a wealth of information on sculpted prims, including the list of for-cost and free programs that support sculpted prim exporting at `https://wiki.secondlife.com/wiki/Sculpted _ Prims`.

CHAPTER 1
CHAPTER 2
CHAPTER 3
CHAPTER 4
CHAPTER 5
CHAPTER 6
CHAPTER 7
CHAPTER 8

CHAPTER 9
CHAPTER 10
CHAPTER 11
CHAPTER 12
CHAPTER 13
CHAPTER 14
CHAPTER 15
APPENDICES

To quickly see some examples of sculpted prims, open your Inventory, go to your Library folder, and look in the Textures folder. There are two folders there, called Sculpt Textures and Surface Textures, that allow you to create the example sculpted prims shown in Figure 8.9.

Figure 8.9: Some of the sculpted prims available in your Inventory's Library folder

DUPLICATING PRIMS

You can duplicate an object by editing it and using the key command Control-D. You can also select the object and, while holding down Shift, drag the object along one of the move handles. If you don't have copy permissions for the object, you won't be able to duplicate it.

DELETING PRIMS

You can delete a prim by selecting it and pressing Delete on your keyboard. By holding down Shift and clicking individual prims, you can select multiple prims at a time and then delete them all. There is no way to automatically undo a deletion. Deleted items go into your inventory's Trash folder, so if you make a mistake you can still recover your object.

USING THE CAMERA

Second Life's camera is far more flexible than the cameras you'll find in most 3D software or games. With just a few keys and your mouse, you can reposition it anywhere, zooming in on details or rotating around the scene from a hundred meters away.

The easiest way to use the camera is with the following keyboard commands and the mouse.

Zoom: Hold down Alt, then left-click and hold your mouse button. Move your mouse to zoom your camera in and out.

Orbit: Hold down Control-Alt, then left click and hold your mouse button. Move your mouse to orbit the camera.

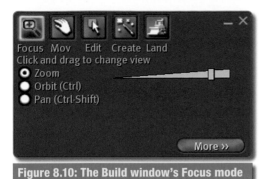

Figure 8.10: The Build window's Focus mode

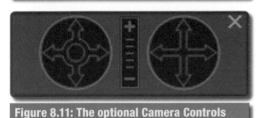

Figure 8.11: The optional Camera Controls interface

Pan: Hold down Control-Shift-Alt, then left-click and hold your mouse button. Move your mouse to pan the camera.

When in Focus mode (accessible from the Tools menu), the camera acts as though the Alt key is already being held down. You can click on objects to zoom, Control-click to orbit, and Control-Shift-click to pan (Figure 8.10).

Another method of controlling your camera is to use the Camera Controls interface (Figure 8.11). Go to View and select Camera Controls to bring up the interface. You can now move your camera using only your mouse.

RESIDENTS SPEAK
LEARNING THE CAMERA

"It's absolutely necessary to learn and understand how to use the camera if you want to build. Once you teach someone how to use the camera to help in their building, you can see that one of the problems limiting them most has just gone away. Their frustration diminishes and their imagination runs wild.

"Most seem to be able to handle the camera once they're taught how to handle it, but many skip that lesson on Orientation Island."

—Mera Pixel

LINKING PRIMS

You can link together multiple prims into a single object. This allows you to move and manipulate the combined object easily. Also, a linked object acts as a single prim in some ways, including the name/description of the object, as well as allowing the object to be copied or sold in a single step. The root prim of the linked object is the one that holds those settings.

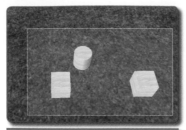

Figure 8.12: Multiple prims selected in a selection box

Figure 8.13: The Menu bar with the Tools menu open and Link selected

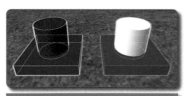

Figure 8.14: Comparison of the selection halo on linked and unlinked prims

To link a group of prims, simply select all the prims you want to link by clicking on them individually while holding down your keyboard's Shift key, or click on the ground or sky while in Edit mode and drag a box out to encompass all the prims you wish to link (Figure 8.12).

When you've selected all the prims you wish to link, link them by selecting Link from the Tools menu or using the keyboard command Control-L.

You may have trouble selecting or linking your prims (Figure 8.13) for a few reasons:

- You may be selecting other people's prims as well. Try checking Select Only My Objects on the Tools menu, or pan your camera around to get a better angle.

- You may be missing some of your prims if you're selecting them individually with Shift-select rather than selecting them by dragging a selection box around them.

- If you have several prims selected already, you may be forgetting to hold down Shift when you click on the next one.

- You're trying to link prims that are too far apart. Prims cannot be linked together if they're beyond a certain distance (which scales according to the sizes of the prims involved). This means you can link two large prims over a greater distance than two very small ones—the maximum distance is proportionate to the prims' size.

- You are trying to link more than 255 prims together. Try making two or more smaller linked sets instead of one large set. You can still move these sets in tandem with each other by simply selecting them both at the same time, and then moving them using the move handles.

See how the highlight changed on your collection of prims? This means that it's now a linked object. The last prim you selected is now highlighted in yellow, indicating that it's become the parent (or root) prim. The prims highlighted in blue are called the child prims. They're all now part of the same object. By deselecting the object and then reselecting it, you can see that all the prims are now highlighted in yellow and blue. You can move the entire object around just as if it were a single prim (Figure 8.14).

⬇ Unlinking Linked Objects

To unlink a linked object, select it then choose Tools > Unlink, or use Control-Shift-L.

ADDITIONAL INFO
UNLINKING PHYSICAL OBJECTS

Be forewarned! If you attempt to unlink a physical object, its component prims will stay physical when you unlink them. If this happens, the prims may explode in all directions when you deselect them. Make sure you uncheck the Physical check box in the Object tab of the Build window before unlinking.

To easily remove a single prim from a linked object, do the following:

1. Select the object.

2. In the Build menu, check the Edit Linked Parts check box.

3. Click the prim you wish to remove from the linked object. It will be highlighted in blue and the other prims will lose their highlight. If you selected the root prim, it will be highlighted in yellow. You may select more than one prim to unlink by holding Shift as you click each prim.

4. Use Control-Shift-L to unlink the selected prim(s); if you unlinked a single prim, that prim will be the only one now selected and highlighted in yellow. If you selected more than one prim to unlink, your entire object will be selected again, with your newly unlinked prims (and the root prim of the remaining linked object) all highlighted in yellow.

5. If you deselected more than one prim, hold down Shift and click the remaining linked object set that you removed your prims from. Just that object should de-highlight, leaving you with your newly delinked prims selected. You can now delete those prims all at once, or modify/link them into their own linked set.

⬇ Working with Linked Objects

Positioning and rotating any object works the same, no matter how many prims it contains. However, scaling linked objects is a little different than scaling an ordinary prim. Edit the object and drag its object handles to make it bigger and smaller. You'll be able to scale the entire object proportionately, but you won't be able to stretch it along the X, Y, or Z axis.

ADDITIONAL INFO
SHRINKING A PRIM IN A LINKED OBJECT

You won't be able to shrink a prim in a linked object beyond the minimum dimension allowed on any axis (1cm). This means that a more-complex object may not shrink as small as you'd prefer. Try unlinking that single prim and repositioning and scaling it individually.

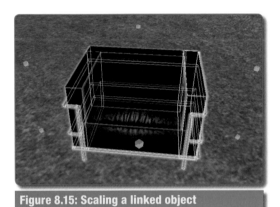

Figure 8.15: Scaling a linked object

Unfortunately, there's no way to scale a linked object without the mouse. You can't just type in the new scale like you can with an individual prim.

When the Stretch Both Sides check box is checked, you can scale the object in place, and it will grow or contract in all three dimensions. Despite what the name implies, you still won't be able to stretch it along the X, Y, or Z axis, though. You can only make linked objects bigger or smaller (Figure 8.15).

⬇ ADDING PRIMS TO A LINKED OBJECT

Prims and linked objects can be linked to an existing object just as a group of individual prims can be linked together. Simply select the prims or linked objects and click Tools > Link from your menu bar, or use the key command Control-L.

Remember that the last prim selected will become the root in the new linked object. If the last object you selected was a linked object, its root prim will become the root for the new linked object.

⬇ WORKING WITH INDIVIDUAL PRIMS IN A LINKED OBJECT

Figure 8.16: The Edit Linked Parts check box

Sometimes you'll want to manipulate individual prims within a linked object. To do so, check the Edit Linked Parts check box in the Build window's Edit mode. This will let you edit each prim in a linked object as if it were a separate prim without having to unlink them first (Figure 8.16).

Figure 8.17: Scaling a single prim within a linked object

Remember that each prim in your linked object is still a separate prim. It has its own parameters and properties, as well as its own inventory. When editing individual prims in a linked object, remember that your prims are still constrained by the limits of linked objects. You won't be able to scale or reposition a prim beyond the limits at which you would be able to link it normally (Figure 8.17).

CHAPTER 1

CHAPTER 2

CHAPTER 3

CHAPTER 4

CHAPTER 5

CHAPTER 6

CHAPTER 7

CHAPTER 8

CHAPTER 9

CHAPTER 10

CHAPTER 11

CHAPTER 12

CHAPTER 13

CHAPTER 14

CHAPTER 15

APPENDICES

TAKING COPIES

Taking copies of your work in *Second Life* is very important. There is no automatic backup feature, so the copies you take of your work might be the only ones you have if you make a mistake.

You can easily take a copy of an object by right-clicking the object and choosing Take Copy from the pie menu. It will appear in your Objects folder in your Inventory. Remember to name your object, either before you take a copy or while it's in your Inventory, so you remember later what it is!

Figure 8.18: The multiple and single icons found next to objects in your Inventory

You can also take backups of nonlinked objects by simply selecting them all at once and then choosing Take Copy from the pie menu. These multiple objects will be saved in your Inventory under one name, but the icon next to them will change. A multiple box icon is shown next to this listing, compared to a single box icon when the object in your inventory is a single prim or linked object (Figure 8.18).

ADDITIONAL INFO
AUTO-SELECT TIP

When you bring copies out of your inventory and rez them in-world, have the Build menu already open before you drag and drop the item to the ground. This way, your objects will automatically be selected when they appear inworld, making placement easier.

USING THE GRID

The Lindens use the term "grid" to describe all of *Second Life* (or alternately, the Main and Teen grids) because of the grid pattern that the different regions make up on the map. In building terms, the grid is an alignment tool to allow you to more easily position prims within a region. Each region within *Second Life* is a 256m x 256m square. (Obviously, there's a third dimension of hundreds of meters of space above this as well, but *SL* follows a two-dimensional map layout.)

Sometimes you'll find that Snap-to-Grid doesn't work as well as you get farther away from the region's origin point, <0,0,0>. When using Snap-to-Grid high up in the air or toward the northeastern corner of the region, you'll still see prims lining up, but they won't be aligned precisely anymore. When we're dealing with decimals, (as we are when building) the larger the number, the less precise it is. The reason for this lies in how *Second Life* stores positioning data for prims.

This isn't a big deal in practical terms, but some builders are frustrated by it. If you're really obsessive-compulsive about your grid positioning, try to limit your precision building to locations near the region's origin point, its southwest corner.

SNAPPING TO THE GRID

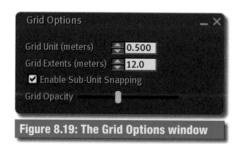

Figure 8.19: The Grid Options window

The Use Grid feature allows you to easily align your objects to points on the grid. This is handy because it allows builders to create and duplicate objects quickly without having to line up prims—they snap into place automatically.

To activate the grid, select the Use Grid check box in the Build window's Edit mode (it should be checked by default). By clicking the Options button next to it, you can open the Grid Options menu (Figure 8.19), in which you can change various properties of the grid:

Grid Unit (meters). Setting the grid unit allows you to snap objects to a smaller grid. When building large structures like houses, many builders opt for a grid line every 0.25 or 0.125 meter. This allows you to drag very large prims into place easily while having the flexibility to line up 0.25m prims precisely. Because measurements in *Second Life* use the metric system, some builders opt for a 0.1m grid. It's up to you to decide what you like best.

Grid Extents (meters). This is how far from the center of the object the grid appears. Changing it from its default setting of 12 meters is rarely necessary.

Enable Sub-Unit Snapping. Check this box to snap to smaller grid divisions when the camera is zoomed in. This feature depends heavily on the camera, and an object's position within the region, and may not divide accurately. For best results, use Sub-Unit Snapping only when you're editing objects close to the region's origin.

Figure 8.20: Show Cross Sections

Show Cross Sections. This option will display colored indicators on the prim you're editing and any nearby prims, helping to show you where in relation to each other your edited prim is being moved (Figure 8.20).

Grid Opacity. This slider allows you to set the transparency of the grid displayed when moving, rotating, or scaling a prim or object. Remember—you'll be able to see the grid only while you're manipulating an object using its object handles. Most builders prefer a low to medium opacity.

For detail work (especially small objects such as attachments), Use Grid becomes ungainly. When it becomes a hindrance, turn it off.

COLLABORATING WITH OTHER RESIDENTS

One of the best features of *Second Life* is the way it allows you to collaborate with other residents. Together, you can work on bigger and more complex projects, build on each other's strengths, and make things that you might not be able to on your own. However, collaborating with other residents can be difficult, and not just when it comes to playing well with others.

There are five options for collaborative building. This section discusses the advantages and disadvantages of each.

⬇ Modify Rights

One way to build collaboratively is to grant another resident modify rights to your objects. Essentially, you're allowing them to edit all your objects. To grant someone modify rights, they must first be on your Friends list. It's not enough to simply have their calling card; they must appear in the Friends window. Open it by selecting Communicate on the toolbar (if you have it turned off, turn it on under View > Toolbar) or by the keyboard command Control-T. Then, select the Contacts tab in the upper left of the window to view your Friends list.

To grant someone else permission to edit your objects, select their name in your Friends list, and select the Can Modify My Objects check box along the bottom of the window. You'll see a dialog box

CHAPTER 1
CHAPTER 2
CHAPTER 3
CHAPTER 4
CHAPTER 5
CHAPTER 6
CHAPTER 7
CHAPTER 8

CHAPTER 9
CHAPTER 10
CHAPTER 11
CHAPTER 12
CHAPTER 13
CHAPTER 14
CHAPTER 15
APPENDICES

asking you to confirm this, and after clicking Yes, you'll see the Modify Rights graphic next to the person's name in your Friends list. Next to the Granted Modify Rights column, there is another column that shows who has granted you modify rights on their objects.

Once you grant someone modify rights, they'll be able to edit anything you own, anywhere in the world. If you don't trust them with everything of yours, consider collaborating with them using an alternate account. Use this option sparingly, and only with people you trust. When building as a group, you can instead use the Allow Group to Modify check box on your objects to give these permissions on specific objects only, rather than on everything you own.

Figure 8.21: The Friends list interface

To *revoke* a resident's modify rights, select the person's name in your Friends list and uncheck the Can Modify My Objects check box. When removing someone from your Friends list altogether, their modify rights will be revoked automatically.

When granting modify rights, the other person will see the chat message "You have been granted the privilege to modify [your avatar name]'s objects." You can easily see who has granted you modify rights and who has modify rights on your objects by checking your Friends list (Figure 8.21).

Figure 8.22: A prim named and ready for group modification

ALLOW GROUP TO MODIFY

If you are uncomfortable with giving out modify rights to other builders for the purpose of a project, consider creating a group specifically for the builders on that project and then using the Allow Group to Modify (and also the Allow Group to Copy) check boxes on your project objects. This will give members of the group the ability to modify and copy your objects, but only the objects you specifically allow.

Using these options along with setting the Next Owner permissions (modify, copy, and transfer) will give you greater control over what objects other people can manipulate and what they can do if they copy those objects.

To make this option even easier to use, prepare at the beginning of a project by creating a single prim, naming it *Group Name* Project Prim—so, for example, Counting Sheep Project Prim as in Figure 8.22—setting the aforementioned permissions on it (including Allow Group to Modify, Allow Group to Copy, and the Next Owner permissions), and then taking the prim into your inventory. Whenever you start to build an object for the project, simply take that prim from your inventory and begin your build with it. By doing this, all the permissions will be already set and you won't have to remember to set them again each time you create something new for the project.

GROUP LAND

When building with other people, it can be a good idea to form a group and set the land to that group. By then setting all your objects to the same group, any group member can edit those objects if you check the Allow Group to Modify check box on the objects; you can return nongroup objects, or even prohibit other people's objects from existing on your group's land.

Figure 8.23: The About Land window

Another option is to deed the land to a group. Deeding land to group ownership also allows you to own 10% more on the same land tier. However, if you sell deeded land, the profits will be split equally among all the group members, and group members in general will have more control over the land itself, such as changing permission settings for the land. If you only want to allow other members of your group to build on your land while preventing other people's objects from being rezzed on your land, choose the Set Group option— deeded land may give group members more abilities to change your land than you're comfortable with. Both of these options can be set in the About Land window (Figure 8.23)

Group land will let you collaborate with other users on larger builds, but to actually link your objects together you'll need to transfer ownership to one person and have that person link the objects. To do that, you have to play with asset permissions, which we'll explore next.

ASSET PERMISSIONS

Asset permissions are set in the General tab of the Build window. They define how future owners of the object (or copies of that object) may use it. Permissions are relatively straightforward to use. When collaborating with other builders, make sure that permissions are granted on all prims, textures, and inventory within each prim that you transfer or sell to your fellow designers, or your fellow designers may not be able to manipulate them when they make copies. If you or a group member needs to link two objects together with different owners, one person must sell their object to the other person—only objects with the same owner can be linked. Setting full permissions—modify, copy, and transfer—for the next owner is very important in this case, as a restriction in any of those fields will carry over when the object that was sold is linked to other prims.

CHAPTER 1
CHAPTER 2
CHAPTER 3
CHAPTER 4
CHAPTER 5
CHAPTER 6
CHAPTER 7
CHAPTER 8
CHAPTER 9
CHAPTER 10
CHAPTER 11
CHAPTER 12
CHAPTER 13
CHAPTER 14
CHAPTER 15
APPENDICES

GROUP DEEDING

Deeding an object transfers ownership of that object to a group. Instead of one individual owning the object, instead it is now owned by the collective group. Some scripted objects require the object be deeded to a group when it is on group-deeded land; more often scripts require only one individual owner to function. Returning a group-deeded object to its owner can also cause the object to vanish completely (rather than appearing in the owner's inventory in the Lost and Found folder, as it would normally). You're generally better off not deeding objects to a group itself, but instead checking the Allow Group Members to Modify check box on each object. This keeps the transfer-of-ownership rate to a minimum and allows you to more easily control your prims' permissions.

ATTACHMENTS

Attachments are what they sound like: objects that can be attached to your avatar. These range from handheld tools, props, or weapons to jewelry and even hair and shoes.

Unlike normal prims, attachments are always phantom, no matter what you do. This means that they'll intersect your avatar, each other, and other objects that are unattached to you. This can pose some problems when making attachments that are likely to intersect, so you'll often need to work around the limits. You'll see more avatars with shorter prim-based hairstyles than with long hair for just this reason—long prim hair frequently intersects the back and tends to look weird.

Attachments can be scripted, which can control your avatar's movement and behavior. Other attachments can act as HUDs—heads-up displays. Such an attachment acts as a customized menu that only the avatar that is wearing it can see. HUD attachments can be interacted with (clicking buttons, etc), just like a traditional user interface menu.

In all these situations, attachments are first created just like any other object, scripts are added (if necessary), and then they are attached to your avatar after you take the finished product into your inventory.

MAKING ATTACHMENTS

For the most part, you'll be working with very small prims, at least compared to those you'd use to build a house or a castle. Because *Second Life* prevents you from making a prim less than 1cm in any dimension, you'll often need to use the Cut and Dimple tools. Cut allows you to slice a section out of your prim, like cutting a slice of pie. Dimple is limited to the sphere primitive and allows you to create a dimple in the top of the sphere.

Holding the avatar still is very important when working with attachments. Ordinarily, your avatar is moving at least a little, and even small movements can make it difficult to position your attachments correctly.

A good tool for immobilizing your avatar is called a *pose stand*, and many varieties are available for free or for purchase within *Second Life*. The CD that accompanies this book contains a document called `simple_pose_stand_script.txt` that you can copy and paste into a script, then put into a prim to create your own pose stand. It allows you to hold your avatar's arms and legs in a stationary position so that you can construct and edit attachments without having to worry about your avatar's pose shifting.

When working with small objects like earrings or body jewelry, you may find that they become "buried" within your avatar. You can get around this in a couple ways. The best way is to link your attachment's prims together, then add a larger prim (not overly large; a 0.125m cube should suffice) to the existing object as a child prim. By ensuring the larger prim isn't the root of the resulting linked object, you can use the larger prim as a temporary handle and delete it later without having to worry that you're deleting the prim that determines the object's position. This will allow you to attach the object to your avatar and move it around by the "handle" prim. After it's where you want it, detach the attachment, rez it on the ground, unlink the handle from the rest of the attachment, take the now handleless object into your inventory, and wear it again. It will reattach to its original attachment point, and in the correct position.

Another option is to use Debug mode to temporarily turn off avatar rendering on your computer. You'll be able to zoom in on and edit your attachments without your avatar blocking them.

To do this, ensure that the Client and Server menu options are available to the right of the Help menu at the top of your window. If they're not active, turn Debug mode on with Control-Shift-Alt-D. Next, select Client > Rendering > Types > Character. When you've positioned your attachment well outside your avatar's body, you can turn avatar rendering back on so you can see what you're doing.

RESIDENTS SPEAK
ATTACHMENTS' PRIM COUNTS

"Attachments really can be built without regard to prim count. Oh, sure, you'll get the complainers and the Hoochie Hair Haters, but if the customer wears the item, it does not count against the land's prim count. But I will say that you can really cut prim usage with textures!"

—Wynx Whiplash

You may encounter some problems with some attachment points. When attaching an object, it is positioned relative to your avatar's skeleton—yes, your avatar really has a skeleton!—not its skin. This can lead to attachments that appear to be floating through your avatar, rather than embedded within it.

CHAPTER 1
CHAPTER 2
CHAPTER 3
CHAPTER 4
CHAPTER 5
CHAPTER 6
CHAPTER 7
CHAPTER 8

CHAPTER 9
CHAPTER 10
CHAPTER 11
CHAPTER 12
CHAPTER 13
CHAPTER 14
CHAPTER 15
APPENDICES

CHAPTER 8

THE BASICS
GETTING
STARTED
REZZING YOUR
FIRST PRIM
EDITING
YOUR PRIM
USING THE
CAMERA
LINKING PRIMS
TAKING COPIES
USING THE GRID
COLLABORATING
WITH OTHER
RESIDENTS
ATTACHMENTS
LANDSCAPING
TEXTURING
CREATING
TEXTURES
UPLOADING
TEXTURES

⬇ MODIFYING ATTACHMENTS

Attachments can be moved, and often modified to better fit your avatar, once you're wearing them. This is handy for attachments that you have purchased, such as prim hair, prim skirts, jewelry, and so on. Again, your posing stand will come in handy here as you make your adjustments.

Right-clicking an attachment on your body and choosing Edit will bring up the same Edit menu you're familiar with from building. You can scale or shrink the size of an attachment (if it's modifiable), reposition the attachment, and so forth using the same tools you use to resize and move prims that you create.

Note that you cannot edit an attachment that is on another avatar's body, nor can other people edit attachments that you are wearing.

LANDSCAPING

There's more to building in *Second Life* than simply manipulating prims. Many residents enjoy landscaping their plots. You can create plant prims only on land that you own, or on group land if you're an officer, but the results can be impressive.

Besides the usual primitives, *Second Life* allows you to use several predefined tree models as primitives. Beyond the two dozen or so types, your options for creating plant life are somewhat limited, however.

In *Second Life* parlance, trees are plants that are affected by wind, whereas grass is a complex model of individual tufts that adhere to the ground surface beneath them. A grass prim will always stay at ground level, no matter how high you attempt to position it.

Even though they look like grass, the Beach Grass and Eelgrass models are actually classified as "tree" prims and will sway in the breeze. Don't be confused by their names!

The specific type and dimensions of a grass or tree model is chosen randomly when you create a new one. This is to give the impression of randomness but can result in odd-looking forests, should you choose to keep the assortment you create. The variety of trees available ranges from palm trees to snow-covered pines. Fortunately, all the plant models exist in your Inventory's Library folder, under Library > Objects > Trees, Plants and Grasses.

Creating a tree through the Build tools causes it to be rezzed with its base at ground level. It doesn't matter if you create it up in the air; the tree will still appear down on the ground. To avoid this, try rezzing trees that already exist within your inventory—from your Library folder, for instance.

To give the effect of a more natural scene, you'll want to rotate and scale trees if you use a bunch of identical tree types clustered together. Introducing a little variety is key. It helps to give the illusion of nature.

CHAPTER 1

CHAPTER 2

CHAPTER 3

CHAPTER 4

CHAPTER 5

CHAPTER 6

CHAPTER 7

CHAPTER 8

CHAPTER 9

CHAPTER 10

CHAPTER 11

CHAPTER 12

CHAPTER 13

CHAPTER 14

CHAPTER 15

APPENDICES

ADDITIONAL INFO
USING SCRIPTED PLANT REZZERS

By using scripted plant rezzers, you can take a few different trees and other plant objects and automatically cover your land with foliage to your tastes.

TEXTURING

Creating untextured primitives is the bulk of what is considered "building" in *Second Life*, but to produce truly stunning content, you'll need to rely on textures. Textures are ordinary image files applied to the sides of objects. They can range from simple patterns used as wallpaper in your virtual house to meticulously hand-drawn clothing. In this section, we'll discuss how to manipulate textures, as well as some ideas for creating your own.

To start, select a prim and then open the Texture tab on your Build window (Figure 8.24).

⬇ TEXTURE

Clicking the Texture box opens the Texture Picker window. The Texture Picker is one part texture previewer and one part special Inventory filter. The inventory half of the Texture Picker works just like your normal inventory, but with a filter applied to allow you to see all the textures and screenshots in your inventory, no matter where they are. Just select them from the Texture Picker's Inventory pane; they'll appear in the texture-preview pane of the Texture Picker.

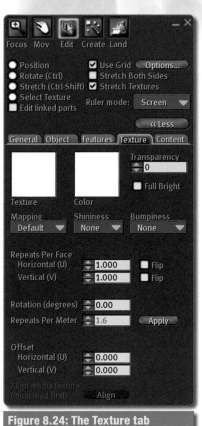

Figure 8.24: The Texture tab

If the 160 × 160-pixel texture previewer is too small, double-click on any texture within the Texture Picker's Inventory panel and open the texture as you would in your normal inventory.

Once you've selected the texture you want, click Select, or if you have the Apply Immediately box checked, just close the window.

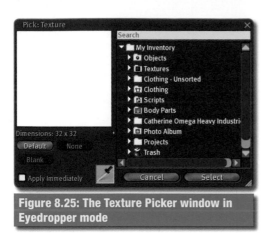

Figure 8.25: The Texture Picker window in Eyedropper mode

Another selection tool is the Eyedropper. When you click on the Eyedropper icon, the mouse pointer changes to allow you to click on any texture face on any object you have edit permissions for, as long as you have a copy of the texture in your Inventory; you can then copy the texture to the Texture Picker. This allows you to apply the texture you just grabbed to your selected faces (Figure 8.25).

> ### ADDITIONAL INFO
> ## AN ALTERNATIVE TO THE TEXTURE PICKER
>
> If you don't want to use the Texture Picker, you can always drag a texture directly from an open Inventory window onto the Texture box of the Texture tab.

COLOR

Clicking the Color box opens the Color Picker. It allows you to select the color you wish to apply to your selected faces.

You'll notice two multicolored areas: the narrow Tint/Shade Picker on the right, and the large square Hue/Saturation/Luminosity Picker to its left. By clicking and dragging your cursor to different positions on these areas, you can quickly select a color. Another option is to manually enter red/green/blue (RGB) values that you've selected from graphics software such as Adobe Photoshop. When working with textures, you may already have some color scheme in mind.

If you're having trouble choosing a color or getting the balance just right, try clicking one of the two dozen or so preset boxes at the bottom of the Color Picker window. Doing so will automatically load the selected color and give you a good starting point. You can also simply click Select to close the Color Picker, and use the preset as your new color.

If you'd like to save a color you've picked, click and drag the Current Color box to the preset squares in the lower section of the window. The four boxes at the bottom right of the Color Picker are blank, but you can replace any of the preset colors with your own custom ones.

CHAPTER 1

CHAPTER 2

CHAPTER 3

CHAPTER 4

CHAPTER 5

CHAPTER 6

CHAPTER 7

CHAPTER 8

CHAPTER 9

CHAPTER 10

CHAPTER 11

CHAPTER 12

CHAPTER 13

CHAPTER 14

CHAPTER 15

APPENDICES

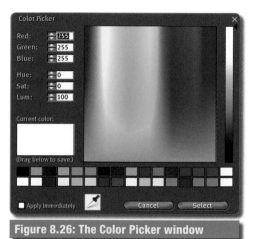

Figure 8.26: The Color Picker window

Like the Texture Picker, the Color Picker (Figure 8.26) allows you to use the Eyedropper tool. The only difference between the Eyedropper tool in the two Pickers is that you don't need edit permissions to grab a color from another resident's objects. This can be particularly handy when collaborating with other residents.

Transparency

By setting the transparency of a prim, you can easily produce translucent windows and effects for all kinds of objects, from waterfalls to light bulbs to crystals to bottles. You can't set an object to more than 90% transparency using the Build tools—that would make it too difficult to find. However, you *can* set it completely invisible by using scripts, which are discussed in Chapter 9. Another option is to use a completely transparent (alpha) texture, which is provided on the CD that comes with this book.

Full Bright

Figure 8.27: A Full Bright cube next to a normal cube

This setting allows you to declare a face immune to the effects of lighting and shadows. It will appear completely unshaded from all angles and will stand out brightly at night. Because of this, Full Bright can be a handy feature to use when making things like signs or boxes in a store. Remember that you can have a Full Bright prim emit light by choosing Light on the Features tab. This lets you create things such as light bulbs or neon signs—light-emitting objects that are completely illuminated, as they would be in the real world (Figure 8.27).

Texturing Individual Faces of a Prim

When making more than the most basic objects, you'll almost certainly want different textures for different faces. This is most easily done by using the Select Texture option on the top of the Edit tab of the Build menu, then clicking a face on your prim to select only that face. You should see the "bulls-eye" crosshairs on that face, indicating it's selected. You can then hold Shift and click additional faces of the prim if you wish.

Dragging a texture out of your inventory and onto a prim's face will apply the texture to only that face, regardless of whether the prim is selected. To apply it to all faces on the destination prim, hold down the Shift key when you release the texture. For safety reasons, there's no way to apply a texture to all prims in an object this way; Undo doesn't work when dragging and dropping textures!

Offsets, Repeats, Flip, and Rotation

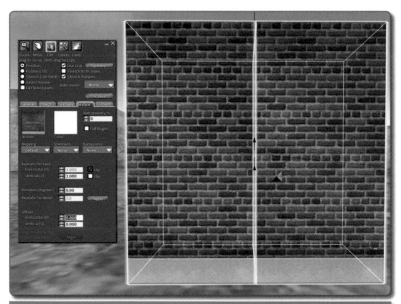

By default, when a texture is applied to a prim face, the texture shows up a single time and is positioned in the center of the prim. By using the Offset and Repeat fields in the Texture tab, you can make a texture repeat many times on a prim or offset it so the texture wraps around, or both. Both these settings are valuable to help you create visual effects, seamless transitions, and more-realistic builds.

Figure 8.28: Stretching a texture across two prims seamlessly

Some experimentation is necessary when using these settings, but practice will quickly help you see the patterns. For example, by setting the Repeat value on a texture to 2 and the Offset value to 0.5, your texture will now appear twice on the prim side-by-side without overlapping. Another example takes two prims, each with the same texture. Set the first prim's texture to a Repeat value of 0.5, and the Offset to a value of −0.25. Set the second prim to the same repeat value, but the Offset value to 0.25. Your texture now stretches across two prims seamlessly (Figure 8.28)!

Texture rotation works something like the Flip Horizontal and Flip Vertical check boxes. While those check boxes literally flip the texture along the horizontal or vertical, creating a mirrored result, the Rotation field allows you to rotate the texture around its center.

⬇ Advanced Texturing Tools

CHAPTER 1
CHAPTER 2
CHAPTER 3
CHAPTER 4
CHAPTER 5
CHAPTER 6
CHAPTER 7
CHAPTER 8

CHAPTER 9
CHAPTER 10
CHAPTER 11
CHAPTER 12
CHAPTER 13
CHAPTER 14
CHAPTER 15
APPENDICES

Some prim shapes are harder to texture than others. Spheres and tori, for example, can seem to distort the texture you apply to it. Other times, setting up customized textures for a simple cube can be difficult if you don't know where exactly parts of the texture will fall once it's applied.

Using a custom grid-mapping texture helps you learn how different prims apply textures to their surfaces, and also helps you create custom textures for a build where precision is important. You can save and upload the Grid Map Texture on the CD included with this book for your own use as you explore texturing.

⬇ Responsible Texturing

Textures are one of the biggest sources of lag in *Second Life*, especially when precautions aren't taken to minimize the amount of data in these image files that are streamed to a viewer's computer. You can help minimize lag in the following ways:

Using smaller files. Textures are automatically resized when you upload them to *SL* to powers of 32—64, 128, 512, and so on. Use the smallest texture you can get away with on your projects. Often a 256 × 256 texture will work fine, and you should never have to go above a 512 × 512 texture unless you're stretching the texture across multiple prims. 1024 × 1024 is the largest texture *SL* will let you upload—anything larger than that will automatically be resized by the server.

Reusing textures. When you can, design your textures so they can be reused in more than one area. Sometimes tinting a texture is all you need to create a visually different effect while still technically only using a single texture file. Experiment with grayscale versions of textures to allow you to tint them more accurately.

Creating texture maps. Game designers will often combine different textures into a single file to minimize loading. You can, too! By creating this special texture and using the Offset and Repeat values, you can create the effect of multiple textures when in fact you're only using a single file. This means faster loading times, and it saves you upload fees. This can take a lot of practice and planning to accomplish, so don't feel bad if it doesn't come naturally, but it's a great skill to work up to.

⬇ Clothing

Clothing in *Second Life* is created in the same way as a normal object is textured: by wrapping a two-dimensional image around a three-dimensional shape. Unlike with normal textures, however, you can't just upload any old texture and hope it fits. Specific parts of a clothing or skin texture correspond to locations on your avatar. The creation process is called UV mapping, and the textures used are UV maps.

As mentioned previously, 3D modeling uses the X, Y, and Z coordinates to determine the position of an object; UV maps are so named because they add two further dimensions: U and V. U corresponds to the right/left on the image that is wrapped around the model, and V corresponds to the image's up/down.

Linden Lab has created a set of templates you can use to make your own textures, but most designers use far more detailed and accurate templates created by Chip Midnight or Robin Wood. All three sets of templates are included on the CD in this book, along with an in-depth guide to using use them.

The most popular software for texture creation is Adobe Photoshop, though many people also use JASC/Corel's Paint Shop Pro, Corel Photo-Paint, or the free image-editing software GIMP. Advanced users may even use 3D-rendering software such as LightWave or Maya to assist in creating clothing.

 RESIDENTS SPEAK
PICKING THE RIGHT TOOLS FOR THE JOB

"For making textures, I use Photoshop CS2 and Eye Candy. Photoshop is my life. I have used it since version 2 and I probably only know how to use half of it, but I use it for everything. Especially because I like fur and scales as opposed to the flat look of an untextured prim. I will add that I am an avid user of Adobe Illustrator and use that for quite a bit of detail work too."

—Wynx Whiplash

"I employ a 'mutt' software system of Photoshop CS2 and LightWave. I use that for both mesh and prim work. I use objects and applied UV-maps in LightWave to work with primitives. But my system is imperfect. I do a lot of blending in Photoshop to reduce the seaming between mesh and prims."

—Ginny Talamasca

"I do all my textures in Corel Photo-Paint—I think it's a superior tool to Photoshop, especially when handling layers and alpha transparencies, at a fraction of the price. I think it's also a much more intuitive tool to learn, especially for novice users."

—Francis Chung

CHAPTER 1
CHAPTER 2
CHAPTER 3
CHAPTER 4
CHAPTER 5
CHAPTER 6
CHAPTER 7
CHAPTER 8

CHAPTER 9
CHAPTER 10
CHAPTER 11
CHAPTER 12
CHAPTER 13
CHAPTER 14
CHAPTER 15
APPENDICES

RESIDENTS SPEAK

BAKING LIGHT EFFECTS INTO YOUR TEXTURES

"Producing realistic shadows and lighting effects in real time is not possible for today's hardware. The process called ray tracing, which produces realistic shadows, is just too slow and would make *Second Life* impossible to enjoy. To compensate, I 'bake' shadows and lighting right into the textures for all my builds. I do this by painting the shadows and light, or using third-party rendering tools like Maya to create a dramatic scene. If I have a stool in one of my sets, I simply draw the shadow of the stool under it and the visual effect can be stunning."

—Aimee Weber

CREATING TEXTURES

Texture creation could take up an entire book on its own—and does! You can find numerous books on creating textures for virtual worlds and game platforms through any online bookstore. Additionally, you can study many free textures available online or follow free online tutorials to help you make better textures.

Second Life has a selection of tutorial links, plus textures you can download and use yourself, located on the official *Second Life* Wiki. Go to `https://wiki.secondlife.com/wiki/Texture_Tools` to start learning more about creating textures.

UPLOADING TEXTURES

To get your textures into *Second Life*, you'll need to upload them from your server to the *Second Life* servers. *Second Life* accepts textures in the Targa (.TGA), Windows Bitmap (.BMP), and JPEG (.JPG/.JPEG) file formats. If the texture you wish to upload is in another format, you'll need to convert it first.

Textures are sized according to a "powers of two" rule. For ideal results, your textures should be 32, 64, 128, 256, 512, or 1024 pixels wide or tall. Your textures don't need to be square, but most are because a square is the best shape for most applications. This means you could have a 512 × 256-pixel texture, for example. Don't worry about fitting the pixels on a prim, though! You can scale a texture to fit any prim, or even show a small fraction of the entire texture.

CHAPTER 8

THE BASICS

GETTING
STARTED

REZZING YOUR
FIRST PRIM

EDITING
YOUR PRIM

USING THE
CAMERA

LINKING PRIMS

TAKING COPIES

USING THE GRID

COLLABORATING
WITH OTHER
RESIDENTS

ATTACHMENTS

LANDSCAPING

TEXTURING

CREATING
TEXTURES

UPLOADING
TEXTURES

Because of the "powers of two" rule, a 640 × 480 image will automatically be resized to 512 × 512 when uploading. Textures will be rounded up or down to the nearest power of two and may look distorted when viewed in the Texture Upload window or placed on a prim that doesn't maintain the original texture's proportions.

The term used to describe an image's proportions is *aspect ratio*. It is a comparison of an image's width and height. For instance, normal televisions and computer monitors use a 4:3 aspect ratio. This means that the width of the picture is 1.333 times the height.

When uploading a photo texture to share with your friends as a billboard, stretch a prim to be 4m across and 3m high, then stick the texture on the side. No matter the resolution of the uploaded image, *Second Life* will rescale the texture to appear at its original resolution.

⬇ Texture Upload Window

To upload a texture, select File > Upload Image. This will open an OS-native File Picker that will look like any other Open File window on your computer. You will have to pay L$10 to upload a texture. (This restriction is intended to discourage residents from filling up the *Second Life* servers with extraneous textures.) The window contains the following options:

Name: This is the name of the texture as it will appear in your inventory.

Description: The Description field is handy for including additional information about the texture, but the texture itself must be viewed to see the description.

Preview Image As: The Preview Image drop-down allows you to change the preview mode, selecting between Image, Hair, Female Head, Female Upper Body, Female Lower Body, Male Head, Male Upper Body, Male Lower Body, and Skirt. Depending on which option you choose, you will see a flat image (in the case of the Image option) or a three-dimensional body part with your texture wrapped around it.

Although *Second Life* uses the same avatar model regardless of which gender you choose, skin and clothing textures will stretch differently based on how the avatar itself is stretched. If you're designing a piece of clothing to be worn by a specific gender, you'll want to make sure it looks good on that gender.

Once you're sure the image looks how you want it to, press the Upload button. It may take a minute or so to upload your texture, depending on how busy *Second Life* is at the time.

You can download a free clothing previewer program provided by John Durant from `http://www.fileden.com/files/2006/10/8/271989/slcp.zip`.

If your texture doesn't look exactly how you pictured it when you actually view it in the *Second Life* world, don't be discouraged. Most designers have to upload several versions before they're totally satisfied.

CHAPTER 9

USING THE LINDEN SCRIPTING LANGUAGE

It is time to look under the hood and dive headfirst into the world of the Linden Scripting Language (LSL). It lets you add behaviors and interactivity to objects inside *Second Life*. Scripting is just another word for programming, so in learning about LSL you will end up learning about programming as well. Do not be afraid, though—between this chapter and the many resources available both online and in-world, you'll be up and scripting in no time. You do not need to write scripts to have fun in *Second Life*, but scripting drives the magic, from vehicles and guns to vendors and HTTP requests.

This chapter walks you through creating your first script and covers the LSL syntax and more-advanced language features. It also teaches you how LSL scripts can sense and communicate with the rest of SL, and how LSL can apply physical forces and move scripted objects onto your screen as heads-up display (HUD) attachments. Finally, it covers the many resources available for when you want to learn more.

CONTENTS

THE ORIGINS OF LSL

So, where did LSL come from? When *Second Life* was still called *LindenWorld* and had small space ships and eyeballs flying around instead of avatars, it did not have a scripting language. Instead, anything created in-world was built via static creations and physics. Thanks to rigid body dynamics, objects in *Second Life* act more or less like real-world objects, colliding with each other, falling under the effect of gravity, etc. This enabled a wide variety of creations, but many types were missing.

Take airplanes, for example. In a few more years (thanks to Moore's Law) we will be able to simulate a wing in real time, solving the many complex equations needed to properly model the interactions of the wing, turbulence, fluid flow, Bernoulli's Principle, etc. However, computers are not yet powerful enough to do that. So full simulation is not the answer. Instead, LSL allows residents to create content that can't be simulated currently within *SL*'s physics system.

Technically, the scripting language that you will be playing with is LSL2, as the language added to *LindenWorld* in August of 2002 was LSL. However, since only a few early alpha users ever had to build using the original LSL, the current language is simply referred to as LSL. The current language is far more powerful and easier to use than the original, so be glad that you never had to play with the first one!

YOUR FIRST SCRIPT

```
default
{
    state_entry()
    {
        llSay(0, "Hello, Avatar!");
    }

    touch_start(integer total_number)
    {
        llSay(0, "Touched.");
    }
}
```

Figure 9.1: The "Hello, Avatar!" script

OK, so you are ready to take the first step. Great! Fire up *Second Life* and go somewhere you can build, such as a sandbox or land you own. Create a box on the ground and select it. Select the Content tab of the Build window and click on the New Script button. The Script Editing window will pop open with the default "Hello, Avatar!" script (Figure 9.1). We'll break down the script in a moment, but for now click the Save button on the lower right of the window. Two lines will appear in the bottom of the window—first "Compile successful, saving…" and then "Save complete." The box then chats "Hello, Avatar!" at you. If you close the Build window and right-click on the box, the script will respond with "Touched."

Congratulations! You have created your first script within *Second Life*! So, what have you done?

Let's break down the script. Right-click the box to pull up the pie menu and select Edit. Again, click on the Content tab. The box will now contain one item, called New Script. Double-clicking on New Script will reopen the Script Editing window. Now we can look at the script:

```
default
{
    state _ entry()
    {
        llSay(0, "Hello, Avatar!");
    }

    touch _ start(integer total _ number)
    {
    llSay(0, "Touched.");
    }
}
```

Even if you've programmed before, few of the keywords will be familiar you to you, so let's break them down one at a time.

The keyword `default` indicates which state the LSL program will begin executing in. You will learn what states are and that LSL programs can have multiple states later in this chapter, but for now you need only know that every LSL program must have at least one state and that it is labeled `default`.

The curly braces, { and }, that follow `default` encapsulate the event handlers within that state—in this case `state _ entry` and `touch _ start`. The `state _ entry` event is triggered whenever execution enters that state, so in our example as soon as you clicked Save to upload the script to the simulator and attach it to the object, the LSL program began to execute and entered the default state. This triggered the `state _ entry` event, meaning that any code sitting within the `state _ entry` was run.

In our example, the only code was the library function `llSay`. `llSay` allows a script to chat text, much like an avatar, onto a channel of its choosing. Channel 0 is the channel that all avatars chat onto and listen to, so by saying "Hello, Avatar!" onto channel 0, the script ensures that any avatars nearby can hear it. What `llSay` does is controlled by the arguments within the parenthesis that follow `llSay`, in this case the integer 0 and the string `Hello, Avatar`. We'll talk about arguments more later.

Of course, what if you forget what the arguments for `llSay` are? One option is to visit the LSL Wiki (`http://lslwiki.net/lslwiki/wakka.php?wakka=HomePage`) or search "llSay" on Google. Fortunately, there is an even easier way, which is to hover your cursor over the word "llSay" in the Script Editor window. This will pop up the following tooltip and remind you what `llSay` does and is looking for:

```
llSay(integer channel, string msg)
Say msg on channel
```

The second event handler is `touch _ start`. Recall that when we clicked on the box, it chatted "Touched." in response? This is what the `touch _ start` event handler does. It is triggered when

CHAPTER 1
CHAPTER 2
CHAPTER 3
CHAPTER 4
CHAPTER 5
CHAPTER 6
CHAPTER 7
CHAPTER 8
CHAPTER 9
CHAPTER 10
CHAPTER 11
CHAPTER 12
CHAPTER 13
CHAPTER 14
CHAPTER 15
APPENDICES

an avatar begins clicking on the object. Again, the only code that exists within the event handler is the `llSay` library function, which we covered a moment ago.

Now let's start making this script our own. If you don't have the Script Editor up, open it by selecting the box, going to the Contents tab, and double-clicking on New Script. Clicking anywhere within the window allows you to edit the text of the script, so go ahead and change "Avatar" in "Hello, Avatar!" to your name. For me, that would be, "Hello, Cory!" As soon as you change the text, the Save button lights up to indicate that the script in the text window does not match the script that has been loaded up to your box. Click the Save button to recompile and save the script.

You should see the same sequence of "Compile successful, saving…" and then "Save complete." displayed in the bottom of the editor and then the box should chat your name at you. Well done!

But what if you wanted to go back to "Hello, Avatar!"? Fortunately, the text editor supports both undo and redo. Click in the text-editor window and hit Control-Z to undo your change. You'll see your name replaced by the text "Avatar" and the Save button lights up since the script has again changed. If you want to redo the changes, use Control-Y.

Remember that until you hit Save, your changes exist only in the text editor and haven't actually been uploaded into *Second Life*. When working on really complicated or critical scripts, it is often a good idea to use a text editor outside of *SL* and then cut and paste the text into *SL*, since that way you'll always have backups. The LSL Wiki has a list of external editors that have syntax highlighting for LSL (`http://lslwiki.net/lslwiki/wakka.php?wakka=AlternativeEditors`).

It is also important to realize that once you have added a script to an object, the script will remain on the object, even if you derez and rez the object into and out of your inventory. If you want to remove the script permanently, the best way is to delete it from the object's inventory.

To fully understand the connection between the text you type and what actually runs on *Second Life*, you need to dig a little deeper into LSL.

DEEPER INTO LSL

Now we'll focus on compilation, uploading, and execution (Figure 9.2). LSL is a scripting language that runs server-side, on a piece of software called the simulator. The simulator does just what its name implies—it simulates the virtual world of *Second Life*. Each simulator runs everything for 16 acres of virtual land—buildings, physics, and of course, scripts. While you manipulate the script text in a form that is somewhat easy to read, the actual code that runs on the simulator is compiled. A compiler is a piece of software that takes the text version of the script and converts it into something that can

CHAPTER 1
CHAPTER 2
CHAPTER 3
CHAPTER 4
CHAPTER 5
CHAPTER 6
CHAPTER 7
CHAPTER 8
CHAPTER 9
CHAPTER 10
CHAPTER 11
CHAPTER 12
CHAPTER 13
CHAPTER 14
CHAPTER 15
APPENDICES

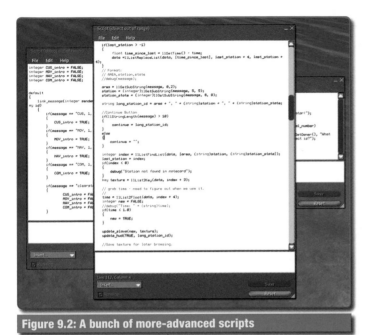

Figure 9.2: A bunch of more-advanced scripts

Figure 9.3: ERROR: Syntax Error

actually run. In the case of LSL, the compiler exists within the *Second Life* viewer itself. In the future, it is likely that the compiler will move from the viewer into the *Second Life* simulators, but where the code is compiled isn't very important. What matters is that the text is converted into a form that can run on the simulators.

Compilers also serve the function of detecting errors in the code you've just written. Although compilers can't detect all errors, it can detect common mistakes like syntax errors (Figure 9.3). Let's return to our "Hello, Avatar!" script. We can introduce a syntax error in many ways, but one example would be to remove the trailing brace, }, from the end of the state _ entry event. Since we have modified the text, the Save button lights up; click on it to attempt to compile the text. Rather than the "Compile successful, saving…" and then "Save complete." we've become accustomed to, we instead see "(7, 4) : ERROR : Syntax error" and the cursor moves to the first letter of the touch _ start event.

What does all this mean? The "(7, 4)" tells us that the error is at or near row 7, column 4 of the script, which we also know because the cursor has been positioned there. The "Syntax error" tells us that we've probably made a relatively simple typing error. If we examine our script, we see that the braces don't match. The compiler, upon reaching the touch _ start event, was expecting a trailing brace, so it flagged this as an error and stopped compiling the script.

Notice something else. If you exit the Build tool and click on the box, it fails to respond with "Touched." When a script fails to compile, *Second Life* stops executing the script on the target object. This is to reduce confusion and prevent broken or mismatched scripts from continuing to operate with *Second Life*. Simply add the trailing brace back in and save the change to both fix the error and to recompile the script.

When a script properly compiles, it generates LSL bytecode. Bytecode is a simple form that is relatively easy to execute. In the future, LSL may compile to a different form for execution, but that won't change how you write scripts. It will simply change how *Second Life* handles things under the hood. Why would we (at Linden) be contemplating these types of changes? Performance, primarily. LSL currently executes quite slowly, so we will continue to make changes to improve what you can do within LSL.

Either way, once the compiled code is on a simulator, it can actually be executed. Execution is simply the process of checking to see whether the script needs to do anything. In our example script, when an avatar clicks on the box, *Second Life* checks to see if any `touch` event handlers exist. Since one does (`touch _ start`), the code within the handler executes. Once that code is complete, the script goes to sleep until it needs to do something else.

This process of doing work only when required is key to both how LSL is structured and to writing good LSL scripts. It requires you to understand states and events, however. We'll discuss states first. As was covered earlier, all LSL scripts need to have at least one state, denoted by the `default` keyword. A state is a collection of code between the opening and closing braces of the state. In its simplest form, a script has a single state and all of its code lives there.

For example, imagine that you are creating a script to manage a very simple door that you touch to open or close. Using states can clarify what your code does:

```
// default state is closed
default
{
    touch _ start(integer tnum)
    {
        // insert code to open the door here
        // . . .
        state open;
    }
}

state open
{
    touch _ start(integer tnum)
    {
        // insert code to close the door here
        // . . .
        state default;
    }
}
```

Note that this is different from the traditional way of writing this, where you would maintain whether the door was open or closed in a global variable, something like this:

```
// default state is closed
integer is_closed = TRUE;

default
{
   touch_start(integer tnum)
   {
      if (is_closed == TRUE)
      {
         // insert code to open the door here
         // . . .
         is_closed = FALSE;
      }
      else
      {
         // insert code to close the door here
         // . . .
         is_closed = TRUE;
      }
   }
}
```

CHAPTER 1
CHAPTER 2
CHAPTER 3
CHAPTER 4
CHAPTER 5
CHAPTER 6
CHAPTER 7
CHAPTER 8
CHAPTER 9

CHAPTER 10
CHAPTER 11
CHAPTER 12
CHAPTER 13
CHAPTER 14
CHAPTER 15
APPENDICES

In this simple case, it may look like the global variable option is easier, but when other behavior also has to change between the open and closed state, splitting the code into multiple states is much simpler than having to wrap everything in if statements.

These code samples illustrate some other basics of LSL syntax. First, the "//" denotes a comment. A comment allows you add text to your script to remind you of why you wrote the code a particular way, to lay groundwork for later coding (such as "insert code to open the door here"), or to make it easier for someone else to follow your work. Note that only the text to the right of the "//" is part of the comment, allowing comments to be added to a line that contains code. For example, in the line

```
state open // this is entered when the door opens
```

"// this is entered when the door opens" is the comment.

Second, we introduce global variables and the variable type "integer." Global variables, like is_closed, are available anywhere in the code. They are similar to global variables in other programming languages, such as C, and they can be any of the types available to LSL (see the section "What Are Types?"). LSL is a statically and strongly typed language, meaning that variables are given types when created and generally require typecasting to convert between types.

FROM LINDEN LAB
AN ANIMATION OVERVIEW

"Animations are the personality of an avatar. They're the finishing touches after you've gotten your hair, outfit, and body just right. Sure, you could use the standard animations to get your point across, but with patience, software, and a bit of luck, you can bring your favorite real-world movements into your *Second Life* experience.

CHAPTER 9

THE ORIGINS
OF LSL

YOUR FIRST
SCRIPT

**DEEPER INTO
LSL**

EVEN DEEPER
INTO LSL

CONNECTING
TO THE WORLD

PHYSICS
AND MORE

CONTROLS
AND DISPLAYS

HOW TO
LEARN MORE

"The first thing needed is software to create the animation outside of *Second Life*. There are several free options; for example, Avimator, Slat, DAZ Studio, Blender, and QAvimator, as well as commercial software like Poser, Maya, and Posemaker. Each system has its own advantages, but all make superb animations. *SL* uses the BVH motion format, so be sure to export this way.

"The jargon related to animations is the same regardless of the software. A key frame is a frame in the animation sequence with a specified joint location, and the program will fill in all the frames between key frames to create a smooth motion. A spline is the set of equations the program uses to generate this smooth motion; if you find that your animation is moving past the key frame or in other odd ways, breaking the spline on the key frames often fixes the problem. Inverse kinematics (IK) is an option that allows you to move the entire arm or leg by moving the hand or foot along the three axes, but if you turn this option on and off, it is important to check your key-frame splines again. Playing with IK can create amazing motions, but it can also have difficult-to-predict consequences, so always save before changing the IK settings.

"Now that you have the software, check that the avatar loaded into it is compatible with *SL*. *SL* cannot accept information from finger, toe, genitalia, or facial joints, so you may have to use an imported or outdated avatar. You can also edit the key frames after creating the animation to delete the information from these joints.

"Let's animate! All joints used in your animation must be in a different position between the first frame and the second frame. The second frame is the first frame you will see in *SL*, and a good first frame often twists the avatar into a ball. If you want to exclude a body part from the animation so that only part of the *SL* movements are overridden, the excluded joints should be in the same position in both the first and second frames.

"In the second frame, the avatar should be in the starting pose for the animation. Depending on your software, each joint can be dragged by the mouse into position or selected and then moved through parameter dials.

"The next key frames will be the different poses your avatar will move through to complete the animation. Remember that humans rarely coordinate moves precisely, so when moving your avatar from one pose to another, set different body parts to arrive in the target pose a few seconds within one another.

"There are a few different ways you can end your animation. The most common way is with the same pose as the second frame (allowing for a seamless loop to be uploaded), or in a unique pose from which the avatar will shift back into normal *SL* animations. You may also create an animation with a beginning animation, a section with matching key frames at each end that can be used as a loop, and a leading-out animation. If you plan on creating this type of animation, write down the numbers the loop begins and ends at.

"Once you have your animation done, export it as a BVH motion and log into *SL*. *SL*'s uploading process allows you to finish customizing the animation. Here you set a priority level for your animation. The higher the number, the higher the priority. The default animations are a two, so to completely override the *SL* default, upload a three or four.

"Timing your loop can make or break an animation. Avoid a jerky animation with a bit of math. Each end of the looped section should have the exact same key frame, and dividing the key-frame number by the total number of frames will give you the in and out percents within a degree or two. Preview the animation a few times from different in and out percents to check the loop, and don't be afraid to make the matching key frames into two or three static frames to give yourself more leeway.

"Hand poses and facial expressions can be set at this stage, and beyond that, ease-in and ease-out settings define how fast your avatar will transition between animations. Now you can upload and begin testing your animation. The test server is a great place to practice. There you won't have to spend your hard earned Lindens getting that hand motion just right.

"There are some limits. Subtle movements aren't always picked up by *SL*, and animations are limited to 30 seconds. While you can upload an animation with 60 frames per second, users will likely only see between 15 and 20 frames per second, so animations are often best in this range. Full-body movements must come from the hip joint, not the body joint, and smaller- or larger-than-normal avatars will require custom animations to maintain the motion. The fastest way to get used to the quirks of the system is to dive right in and start testing it out for yourself. In no time, your avatar will be able to do your favorite dance move or develop a signature walk or strut as unique as the rest of you."

—Kiari Lefay and Leslie Havens

CHAPTER 1
CHAPTER 2
CHAPTER 3
CHAPTER 4
CHAPTER 5
CHAPTER 6
CHAPTER 7
CHAPTER 8
CHAPTER 9

CHAPTER 10
CHAPTER 11
CHAPTER 12
CHAPTER 13
CHAPTER 14
CHAPTER 15
APPENDICES

⬇ What Are Types?

A type determines what kind of data can be stored and LSL supports seven distinct types:

INTEGER

An integer is a whole number between −2,147,483,648 and 2,147,483,647. The following are some examples of integers in use:

```
integer int = -23; // in the language C, integers are called int. Don't be confused
    by this!
integer foo = 235632;
integer blar = 0;
```

CHAPTER 9

THE ORIGINS
OF LSL

YOUR FIRST
SCRIPT

DEEPER INTO
LSL

EVEN DEEPER
INTO LSL

CONNECTING
TO THE WORLD

PHYSICS
AND MORE

CONTROLS
AND DISPLAYS

HOW TO
LEARN MORE

FLOAT

This is a *floating-point* (or decimal) number with seven significant figures that can be positive or negative. The largest positive or smallest negative number that can be represented is ± 3.4028235E38 (around 34 with 37 zeros after it), while the smallest positive or largest negative number that can be represented is ± 1.17549351E-38 (0.0 followed by 36 zeros then 117549351). Floats (another name for floating-point numbers) are very accurate for numbers close to zero, but are less accurate for huge numbers. Examples of floats are as follows:

```
float e = 2.718128; // the decimal point indicates that this is a float
float f = 0.f; // a trailing ".f" can also be used
float one = 1; // even though the literal "1" is an integer, this assignment will
    work.
integer i_one = 1; // note: if (one == i_one) is a BAD idea! More on this later.
```

STRING

A string is a collection of characters, such as the following:

```
string name = "Exposition Linden";
string character = "c"; // single characters in LSL are just string
string number = "1"; // note: "1" != 1
```

VECTOR

A vector is three floats representing x, y, and z components. A vector is generally used as a position, velocity, acceleration, or color. All three values can be set simultaneously, or they can be set as individuals:

```
vector pos = <123.3, 54.0, 32>; // vectors will promote entries into floats
vector vel;
vel.x = 12.0; // this is much
vel.y = 23.0; // slower than initializing via a
vel.z = 36.0; // vector!!
```

LIST

Since LSL doesn't have arrays or structures, the primary method for storing collections of data is lists. All the other data types may be placed in lists (but a list can't be placed in a list). There are many different ways to work with lists; this chapter will cover some of them, and the LSL Wiki (http://lslwiki.net/lslwiki/wakka.php?wakka=list) has excellent examples. More on lists later.

ROTATION

A rotation is four floats representing the x, y, z, and s components of a quaternion rotation. Although quaternions are extremely complicated and often confusing, LSL allows them to be used without your having to master the underlying theory. We'll talk more on rotations later, and you can check out `http://lslwiki.net/lslwiki/wakka.php?wakka=rotation`. Here are some sample rotations:

```
rotation rot = <0.0, 0.0, 0.0, 1.0>; // Rotations in LSL are internally normalized
rotation rot = <32, 2, -9, 128>; // even if your initialization is not
```

KEY

A *UUID*, or Universally Unique Identifier, is used to identify many objects within *Second Life*. Like rotations, keys allow you to use UUIDs without having to write a lot of code to support them. We'll go over details later, but you can also consult `http://lslwiki.net/lslwiki/wakka.php?wakka=key`.

```
// you almost never need to initialize keys with literals like this.
key object_id = "00000000-0000-0000-0000-000000000000";
```

Typecasting is used when variables of different types are assigned to each other. LSL supports two implicit conversions: integer to float and string to key. These allow the following statements to work correctly:

```
float my_float = 4; // although you really should write this as 4.0
// data between " and " can be either a string or a key.
key object_id = "00000000-0000-0000-0000-000000000000";
```

For any other conversions, explicit typecasting is needed. Like C, a typecast is the type you wish to cast to inside parentheses:

```
integer bad_pi = (integer)3.1425926; // bad_pi == 3
float good_pi = (float)"3.1415926"; // good_pi == 3.1415926
```

Now let's discuss the `if` statements. The `if` statement is the simplest of the conditional, or flow control, statements in LSL. If the code within the parentheses evaluates to `TRUE`, then the code within the braces is executed. The `if` statement is not the only type of expression in LSL for flow control. Flow control allows you to make decisions about whether pieces of code are executed (for more detail, consult `http://lslwiki.net/lslwiki/wakka.php?wakka=FlowControl`). LSL's flow-control statements are as follows:

```
integer expression = TRUE; // TRUE is an integer constant in LSL. TRUE == 1
if (expression)
{
    // do something if expression == TRUE
}
else
{
    // do something else if expression == FALSE
}

if (expression)
    // do something in one line
else
    // do something else in one line
```

CHAPTER 1
CHAPTER 2
CHAPTER 3
CHAPTER 4
CHAPTER 5
CHAPTER 6
CHAPTER 7
CHAPTER 8
CHAPTER 9
CHAPTER 10
CHAPTER 11
CHAPTER 12
CHAPTER 13
CHAPTER 14
CHAPTER 15
APPENDICES

CHAPTER 9

THE ORIGINS
OF LSL

YOUR FIRST
SCRIPT

DEEPER INTO
LSL

EVEN DEEPER
INTO LSL

CONNECTING
TO THE WORLD

PHYSICS
AND MORE

CONTROLS
AND DISPLAYS

HOW TO
LEARN MORE

```
while(expression)
{
    // do something until expression == FALSE.   FALSE == 0
}

do
{
    // do something until expression == FALSE.   FALSE == 0
} while(expression);

integer i; // an iterator

for (i = 0; i < 100; i++)
{
    // do something 100 times, where i starts at 0 and counts
    // up to 99
    // this code will exit when i == 100
}

@again; // this is a label
// this code will be executed forever
jump again; // move execution to the @again label
```

There are two additional flow-control mechanisms. The first is the `state` transition, which we already covered. The second is the `return` command, which we will cover in the section "Advanced Language Features."

In all of the flow-control examples, the decision of which path to take was determined by the value of an expression. In LSL, an expression is a combination of operators and functions. Functions will be explained in more detail in the "Advanced Language Features" section. Operators are divided into several broad categories. As with other categories, the LSL Wiki covers this in great detail (`http://lslwiki.net/lslwiki/wakka.php?wakka=operators`).

⬇ OPERATOR TYPES

Operators take one or two values, perform a mathematical operation on them, and produce a new value.

UNARY

Unary operators are arithmetic operators that modify one value, as in the following example:

```
integer  count = 1; // create a new integer variable and assign it the value of 1
    count++; // the "++" operator adds 1 to "count" and assigns the result to
    "count"
llSay(0, (string)count); // says "2"  -- note the type conversion
```

BINARY

Binary operators are arithmetic operators that act on two values to produce a third, as shown here:

```
integer a = 5;
integer b = 2;
integer c = a + b; // compute a plus b, so c = 7
```

BOOLEAN

Boolean operators always generate TRUE (1) or FALSE (0) results:

```
integer a = 5;
integer b = 2;
integer c = a != b; // "!=" returns TRUE if its arguments are not the same.
```

BITWISE

Bitwise operators act on the bitfields that make up integers. Here are some examples:

```
integer a = 5; // 0x101 in binary
integer b = 2; // 0x010
integer c = a | b; // a or b = 0x111, so c = 7
```

ASSIGNMENT

Finally we have the assignment operators, which take the result of an expression and assign it to a variable. In addition, LSL supports several variants of the assignment operator that perform an arithmetic operation along with assignment, as in the following example:

```
integer a = 5; // assigns 5 to a
a += 5; // adds 5 to a, then assigns the result, so a = 10
```

EVEN DEEPER INTO LSL

Let's look a little deeper in to LSL. One of the most powerful features of a programming language is the ability to define and then call *functions*, chunks of code that can be reused in different contexts. This listing defines a few functions that provide some useful vector operations.

CHAPTER 1
CHAPTER 2
CHAPTER 3
CHAPTER 4
CHAPTER 5
CHAPTER 6
CHAPTER 7
CHAPTER 8
CHAPTER 9

CHAPTER 10
CHAPTER 11
CHAPTER 12
CHAPTER 13
CHAPTER 14
CHAPTER 15
APPENDICES

```
// Get the vector from position a to position b.
// If we call the vector returned by this function 'c' then
// a + c = b.  Since vector addition and subtraction work
// similar to the way it works with number, c = b - a
vector vectorTo(vector a, vector b)
{
    return b - a;
}

// Get the vector from this object's current position
// to position 'dest'
vector vectorFromMeTo(vector dest)
{
    return vectorTo(llGetPos(), dest);
}

// Get the direction vector with a length of 1 meter from
// this object to position 'dest'
vector directionFromMeTo(vector dest)
{
    return llVecNorm(vectorFromMeTo(dest));
}

// Return the distance from this object to position 'dest'
float distanceTo(vector dest)
{
    return llVecMag(vectorFromMeTo(dest));
}

default
{
    state _ entry()
    {
        llSay(0, "The distance from this object to the region corner is: " +
            (string) distanceTo(<0.0, 0.0, 0.0>) +
            " meters");
    }
}
```

The function `vectorTo` does a simple calculation:

```
vector vectorTo(vector a, vector b)
{
    return b - a;
}
```

A function can be called from a state or another function to do some work. The first line of the function gives the return type of the function (in this case, a vector), then the name of the function (in this case, `vectorTo`), then the arguments the function takes (in this case two vectors, named `a` and b). *Arguments* are the values that a function works on. If the function doesn't need to return a result, the return type can be omitted. If the function doesn't need any arguments, they too can be omitted, as shown here.

```
// This function takes no arguments and returns no value
sayHi()
{
    llSay(0, "Hello there");
}
```

The body of a function is enclosed in a set of curly braces, {}. The body consists of any number of LSL statements. If the function needs to return a value, it must contain a *return statement.* A return statement stops the function immediately and, optionally, returns the return statement value. A function always stops at either a return statement or the closing curly brace, and the script continues running where the function was first called.

LSL uses *call by value*; this means that functions get copies of the arguments passed to them. A function can do whatever it wants with its arguments, without changing any values in the event handler or function that called it. Functions can call other functions. Here the `vectorFromMeTo` function calls two other functions, the `vectorTo function` defined earlier in the script, and the built-in function `llGetPos`.

```
vector vectorFromMeTo(vector dest)
{
    return vectorTo(llGetPos(), dest);
}
```

The following code shows a more involved script that detects if a resident is currently online. It uses *global variables*, variables that can be set or used in any function or event handler to store the UUID of the resident to check for, as well as two time values. It defines three functions: one that queries the online status of a resident, one that performs whatever action we want to do when the resident is online, and one that performs the action we want when the resident is offline.

```
// Script to check if a resident is online or offline.

// The key of the resident to check is stored in this global
// variable. It is set when a resident clicks and holds
// on this object for more that minHoldTime seconds.
key residentToCheck = NULL _ KEY;

// Amount of time in second a resident must click and hold
// on this object to change the residentToCheck variable
float minHoldTime = 3.0;

// How often (in seconds) to check to see if the resident
// is online.
float checkTimeout = 5.0;

// Query the online status of resident with UUID resident _ id.
// causes a dataserver event
queryIfOnline(key resident _ id)
{
    llRequestAgentData(id, DATA _ ONLINE);
}

// This function is called when residentToCheck is online,
// it's called over and over again, every checkTimeout seconds
doIfOnline()
{
    llSay(0, "online");
}

// This function is called when residentToCheck is offline,
// it's called over and over again, every checkTimeout seconds
doIfOffline()
```

CHAPTER 1
CHAPTER 2
CHAPTER 3
CHAPTER 4
CHAPTER 5
CHAPTER 6
CHAPTER 7
CHAPTER 8
CHAPTER 9

CHAPTER 10
CHAPTER 11
CHAPTER 12
CHAPTER 13
CHAPTER 14
CHAPTER 15
APPENDICES

```
{
    llSay(0, "offline");
}

default
{
    // This event is called when the script starts running
    state _ entry()
    {
        // request a timer event every checkTimeout seconds
        llSetTimerEvent(checkTimeout);
    }

    timer()
    {
        // if the script has residentToCheck set, check
        if (residentToCheck != NULL _ KEY)
        {
            queryIfOnline(residentToCheck);
        }
    }

    // This event is called when we have data about the resident's
    // online status, data is either "1" or "0"
    dataserver(key queryid, string data)
    {
        if ((integer)data == 1)
        {
            // resident is online, call the online function
            doIfOnline();
        }
        else
        {
            // resident is offline, call the offline function
            doIfOffline();
        }
    }

    // called when a resident starts touching this object
    touch _ start(integer n)
    {
        // Reset the scripts timer, calling llGetTime will
        // give the number of seconds since llResetTime was
        // called.
        llResetTime();
    }

    // called when a resident stops touching this object
    touch _ end(integer n)
    {
        // if the resident clicked and held on the object for more
        // than minHoldTime, store that resident's key
        if (llGetTime() > minHoldTime)
        {
            // The llDetected... functions give information about
            // the resident touching the object.
            residentToCheck = llDetectedKey(0);
            llSay(0, "Now checking the status of " + llDetectedName(0));
        }
    }
}
```

llAbs
llAcos
llAddToLandBanList
llAddToLandPassList
llAdjustSoundVolum...
llAllowInventoryDrop
llAngleBetween
llApplyImpulse
llApplyRotationalImp...
llAsin
llAtan2
llAttachToAvatar
llAvatarOnSitTarget
llAxes2Rot
llAxisAngle2Rot
llBase64ToInteger
llBase64ToString
llBreakAllLinks
llBreakLink
llCSV2List
llCeil
llClearCameraParams
llCloseRemoteDataC...
llCloud
llCollisionFilter
llCollisionSound
llCollisionSprite
llCos
llCreateLink
llDeleteSubList
llDeleteSubString
llDetachFromAvatar
llDetectedGrab
llDetectedGroup
llDetectedKey
llDetectedLinkNumbe...
llDetectedName
llDetectedOwner
llDetectedPos
llDetectedRot
llDetectedType
llDetectedVel
llDialog
llDie
llDumpList2String
llEdgeOfWorld
llEjectFromLand
llEmail
llEscapeURL
llEuler2Rot
llFabs
llFloor
llForceMouselook
llFrand
llGetAccel
llGetAgentInfo
llGetAgentSize
llGetAlpha

Figure 9.4: Library-function list

In addition to user defined functions just described, LSL provides a number of *library functions* (Figure 9.4). They are built-in functions that are there to perform common tasks or to provide functionality that would be difficult to write in LSL directly. More than 300 functions are built into LSL, and more are being added regularly.) For a comprehensive description of all of the functions, check out `http://lslwiki.net/lslwiki/wakka.php?wakka=functions`.) It is important to recognize that LSL functions operate just like the user-defined functions. They are available within any event handler or user-generated function, their arguments are passed by value, and they may or may not return a value. One additional aspect is that some of them have a delay value associated with them. This delay exists to protect *Second Life* from certain types of abuse.

CONNECTING TO THE WORLD

LSL's real power is in its ability to allow an object to communicate and interact with the rest of the world. To cover everything you can do with it would require a separate book, but the following should get you started.

CHAT

In our first example, we showed that an object can chat to the rest of the world using the `llSay` function. This is handy for communicating to people near the object, and it can also be useful for local object-to-object communication.

```
default
{
    state_entry()
    {
        llListen(0, "", llGetOwner(), "");
    }

    listen(integer channel, string name, key id, string message)
    {
        llSay(0, message);
    }
}
```

The preceding script is a simple chat repeater that illustrates the basics of scripted chat. All it does is repeat everything the object's owner says. When the script starts, `llListen` sets up the `listen` event so that the object can listen for chat. `llListen` lets you filter what you want to listen for by chat channel, name, UUID, and message.

195

CHAPTER 9

THE ORIGINS
OF LSL

YOUR FIRST
SCRIPT

DEEPER INTO
LSL

EVEN DEEPER
INTO LSL

CONNECTING
TO THE WORLD

PHYSICS
AND MORE

CONTROLS
AND DISPLAYS

HOW TO
LEARN MORE

```
integer llListen(integer channel, string name, key id, string message)
```

In the example, the script listens on channel 0, which is the public chat channel that all avatars chat on. There are a few billion chat channels so that objects can chat to each other without fear of message collision. The name and message parameters are left blank in this case so the script will listen for all names and messages. `llGetOwner` returns the UUID of the owner, so in this case the script ends up listening for public chat made by the script's owner.

When the script "hears" something that matches the requirements set in `llListen`, the `listen` event will be triggered. In this case we just pass the message that was heard to `llSay`. Notice that even though the script listens on channel 0 and chats on channel 0, the script never hears its own messages.

Chat sent with `llSay` can be heard in a radius of 20 meters; alternatively, chat can be sent with `llWhisper` (10 meters) or `llShout` (100 meters). Chat sent with `llRegionSay` can be heard anywhere in the region, but this function cannot chat on the public chat channel, 0.

Because there are times when you want to use chat but keep it private, there is also `llOwnerSay`—a special chat that only the object's owner can hear.

IM

There are times when you want to send a message to someone who is not within Whisper, Say, or Shout radius, or you want to keep your message private. The easiest way to do this is through an instant message (IM). IMs can be "heard" anywhere in *Second Life*, but only by the intended recipient. To send an IM, you need to know the intended recipient's UUID.

```
llInstantMessage(key uuid, string message)
```

If the resident is offline, the message will be saved until they log in next. Objects cannot IM other objects.

SENSORS

Sensors allow you to gather information about avatars and objects near your object. Setting up a sensor is somewhat like setting up a listen for chat. When `llSensor` is called, the parameters filter out the results, and if there are any matches a `sensor` event is called. The major difference is that whereas `llListen` is continuous, `llSensor` is a single request. `llSensorRepeat` creates a sensor that fires periodically. The following script is an example using a sensor.

```
default
{
    state _ entry()
    {
//Set up a repeating sensor, that once a second looks for any
//avatars within a sphere with a 20 meter radius.
        llSensorRepeat("", "", AGENT, 20.0, PI, 1.0);
    }
```

```
        //A sensor returns the first 16 items detected.
        sensor(integer detectedCount)
        {
            // Say the names of everyone the sensor detects
            for(i=0;i<detectedCount;i++)
            {
                llSay(0, llDetectedName(i));
            }
        }
}
```

CHAPTER 1
CHAPTER 2
CHAPTER 3
CHAPTER 4
CHAPTER 5
CHAPTER 6
CHAPTER 7
CHAPTER 8
CHAPTER 9

CHAPTER 10
CHAPTER 11
CHAPTER 12
CHAPTER 13
CHAPTER 14
CHAPTER 15
APPENDICES

ADDITIONAL INFO
ANGLES, RADIANS, AND SENSORS

Angles in LSL are measured in radians. Radians are just a different way of measuring angles, like feet and meters are different ways of measuring distance. 360 degrees is equal to 2 pi radians (about 6.28), 180 degrees is pi radians (about 3.14). You can convert an angle in degrees to radians by multiplying it by the built-in constant RAD _ TO _ DEG, and you can convert degrees to radians by multiplying by DEG _ TO _ RAD.

```
integer deg = (PI / 4.0) * RAD _ TO DEG; // deg is 45
integer rad = 360 * DEG _ TO _ RAD; // rad is PI * 2
```

The fifth argument to llSensor and llSensorRepeat is an angle, the area to search in front of the object. The sensor functions search this angle to the left and to the right, so setting it to pi radians searches pi radians (180 degrees) to the left and pi radians to the right, for a full 360-degree sensor sweep.

⬇ PAY

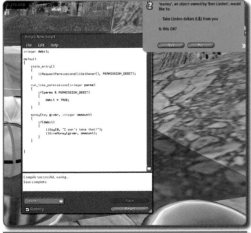

Figure 9.5: Giving and taking money

Scripts can also give and take L$ (Figure 9.5). This is handy for creating vendors, gambling games, and more. In order for an object to accept money, the script must have a money event:

```
default
{
    money(key giver, integer amount)
    {
        llSay(0,
            "Thanks for the " + (string)amount
                + "L$ donation!");
    }
}
```

197

CHAPTER 9

THE ORIGINS
OF LSL

YOUR FIRST
SCRIPT

DEEPER INTO
LSL

EVEN DEEPER
INTO LSL

CONNECTING
TO THE WORLD

PHYSICS
AND MORE

CONTROLS
AND DISPLAYS

HOW TO
LEARN MORE

Giving money via a scripted object is a bit more complicated. The script needs to request permission from the object's owner to debit L$ from their account.

```
default
{
    state _ entry()
    {
        llRequestPermissions(llGetOwner(), PERMISSION _ DEBIT);
    }

    touch _ start(integer number _ touching)
    {
        llGiveMoney(llDetectedKey(0), 1);
    }
}
```

The preceding script gives L$1 to whomever clicks on the object that's using `llGiveMoney`. This script will not work unless when the `llRequestPermissions` function is called, the owner grants permission to let the object give money.

⬇ INVENTORY

An object has an inventory (Figure 9.6)—this is where the script lives, but it can also contain most of the things a resident's Inventory can. The script can give, take, and use inventory. For instance, a gun would use `llRezObject` to rez a bullet from its inventory. A vendor would use `llGiveInventory` to give a single item, or `llGiveInventoryList` to give a folder.

The following is an example of a drop box that shows how to give and take inventory:

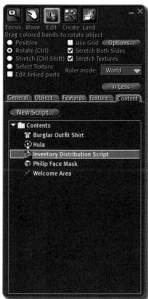

Figure 9.6: Object inventory

```
default
{
    state _ entry()
    {
        //Allows anyone to drop inventory
        llAllowInventoryDrop(TRUE);
    }

    touch _ start(integer number _ touched)
    {
        //Only the owner can take it out.
        if(llDetectedKey(0) == llGetOwner())
        {
            //Make a list of all the objects in the inventory
            list contents = [];
            integer i;
            for(i=0;i<llGetInventoryNumber(INVENTORY _ OBJECT);i++)
            {
                contents += llGetInventoryName(INVENTORY _ OBJECT, i);
            }
```

```
            //Give all the objects in a folder
            llGiveInventoryList(llGetOwner(), "Drop Box", contents);
        }
    }

    changed(integer change)
    {
        if (
          (change & CHANGED _ INVENTORY) ||
          (change & CHANGED _ ALLOWED _ DROP)
          )
        {
            llSay(0, "Thanks for adding an item to my inventory!");
        }
    }
}
```

CHAPTER 1

CHAPTER 2

CHAPTER 3

CHAPTER 4

CHAPTER 5

CHAPTER 6

CHAPTER 7

CHAPTER 8

CHAPTER 9

CHAPTER 10

CHAPTER 11

CHAPTER 12

CHAPTER 13

CHAPTER 14

CHAPTER 15

APPENDICES

PHYSICS AND MORE

Second Life has a server-side physics simulation, which means objects will fall, bounce, and collide correctly. A script can change how the built-in physics affect an object.

By default, an object in *Second Life* is "pinned." This means that if you lift it up and let go, it will not fall down. To make it fall, you can set its status to physical:

```
default
{
    state _ entry()
    {
        llSetStatus(STATUS _ PHYSICS, TRUE);
    }
}
```

An object can also change its collision status by becoming "phantom" with the `llSetStatus` function:

```
llSetStatus(STATUS _ PHANTOM, TRUE);
```

Phantom objects to not collide, so physical objects and residents can move through them.

APPLYING FORCES

By changing the forces on a physical object, you can control how it moves. There are several ways to do this; the easiest way is to use `llSetForce` or `llApplyImpulse`. These work just like your high-school physics class taught you: a force is a continuous push, and an impulse is a single, instant push. A simple example:

CHAPTER 9

THE ORIGINS
OF LSL

YOUR FIRST
SCRIPT

DEEPER INTO
LSL

EVEN DEEPER
INTO LSL

CONNECTING
TO THE WORLD

PHYSICS
AND MORE

CONTROLS
AND DISPLAYS

HOW TO
LEARN MORE

```
default
{
    touch _ start(integer touched)
    {
        // bounces the object up in the air.
        llApplyImpulse(<0,0,100>, FALSE);
    }
}
```

⬇ VEHICLES

Figure 9.7: A scripted airplane in flight

For more control, there is a suite of functions that let you change over 20 parameters to alter every aspect of how a physical object moves, from buoyancy to friction (Figure 9.7). The vehicle code is much more complex but correspondingly more powerful. For more information, check out the vehicle page at `http://lslwiki.net/lslwiki/wakka.php?wakka=vehicles`.

⬇ CONTROLS AND DISPLAYS

You probably don't want to interact with an object via text and clicks alone. Flying a jet across a sim will be tough if you have to type "up" over and over again. Likewise, no one wants to watch your slide show if it is just text describing the pictures you put inside.

⬇ TAKING CONTROL

A scripted object can take over the normal movement controls from an avatar. This makes it easy to create guns that shoot when you click the mouse, or a car that drives when you use the arrow keys.

A script needs to request permission to take over the controls from the avatar. In the special case of attachments and vehicles, permission is granted automatically, but the script still needs to make the request.

The following example is a portion of a very basic gun script:

```
// Chat a random gun onomatopoeia
fire()
{
    list noises = ["Blam!", "Kapow!", "Bang!", "Peechoo!"];
    llSay(0,
```

```
            // This is a good way to get a random element from a list
            llList2String(
              noises,
              (integer)llFrand(llGetListLength(noises))
              )
            );
}

default
{
    // If we attach the gun, request permissions; if we
    // detach, release control.
    attach(key attachedAgent)
    {
        if (attachedAgent != NULL_KEY)
        {
            llRequestPermissions(
                llGetOwner(), PERMISSION_TAKE_CONTROLS);
        }
        else
        {
            llReleaseControls();
        }
    }

    // When permission is granted, the run_time_permissions
    // event is triggered. Use this as a cue to take controls.
    run_time_permissions(integer permissions)
    {
        if (permissions == PERMISSION_TAKE_CONTROLS)
        {
            //We want to take the left mouse button in mouselook.
            llTakeControls(CONTROL_ML_LBUTTON, TRUE, FALSE);
        }
    }

    control(key name, integer levels, integer edges)
    {
        // After taking controls, if those controls are used,
        // take the appropriate action.
        if (
            ((edges & CONTROL_ML_LBUTTON)) &&
            ((levels & CONTROL_ML_LBUTTON))
            )
        {
            //  If left mouse button is pressed, fire
            fire();
        }
    }
}
```

⬇ DISPLAY

Scripts can also control the appearance of an object. Probably the most used example of this is changing textures for things like slide shows. To change a texture, it is easiest to use a texture in the object's inventory. If you have a bunch of great snapshots, you can drop them into a box with the following script to watch them display:

```
integer i;  // counter used in the timer() event

default
{
    state _ entry()
    {
        // Change image every 10 seconds
        llSetTimerEvent(10.0);
    }

     timer()
    {
        // Make sure there is at least one texture in inventory
        if (llGetInventoryNumber(INVENTORY _ TEXTURE) > 0)
        {
            // Use the modulus operator, %, to make i cycle
            // over a range of values. If the number of textures
            // was 5, the value of i would be
            // 0, 1, 2, 3, 4, 0, 1, 2, 3, 4, 0, 1...
            i =
                (i + 1) % llGetInventoryNumber(INVENTORY _ TEXTURE);

            // set the texture on the "0" face of the object.
            llSetTexture(
                llGetInventoryName(INVENTORY _ TEXTURE, i), 0);
        }
    }
}
```

HOW TO LEARN MORE

If this brief introduction to LSL has left your head spinning, don't worry! If you haven't programmed before, the promise and power of adding code—of adding behavior—to objects in *Second Life* can be overwhelming. Even if you are an experienced software developer, the quirks and unique aspects of LSL can take a while to wrap your brain around, but once you do you will have opened up entirely new worlds of possibilities. No matter what, you're going to be hungry for more—more knowledge, more examples, more people to learn with. Fortunately all of these exist, both within *Second Life* and on the Web.

Let's begin inside *Second Life*. The Event Calendar is a great place to start looking for help about LSL. Every week there are many classes on LSL, ranging from Scripting 101 to Advanced Vehicles. Not only do these classes provide concrete information on the mechanics of scripting in *Second Life*, but they also can connect you to the community of scripters within the world. By meeting the other students and instructors, you can build a strong network of friends and fellow scripters to question, to collaborate with, and to find new challenges.

There are many different communities of scripters within *Second Life*, from the professional content developers doing large real-world projects to the beginners gathering to play in the sandboxes. You are certain to find one that matches your skills and interests. Like other forms of creation within *Second Life*, scripting is the most fun when done with others, so use the time when you're learning LSL to meet other people and groups.

Classes in *Second Life* are only one resource for learning about scripting. Two *Second Life* forums exist as resources for scripters; The Scripting Library forum (`http://forums.secondlife.com/forumdisplay.php?f=15`) acts as a repository for various scripts, new ideas, and the basic building blocks every scripter would otherwise have to reinvent. The Scripting Tips forum (`http://forums.secondlife.com/forumdisplay.php?f=54`) allows scripters to share knowledge on a daily basis. Both forums see daily contributions by a many scripters, and both are worth reading and contributing to. They will connect you to other scripters rapidly.

A more specialized support option is the *Second Life* Scripters mailing list (`http://secondlife.com/community/mailinglists.php`). It tends to cover very specific questions about or problems with LSL, often before they show up on either the forums or the LSL Wiki. The mailing list is a good place to lurk as an intermediate scripter, but really it's best used by expert scripters looking to connect with other advanced scripters. However, like mailing lists in general, it isn't the best resource for general searches or broad questions. Fortunately, another option exists.

That resource is the LSL Wiki (`http://lslwiki.net/lslwiki/`), a wonderful resource for all things *Second Life*. Beyond the most comprehensive documentation of all LSL functions (`http://lslwiki.net/lslwiki/wakka.php?wakka=functions`), it also calls out known bugs (`http://lslwiki.net/lslwiki/wakka.php?wakka=KnownBugs`) and gotchas (`http://lslwiki.net/lslwiki/wakka.php?wakka=annoyances`). Moreover, it has numerous tutorials (`http://lslwiki.net/lslwiki/wakka.php?wakka=LSLTutorials`) and links to many of the scripting groups, mentors, and teachers (`http://lslwiki.net/lslwiki/wakka.php?wakka=ScriptingMentors`) in *Second Life*. Most importantly, the LSL Wiki is a wiki, so it is constantly being added to, always being updated by the *Second Life* community. As you begin to learn about LSL, you should become familiar with the LSL Wiki and contribute to it yourself. It is yet another way to meet other scripters and to become part of the LSL community within *Second Life*.

A final resource for LSL is the *Second Life* Education Wiki (`http://www.simteach.com/wiki/index.php?title=Second_Life_Education_Wiki`). The *Second Life* Education Wiki provides up-to-date information on the education and research projects going on in *Second Life*. Educators and researchers provide both a resource to scripters and a market for specialized scripts and builds. Campus:*Second Life* (`http://www.simteach.com/wiki/index.php?title=Campus:Second_Life`), as well as other university and education builds within *SL*, often brings groups into contact with LSL, either because their students are exploring LSL or because of specialized needs. As you become more confident with LSL, you will find educators to be some of the most collaborative and open scripters in *Second Life*. If you are looking for interesting and unusual projects to apply your budding scripting skills to, look no further than the Education Wiki.

Of course, no book can keep up with the resources constantly appearing on the Web in support of LSL, so new options will have appeared by the time this book is on shelves. Seek them out!

CHAPTER 1
CHAPTER 2
CHAPTER 3
CHAPTER 4
CHAPTER 5
CHAPTER 6
CHAPTER 7
CHAPTER 8
CHAPTER 9
CHAPTER 10
CHAPTER 11
CHAPTER 12
CHAPTER 13
CHAPTER 14
CHAPTER 15
APPENDICES

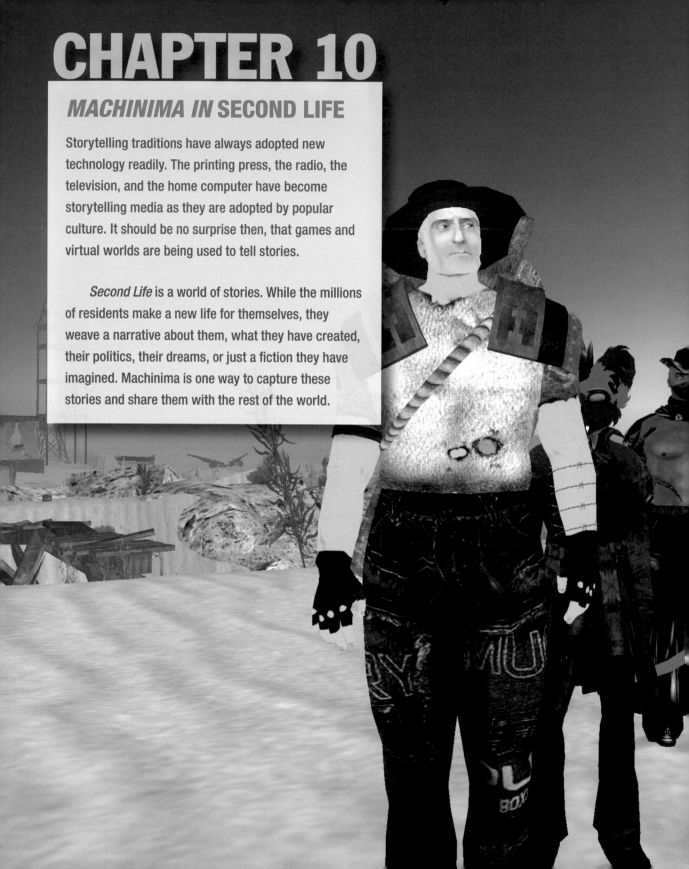

CHAPTER 10

MACHINIMA IN SECOND LIFE

Storytelling traditions have always adopted new technology readily. The printing press, the radio, the television, and the home computer have become storytelling media as they are adopted by popular culture. It should be no surprise then, that games and virtual worlds are being used to tell stories.

Second Life is a world of stories. While the millions of residents make a new life for themselves, they weave a narrative about them, what they have created, their politics, their dreams, or just a fiction they have imagined. Machinima is one way to capture these stories and share them with the rest of the world.

CONTENTS

WHAT IS MACHINIMA?

Machinima is the art of making a movie using a real-time rendering engine. *Rendering* is what your computer is doing when it draws an image. Any computer-generated imagery is considered "rendered," whether it is the icons on your home PC's desktop or a complex special effect created for a big-budget action film. In the conventional film industry the bar for quality computer graphics is so high that a single frame of a film can take hours to render. To maintain the illusion of motion, a film will show 24 static frames per second. Creating a feature-length computer-generated movie in this fashion takes a lot of time and a lot of resources.

Video games and virtual worlds like *Second Life* render their images in real time. That means that each frame is rendered in a fraction of a second. To make a virtual environment that feels truly interactive, the picture must update faster than 15 times per second. Unfortunately, this means that the quality will be lower than what you see in a movie.

Originally machinima was a movie made using a video game engine (or a modified version of it), but the definition has expanded in the last several years as specialized rendering engines and non-game virtual worlds have been used to produce movies.

A HISTORY OF MACHINIMA

In the early 1990s game developers started experimenting with letting players record sequences of gameplay. The best known of these was id Software's game *Doom*, which would let you then replay a sequence in real time using the game engine. *Doom* also let players "mod" it—allowing them to create their own maps and gameplay. id Software continued to develop tools for recording and customizing their games. In 1996 a group of *Quake* (another id game) players called the Rangers released a recording titled "Diary of a Camper," which is credited as being the first machinima film, meaning it's the first example of narrative storytelling using these tools.

In 2000 Hugh Hancock launched the website Machinima.com as a community resource for these movies, simultaneously giving the genre the name—a slightly misspelled contraction of *machine* and *cinema*. The site was hosting a film created in *Quake III Arena*, Tritin Films's "Quad God," which broke away from making movies that could only be replayed using the game engine. Tritin Films had recorded the frames instead, which could be converted into any digital movie format.

Figure 10.1: A still of an early *Second Life* **promotional movie**

In 2002 Linden Lab created a promotional film in-world (Figure 10.1), the first example of machinima in *Second Life*. Soon afterward, they added a feature to the *Second Life* client that allowed a user to record a video of their *Second Life* experience to their hard drive. Soon enough, users were creating videos documenting their experiences, as well as telling original stories.

Second Life proved to be fertile ground for machinima due to the ease of content creation. Even more important was the ability to collaborate on a project in-world. Several communities have formed around making movies, teaching others how to make them, and organizing festivals and galleries.

CHAPTER 1

CHAPTER 2

CHAPTER 3

CHAPTER 4

CHAPTER 5

CHAPTER 6

CHAPTER 7

CHAPTER 8

CHAPTER 9

CHAPTER 10

CHAPTER 11

CHAPTER 12

CHAPTER 13

CHAPTER 14

CHAPTER 15

APPENDICES

MAKING YOUR OWN MACHINIMA

Machinima appeals to a lot of content creators because it is very multidisciplinary. In previous chapters you learned a lot about building, scripting, texturing, and more. A machinima made in *Second Life* can derive benefit from all of these skills. So let's start making one!

We are going to start with the basics of making a movie in *Second Life*—you'll see how easy it is. After that, we can start making it more complicated. New machinimatographers (my own word) often get hung up on what they can't do. Don't fall into that trap! Making a machinima in *Second Life* is only as hard as you make it.

YOUR FIRST MOVIE

Figure 10.2: Changing the size of the window

The first celluloid film, shot by Louis Le Prince, captured a group of people walking around in circles in a British garden. Your first machinima will be at least as interesting! The first step is probably the hardest—log into *Second Life*, and find something interesting to look at. Move the camera to a point where you can easily capture the scene.

Now, from the file menu, change the size of the *Second Life* window to something smaller (Figure 10.2). When we record the movie, it will be saving a lot of information to your hard drive—up to a gigabyte per minute. The larger the window, the more data to save, so to spare your computer, go to File > Set Window Size > 640×480. Your view will quickly resize.

CHAPTER 10

WHAT IS
MACHINIMA?

A HISTORY OF
MACHINIMA

**MAKING YOUR
OWN MACHINIMA**

SCREENING
YOUR FILM

Now we can capture the scene. When you were resizing the window, you may have noticed another option in the File menu: Start/Stop Movie to Disk. When you choose it, *Second Life* will ask where you want to save the final movie file. Choose a location you can remember. Anything you record this session will be saved there—if you want to save your movies to a new location, you will need to relog in.

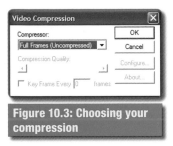

Figure 10.3: Choosing your compression

A second dialog will appear, from which you can choose how to compress your movie (Figure 10.3). For now, we opt for simplicity and choose Full Frames (Uncompressed). As soon as you choose the compression, everything you see in the *Second Life* window will be saved to a `.avi` video file to your computer using the built-in recorder. You may notice that *SL*'s performance worsens considerably. To stop recording, choose File > Start/Stop Movie to Disk again.

Congratulations! You have just made your first machinima. I told you it was easy. Go ahead and watch it. Of course, your movie probably won't win you an Oscar—but don't despair; the rest of this chapter should help with that.

Your Second Movie

This section is a fairly complete look at how to start with a story, and make a machinima out of it. It might seem a little intimidating because you will see how much can go into making a machinima—but just remember that your second, third, and *n*th movie has to be only as complex as you want it to be. Making machinima in *Second Life* is easy, but making a complicated machinima will always be complicated.

PREPRODUCTION

The first thing you will need is a story. Every machinima should have one, but many don't. Ensuring that you have a story will mean that you are well on your way to acquiring the final thing a machinima needs: an audience. Even if your machinima is as simple as an advertisement for your used-plywood cube dealership, a story will make it more interesting to any viewer—we all want to know how the story ends.

Treatment

Write down your story in a few paragraphs, as a summary. In the real world, this summary is known as a *treatment*. This will be handy to share with others to get them excited about working on your project with you.

CHAPTER 1
CHAPTER 2
CHAPTER 3
CHAPTER 4
CHAPTER 5
CHAPTER 6
CHAPTER 7
CHAPTER 8
CHAPTER 9
CHAPTER 10
CHAPTER 11
CHAPTER 12
CHAPTER 13
CHAPTER 14
CHAPTER 15
APPENDICES

ADDITIONAL INFO

STORYTELLING

Coming up with a story is the first hurdle for any machinima maker, and often the hardest. Here are some tips for coming up with a story.

Draw from your own experience. Maybe it's something that happened to you, maybe to a friend. Play around with the setting—sure, everyone likes to hear about your love triangle gone horribly and hilariously wrong, but what if your love triangle goes horribly and hilariously wrong *in space*?

Draw from the classics. There is an old saying that there are only so many stories, and they've all been told. So take one and tell it your own way. Maybe something about a tragic, forbidden romance between a Furry and a Gorean; set in Verona.

Throw darts. Write down interesting characters, places, and events, and choose them randomly. It will probably turn out weird (I once made a movie about a bearded lady who fell in love with a missionary alien using this technique) but it will help you practice your filmmaking until you reach a point where the stories come more easily.

Script

Once you have a treatment, expand it into a script. You may have everything about your movie memorized, but chances are that you will be working with other people on it, and they can't read your mind. A typical shot is complex, and organizing a movie with potentially hundreds of shots is difficult enough even if you do have everything written down.

Your script should at least contain any dialog, settings, chronology, and important action that will happen in your movie. A good rule of thumb is that one page of script is equivalent to one minute of final machinima, so try and keep it short. As tempting as it might be to try to make that 90-minute feature-length film, you should work your way up to that instead of jumping straight in.

You don't need to write *everything* down. If you are not the director of your movie, you might find that the director cherishes a lean script, which gives him more artistic leeway. Concentrate on making sure the story comes through as clearly as possible, because, as you will soon find, the actors in *Second Life* can leave something to be desired.

Setting

Everything takes place somewhere, and in *Second Life* there are a lot of somewheres. You have a script, and in it is a description of a setting. There are two ways to go about creating that setting.

CHAPTER 10

WHAT IS
MACHINIMA?

A HISTORY OF
MACHINIMA

**MAKING YOUR
OWN MACHINIMA**

SCREENING
YOUR FILM

The first, of course, is to find a setting that already exists in *Second Life*. This is a good option for those who don't own land or don't have the time to build. In the glorious anarchy that is *Second Life's* architecture, you can find any area you can imagine—from a fantasy castle to a space station. If you find that perfect place and you want to use it in your movie, it is very important to ask for permission to film there. Most of the time you will find that the owner of the build is more than happy to have you there, but not always. There are intellectual-property issues surrounding what is shown in your movie, and you may end up infringing on another resident's rights if you shoot their content without their permission. It is also polite—no one wants you to be filming a steamy romance scene in their living room when they were planning to have a quiet night in. When you are finished filming there, be sure to thank your host, as well as clean up any mess you may have left—you never know when you might want to film a sequel.

A better option, if you have the budget, is to build the set from scratch. Building the set gives you a few advantages. Primarily, you have full control over the set, so if you need to fill it full of rats, blow it up, or otherwise change it, you can. Secondly, you always have it when you need it. You will find that sometimes you need to get some extra footage or recapture a flawed shot—knowing your set will be there for you to use, and not replaced with a dance club, is comforting.

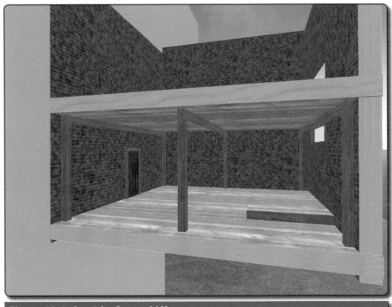

Figure 10.4: A set in *Second Life*

If you are building your own sets, here are a few tips. First, build only what you need to. You may have seen photos of a Hollywood set where all the buildings look real from the front, but from behind it's all plywood (Figure 10.4). If you have a scene set in the throne room of the castle, you don't need to build the dungeons. There are two reasons for this—first, it will take a lot of time and energy to build things that the audience will never see, so all that time will be wasted. Second, just because you can't see it doesn't mean the *Second Life* client isn't rendering it.

Another good idea is to turn on Phantom on anything you can in the scene by checking the Phantom check box in the Object tab of the Build panel. If it is a crowded scene, it will be hard for clumsy avatars to move smoothly through it. If they can't collide with the object, it is that much easier to move around. Similarly, if you have a tight interior scene, make the walls on the outside transparent to be sure your cast and crew can see what is going on.

Characters

You have a story and the place where it will happen; now you need someone to tell it. Character development is one of the most challenging aspects of storytelling, and in some ways *Second Life* makes it even harder. One of the first films I made in *Second Life* starred primitives rolling and shuffling across the plains because it was so hard to make avatars act.

Sometimes you'll use just a single avatar to play multiple roles with different skins, but other times you'll work with other people in creating characters. The most important thing to keep in mind when working with other people on a movie is the need to communicate. Share your script, storyboards, and any other concept material with them. To realize your vision, they need to know what your vision is. During a shot, use voice chat to coordinate your actors, and let them see the script. The more they know what they are doing, the better they will do it.

Costumes

I don't need to say too much about making avatars look good; Chapter 5 covered that in detail. Some good general advice is to design your characters to be distinctive, make sure they have unique silhouettes, and be certain that any changes to their appearance are shown explicitly. Don't go crazy with high-prim hair and jewelry, as they will take more time to render.

More importantly, if it is possible, make sure that all the assets for a character are transferable and copyable. Unlike the real world, any avatar can look like Tom Cruise, and you don't have to worry about your star's schedule if anyone can be your star.

Animations

Unfortunately, as strong as *SL* is for the other aspects of moviemaking, character animations are its weakness. Body language is at the core of acting—the most inspired voice acting will fall flat if your sexy female lead walks like a duck (unless, of course, she is a duck).

There are two types of animations in *Second Life*. The first are the built-in Linden Lab–created animations. The default motion animations feel like placeholders until better animations are put together, and yes, your avatar will walk like a duck with them. There is also a list of triggered animations, which are generally coarse emotive motions—overblown but effective in a slapstick way. There are also a list of facial animations that you can trigger. These are effective for communicating typed emotes, but are too coarse to be used for subtle or complex emotion.

The second type of animation is the user-uploaded variety. These range, predictably, from not very good to *very, very* good. Unfortunately, the really good ones can be hard to find, and you will be lucky if you can find all the animations you need. If you can't find ready-to-use animations for your purposes, you can, of course, create your own animations.

CHAPTER 1
CHAPTER 2
CHAPTER 3
CHAPTER 4
CHAPTER 5
CHAPTER 6
CHAPTER 7
CHAPTER 8
CHAPTER 9
CHAPTER 10

CHAPTER 11
CHAPTER 12
CHAPTER 13
CHAPTER 14
CHAPTER 15
APPENDICES

CHAPTER 10

WHAT IS
MACHINIMA?

A HISTORY OF
MACHINIMA

**MAKING YOUR
OWN MACHINIMA**

SCREENING
YOUR FILM

ADDITIONAL INFO
BETTER TOOLS ON THE HORIZON

Custom animations are probably one of the hardest things to do well, and even if you are good at it, it will take quite a bit of time. Unfortunately, as of this writing, there is not a way for users to create facial animations or mouth motion in *Second Life*. (The software CrazyTalk offers some such functionality; more on that in the "Visual Effects" section of this chapter). Both Linden Lab and the *Second Life* community are currently working on methods to better animate avatars in *Second Life*, so making machinima will only get easier in the future.

Storyboarding

You have a story and a script, and the assets for your film, but you still need to visualize it. The best way to do this is by storyboarding. Think of it as making the comic-book version of your movie.

Storyboarding forces you to go through your script and plan every shot. When we start talking about actually shooting a scene in *Second Life*, you will understand why it is a good idea to plan as much as possible. While it means taking a bit more time early on, storyboarding will save you time in the long run.

Storyboarding in *Second Life* is very easy. All you need to do is place the characters in the setting and take a screenshot. Your screenshot needs to reflect the composition of the final recorded shot, making sure all the important elements are included. Once you have taken them, slap them on boards in *Second Life* and arrange them in order—make sure that the story makes sense visually, and there aren't any glaring gaps. You can also take the screenshots into your editing software and make up an *animatic*—basically a movie composed of the still images—to figure out the timing for each shot.

Cast and Crew

We are almost ready to actually start recording your movie, but first we'll discuss the most important part of making a machinima in *Second Life*: other people.

Some people are geniuses at everything, but for those of us who aren't and could use a little help in any of the myriad aspects of producing a movie, we need look no further. *Second Life* is full of talented individuals who can help you make your dream a reality. Check out the Machinimatographers group in *Second Life* (find it using the search tool under the Groups tab), as well as the machinima wiki portal at `http://wiki.secondlife.com/wiki/Machinima` to find people who want to help.

Finally, make sure you credit anyone who helps. It will make it more likely they will want to help again.

CHAPTER 1

CHAPTER 2

CHAPTER 3

CHAPTER 4

CHAPTER 5

CHAPTER 6

CHAPTER 7

CHAPTER 8

CHAPTER 9

CHAPTER 10

CHAPTER 11

CHAPTER 12

CHAPTER 13

CHAPTER 14

CHAPTER 15

APPENDICES

ADDITIONAL INFO
OPEN THE LINES OF COMMUNICATION!

Again, be sure to communicate with other people on set. The more information they have about your vision, the better they'll be at helping realize it.

PRODUCTION

Now that you have a story to tell and you know how you want to tell it, it's time to start shooting. Depending on the complexity of your story, each shot may require the coordination of multiple people. The preproduction work you have done should smooth out most of the bumps, but the better prepared you are for a shot, the faster you can actually make it happen. Acting in a movie will sound fun to your friends until they realize that it's really a matter of 10 minutes of setup for 10 seconds of action. Nothing is more distracting than a bored extra.

Setting Up a Shot

The first thing you need to do is set up a shooting schedule. This doesn't have to be anything complex, but if you have other people helping you out, you need to make sure everyone can be at the scene at the same time. Go through your script and storyboards and organize the scenes by setting. It's easier to shoot all of the scenes for a single set at once than to move between multiple sets. Figure out which characters need to be there, what props and costumes they will need to have, and what shots you will be taking. Write it all down.

Get to the set early; make sure it is still there and that it is ready for your shooting. Take a good look around—*Second Life* loads the textures faster if you are looking at them, and you want everything to look its best. As your cast and crew arrives, make sure they have everything they need—costumes, props, and fajitas from the caterers.

Pull up the storyboard of the scene, and show it to your actors so they understand what is going to happen. Make sure that the props are placed correctly. Block out your actors' locations and movements—that is, mark in the scene where they should stand, and if they are moving, where they should move to. Small markers on the floor usually do the trick, but make sure that they won't show up in your final shot.

Set up the lighting for the shot. In *Second Life* you can move the sun, so if it is a night shot and you are shooting when the sun is in the sky, select World > Force Sun > Midnight. You can also place light objects around the scene to create more mood and atmosphere. Most importantly, make sure that it's not too dark—too often a dark, moody scene is ruined by the inability to discern what the heck is going on in there. You can always make it darker in postproduction, but it is harder to make it light again.

If you are using a scripted camera, set it up. Test it with the actors standing on their marks. Do a few test runs to warm everyone up and keep them awake. If everything looks good, you're ready to record!

CHAPTER 10

WHAT IS
MACHINIMA?

A HISTORY OF
MACHINIMA

**MAKING YOUR
OWN MACHINIMA**

SCREENING
YOUR FILM

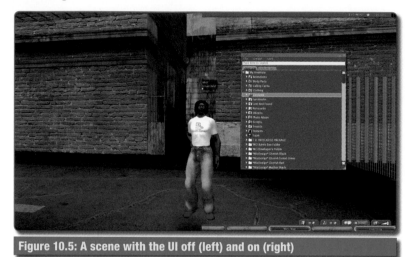

Figure 10.5: A scene with the UI off (left) and on (right)

If you have done everything already covered in this chapter, the actual recording should be very easy. You just need to turn off your UI (Figure 10.5), start the recording, and then start the action. Turning off the user interface is a good idea for a few reasons—it doesn't look very good, and it reminds everyone that the action took place in *Second Life* instead of the fictional setting. Finally, it's annoying to have to do a second take of a shot because your mother instant-messages you in the middle of the steamy romance scene.

To turn off the UI, you will need to have the Client menu revealed. To do this, press Control-Alt-D; you will see two new menus appear: Client and Server. The user interface can then be toggled with the shortcut Control-Alt-F1. It is possible to navigate to this option in the Client menu, but it is impractical, especially given that when the shot is over, you won't be able to see the menu to turn the UI back on.

Now that the interface is off, start recording. Depending on which method you use, this will probably be another keyboard shortcut. The easiest way is to use the built-in recorder, as we described for your first movie. There are better options though, described in the "Recording Tools" sidebar.

ADDITIONAL INFO
RECORDING TOOLS

Sometimes you will need a helping hand getting that shot juuuust right. Here are some tools in and out of *Second Life* that can make things easier.

Pose balls/pose stands. Animation is hard, but it's critical for transforming an avatar to an actor. There are hundreds of people in *Second Life* who are creating animations that a director can put right into a scene. Rumor is, when filming a fight scene you can get a lot of mileage out of some of the more … adult … animations.

TeamSpeak or Ventrilo. These voice-chat programs were originally developed for gamers who needed to communicate quickly with each other. While *Second Life* now has its own voice-chat system, you may want to communicate quickly using voice without polluting the audio in *SL*.

The Alt-Zoom Machinima Starter Kit. This is a little kit I put together a few years ago that's full of goodies that help me on the job. Included is a random story generator, some blocking tools for keeping your actors where you want them, and a scripted dolly for smoother camera motions.

An extra computer. A must for the professional machinimist. When you are running a shot, sometimes you need an extra actor, or maybe you just need to see the user interface to keep track of what your crew is up to. Your primary machine will be busy capturing the scene, and putting any extra load on a second one can help.

CHAPTER 1

CHAPTER 2

CHAPTER 3

CHAPTER 4

CHAPTER 5

CHAPTER 6

CHAPTER 7

CHAPTER 8

CHAPTER 9

CHAPTER 10

CHAPTER 11

CHAPTER 12

CHAPTER 13

CHAPTER 14

CHAPTER 15

APPENDICES

Let the scene record for a few seconds before you start the action. When you start editing, having some footage on either side of the action is very helpful. Make sure to let everyone involved in the scene know when the action starts. I do this with a gesture that shouts "Action" when I hit the F12 key. I can't see what I am typing with the UI off, so having a single keypress is helpful. I also have the action gesture trigger any scripted effects I want to happen, like camera motion and special effects.

ADDITIONAL INFO
THE CAMERA

The camera is the defining tool of any moviemaker. In *Second Life*, it's easy to get home-video-quality camera work by going into mouselook and just looking around, but if you want to get more cinematic shots, you will probably need some outside assistance.

Scripted cameras. These cameras take control of your avatar and move it through a scene. Many of these use waypoints that allow you to quickly visualize and change a shot. Two notable examples are the Alt-Zoom Camera found in the Machinima Starter Kit in Lukanida, and the Filming Path camera sold by Geuis Dassin.

Joystick flycam. There is a stealth feature in *Second Life* that lets you move the camera using an analog control, such as a joystick or a 3D mouse. You can access this by opening the client menu and choosing Joystick Flycam. This will bring up a panel that lets you configure your control to work with the camera in *Second Life*. It's a bit complex and every device is different, but there are some good walkthroughs on the *Second Life* wiki at `http://wiki.secondlife.com/wiki/Flycam`.

When the shot is complete, remember to turn off the recording, and to turn your interface back on. Go ahead and find the clip you just shot, and take a look at it. If it looks good, awesome! It is important to rename it with the scene name, shot number, and take number—by the time you are done shooting, you will have a lot of footage to sort through. You won't always get perfect first takes, but don't throw out bad

CHAPTER 10

WHAT IS
MACHINIMA?

A HISTORY OF
MACHINIMA

**MAKING YOUR
OWN MACHINIMA**

SCREENING
YOUR FILM

ones right away—you might find that when you get into the editing room, you need extra footage or that take one was perfect for the first half, and take two was perfect for the second, but neither was good for the whole.

Move onto your next shot, until your time for the day is up. Thank anyone who was helping, and let them know when you will need help for any more shots. Repeat until you have everything filmed.

ADDITIONAL INFO
YOUR COMPUTER'S PERFORMANCE

Second Life likes to chew computers up and spit them out. This will become even more of an issue when you start to record. Your computer needs to render a scene twice—once to your screen and once to your hard drive. Most hard drives are notoriously slow. If you find that the frame rate of your capture falls to unacceptable levels, try the following tricks:

Reduce your resolution. It is natural to want to capture at the resolution you use in *Second Life*, but that is a lot of data to write to your hard drive every second. Dropping the resolution from 1280 × 960 to 640 × 480 will quarter the amount of data you are writing every frame.

Simplify the scene. The more complex the scene the computer has to draw, the more time it will take to draw it. Cut down on the number of avatars in a scene. Turn off rendering of anything you can't see—trees, water, and land if you are indoors. Build your set facing the ocean beyond the region's borders.

Use a different recorder. *Second Life*'s built-in recording tool is convenient, but not very high-performance. Try Fraps for the PC, and Snapz Pro or iShowU for the Mac. These programs are optimized to capture images as quickly as possible, but they will still be limited. If you need to capture as fast as possible, find a video camera and point it at your monitor—it seems a bit much, but there are machinima makers out there who have done great work this way.

POSTPRODUCTION

Once you have all your footage, all that is left is to put it together into a single cohesive movie. Unfortunately, you can't do most of this work in *Second Life*—it has to be done offline using editing software.

Editing

Editing a movie is easy to learn, but difficult to master. On the surface, it is just a matter of arranging your shots so that they make chronological sense. In practice, however, good editing is much more. The timing and pacing of a scene will be perfected here, transforming your movie from slow and boring to fast and suspenseful!

ADDITIONAL INFO
EDITING TOOLS

CHAPTER 1

CHAPTER 2

CHAPTER 3

CHAPTER 4

CHAPTER 5

CHAPTER 6

CHAPTER 7

CHAPTER 8

CHAPTER 9

CHAPTER 10

CHAPTER 11

CHAPTER 12

CHAPTER 13

CHAPTER 14

CHAPTER 15

APPENDICES

Since you can't edit directly in *Second Life*, here are some tools to help you out.

Free editing. Windows Movie Maker is free for the PC, and iMovie comes with the purchase of any Mac that can run *Second Life*. These are great programs for getting started, but the free stuff is understandably limited.

Not-so-free editing. There are many feature-rich editing packages out there. Mid-level programs include Vegas, Final Cut Pro, and Adobe Premier (shown here). For the very high end, check out Avid DV. QuickTime Pro is a great tool for getting your movies ready to screen in *Second Life*. The default export settings are already close to perfect, as they are set up for iPod Video.

You can find free editing software for any operating system. Most of these are easy to use, and require the editor to simply drag a clip onto a timeline. For your second movie, simply trimming the extra footage off your shots and putting them in the right order, adding titles and credits, and exporting the results should be enough. As you get more comfortable, working with transitions, audio, and effects will allow you to considerably deepen your machinima vocabulary.

CHAPTER 10

WHAT IS
MACHINIMA?

A HISTORY OF
MACHINIMA

**MAKING YOUR
OWN MACHINIMA**

SCREENING
YOUR FILM

Sound

Watching a movie is such a visual experience that it's easy for a viewer to forget that they are using another sense: hearing. You tend not to notice good sound design because it is meant to make a scene sound natural. You will notice *bad* sound design, though—doors that don't slam, the lack of footsteps in the empty hall, voice work that sounds like the actor is on the other side of a phone call.

Unfortunately, *Second Life* has a pretty dismal soundscape most of the time. The clicks and thunks of the UI rise above the roar of the ever-present wind. Footsteps clatter strangely on stairs. To get a natural sound, you will need to acquire the sounds yourself.

Sit down and watch the scene carefully. First look at the setting. What sounds would you hear there? If the scene is inside a busy restaurant, you would hear the clatter of cutlery against plates, and the low mumble of people talking among themselves. Out on the street, you might hear cars passing, construction noises, and the beeping of a large truck reversing. Write down the sounds you would expect, then watch the scene silently, looking for specific noises. A door opens, and the sounds of the party next door come in louder. You hear glass breaking as a mirror is dropped. Write those down.

Once you know what sounds a scene should have, it's just a matter of finding them. A lot of noises can be captured with a decent microphone and a digital recorder. If those are out of your budget, there are resources on the Internet that offer free sounds. Be careful with others' audio, though; you will need to make sure you have permission to use those sounds in your movie.

ADDITIONAL INFO
THE FREESOUND PROJECT

The Freesound Project at `http://freesound.iua.upf.edu/` offers great sounds you can use to create your audioscapes. Pay attention to the various usage licenses, though, and make sure you aren't encroaching on the creator's rights.

After you have all the noises, think about how music can enhance the mood of a scene. A good soundtrack can amplify the emotion of your story through tempo and foreshadowing. Very few of us can command the resources of Hollywood and get a composer with a full orchestra to provide a score, but *Second Life* has a large community of musicians who are eager to get their music heard. Ask around, and you will probably have no problem finding music for your machinima.

ADDITIONAL INFO
CATCHY CLIPS

Remember that you don't need to use a whole song in your movie. Sometimes using a shorter clip can have a greater effect.

Visual Effects

Some visual effects are difficult to achieve using *Second Life*'s rendering engine. Sometimes you can get around these limitations by using effects generated by other software. The two most common examples are green-screening and lip-synching.

Figure 10.6: An avatar green-screened into a scene

Green-screen, or chroma-key, is a production technique that lets you substitute a color with other imagery. This allows you to put together more complex imagery than you typically would be able to—including allowing you composite *Second Life* footage with non–*Second Life* footage. To do this, simply film a subject in front of a well-lit, colored background.

(Traditionally a bright green is used; hence the term *green-screen* (Figure 10.6). In practice, however, any color can be used. The color of your background should not be found on your subject anywhere, or else that will also be substituted!

While the free editing software available today does not support chroma-key substitution, there are reasonably affordable options, such as Sony's Vegas, that do. These editors simply let you choose the color to substitute, along with a few parameters for cleaning up edges.

The inability to make an avatar's lips move realistically has frustrated a lot of machinima-tographers who wish to work with dialog in their movie. Quite a few have worked around this limitation by using Reallusion's CrazyTalk software. CrazyTalk allows you to take a still image of a face and pair it with an audio clip, and the software emulates the facial motion that would result. When combined with the green-screen technique, you can combine the animated face exported from CrazyTalk with a motion clip from *Second Life*, allowing you to have facial animation on a shot with a moving camera and/or actor.

There are far more effects that are achievable—and the more expensive the editing software, the more bells and whistles it will have. However, just because someone gives you a fancy neon-glow-around-everything filter, it doesn't mean you have to use it. Make sure that any effect you use in your film assists you in telling your story. If it doesn't, at best it is a waste of time, and at worst it will make your movie look silly.

CHAPTER 1
CHAPTER 2
CHAPTER 3
CHAPTER 4
CHAPTER 5
CHAPTER 6
CHAPTER 7
CHAPTER 8
CHAPTER 9
CHAPTER 10

CHAPTER 11
CHAPTER 12
CHAPTER 13
CHAPTER 14
CHAPTER 15
APPENDICES

Now that you are finished editing your movie together, you will need to render the entire thing into a single file. If you are not careful, that file is going to be huge. I once delivered 30 minutes of uncompressed footage to a client; it had to span across seven DVDs. You won't be able to show anyone your film if it fits only on your hard drive.

Luckily, a lot of work has been put into making video files smaller—these days you can make a good-looking DVD-quality movie that can be streamed in real time across the Internet. Of course, there are a lot of options out there, and depending on how you plan on having people watch your movies, there are different methods for preparing your movie. This section will focus on two common scenarios and provide some resources for learning more about what is considered a dark magic to many.

The first scenario is to create a master copy. This will be the best-quality copy of your movie, and you will create any other versions from it. It is easy to go from a large, high-quality version to a smaller version, but it is almost impossible to get good results going from a small version to a larger one. This means it is important to keep a high-quality version around in case you ever want to make other compressed versions. Depending on the software used for editing, you may or may not have all of the options outlined in this section. Don't worry—as long as you can output a high-quality copy, it will be possible to convert it as needed.

Your high-quality version should be exported at the maximum resolution of your clips. If you captured at 640 × 480, keep that resolution for the output. Many pieces of editing software are built to output for broadcast television. For your master copy, assume that it will be shown on a computer screen. Televisions use a bunch of tricks to broadcast information more effectively—changes in pixel shape and interlacing are a couple. For our purposes, if you have the option, output with square pixels and noninterlaced. You will also be able to choose your frame; for most of us this won't matter too much, as the frame rates you will be getting in *SL* are lower than those you will find in a movie or TV. I like to output at 30 frames per second (fps), which can be downsampled for any other uses. While exporting uncompressed footage will maintain the full image quality, it will also result in a file that is too large to be of much use. I usually export my movies using the H.264 codec at full quality, which is one of the better MPEG-4 video compressors, and also happens to be the codec that Apple uses to compress video for QuickTime.

The second scenario is to prepare a movie to be shown in *Second Life*. Videos can be streamed on a parcel, allowing for multiple residents to watch a movie together. Naturally, after you finish your film, you will want to show it to everyone who helped. *Second Life* uses Apple's QuickTime software to display streamed movies, so anything you want to show needs to work with QuickTime. Most of the options will stay the same from your master copy, but there are three changes. First, drop the resolution—as nice as it is to watch high-quality movies, most people won't notice as long as the resolution is 320 × 240 or greater. This means smaller file sizes, which means faster loading, and that more people can watch at once (Figure 10.7). Use the H.264 codec again, but at medium quality. Also, most importantly, find the option to prepare it for Internet streaming/fast start. The easiest tool I have found to do this all is QuickTime Pro, which has a converter built in.

Figure 10.7: An audience watching a movie in *SL* (Image courtesy of Anya Ixchel)

CHAPTER 1
CHAPTER 2
CHAPTER 3
CHAPTER 4
CHAPTER 5
CHAPTER 6
CHAPTER 7
CHAPTER 8
CHAPTER 9
CHAPTER 10

CHAPTER 11
CHAPTER 12
CHAPTER 13
CHAPTER 14
CHAPTER 15
APPENDICES

 ADDITIONAL INFO
TEST-WATCH YOUR CREATION

Always remember to watch your movie after you export it, to make sure everything looks and sounds right. Then show it off to others, even outside *SL*. Upload it to YouTube and submit it to the various machinima festivals and galleries in *Second Life*.

FROM LINDEN LAB
OUR FAVORITE MACHINIMA

"My favorites are Robbie Dingo's canon (some are on this book's CD) because it appeals to the artist in me, the Natural Selection Studios' oeuvre for its ludicrously valuable sense of humor, (that Kronos Kirkorian 'Lip Flap' one is a hoot too—observational humor). And I'm really fond of Amras Aldar's video tutorials and hope he'll keep doing them."

—Torley Linden

"'Better Life' by Robbie Dingo (on this book's CD) never fails to strike a chord with me. *Second Life* touches people's lives in so many ways. For me, this poignant video captures this in a way that touches me every time."

—Jill Linden

SCREENING YOUR FILM

If you make a movie in the woods and don't show it to anyone, does it make a sound? Hopefully you will never need to know the answer, because there are great places in *SL* and on the Net to screen your film.

YouTube. The biggest video-sharing site on the Net. A good video here can get thousands of views.

Blip.tv. While YouTube hosts videos only in Flash format, blip will host them in QuickTime as well—which means you can stream video hosted at blip in *Second Life*!

Your parcel. If you own land in *Second Life*, why not set up that private screening room you have always wanted? You can use the free Linden-made media player in your Library, or any of the other readily available video-streaming options in *SL*.

Festivals. Every month there are a few machinima festivals in *Second Life*—keep your ear to the ground, and enter them as you can—who knows, you might make a few L$!

CHAPTER 11

WHO ARE YOU? IDENTITY IN THE VIRTUAL WORLD

So you're a *Second Life*r. But what does that mean? What really makes a Furry different from a Goth? A businessman different from a club singer? Each of us has a unique identity in this virtual world, carefully and intricately crafted. We come from a spectrum of backgrounds and have a wide range of dreams. How does this play out inside the virtual world?

In this chapter, we'll walk you through the process of creating your virtual identity and what it means to build a virtual you inside *Second Life*. We'll explain how identities can be constructed in a place where the only clues you have about the people on the other side of the screen is what their avatars look like. We'll point out the hurdles you'll have to leap and lead you around the inevitable bumps. Finally, we'll give you the low-down on how to make friends and influence people in-world and we'll give you a tantalizing look at some of the most influential people in the virtual world. Put on your pop-psychology hats; it's time to take a look at who you are when you're online.

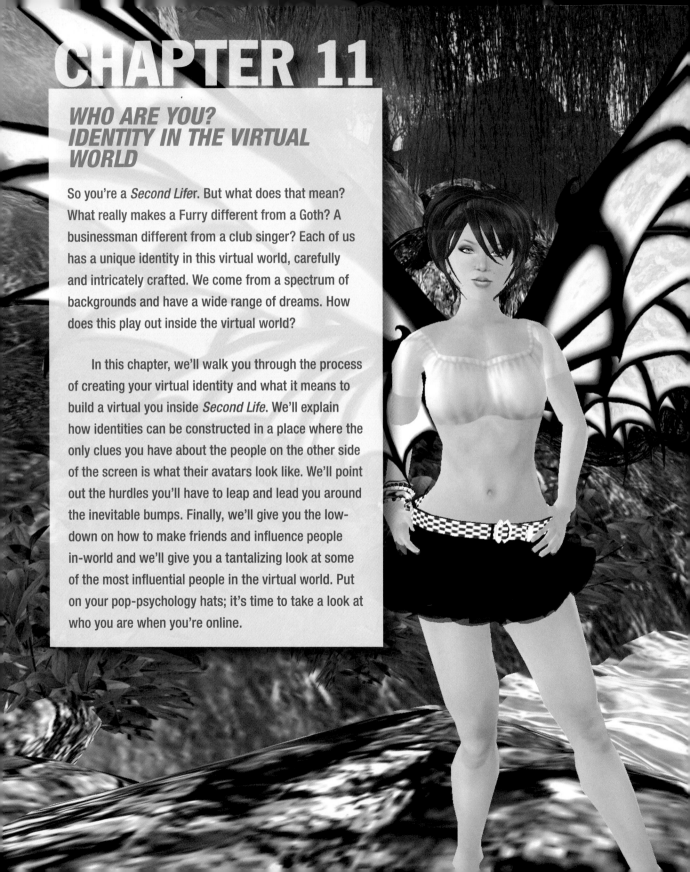

CONTENTS

CHAPTER 11

CONSIDERING
YOUR REAL-
WORLD SELF

EXPRESSING
YOURSELF IN THE
VIRTUAL WORLD

MAKING FRIENDS
AND INFLUENCING
PEOPLE

FINDING THE
SOCIAL LADDER
AND CLIMBING IT

CONSIDERING YOUR REAL-WORLD SELF

Before you discard your meat-space self in favor of a virtual you, you might want to take a look at who you are offline (see the sidebar "Real-Life Demographics"). Sure, it may seem strange to un-suspend your disbelief in a world where you should have complete control over every little bit of your identity, but your offline self has a crucial role to play in who you are when you're online.

Figure 11.1: Where you come from has an effect on who you are in *Second Life*.

First things first: where do you come from? Are you North American? African? European? Asian? Your cultural make-up places inevitable boundaries on who you might imagine yourself to be and how you adapt to this brave new world (Figure 11.1). Most of the millions of people who've signed up for accounts come from English-speaking countries, but there's an increasing number of Germans, French, Brazilians, Japanese, and Chinese people tipping the cultural balance in new and fascinating directions, adding spice and substance to this burgeoning international community. With so many people from so many places, *Second Life* really is the ultimate online melting pot.

 FROM LINDEN LAB
SECOND LIFE VS. REAL-LIFE

"How does my in-world identity differ from my out-of-world one? I tend to wear fewer wings in real life."

—Morpheus Linden

"Truth to be told, my *Second Life* identity isn't much different than my first life one. The only difference is that I'm more of an instant celebrity in-world, because I've got that 'Linden' at the end of my name. When I'm in-world as my alt (Prospero Frobozz), I'm very much the *Second Life* projection of Rob Knop. Obviously, when I'm in-world as a Linden, I need to be a little bit careful, for I'm representing the company—but as companies go, Linden grants a lot of autonomy to its employees, and as such only rarely do I find that I really need to catch myself and think about what I should or should not say."

—Prospero Linden

Next, what are your personal defining factors? Your age? Gender? Religion? Political leaning? These are phenomena we think we should be able to slough off when we're online, but they have a huge impact on the decisions we make when we're inside *Second Life*—just like they do when we're offline. We're enveloped in stereotypes, coping mechanisms, and reflections from our offline lives; it's impossible to imagine that we could get rid of them completely. So rather than totally reinventing ourselves when we enter a world like *Second Life*, what we're really doing is extending ourselves—our existing hopes, ambitions, and ideals—and adapting them within the newfound communities of people that the online space affords.

What do you do for a living? Your professional experience also has an impact on the world we make for ourselves in *Second Life*. After all, as we advance through life we develop personal systems of learning, communicating, and making sense of the world around us. These affect how we make new friends, form new groups, and solve problems when we're online.

CHAPTER 1
CHAPTER 2
CHAPTER 3
CHAPTER 4
CHAPTER 5
CHAPTER 6
CHAPTER 7
CHAPTER 8
CHAPTER 9
CHAPTER 10
CHAPTER 11

CHAPTER 12
CHAPTER 13
CHAPTER 14
CHAPTER 15
APPENDICES

 ADDITIONAL INFO
THE IMPACT OF THE FOUNDING FATHERS (AND MOTHERS)

Take a look around you when you're in-world: if you're pleased with the ways *Second Life* works, you can thank the architects, artists, designers, scientists, dreamers, and other digital pioneers with high-powered computers and frontier spirits who inhabited and laid down the foundations for *Second Life* in the early days. These folks came to *Second Life* with crazy dreams of commerce and community, architecture and aspiration. They created the markets, the landscapes, and the social environments that dominate the headlines which capture the attentions of the populations of the real world today.

Nephilaine Protagonist is an experienced clothing designer in *Second Life* and was one of the first to develop an in-world brand that transcended the high quality of her clothing. Her label, Pixel Dolls, became so popular that Protagonist's real-life counterpart considered taking the fashions outside the virtual world.

Contradictorily, **Francis Chung** brought the virtual world both the gun and the hug (among other marvelous inventions). Her scripting and building skills established a gamut of interpersonal interaction that was previously unattainable.

(Continued)

CHAPTER 11

CONSIDERING
YOUR REAL-
WORLD SELF

EXPRESSING
YOURSELF IN THE
VIRTUAL WORLD

MAKING FRIENDS
AND INFLUENCING
PEOPLE

FINDING THE
SOCIAL LADDER
AND CLIMBING IT

Eggy Lippmann is a talented builder, *Second Life* archivist, and gregarious socializer. As one of the earliest residents, he is perfectly suited to curate the *Second Life* history wiki (`http://history.secondserver.net`).

Fizik Baskerville brought real-world business into *Second Life*. Through his London-based company Rivers Run Red and its in-world counterpart, Avalon, he has transitioned several dozen real- and virtual-world brands between the two.

Before **Pathfinder Linden** joined *Second Life*, he laid the groundwork for the development of education and therapy in the virtual world. Having previously worked to develop therapeutic online communities, he saw the simulation potential of *Second Life* and established Brigadoon (a community for people with cerebral palsy) and Live to Give (a community for people with autism and Asperger's syndrome).

The founding fathers and mothers are responsible for who we as residents of *Second Life* are, who we can be, and what we'll be in the future. They brought with them a sense of freedom and of creative purpose, and that ideal lives on in the new generations of *Second Life*rs who continue to push their ways through the gates in droves today.

So before you discard yourself at the digital doors, remember that who you are inside of *Second Life* is part of who you want to become when you're offline. Don't reject it—embrace it! *Second Life* residents are part of a movement that re-imagines identity and community, where offline dreams fuel digital passions as varied as the millions of people who have already landed in-world.

ADDITIONAL INFO
REAL-LIFE DEMOGRAPHICS

Here's a look at the real-life stats of Second Life residents.

REAL-LIFE AGE OF RESIDENTS (IN YEARS)*

- 13-17: 1%
- 18–24: 26%
- 25–34: 37%
- 35–44: 22%
- 45+: 13%

REAL-LIFE GENDER OF RESIDENTS

- Male: 58%
- Female: 42%

Avatar Gender of Residents**

- 🔹 Male: 43%
- 🔹 Female: 57%

Top 10 Countries of Resident Origin*

- 🔹 United States: 26%
- 🔹 Germany: 12%
- 🔹 France: 8%
- 🔹 UK: 6%
- 🔹 Spain: 5%
- 🔹 Italy: 5%
- 🔹 Brazil: 5%
- 🔹 Japan: 4%
- 🔹 The Netherlands: 3%
- 🔹 Canada: 2%

*Real-Life Age of Residents: 1% unknown. Based upon the August 2007 Key Metrics, released September 2007 on the Official Linden Blog (`http://blog.secondlife.com/2007/09/25/august-2007-key-metrics-released/`)

**Based upon an independent survey of 750 residents April–December 2006

CHAPTER 1
CHAPTER 2
CHAPTER 3
CHAPTER 4
CHAPTER 5
CHAPTER 6
CHAPTER 7
CHAPTER 8
CHAPTER 9
CHAPTER 10
CHAPTER 11

CHAPTER 12
CHAPTER 13
CHAPTER 14
CHAPTER 15
APPENDICES

EXPRESSING YOURSELF IN THE VIRTUAL WORLD

Figure 11.2: You express yourself through your avatar.

While the real-world demographics of online citizens are fascinating, it's when people start to express themselves inside *Second Life* that things get interesting. Anyone who's set foot in *Second Life* knows that this virtual world is rife with self-expression. Everywhere you turn there are little signs of the people who've come before (Figure 11.2). Everything, from a prim lamp to prim hair, represents a little bit of who someone is and who they want to be.

CHAPTER 11

CONSIDERING
YOUR REAL-
WORLD SELF

**EXPRESSING
YOURSELF IN THE
VIRTUAL WORLD**

MAKING FRIENDS
AND INFLUENCING
PEOPLE

FINDING THE
SOCIAL LADDER
AND CLIMBING IT

But objects tell only part of the story. We are also part of sub-communities that challenge and stretch our imaginations. Our affiliations—from friendships to group memberships—become part of our identities and help to define who we are and what we can do.

In *Second Life*, the most important things to think about when developing an online identity have to do with interacting with other people. After all, in a virtual world like this one, we're part of a thriving social world. Yet the Internet is less than obliging at providing the mechanisms necessary for fruitful relationships to form and flourish. It's a computer-mediated medium with only a lean standard of communication; most interaction occurs via keyboard and mouse. It's not surprising that outsiders may think developing meaningful relationships with people in-world is impossible. In fact, there are a few crucial cues missing that we rely upon when interacting face to face.

FROM LINDEN LAB
LET IT ALL HANG OUT

"Don't constrain yourself. If you have a childhood dream you want to manifest in your *Second Life*, do it. This has worked very well for me. Two words: 'Hyperbolize vociferously.'"

—Torley Linden

In this section we tackle the biggest assumptions about online relationships and burst the bubble of the critics. Here you'll discover what it means to be part of an online collective and how, as human beings, we manage to bring thriving humanity and unique online identities to the cold computer screen.

Figure 11.3: You can hide behind a digital mask in the virtual world.

⬇ ANONYMITY

The biggest hurdle is undoubtedly that we have to interact behind well-constructed identity masks. Our real-life selves are effectively totally anonymous, but anonymity, while a stumbling block, doesn't prevent us from developing meaningful relationships at all.

In fact, the anonymity of *Second Life* can be a huge release (Figure 11.3). You can completely reinvent yourself in a safe place, without real-world relationships and restrictions holding you back. Research into virtual environments points out that people are more willing to be open and honest with each other when hiding behind a virtual mask than when they're face to face, just like on a train ride over the course of which a stranger tells you his life story. Virtual worlds like *Second Life* are filled with encounters of personal disclosure. That kind of sharing breeds trust and, ironically, the opportunity to be more like our real selves.

So why should people care about who's behind the mask? Well, knowing a bit about the offline identity of other people does makes interacting with them a lot easier. Whether we like to admit it or not, we rely on certain patterns of behavior to make social situations flow more smoothly. Many of these are based on social stereotypes like age, gender, and place of residence. So when someone asks you where you're from and how old you are, rather than trying to get personal, they may actually be trying to form an impression of how to interact with you so they can avoid making any embarrassing gaffs. These probes don't just keep people out of trouble—a quick poke around personal preferences could establish common ground that might promote further contact in the future.

Figure 11.4: A virtual hug can be a real display of affection.

But aside from that basic information, people give away loads of information about themselves through standard communication. Hundreds of subtle cues in even the most basic text-based chat signal to others your gender, your age, and your religion. For example, some research says that women tend to ask questions more often than men. They also like to add emoticons to their communication. Researchers think this demonstrates empathy and acts as a way to express closeness and friendship in lean media like the Internet. (For more on the idea of giving away information about yourself, see the sidebar "A World with Voice.")

Throw in a 3D environment with its gestures and hugs (Figure 11.4), and you're sending out even more information about who you are and who you want to be. Add in a fully personalized avatar, and you've got yourself a pretty transparent virtual persona. So much for the anonymity of the Internet.

ADDITIONAL INFO
A WORLD WITH VOICE

In June 2007, Linden Lab launched one of the most controversial technological advances to arrive in *Second Life* in its four year history: voice communication. In one update, they lifted the veil on a thousand conversations. Its impact has rippled throughout the virtual world.

Up to that point, communication was exclusively text-based. People typed what they wanted to say, shout, or whisper and the words scrolled up the screen. There was no accent, no pitch— only the cold white letters on a soft gray background. And a lot of people liked it that way.

(Continued)

CHAPTER 1
CHAPTER 2
CHAPTER 3
CHAPTER 4
CHAPTER 5
CHAPTER 6
CHAPTER 7
CHAPTER 8
CHAPTER 9
CHAPTER 10
CHAPTER 11

CHAPTER 12
CHAPTER 13
CHAPTER 14
CHAPTER 15
APPENDICES

CHAPTER 11

CONSIDERING
YOUR REAL-
WORLD SELF

**EXPRESSING
YOURSELF IN THE
VIRTUAL WORLD**

MAKING FRIENDS
AND INFLUENCING
PEOPLE

FINDING THE
SOCIAL LADDER
AND CLIMBING IT

Once voice was launched, there was a massive uproar as the text-faithful recognized how the introduction of a voice client would affect their online personas. Macho men could suddenly be undermined with a weedy accent. Closet gender-benders would be instantly unmasked. Speculation was rife: relationships would most certainly transform. One of the bastions of anonymity was gone.

Other people thought the text-based medium had been cumbersome and slow. Indeed, the average speaking speed far outstrips the rate of a typical typed word, and many people new to Internet communities and accustomed to the immediacy of telephone conversations preferred the new tool. They also liked the amount of nonverbal communication that could be hidden in a person's tone.

Something shifted in the nature of online identity in *Second Life* the first day a resident breathed into a USB headset, but it will take several years before the ultimate impact will be seen.

SOCIAL CUES

Another important element missing from the online space is the library of social cues we use—often without realizing it—to determine if someone's trustworthy. All of the nonverbal interaction we take for granted when we're interacting with other people face-to-face is absent when we're online. Offline we've got smiles and frowns, eyebrow raises and furrows. Online we don't even know if when someone's paying attention or, crucially, whether they've left the keyboard to make a cup of tea.

There are incredible subtleties in the human face that signal hundreds of different emotions that can tip the observer off about another person. Every day, we make snap judgments based on clothing, accent, smell, vocal tone, and facial expression. We can recognize if someone approves or disapproves, is looking at us with like or dislike, wants to speak, or is happy to listen. Online, most of these cues are absent. Yet anyone who's ever been involved with a virtual community recognizes that even without these things, people not only cope but they positively thrive. As social animals, we've developed some sophisticated digital nonverbal mechanisms to deal with these absent elements.

How do you cope when you've got no idea who's on the other side of the screen? What do you do to assure someone you're trustworthy when all they can see are a name and a fluffy avatar? The Internet provides several challenges, but human nature has served up a helping of work-arounds that are pretty successful at doing the trick.

Figure 11.5: What you wear says a lot about who you are.

Virtual worlds like *Second Life*, in contrast to traditional, text-based computer-mediated communication, provide some basic mechanisms, like gestures and emoticons, that fill in the gaps. They also offer a visual cornucopia of costuming that says one thing or another about avatars (Figure 11.5).

The joy of a virtual world is that residents are able to costume their avatars to match their desired online personas. Thanks to the bonanza of shopping outlets and digital modeling tools in *Second Life*, one of the nonverbal elements missing from many online communities is present in *SL*. You'll encounter all manner of elaborately dressed avatars, each unique but most falling into familiar offline categories. There are businessmen in suits, Goths in black and chains, emos in eyeliner, film directors in baseball caps, 1950s pin-ups in skimpy outfits, club princesses in killer heels drenched in bling, hippies with long flowing scarves, and Harajuku girls in elaborate frills. Every social niche you find offline has a boutique somewhere in the virtual world. There are even some subcultures you might never have heard of (see the sidebar, "The Furries").

ADDITIONAL INFO
THE FURRIES

One of the most prominent subcultures in the *Second Life* social scene is the Furries, a group thousands strong who get together to role-play in areas like Luskwood and FurNation. It's not difficult to miss a Furry even when they're prowling away from these areas; they have anthropomorphic animal avatars to represent their affinity with the group, and to demonstrate their affection for a particular type of animal.

Furries arrived in *Second Life* at the beginning of the virtual world's history, and settled in beautiful woodlands on the mainland. Since that time, the community has purchased several islands for their fur-based fun and Linden Lab has included Furry avs in the default selection.

Furry creatives have spearheaded some of the most dramatic modifications of avatar models, transforming the traditional humanoid characters into all manner of beasts—male, female, and otherwise. The creatures come in various sizes, species, and orientations. Most are dedicated to a thriving offline community, and use *Second Life* as a tool to express their inner animal and to interact with those who feel the same way.

Figure 11.6: "Newbie" clothing is discarded in favor of something more individual.

Just like offline, these external decorations act as signals to other people, sending out cues to folks interested in similar things. In fact, the first thing most people do when they arrive in *Second Life* is to shed their cookie-cutter newbie getups and slip into something with a little more personality (Figure 11.6). (There's big money in personalization, and it is the easiest way to express yourself in the virtual world.)

Avatar creation allows us to circumvent the loss of social cues and identify people we might have something in common with. But to develop long-term relationships we use much more sophisticated means: we allow online pseudonyms to represent in-world identities.

⬇ PSEUDONYMITY

Figure 11.7: People develop identities despite their digital masks.

Sure, you might not know where the real-life person on the other side of an avatar lives, their gender, or even what they look like, but after interacting together over a period of time, that avatar develops what's called a *pseudonymous* identity. Particularly in an environment like *Second Life*, where people interact over months and even years, people may not know who you are offline, but they *do* know who you are *online* (Figure 11.7).

Here's an example. One of *Second Life*'s most famous residents is Anshe Chung, a virtual real-estate agent. Almost everyone in the online world knows Anshe or at least has heard about her. She is an accomplished businesswoman who started her long and illustrious career with only a few Linden dollars and her official allotment of First Land. Over the years, she's grown her business into one of the most prosperous enterprises in-world.

Not very many people know that "she" is actually two people, a husband-and-wife team based in both Germany and Hong Kong. Their offline lives are of little consequence to what they do online: it's Anshe's actions inside *Second Life* that matter in the virtual world. And that is the power of pseudonymity. Anshe's reputation demonstrates that what you do when you're in *Second Life* has implications for the rest of your tenure there. Because it's a social environment, and the people on the other side of the avatars are human beings with feelings and memories, what you do becomes who you are. So your choices form the basis of your virtual pseudonymous identity.

The likelihood is that over time your pseudonymous identity will come to resemble the real you. This is because after hanging out for a while and getting to know another person's sense of humor and conversational style, the subtle information we give away about ourselves becomes extremely important. And the fewer inconsistencies you present, the more other people will trust you and the more likely it is that you'll develop solid relationships.

Of course, because *Second Life* is a virtual reality, we can have as many identities as we can handle, discarding one when an avatar gets into social hot water. But at the heart of pseudonymous identity is the time and energy people invest in their online selves. Doing it all over again on a whim or because of a silly social foible is a pretty discouraging prospect. In *Second Life*, most people stick with just one or two avatars, juggling them according to the characteristics they've developed in each. One avatar might be worn as part of a thriving social scene and another could be worn like work clothing.

You don't experience your *Second Life* in a vacuum, and your relationships with people online affect who you can be when you're logged on. Their social influence—both subtle and overt—contributes as much to the construction of your online identity as you do. Online, just as offline, you are part of a larger world that surrounds you.

CHAPTER 1
CHAPTER 2
CHAPTER 3
CHAPTER 4
CHAPTER 5
CHAPTER 6
CHAPTER 7
CHAPTER 8
CHAPTER 9
CHAPTER 10
CHAPTER 11
CHAPTER 12
CHAPTER 13
CHAPTER 14
CHAPTER 15
APPENDICES

MAKING FRIENDS AND INFLUENCING PEOPLE

Your avatar's identity in *Second Life* is inextricably intertwined with the social features of the virtual world. It's used to make friends and to influence people, but the community at large similarly affects who you are and who you can be in this online space.

Click the ground to "rez" (create) a cube

Figure 11.8: Object building is another way people express themselves in the virtual world.

⬇ IT'S WHAT YOU DO THAT COUNTS

Everything you do in *Second Life* is an explicit display of identity. Because *SL* is a pervasive virtual world, you leave traces of yourself every time you log off, whether you spend your time creating objects, performing, developing scripts, or just hanging out (Figure 11.8). In this frontier, you are what you do. And the groups you join and the events you take part in form the community that helps to define who you are in-world.

CHAPTER 11

CONSIDERING
YOUR REAL-
WORLD SELF

EXPRESSING
YOURSELF IN THE
VIRTUAL WORLD

**MAKING FRIENDS
AND INFLUENCING
PEOPLE**

FINDING THE
SOCIAL LADDER
AND CLIMBING IT

Your pseudonymity carries a burden, and that is consequence. If you're a builder, the objects which you create will bear your name, and their quality, design, and style will be a testament to your personal portfolio and the contribution you make to *Second Life*. If you're a performer, the quality of your performance will represent you in the club circuit. If you're a rabble rouser, a schemer, a charlatan, or a griefer, those stereotypes will follow you into new interactions and might make it more difficult for you to get things done.

⬇ SECOND LIFE NETIQUETTE

The Internet has a reputation as a lawless frontier with scant regulation and danger around every corner. Its detractors claim it has no policing, no regulation. External entities, the critics argue, should get in and create law and order.

What they don't realize is that regulation abounds in online worlds like *Second Life*. There's a Terms of Service (`http://secondlife.com/corporate/tos.php`), which binds every resident to a social contract. Noncompliance with these terms carries a penalty. At its extreme, having an account banned is the equivalent of avatar death.

Then there's the informal governance that rules the social world of *Second Life*. Sure, there may not be a series of statues in a rule book for local laws within sub-communities, but the subtle social norms which have evolved decree how indiscretions should be dealt with. Punishment in this space can be unrelenting. Ultimately, because *Second Life* is all about the community, the rules which hold it together also regulate who each resident can be.

WHAT MAKES THE *SECOND LIFE* COMMUNITY

Part of getting involved with *Second Life* is developing an understanding of what makes it unique. As you hear the lore, adopt the language, and make emotional connections, these become part of your online identity. As you evolve into an active member of this new society, you can truly take part in everything it has to offer.

Common Symbols

The language of *Second Life* is unique to its population. Words like *av*, *alt*, *grid*, and *rez* roll off the tongues of old-timers, and set them apart from people who've just made the leap from Orientation Island. They act as common symbols for residents, identifying the people who use them as part of the larger community.

Likewise, avatars and clothing create local affiliations. Certain brand names of locally and externally developed products represent high quality. Gestures and greetings indicate that you understand the social rules of the context. Recognizing and adopting these into your inventory or your vocabulary demonstrates that you participate in the *Second Life* world and helps other residents identify you within the virtual universe.

Shared Stories

**Figure 11.9:
The *Second Life*
Historical Museum
archives the stories
of residents for later
generations.**

*Second Life*rs share stories that they pass down through "generations."
(Figure 11.9)

As you ascend from newbie to full-fledged community member, you'll
hear all kinds of legends from established residents. People who arrived
in 2003 may hark back to the heady days of the Prim Tax Revolt and the
demise of a sim called Americana. The people who landed in 2004 may talk
about a mysterious resident named Torley Torgeson, an avatar obsessed with
watermelons and with a *joie de vivre* which made her the first home-grown
star. Those who arrived in 2005 may tell tales of Tringo, a game that swept the
virtual land and crossed the divide into real-world popularity. For those who
joined in 2006, the stories might be about CopyBot and its ill effects on the
economy of the burgeoning nation.

Every year and every community has its anecdotes. As you add them to
your repertoire and share them with new residents, the slant you put on these
stories will represent who you are and what you perceive to be important in
Second Life.

Emotional Connections

The emotional connection residents feel with one another is a crucial element in maintaining the sense of
community in this virtual world. Friendships emerge in online communities for the same kinds of reasons
as they do offline: people seek others who are like-minded and who will offer support. There are several
prerequisites that determine if two people will become close. First, they must share space at the same
time. While in the real world this might mean grabbing a drink at the water cooler at a particular time of
day or attending the same class, in *Second Life* it means being online together and in the same location.

**Figure 11.10: Groups help people develop
emotional connections.**

Second, people have to have something in common.
In-world groups (like The Thinkers, which brings together
people interested in discussing digital culture and
philosophy, or I'm French, a group of French nationals
and French speakers) help to filter out the many potential
friends from the vast population (Figure 11.10); regular
meetings, discussions, or events bring strangers together
and provide a context that may inspire more discussion
and, ultimately, more contact. Before you know it, you've
swapped Calling Cards—like virtual business cards—and
are on each other's Friends lists. Putting someone on a
Friends list is like adding them to a buddy list in a web
instant messaging service: you can see when a friend is
online, and they're granted special permissions, like seeing where you are on the grid. A friend is halfway to
being an in-world *partner*, a special public relationship between two people. Kind of like marriage!

CHAPTER 11

CONSIDERING
YOUR REAL-
WORLD SELF

EXPRESSING
YOURSELF IN THE
VIRTUAL WORLD

**MAKING FRIENDS
AND INFLUENCING
PEOPLE**

FINDING THE
SOCIAL LADDER
AND CLIMBING IT

Figure 11.11: Residents band together to fight common enemies.

Interpersonal relationships are fantastic, but to create a passionate and connected community, you've got to have common enemies (Figure 11.11). The important thing about bad guys is that they help people define who they aren't. For example, most of the residents in *Second Life* aren't Front Nationale members, as massive protest actions by hundreds of active residents against the far-right French conservative party in 2007 demonstrated. (See the sidebar "The Top Five Bad Guys of *Second Life*.")

However, most conflicts aren't so cut and dried. There are many gray areas which demand affinity with one or another side at a local level. These groupings may be formalized, or they may simply be amorphous collectives tied together by similar attitudes. For example, the community was torn apart in 2006 when the CopyBot program infiltrated the virtual marketplaces. There were two main camps: those who cried for copyright protection as security against potential intellectual-property theft, and those who favored no copyright, little regulation, and the right to transfer objects.

Such conflict forced many residents to choose sides and question which ideas they wished to promote inside the virtual world. Bad guys can indeed bring people together, but they also have the awesome power to polarize and occasionally destroy a population.

ADDITIONAL INFO
THE TOP FIVE BAD GUYS OF *SECOND LIFE*

Linden Lab: Early in 2003, *Second Life* witnessed its first upsurge by an angry mob. Before the current economic system had settled into place, a gaggle of builders declared war on Linden Lab for unfair "taxation" on primitives, the basic building blocks of the virtual world, and dressed in colonial garb, they littered the virtual landscape with tea crates and protest placards. The Prim Tax Revolt was the first indication that the online gathering had become a viable and powerful community.

W-Hat and the V5: In 2004, a group of self-proclaimed goons arrived from the notorious Something Awful forums intent on causing a virtual ruckus within *Second Life*. The tribe, with its headquarters in the Baku region of the grid, was repeatedly held responsible for griefing attacks that shut down several areas of service. While they proclaimed their innocence, many accounts were banned. W-Hat subsequently split from V5 and now carries on their goonish activities without intent to disrupt.

American Apparel: As publicity about *Second Life* ramped up in 2006, businesses began opening virtual shops to cater to the needs of potential avatar consumers. American Apparel was one of the first major brands to arrive in the virtual world, and was subsequently the setting for many angry protests by members of the community keen on keeping commerce and creativity free from external pressure.

CopyBot: The economic system of *Second Life* was challenged when a controversial debugging tool was let loose on the grid in late 2006. CopyBot, which made unauthorized replications of objects for the owner of the hack, left in-world shopping malls bereft of stores as shop owners quickly barricaded their intellectual property from its effects.

Front Nationale: In January 2007, the ultra-right French political party Front Nationale opened up offices inside the virtual world and was welcomed with bombs, exploding pigs, protests, and a very angry mob. Fearing it had lost control of its core beliefs, the community battered the new construction until the party representatives retreated into the real world.

SOCIAL RULES

While the social side of things can help you to clearly identify who you want to be and who you'd like to meet in the virtual world, it can also restrict creation. *Second Life* has rules and regulations that residents must abide by if they want to remain there. The formal ones, like the Terms of Service, are pretty straightforward, but the informal rules have the greatest effect on who you can be in the virtual world.

Unspoken norms in a community define how members should react to situations. For example, in offline situations there are no signs demanding that we say "please" and "thank you," but in most situations it's polite if not expected. Similarly, you wouldn't stand up and sing a song in the middle of a real-world lecture (unless it was that kind of class). The same subtle social rules apply in virtual space, and to succeed in the *Second Life* community, you've got to figure out what they are and stick with them.

For example, even though it's a virtual world, the rule of politeness still stands. Every time you enter a new environment where people are already gathered, you can expect to hear greetings from all sides. Give a shout back! If someone gives you a gift, don't forget to acknowledge it with a "thank you," and see what you've got in your inventory to give back.

CHAPTER 11

CONSIDERING
YOUR REAL-
WORLD SELF

EXPRESSING
YOURSELF IN THE
VIRTUAL WORLD

MAKING FRIENDS
AND INFLUENCING
PEOPLE

FINDING THE
SOCIAL LADDER
AND CLIMBING IT

If you're coming into *Second Life* to sell a service or product, that's a particularly important unspoken rule. Make sure you've got something that you can give to the community that's relevant to them; do your research and see what the population feels is important. Otherwise, you'll flounder. Residents don't like to feel like they're giving but not receiving anything in return.

Another unspoken rule is to avoid asking people about their first lives. They'll tell you if they want to, but asking a stranger how old they are, if they're male or female, or where they're from is considered rude, and a little too intimate!

While these are only a few examples, the unspoken rules have significant power over the actions and attitudes of the virtual world's residents. New residents look at others to determine how to act when a novel situation arises. We watch people we admire and mirror their responses. We learn who it's appropriate to be, and we try on these identities.

So, the social life of *Second Life* has a double-role in the creation of our online selves. On the one hand, it offers a way to nurture relationships and other affinities. On the other hand, it restricts us. This demonstrates that our second lives aren't really that different from our first ones. More often than not, our identities in-world aren't huge leaps from our identities elsewhere.

FINDING THE SOCIAL LADDER AND CLIMBING IT

So, what's the secret to success in *Second Life*? The answer lies in how you interact with other people. Do you want to be a successful businessperson? A successful educator? A successful performer or artist? It's all about finding your niche and making sure you're an indispensable part of the social life.

The people who've received the most notoriety in *Second Life* come from all kinds of backgrounds. Some entered the virtual community with a crazy dream and a bit of computer experience, and have built commercial empires. Others arrived with intent and made masterpieces that captured the zeitgeist. (Others are the creators of the world itself; see the sidebar "The Lindens.")

Interestingly, those highest in status aren't necessarily those with the most friends. No, the people who rise to the top tend to be those folks who are most dedicated to their second lives and are willing to put time and energy into creating something useful and relevant for the rest of the community.

Here are a few tips and tricks for creating a successful *Second Life* persona:

Participate. If you're interested in building up your online identity, get involved with the community as much as you can. Find out what people need and how you might be able to offer something. Collaborate!

Join a group. There are so many groups in *Second Life*, it's sometimes hard to decide which ones to join! But if you dive in, you'll inevitably meet people who are interested in similar things, and voilà, a community is formed.

Talk. Don't be afraid to speak up! No one bites in *Second Life*, unless you ask them to.

Listen. Take the time to hear what other people are trying to say. You may walk away with a whole new perspective.

Be consistent. Online interaction is all about trusting other people, and one of the biggest give-aways that someone can't be trusted is if they are inconsistent. If you say you're going to do something, do it!

Find your niche and fill it. *Second Life* is still a new frontier with many niches to be discovered and filled. Find yours and experiment!

Be creative. There is no limit to the imagination inside *Second Life*, and truly new adventures—whether in jewelry making, performance, architecture, knowledge transfer, charity fundraising, or weapon design—are met with wonder and awe. There are so many people inside the virtual world replicating what's already offline that new and creative enterprises are always greeted with widespread acclaim!

Offer something of quality. Don't just throw something together and expect the virtual world to fall at your feet! There are plenty of residents willing to help others realize their ideas in sophisticated ways that utilize the environment to its utmost. As your indelible mark on the virtual world, make sure you can be proud of what you offer.

Be polite. It doesn't hurt!

ADDITIONAL INFO
THE LINDENS

If there is one sign of ultimate status in the virtual world, it is the surname *Linden*. Bestowed only upon employees of Linden Lab, the family Linden is possibly the best-recognized group of avatars in *Second Life*.

Regularly referred to in the collective, "The Lindens" are as close to virtual-world gods as you'll get. As such, they are both heralded and despised, at once celebrated for their creation, acclaimed for their leniency, and detested for too much regulation (or not enough). These gods do indeed have ultimate power, and while they currently run a benevolent dictatorship, they do have authority to smite anyone who crosses the Terms of Service.

Thankfully, the Lindens are not a terrible and faceless entity. More than 100 of them are wandering around the grid, and only a few carry whips. They do, however, possess a precious object unique to each of them: the Linden Bear. These virtual plush toys are built by every employee to represent his or her role in the virtual community and they are distributed to friendly residents. Boost your personal celebrity by collecting them all!

CHAPTER 1
CHAPTER 2
CHAPTER 3
CHAPTER 4
CHAPTER 5
CHAPTER 6
CHAPTER 7
CHAPTER 8
CHAPTER 9
CHAPTER 10
CHAPTER 11

CHAPTER 12
CHAPTER 13
CHAPTER 14
CHAPTER 15
APPENDICES

ADDITIONAL INFO
THE FETED INNER CORE

Being an opinion leader in a close community can occasionally work against you, particularly if other members of the public view your leadership as a bit too cozy with the powers that be. In 2003, just around the time of the Prim Tax Revolt, rumors spread around the grid that a cabal of privileged residents had more than their equal say in the goings on of *Second Life*. The buzz, propagated by virtual-world skeptics, was that certain dedicated creatives and accomplished builders had inequal access to the Lindens, who paid more attention to their needs and requests than to the rest of the in-world population.

Discovering the members of this Feted Inner Core, or FIC, became a worldwide witch hunt. Most pointed to the unacknowledged aristocrats, successful business owners who were already supplementing their offline incomes in the fledgling economy of the early virtual world. Names bandied around included well-known fashion designers, real-estate agents, animation and pose builders, avatar modifiers, and marketplace owners. Some of the more vocal political upstarts were not implicated, which may explain why the gossip was propagated with such animosity.

But as *Second Life* grew, the search for members of the FIC fell quiet. They may still exist in the shadows, feeding requests to the Lindens in return for newbie blood, yet to this day their true identities are unknown. Most residents now think that the power has evolved from a localized group of people to a more distributed group. These folks are often the subject of *Second Life* tabloid headlines pointing out the so-called Power Elite.

So now you know who you are and who you can be inside *Second Life*. You've accepted that your online self likely won't be terribly far from your offline self, but that it's OK. You've leapt over the hurdles of anonymity and the loss of social cues by wearing your heart on your digital sleeve and developing a pseudonymous identity. You've discovered the common symbols and passed on the *Second Life* legends. You've bonded with other people and have stood firm against adversity. You've been formed by the community and have helped it form around you. You're now ready to take on the world.

CHAPTER 12

SHOPPING

One of the most interesting features of *Second Life* is that it allows user-generated content to flourish. Whether you're looking to stock your new virtual house with just the right furniture style or trying to find a pair of bat wings to add the finishing touch to your vampire avatar, shopping is an activity that all *Second Life* residents are very familiar with. This chapter covers the basics, from acquiring a supply of *Second Life*'s currency, the Linden dollar, to helping you learn how to find exactly what you're looking for without spending fruitless hours traversing the *Second Life* grid.

CONTENTS

ACQUIRING LINDENS

As a brand-new resident of *Second Life*, you'll need some money to start shopping. Although a number of places offer goods for free, the quality, scope, and variety of goods offered at those places is somewhat limited. (We will, of course, cover these freebie shopping palaces in just a few more pages.)

Linden dollars (also just called Lindens) are traded on a public currency exchange called the Lindex that's operated by Linden Lab. Here sellers of Lindens can cash them out for US dollars to buyers of Lindens. As of this writing, the 90-day average exchange rate was 266 Linden dollars to one US dollar. (A good way to convert in-world prices to real-world prices is to remember that L$1,000 is just a bit less than US$4.)

There are a couple of ways to buy Lindens—one from the Web and one from inside *Second Life*—but first you need to set up the payment information for your account as follows.

1. Navigate to `http://www.secondlife.com` in a browser.

2. Choose the Resident Login link from the upper-right corner of the page.

3. Log into your account.

4. Click on the Update Payment Method link on the right-hand sidebar.

5. Choose your payment method: PayPal or a major credit card.

6. Enter the appropriate details for your payment method.

BUYING LINDENS FROM THE WEB

Since you're already logged into the *Second Life* website, it makes sense to place your first Lindens order directly from the website. To do this, click on the Buy L$ link on the left sidebar.

You'll soon see a page (Figure 12.1) that presents some economic statistics about the Linden and the top 20 best sell-order rates. You don't need to worry about the rate at this stage because the Lindex automatically fills buy orders from the best available rate. (Remember, as a buyer you want the ratio of Lindens to US dollars to be high; sellers want the ratio to be low.)

To proceed, type in the amount of Lindens you want to purchase. L$2,500 (about US$10) is a good amount of money to carry around for starters. That sum will let you fully kit out your avatar, if you so choose, and provide some purchasing power if you see something (or some things) you absolutely cannot live without in the virtual world.

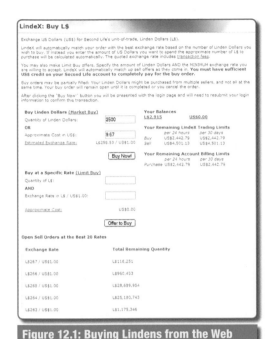

Once you click the Buy Now! button, you'll get a confirmation screen. Click Place Buy Order. You'll then be asked to log in to your account again as a security measure. (After all, someone could've found your browser open while you were at lunch.) Finally, assuming all goes well, you will see a buy confirmation screen (Figure 12.2).

Figure 12.1: Buying Lindens from the Web

Figure 12.2: Buy order success!

ADDITIONAL INFO
FIGHTING FRAUD

It can take several minutes—even hours—for Linden Lab to authorize a payment method for buy orders through its antifraud software. If your buy order doesn't work immediately after you update your payment information, try entering your buy order again a bit later. (If a transaction fails you won't be charged, so a second try is safe.)

Congratulations; you've just acquired some walking-around money.

BUYING LINDENS FROM INSIDE *SECOND LIFE*

Imagine you've just found the perfect house for your brand-new rental property. It costs L$2,500, but you've only got L$500 on hand. What to do? Close *Second Life*, fire up a browser, log into your account, and place a buy order, right?

Figure 12.3: In-world Linden button

Fortunately, there's a convenient way to buy Lindens from inside *Second Life*. In the upper-right corner of your viewer menu bar, near your account balance is a light-blue circle inscribed "L$"(Figure 12.3). Clicking this button allows you to place a buy order for Lindens from inside *Second Life*.

CHAPTER 1
CHAPTER 2
CHAPTER 3
CHAPTER 4
CHAPTER 5
CHAPTER 6
CHAPTER 7
CHAPTER 8
CHAPTER 9
CHAPTER 10
CHAPTER 11
CHAPTER 12

CHAPTER 12

ACQUIRING
LINDENS

**VIRTUAL-GOODS
TAXONOMY**

SHOPPING ON A
TIGHT BUDGET

SHOPPING AS A
SOCIAL ACTIVITY

IN-WORLD
SHOPPING
OUTSIDE OF
SECOND LIFE

TROUBLE-
SHOOTING
SHOPPING WOES

FINDING
WHAT YOU'RE
LOOKING FOR

MORE SHOPPING
RESOURCES

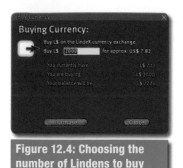

**Figure 12.4: Choosing the
number of Lindens to buy**

After you click that button, a dialog box allows you to enter a quantity of Lindens to purchase (L$1,000 by default) and estimates how much it will cost in US dollars to fill that order (Figure 12.4).

After you click Purchase, a confirmation dialog asks if you're sure you want to proceed with this buy order. Choose Yes and the Lindex order will be placed automatically and filled at the best available exchange rate—and the money will show up in your account within seconds.

VIRTUAL-GOODS TAXONOMY

Now that you have some spending money, what is there to buy? With the content-creation freedom in *Second Life*, it's generally a safe bet that most anything can be purchased or found in-world. Some of the things we'll cover include vehicles, weapons, houses, furniture, avatar kits (including, for example, werewolves, robots, and real-world celebrities), and fashion items (including garments, hair styles, shoes, and accessories such as sunglasses).

Generally, these items can be placed into three categories: goods that your avatar lives in or around, goods that your avatar sits on or in, and goods that your avatar wears or displays.

Goods that Avatars Live In or Around

Many *Second Life* residents enjoy owning a parcel of virtual land as a place to further express their online identity. They may landscape the land into a lush tropical garden, create the house of their dreams, or display a collection of resident-created experimental artworks. Here we'll go through some of the things that avatars live in (such as houses) or around (such as landscaping.)

LAND

Aside from personal appearance, a place to call your own is probably one of the most popular things to shop for in *Second Life*. Whether you're looking for a lush green meadow or a dark and forbidding mountain to call home, you can find it if you look.

In *Second Life*, land is bought and sold in units of square meters. These plots are sometimes called *parcels*. At the time of this writing, land was hovering around L$6.50 per square meter at its least expensive. The smallest parcel a Premium account holder can own without incurring additional monthly land-use (or *tier*) charges from Linden Lab is 512 square meters.

Just like in real life, *Second Life* has two zoning ordinances: PG land is considered "all ages appropriate." Such land restricts adult themes, profanity, sexual activities, and nudity. Mature land is considered adult-oriented—but not every parcel zoned Mature contains the things prohibited from PG parcels.

There're also two different types of land—"mainland," which is created, owned and maintained by Linden Lab, and "estates," which are owned and maintained by third parties unaffiliated with Linden Lab. If you purchase land in an estate, the initial land purchase price and on-going land usage fee (or tier payment as it's known) goes to your landlord (or one of his agents), not Linden Lab.

ADDITIONAL INFO
MAINLAND VS. ESTATE LAND

Only users who sign up for a Premium account can buy and sell land directly on the Linden Lab–owned mainland or purchase an entire estate. Holders of any account type can own land on an estate parcel, which is a region controlled by a third party not affiliated with Linden Lab.

You can find land for sale in *Second Life* by choosing Search from the lower part of your viewer, and then selecting the Land Sales tab. Two drop-down boxes allow you to refine your search. One box sorts available parcels between estates and mainland, and the other sorts between Mature and PG parcels.

You can further narrow your search by checking the boxes to the right of these drop-downs. These check boxes set a maximum price of the parcel in Linden dollars and a minimum size in square meters.

Some of the best-known *Second Life* entrepreneurs have set up real-estate development and rental businesses in *Second Life*. One of the best ways to learn more about the land they have available is by visiting their websites:

Dreamland: `http://dreamland.anshechung.com/`

Otherland Group: `http://otherland-group.com`

Azure Islands: `http://azureislands.com/`

ADDITIONAL INFO
HOW MUCH LAND SHOULD I BUY?

Each parcel in *Second Life* supports a defined number of prims—or in-world objects. If you try to use more prims than your parcel supports, *Second Life* will notify you that you've used as many prims as your land can support, and refuse to place whatever object exceeded the limit on your parcel.

CHAPTER 1
CHAPTER 2
CHAPTER 3
CHAPTER 4
CHAPTER 5
CHAPTER 6
CHAPTER 7
CHAPTER 8
CHAPTER 9
CHAPTER 10
CHAPTER 11
CHAPTER 12

CHAPTER 13
CHAPTER 14
CHAPTER 15
APPENDICES

CHAPTER 12

ACQUIRING
LINDENS

**VIRTUAL-GOODS
TAXONOMY**

SHOPPING ON A
TIGHT BUDGET

SHOPPING AS A
SOCIAL ACTIVITY

IN-WORLD
SHOPPING
OUTSIDE OF
SECOND LIFE

TROUBLE-
SHOOTING
SHOPPING WOES

FINDING
WHAT YOU'RE
LOOKING FOR

MORE SHOPPING
RESOURCES

The larger the parcel size, the more prims it can support. If you plan to own and decorate a modest cottage with efficiently designed low-prim furniture, a 512-square-meter parcel will fit the bill. If you plan to own a sprawling 17th-century castle with elaborately ornate house décor, you will need a substantially larger parcel.

As the parcel size increases, so does the monthly land-usage fee charged by Linden Lab or estate owners. (If you purchase more than 512 square meters on the mainland, you'll have to pay a land-use fee to Linden Lab.) As of this writing, Linden Lab does not accept Linden dollars to pay tier fees. If you sell content in *Second Life* to cover the cost of your land usage, you will have to sell the Lindens on the Lindex to cover your tier.

RENTAL PROPERTY

It's possible to find land parcels on estates for sale for L$0—they charge only the tier fees month-to-month—and if you're especially patient you can find rentals that cost far less than you'd pay in tier fees. Keep in mind that with rental land you can't resell the land in the future—when you decide to leave your rental your landlord simply reclaims the land parcel from you. If you view your *Second Life* land purchase as an investment and want to sell it for a profit later, you will probably not want to look for a rental.

Sometimes these rental parcels come furnished with landscaping, a cottage, and even furniture. There are also various high-rise developments that will rent you an apartment. These types of rentals can often be extremely affordable because many residents chip in to pay the tier fee for the parcel the high-rise sits on (for example, instead of one resident paying the entire cost of a US$15 land-use fee, in a high-rise perhaps five residents each pay $3 per month.)

If you're interested in rentals, check out the following:

Ravenglass Rentals, Prokofy Neva, Alston (113, 22, 37): A very old and well-known rental company run by one of *Second Life*'s most outspoken residents. Helping new residents with rentals is a passion.

Crystal Islands, Doeko Cassidy, Kidoko East (12, 124, 24): A large private-estate-parcel-rental company with many different landscaped themes and parcel sizes.

Great Spaces, Zal Chevalier, Pyewacket (117, 154, 57): Most of these rentals come beautifully landscaped and with a custom house, ready to move in and enjoy.

CHAPTER 1

CHAPTER 2

CHAPTER 3

CHAPTER 4

CHAPTER 5

CHAPTER 6

CHAPTER 7

CHAPTER 8

CHAPTER 9

CHAPTER 10

CHAPTER 11

CHAPTER 12

CHAPTER 13

CHAPTER 14

CHAPTER 15

APPENDICES

ADDITIONAL INFO
A NOTE ABOUT VENDOR LISTINGS

Because businesses often change locations in *Second Life*, it's often more convenient to find and visit a business location by searching for the name of the owner in-world and finding the current business location in his or her picks.

For that reason, the avatar name of the business owner appears alongside the name of the business in each category. This will help you find businesses even if they've moved from the noted location since this book was published.

PREFABRICATED HOUSES

Second Life has long been the refuge of the frustrated architect. From soaring skyscrapers to beautiful log cabins straight from the pages of *Architectural Digest*—there's a prebuilt house for your personal style and taste somewhere in *Second Life*. These prebuilt houses (or house-construction kits) are commonly called *prefabs*.

The following are some of the most innovative and talented prefab construction artists:

HOMESTORE, Ingrid Ingersoll, Tableau (201,80, 26): One of two locations in *Second Life*, this one features Ingrid's fun and "only in *Second Life*" adult tree house with two rooms, a wrap-around deck, and the tree base the house is perched in.

Dominion Custom Homes, Sam Portocarrero, Dominion (211, 180, 25): Along with several styles and designs of prefabs, Sam also will take on custom build work designing everything from stores to huge, custom-everything mansions.

RESIDENTS SPEAK
FINDING THE PERFECT PREFAB HOUSE

"Shopping for prefab housing in *Second Life* can be quite difficult unless you know what you're looking for. Many factors go into buying your home, such as cost, number of prims, plot size, and style. Whether you are on a 512-square-meter parcel or own an entire sim, it is best to visit multiple stores to assess your overall needs in housing.

(Continued)

"There are many styles of housing in *Second Life*. For example, Rem Koolhaas builds low-prim modern structures designed to fit on tiny plots while maximizing space. On the opposite end of the spectrum, Asri Falcone's mansions are larger than life and fit for a rock star. They often require more than a quarter of a sim just to place them! If you are looking for something in between, Barnesworth Anubis offers affordable housing in many different designs.

"The last thing to look for is permissions. Chances are that at some point, you will mess up or accidentally delete your house. It helps to have a copy/mod/no transfer version of a house because if it can't be fixed, you can easily rez a new one and replace it. If you have to contact a designer to correct your mistake, not only will it delay your decorating process, but they may even charge you!"

—moo Money

ARTWORK/INTERIOR DECORATIONS

No one wants to live in a house with bare walls—not in their real life, and not in *Second Life*. Fortunately, *Second Life* has a really thriving art scene, including over 300 galleries where you can see original works of art unique to *Second Life* (like prim sculpture) and traditional art media brought into *Second Life* (like photography.)

Even if you decorate your place with your own snapshots taken inside *Second Life*, you might want to shop for accessories to make your house truly a home, whether it's a set of decorative vases or a beautiful flower arrangement. Here are some shopping resources:

Morphing Sculptures, Sasun Steinbeck, Mauve (160, 70, 34): You can check out one of *Second Life*'s original art forms (prim sculpture), buy your own morphing sculpture, and pick up a free list of over 50 other art exhibits and galleries.

Digital Bamboo, Digital Bamboo, Samurai Island (205, 203, 33): Beautifully detailed Asian-themed interior décor and furniture.

House of Creations, Lina Vandeverre, Optimal (129, 176, 24): A really nice selection of decorative panels, artwork, vases, and lighting.

EXAKT, Petgirl Bergman, Verloren (217, 32, 33): *Second Life*'s answer to IKEA is this store from Swede Petgirl (Tina) Bergman.

Arda's Home Décor, Arda Fauna, Solang (120, 152, 25): Gorgeous flower arrangements and other decorative interior plants, along with a nice collection of art and furniture.

LANDSCAPING SUPPLIES

CHAPTER 1
CHAPTER 2
CHAPTER 3
CHAPTER 4
CHAPTER 5
CHAPTER 6
CHAPTER 7
CHAPTER 8
CHAPTER 9
CHAPTER 10
CHAPTER 11
CHAPTER 12
CHAPTER 13
CHAPTER 14
CHAPTER 15
APPENDICES

Whether your parcel is mountainous or beachside, you'll want to keep the exterior of your house looking as good as the interior. If you're looking for some plants, trees, or flowers to spruce up your virtual yard, you'll be sure to find something green that fits your needs.

Figure 12.5: Fallingwater Flowers

Heart Garden Center, Lilith Heart, Heart 1 (124, 125, 29): Incredible botanical creations and other landscaping items.

Fallingwater Flowers, Fallingwater Cellardoor, Shiny Falls (82, 186, 27): Beautiful, fantastical, and whimsical flowers, plants, and shrubs (Figure 12.5).

GOODS THAT AVATARS SIT ON OR IN

Do you want to blast around *Second Life* in a rocket ship? How about piloting a submarine through an inky, icy sea? Maybe you just want to equip your fabulous new glass-and-steel skyscraper with some office furniture. Here is a selection of items avatars sit on or in.

VEHICLES

In *Second Life* you're not limited to choosing between a plane, train, or automobile; you can select a hover car, submarine, or science-fiction-inspired space marauder. You'll find plenty of traditional vehicles too, though. Here are some of the creators who specialize in making vehicles in *Second Life*:

Figure 12.6: HD Custom Cycles

Abbotts Aerodrome, Cubey Terra, Abbotts (159, 152, 71): The flagship store of one of *Second Life*'s leading flying vehicle creators.

Dominus Motor Company (DoMoCo), Francis Chung, Drive In (24, 217, 26): Home of the Dominus Shadow, a thoroughly beautiful, thoroughly fun classic muscle car in the style of the famous Ford Mustang fastback.

HD Custom Cycles, HD Pomeray, Lil Slurgis 1 (55, 47, 34): Exceptionally cool heavyweight cruisers and choppers, complete with custom sounds and riding animations (Figure 12.6).

FURNITURE

A house without furniture is a not really a home, is it? Most people in *Second Life* like having a home full of beautiful furniture. Whether you want to decorate in a supertrendy mid-century modern style with lots of chrome and glass or find something such as a piece Queen Victoria might've stocked in her own virtual castle, it's out there for your shopping pleasure.

RELIC, Baron Grayson, Sanctum Sanctorum (79, 185, 125): Elegant old-world and Gothic-themed furniture for sale in one of *Second Life*'s most photogenic and atmospheric sims.

Herman Miller, Real HermanMiller, Avalon (68, 125, 25): The legendary furniture company has opened a branch in *Second Life* offering residents the same amazing mid-century modern and thoroughly modern furniture that made the company famous. For a limited time, this store is offering several *free* Herman Miller designs including the iconic Aeron chair.

Mission Home Store, Troy Vogel, Tilitr (206, 47, 22): Fantastic-quality Arts and Crafts and Mission-style furniture and décor.

🔽 Goods that Avatars Wear

Avatar customization is the broadest form of content in-world. Residents often spend hours putting together their own style scene. That makes virtual goods that avatars wear some of the most popular things to shop for. Whether you're looking to make your avatar a futuristic cyborg, a pale-skinned vampire, or a world-class supermodel with the shoe collection to match, *Second Life* lets you explore and express your personal style. Who do you want to be today?

WEAPONS

Samurai swords, Excalibur siblings, futuristic light sabers, Old West six shooters, and thoroughly modern assault rifles all exist inside *Second Life*. If you feel the need to be well-armed, here are some places to find those things.

ADDITIONAL INFO
FIREARMS AS FASHION

Weapons—especially firearms—in *Second Life* are *generally* fashion accessories, as land owners have the option to make their land "safe." Turning on the Safe flag means that being attacked by weapons won't cause any damage to the people on that parcel. And death—if you're in an area that isn't marked as safe—means that your avatar teleports home, with all of his possessions intact. If you want to play shoot-'em-up with some friends, check out Saijo City—a sim-sized postapocalyptic city of the near future. Vast swaths of the city are unsettled "no man's land" where anything can happen, even gun battles.

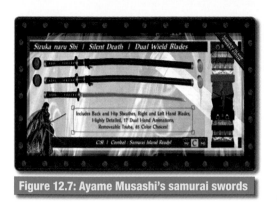

Figure 12.7: Ayame Musashi's samurai swords

Samurai Island, Ayame Musashi, Samurai Tokyo (183, 183, 25): Samurai and other swords, many of which include a scripted dueling game for use with other duelists (Figure 12.7).

Carlos, Inc., Jenny Carlos, Nogojiri (48, 28, 56): Modern firearms.

Dictatorshop, Lillani Lowell, Matriarch (110, 28, 29): Futuristic weapons inspired by sci-fi and video games.

MUSICAL INSTRUMENTS

Even if playing *Guitar Hero 3* is the extent of your musical talent, you can look like an absolute rock star in *Second Life*. Wild guitars—both re-creations of famous real-world brands and some instruments that could truly exist only in *Second Life*—come complete with wicked-cool animations. There are keyboards, string basses, and even mic stands for your new virtual band's lead vocalist. Even if your drummer keeps exploding like in *Spinal Tap*, at least you know his drum kit will be ready for the next gig.

Hyper-Instruments, Robby Dingo, Scafell (68, 144, 48): Realistic-looking musical instruments that can play actual music in-world.

Guitar Palace, Bill Havercamp, Sunset Beach (131, 147, 22): A huge selection of musical instruments and accessories.

Serendipity Studios, Sue Stonebender, Intemptesta Nox (163, 76, 77): Beautiful pianos in every size, color, and shape.

AVATAR KITS

Most avatars in *Second Life* are humanoid, whether they're cyborgs, vampires, or fashion models. But what if you want to be a dragon, an anthropomorphic fox, a mermaid, or a tiny panda? Using prims and some very clever textures, you can join the ranks of the non-human avatars in *Second Life* by using one of the incredible creations made by the following organizations:

Luskwood, Michi Lumin, Lusk (226, 125, 60): One of *Second Life*'s original anthropomorphic animal avatar makers, with over 80 different designs.

Grendel's Children, Flea Bussy, Avaria Tor (204, 234, 251): An incredible assortment of avatars from wind-up mechanical animals to complete 30-meter-tall dragon avatars.

Isle of Wyrms, Daryth Kennedy, Cathedral (123, 221, 101): Stunning dragon avatar kits are available at this incredibly detailed and beautifully atmospheric sim-sized store. Nearby sims offer other fantasy avatars such as drow, hobbits, and other swords-and-sorcery fun.

FROM LINDEN LAB
A FAVORITE SHOP

"My favorite shop is Grendel's Children (`http://slurl.com/secondlife/Avaria%20 Tor/204/240/252`), by far. I love that place. The avatars are extremely well designed, they're often amusing, and they're at extremely good prices given how well made they are."

—Prospero Linden

FASHION ITEMS

From couture ball gowns to sizzling latex, *Second Life* has a dynamic and vibrant fashion scene. Do you want to unleash your inner diva with extravagant flair or let your inner wild child come out to play on the darker side of fashion? The choice is yours in *Second Life*.

ADDITIONAL INFO
THE QUAD: WOMEN'S FASHION MECCA IN *SECOND LIFE*

No fashionista who spends much time in *Second Life* can resist the powerful tug of The Quad—a super-island of four sim-sized stores created by some of the very best creative minds of *Second Life*. The Quad consists of sims Dazzle, ETD Isle, Celestial City, and Canimal, and they are all together for your shopping convenience.

Dazzle (66, 14, 26) houses a store called Last Call that features high-end fashions for men and women created by lead designer Ginny Talamasca, one of the most talented virtual fashion creators in *Second Life*. Ginny's formals are among the very best available in *Second Life*. Last Call also offers jewelry, accessories, and shoes by talented prim artist Lyra Muse.

ETD Isle (198, 178, 30) houses the hair and clothing creations of Elikapeka Tiramisu. ETD is widely regarded as offering some of the best prim hair styles. Elikapeka's hair texturing has recently been redesigned to be even more realistic, and her many devoted customers make Elika's store one of the most popular shopping destinations anywhere in world. ETD sells hairstyles for both men and women. Once a month Elika chooses an up-and-coming designer to feature in a store next to her own, which is a great way to find and sample new fashion talent in *Second Life*.

Celestial City (67, 240, 26) houses Celestial Studios, a store by Starley Thereian that offers women's hair, women's clothing, and some of the best women's skins. The clothing-design vibe at Celestial Studios is classy casual. You can also check out Oxygen Designs on the Celestial City sim, a clothing and pose line by Vee Grace.

CHAPTER 1

CHAPTER 2

CHAPTER 3

CHAPTER 4

CHAPTER 5

CHAPTER 6

CHAPTER 7

CHAPTER 8

CHAPTER 9

CHAPTER 10

CHAPTER 11

CHAPTER 12

CHAPTER 13

CHAPTER 14

CHAPTER 15

APPENDICES

Finally, if you like clothing with more of a punk/street edge, you will enjoy shopping at **Canimal** (209, 62, 26) by Canimal Zephyr. With styles for both men and women, the clothing at Canimal will indulge your inner emo Goth punk rocker. Canimal also offers a beautiful line of skins and the occasional must-have jewelry collection.

You can visit The Quad by clicking on the Map button in your viewer and typing one of the sim names into the Search box on the right-hand side of the pop-up window.

Mainstream Clothing

These designers feature clothing you'd find on a red-carpet runway or in any glossy real-world fashion catalog.

Simone! Design, Simone Stern, Simone (112, 156, 36): One of *Second Life*'s most accomplished fashion designers for women, Simone offers clothing that encompasses many, many styles and time periods.

Pixel Dolls, Nephilaine Protagonist, Port Seraphine (182, 36, 21): One of *Second Life*'s original fashion designers is still going strong with formals, casuals, lingerie, and anime-inspired clothing.

Blaze, Blaze Columbia, Blaze (71, 117, 22): Especially well known for formal and business wear for men and women.

Fetishwear

These vendors specialize in creating sexy skin-tight latex and leather outfits.

Sweet Dreams, Vanity Glitter, Port Seraphine (197, 150, 22): Latex, lingerie, and more latex.

Draconic Kiss, Draconic Lioncourt, Koreshan (193, 93, 25): Latex wear and a selection of Japanese street fashion styles called "elegant Goth Lolita."

KDC, Kyrah Abattoir, dead realm (87, 178, 594): One of *Second Life*'s first and best fetishwear vendors, this store features sleek, shiny realistic latex outfits and plenty of bondage gear.

Skins

In *Second Life* a skin is the bottom-most texture layer around your avatar's wireframe mesh. It dramatically affects characteristics such as skin tone, makeup, body hair, and lip size. Here are some of *SL*'s best skin creators.

Naughty, Lost Thereian/Ambyance2 Anubis, Naughty (80, 168, 24): Featuring some of the most popular skins and hair designs for male and female avatars in *Second Life*.

Figure 12.8: Tete á Pied main store

Tête á Pied, Roslin Petion/CJ Carnot, Nouveau (200, 156, 22): The store offers the brand-new Vivant skin line for women. Roslin is a professional makeup artist in real life, and it shows on these beautifully done skins (Figure 12.8).

FKNY, Funk Schnook, FNKY Cake (128, 43, 24): Creator of the Antonio skin line for men, FKNY has quickly become one of the most popular male skins in *Second Life*.

FROM LINDEN LAB
OUR FAVORITE PURCHASES

"This changes and expands with age (not unlike wine), so here are a few of my favorite purchases: I really dig Nicky Ree's clothes … and the many of 'em they are. Lilith Heart makes some of the bestest prim plants, Intemptesta Nox with Baron Grayson and Sue Stonebender's creations have such ancient-looking goods. Luxe Island is prime for sculptie innovations (where I got one of my fave sculptie chairs from Xenius Revere)."

—Torley Linden

"My best buy ever was my house in Linden Village, designed by the brilliant Scope Cleaver. Innovative architecture and gorgeous nighttime lighting! I also love my OmniTech OmniPhaze—it lets me fly through walls!"

—Benjamin Linden

"My best purchase is probably the skin that I bought for my alt. It's got a great beard on it that even looks like my real-life beard—albeit slightly redder in color. While I'm not fond of the overly articulated musculature on the chest, I'm very happy with the way the face looks on this skin. It made a huge difference in making my avatar look halfway decent when I went from the default 'plastic ken doll' skin that avatars start out with to this skin."

—Prospero Linden

"My best purchase ever was my skin. For me, since I choose to not role-play, the core of my online identity is my appearance. The core of my appearance is my shape and skin."

—Jill Linden

Hair

The hair model that the default *Second Life* avatar possesses leaves a lot to be desired. Most residents purchase hair made from prims such as those created by the following designers. Don't worry about that counting against your parcel prim limit, as prims that are attached to your avatar are exempt from the parcel limit.

Calla, Haedon Quine/Tigerlily Koi, Callatropia (125, 194, 24): Dynamic duo creates beautiful and unique hairstyles for women and men.

Gurl6, Six Kennedy, GuRLyWood (110, 108, 22): Creates some of the truly wild and fantastical hair styles to be found in *Second Life*; Six Kennedy's boyfriend Dominik Bauer makes hairstyles for men.

BooPerFunk, Booperkit Moseley, BooPerFunk (232, 26, 22): Excellent African, African-American, and West Indes hairstyles for men and women.

Shoes

From fancy dress shoes to combat boots, footwear in *Second Life* encompasses the same variety and creative diversity as everything else in-world.

Shiny Things, Fallingwater Cellardoor, Shiny Falls (163, 181, 37): Beautifully realistic pumps, sandals, boots, jewelry, and handbags for women; boots and dress shoes for men.

Sylfie's Prim Seduction, Sylfie Minogue, Sylfie (70, 35, 22): Over 100 women's shoe and boot styles set in a tropical tiki hut–themed shopping sim.

Maitreya, Onyx LeShelle, Superieure (99, 47, 451): Onyx is a newcomer who has taken boots and shoes to a new level by incorporating sculpted prims into her design work; she also offers some amazing animations and poses.

 RESIDENTS SPEAK
GLOBAL STYLE IN *SECOND LIFE*

"One of the biggest selling points of shopping online for my clothing has always been getting interesting imported designs that wouldn't be available locally. The effect of different cultures on fashion, from as minor a shift as England to as major a shift as India, is a valuable asset to those interested in cultivating a well-rounded and, more importantly a unique wardrobe. Shipping, however, can be murder. A world where the cost of materials and shipping is no object, and designers from every nation on earth are presenting their perspectives to the consumer, is fertile ground for truly inspiring fashions to take root.

(Continued)

CHAPTER 1
CHAPTER 2
CHAPTER 3
CHAPTER 4
CHAPTER 5
CHAPTER 6
CHAPTER 7
CHAPTER 8
CHAPTER 9
CHAPTER 10
CHAPTER 11
CHAPTER 12
CHAPTER 13
CHAPTER 14
CHAPTER 15
APPENDICES

"It would be a lie to say the market of international fashion in *Second Life* is a model one. As in our first lives, language barriers can cause problems in getting widespread exposure and recognition. Fashion in *SL* is without a doubt dominated by English. However, there is so much amazing work going on outside of the English-speaking fashion communities that it can no longer be overlooked. A great example of this is the Japanese community, which is designing items that catch on in mainstream fashion and spread like wildfire.

"There's an incredible thirst for the unique creations that come from different cultures, and we're in the midst of a great movement to embrace a greater number of international fashion and design influences. This market will only continue to grow and become more diverse and inspiring for the consumers as the popularity of *Second Life* rises around the world."

—Iris Ophelia

Accessories (Jewelry, Sunglasses, Handbags)

Don't forget about the finishing touches for your style statement. Shop for accessories at these locations.

Figure 12.9: Paper Couture in Barcola

Paper Couture, Prue Lu, Barcola (79, 125, 25): Incredibly stylish sunglasses, purses, and jewelry complements a line of couture fashion designs (Figure 12.9).

Muse, Caliah Lyon, Linji (143, 152, 49): Stunning attention to detail and flair for fashion drama makes Muse a great place to find jewelry to complement your wardrobe.

Miriel, Miriel Enfield, Nouveau (114, 201, 33): Formal and casual jewelry in a variety of metal textures and stone color choices; also some of the best eyes to be found in *Second Life*.

Animation Overrides

An animation override replaces the default animations in *Second Life* with alternative, usually more-realistic-looking animations. Most *Second Life* residents find the default animations to be somewhat clunky, so new animations are popular.

Torridwear, Torrid Midnight, Chartreuse (177, 69, 22): Several male and female animation overriders are available here, as well as an inexpensive line of cute casual women's fashions.

ANA-motions, Surealia Anatine, Sterling Heights (120, 94, 22): Fun, fresh animation overrides include "broken doll," "emo girl," and "music box ballerina."

Miscellaneous

There are other miscellaneous fashion items available, such as wings, tails, and neko (cat/human hybrid) ears to spice up your avatar.

Material Squirrel, Kala Bijoux, Winged Isle (22, 110, 47): Some of *Second Life*'s best-looking wing designs, plus scripted tails and horns.

Hybrid, Philo Sion, Glass Earth (136, 185, 23): Beautifully textured and constructed tails, ears, and complete kits including skins for nekos.

ADDITIONAL INFO
THE BLOCK: STYLE FOR GUYS

Although it's generally true that the fashion scene in *Second Life* revolves around female avatars (who shop more frequently and avidly than male avatars, as a rule), Zabitan Assia's shopping region The Block caters mostly to men. From skins to shoes to really cool shades, if it's something guys want to wear in *Second Life*, one of the vendors on The Block will likely be offering it for sale. The block is located at Varado (79, 128, 31).

Another great place to shop for male fashion is on the sim Kmadd Enterprise (128, 128, 0). Virtually every major male-fashion content creator has a branch on Kmadd. It's a great spot to do some serious wardrobe upgrades.

ADULT ITEMS

Second Life has always been a place where consenting adults can do everything consenting adults do in the real world. As such, there is a wide range of adult items available in *Second Life*, from sex toys and scripted genitals to elaborately detailed sexual props like beds with sex-act animations built right into them. If you feel the need to get your virtual freak on, you might want to shop at some of these stores:

Eros, Stroker Serpentine, Eros (183, 193, 23): One of *Second Life*'s original adult-item vendors, Eros sells everything from scripted genitals to "sexbeds" with adult animations built in to them.

Xcite, Javier Puff, Eventide East (108, 125, 34): Probably the best-known vendor of scripted genitals in *Second Life*, Xcite also sells sex toys and other adult gadgets.

Sensations, Amethyst Rosencrans, Sensations (150, 152, 48): Probably best known for locking collars that allow other users to control a collared avatar, locking cuffs, and scripted "alternative" sexual objects like tentacles.

CHAPTER 1
CHAPTER 2
CHAPTER 3
CHAPTER 4
CHAPTER 5
CHAPTER 6
CHAPTER 7
CHAPTER 8
CHAPTER 9
CHAPTER 10
CHAPTER 11
CHAPTER 12

CHAPTER 13
CHAPTER 14
CHAPTER 15
APPENDICES

SHOPPING ON A TIGHT BUDGET

When you first start in *Second Life*, you might be tempted to sink some money into virtual goods. There's a still a huge amount of content in *Second Life* that's free (or nearly so) for the taking, so be sure to check that out as well. Some of the best places to start your low-budget shopping extravaganzas are listed here.

> **ADDITIONAL INFO**
> ## THE GULF BETWEEN NO COST AND FREEBIE
>
> Although there is a lot of content available at no cost in *Second Life* (technically for sale but priced at L$0), much more of the "free" content is set for sale at L$1. Although these items cost money, they're still commonly called *freebies* (L$1 is about one-third of a US penny). So you may find that you're in need of some Lindens even if you're shopping for freebies.
>
> How can you get small amounts of Lindens in *Second Life*?
>
> **By camping.** One of the best ways to earn very, very small quantities of Lindens is by camping. Some venue owners in *Second Life* pay campers (people who have mastered the art of just sitting around) to get their venues ranked in the Popular Places search tab—the more avatars in a region, the higher that location's rank in the search engine. Most camping spots in *Second Life* pay a rate of approximately L$2 per 10 minutes, or L$12/hour. Unless you think your time in *Second Life* is worth about 3 cents an hour, you probably should just buy a couple of real dollars' worth of Lindens. But if you only need L$2, then taking a coffee break is probably not a bad idea. You can find a lot of camping sites by searching for the word *camping* in the Classifieds.
>
> **From money trees.** New residents can look for money trees in *Second Life*, which generally pay out a bit more than camping (between L$5–30 depending on the tree). You can find money trees by searching for *money tree* in the Classifieds.

GNUbie Store, Indigo (199, 63, 38): The GNUbie store in Indigo has long been a place for new residents to stock up their inventories with a very minimal outlay of Lindens. The GNUbie store comes complete with prefabs, furniture, interior décor, vehicles, scripting kits, textures, and a lot of fashion items, all in a very neatly organized set of displays. Many of the items in the store come with permission to disassemble the items, which you can use as a template or model to make your own content that matches how you picture it in your mind.

New Citizens Incorporated (NCI), Kuula (54, 175, 29): NCI has been helping new residents in *Second Life* learn more about this amazing virtual world for a long time. NCI offers classes in everything from "How to modify your appearance" to "How to start scripting with LSL." They also help support The Shelter, a great social hangout for residents new and old. NCI also has an extensive collection of true freebie items—everything from libraries of LSL scripts to hundreds of free shoes.

Free Dove, Gallii (113, 53, 33): This location is always busy—full of new residents looking for fashionable goods at no cost. Free Dove has special content for residents at L$0, regardless of avatar age. The range of fashion goods for both men and women is probably the best collection to be found in *Second Life*. This is always a good stop for a brand-new avatar to find decent shoes, prim hair, clothing, and more for free.

Figure 12.10: Nyte'n'Day's L$1 newbie kit

It's worth noting that some vendors also have special low-priced content for new residents—but most of them have some strings attached, from joining their new-item announcement list to having an avatar of a certain age or younger. This time period is typically 30–60 days, so if you're a new resident, swing through some of the stores and see if they have high-quality free goods available at a very low cost. Some other creators don't put any restrictions on their freebie items. See Figure 12.10—find this kit at Couture Isle (44, 159, 49). It includes a skin, two shapes, two outfits and more.)

Another great resource for low-cost or free shopping is the Fabulously Free in *Second Life* blog (`http://fabfree.wordpress.com`) written by Cherlindrea Lamont. Cherlindrea constantly updates her site with the newest giveaways, L$1 fashion finds, and more.

RESIDENTS SPEAK
INDULGENT SHOPPING ON A TIGHT BUDGET

"I'm on a tight budget in real life. There's no room for department-store shopping, let alone designer-boutique shopping. Unfortunately, I have champagne tastes and a beer budget; actually, it's more of a tap-water budget. Three-hundred dollar shoes are out of the question for me, no matter how much I may want them. It's no use even visiting the high-end stores that I love because the sales help sizes me up right away and they know I can afford to do nothing more than visit the merchandise. It's a completely different story in *Second Life*, where I can indulge every whim. I can afford to teleport over to Shiny Things, Lassitude & Ennui, or Paper Couture and pick up gorgeous shoes, a matching bag, and some great jewelry for less than US$10.

(Continued)

"*Second Life* designers are amazingly creative; their designs are as innovative and as fresh as those of real life designers. However, when it comes to pricing, *Second Life* designers have a definite advantage. While they have to invest in design tools and spend a lot of time designing, just like real-life designers, they don't have to pay for materials. It costs a *Second Life* designer the same amount to produce one pair of shoes as one thousand pairs of shoes. What that means for me is that *Second Life* designs are incredibly affordable and that I can have the wardrobe of my dreams in *Second Life* while shopping sale racks in real life."

—Tamara Kirshner

SHOPPING AS A SOCIAL ACTIVITY

Like most things, shopping in *Second Life* is more fun with friends around. Whether you're looking for a BBQ grill, a yacht, or a new hairstyle, having your *Second Life* friends help you choose from among the huge range of choices in style is always a good time.

Because *Second Life* offers teleportation, that's the main way people move between sims. (By contrast, once they're at a destination sim, most people walk or fly their avatar around to shop.) Unfortunately, there is not (yet) a group teleport function, so when you go to a shop, you will have the manually look up your friends from your Friends tab and then click the Teleport button on the right side of the Communicate window.

ADDITIONAL INFO
TELEPORTING MISHAPS

When you teleport multiple people to a destination and you remain in the same location, incoming avatars will "stack" on top of each other—each one standing on the head of the previous teleportee. Sometimes you can teleport avatars (usually accidentally!) into a lake or the middle of a building. Teleport mishaps are part of the funny side of *Second Life*, so grin and bear it if one happens to you while you're out for an evening of shopping.

Keep in mind that normal chat in *Second Life* has a range of 20 meters. So if you see someone making the typing animation at a reasonable distance from your avatar but you can't see their chat text, they might be too far away to "hear." If this happens to you, try to move closer to the typist so you'll be in hearing range again.

CHAPTER 1

CHAPTER 2

CHAPTER 3

CHAPTER 4

CHAPTER 5

CHAPTER 6

CHAPTER 7

CHAPTER 8

CHAPTER 9

CHAPTER 10

CHAPTER 11

CHAPTER 12

CHAPTER 13

CHAPTER 14

CHAPTER 15

APPENDICES

RESIDENTS SPEAK
PIXEL SHOPPING WITH FRIENDS FOR THE WIN

"I consider myself to be an expert shopper. It's a sport to me; purely recreational and for the thrill of the hunt. Hunting bargains and finding that perfect item are victories to be celebrated. And, of course, it's always better when done in teams. I have spent many years finely tuning my shopping abilities in real life; knowing who to take with me when hunting for different items, where to look, and how to spot a sale. So when I discovered shopping in *Second Life*, it was love at first Linden spent.

"Now, I have heard some people say that they prefer real shopping as opposed to the virtual variety, and vice versa. For me, it's all virtual all the time. Sure, shopping in *Second Life* doesn't help me find something to wear to work in the morning, but that's just about the only drawback. On the plus side, everything always fits perfectly (or can be made to without visiting a tailor), and it's much less expensive. There are still sales to be hunted down and celebrated. And best of all, my virtual closet will expand to hold whatever I can manage to buy. Just as in real life, I have found a group of like-minded folks who are fun to talk to and similarly inclined toward retail sport, so the social aspect keeps me satisfied as well. And best of all, in *Second Life* I can wear what I want when I want and not disturb the general public.

"It's pixels for the win in my shopping world!"

—Madison Carnot

IN-WORLD SHOPPING OUTSIDE OF *SECOND LIFE*

The seriously shopping-addicted can browse *Second Life* goods while browsing the Web (say, like at work!). Two Web-based e-commerce portals display goods and accept Lindens that you've deposited into your account to pay the vendors for the merchandise. These are OnRez (`http://shop.onrez.com`) and SL Exchange (`http://www.slexchange.com`) also sometimes written as SLX.

A relatively recent interesting phenomenon is the sale of real-world goods and services through these sites in Linden dollars. Computers, video cards, monitors, and other software has been offered for sale through these sites, with the vendors of these real-world goods accepting Lindens as payment.

Creating an account on both sites is very straightforward. Once your accounts are active, you can shop online and your new items will be automatically sent to your avatar, held until the next time you login.

The two sites are virtually equivalent in terms of functionality, and like most Web shopping sites, both are fun to browse. Plus, it's always amusing to see what other shoppers had in their carts when they bought the same item you're thinking of purchasing.

ADDITIONAL INFO
ACTIVATING YOUR SL EXCHANGE ACCOUNT

SL Exchange requires that you validate your avatar's identity in-world to fully activate e-commerce shopping. To complete this step, simply find an SL Exchange kiosk on the SL Exchange island (named appropriately, Exchange) and have your avatar say an alphanumeric code generated from the SL Exchange website.

TROUBLESHOOTING SHOPPING WOES

Second Life is a technical marvel, and like all technical marvels, everyday events can sometimes go wrong.

UNPACKING BOXES

Once you've shopped for a while, you'll notice that some items you buy come packaged not in folders but in prims commonly called *boxes* (even if they're not a cube shape). A question that new residents often ask is, how do I get the stuff I just bought out of this box? It keeps attaching to my hand if I wear it!

1. Locate and drag the box from your inventory onto the ground.

2. Right-click on the box once it is rezzed and choose Open from the pie menu.

3. A dialog box will appear showing you the contents of the box.

4. Click Copy to Inventory.

5. Right-click on the box, choose More from the pie menu, then choose Delete.

6. You may get a warning about something set to No Copy permissions, but you can ignore it; you've already pulled the contents from the box into your inventory safely, so click Yes.

CHAPTER 1

CHAPTER 2

CHAPTER 3

CHAPTER 4

CHAPTER 5

CHAPTER 6

CHAPTER 7

CHAPTER 8

CHAPTER 9

CHAPTER 10

CHAPTER 11

CHAPTER 12

CHAPTER 13

CHAPTER 14

CHAPTER 15

APPENDICES

ADDITIONAL INFO
IS BUILD ENABLED?

You will need to be in an area where Build is turned on to unpack boxes. If you see a box with a slash through it at the top of your viewer window, you are in an area where building is not allowed—and these steps will not work in such a place. You will get an error message when you try to drag the box from your inventory onto the ground.

If you don't own land or rent a place to stay, you can find a building area called a sandbox where building is permitted for all *Second Life* residents. Search for one by clicking on Search in the bottom of your viewer, selecting the All tab, and typing in *Sandbox*.

ASKING FOR CUSTOMER SERVICE

If something goes wrong with your shopping experience, you can often contact the content creator for help. Most content creators are busy making new items or helping other customers with issues, too, so be as patient and respectful as possible.

Your first course of action when seeking help is to check the content creator's profile—many content creators have store policies and customer-service FAQs that can save you a lot of time and frustration.

When your question or problem isn't covered by an FAQ, it's time to create a notecard. (Since *Second Life* caps the number of instant messages that it will hold for residents, an IM sent to a content creator can often get lost among the other offline IMs that person has received.) A more reliable way to request help is to create a notecard and write your request on it.

Figure 12.11: Creating a new notecard

You can do this by opening your inventory and selecting Create then New Note (Figure 12.11). The first thing you'll want to do is type your name—many customer-service notecards don't include the author's name, and that makes it hard to get a response! After that, explain your problem politely and suggest a course of action you'd like the content creator to consider to resolve the issue. Once you're finished, click Save and drag and drop the notecard (renamed from New Note to something like Help Request from [your avatar's name]) on to the content creator's profile.

Some content creators don't log into *Second Life* every day, so it may take a day or two to get a response. Don't be discouraged if your problem isn't resolved immediately. Most content creators want to be fair to their customers and help them resolve issues as quickly as they can.

ADDITIONAL INFO
GET YOUR TRANSACTION-HISTORY DETAILS

It's often helpful to cut and paste your purchase record for a particular item from the master transaction history Linden Lab maintains on the *Second Life* website when you write for customer service assistance. You can access this history (a rolling 30-day log of everything you've bought, sold, given, or been given) by logging into the *Second Life* website and choosing Transactions History from the right sidebar under Account.

FINDING WHAT YOU'RE LOOKING FOR

Second Life has become so large and so full of content that sometimes you *know* what you want to buy—if only you could figure out who made it! The first place to turn is to the in-world search engine. If you shop a lot, it's quickly going to become a staple in your journeys around the grid. Simply click Search and then select the Classifieds tab. This will let you search through the paid ads that content creators submit.

ADDITIONAL INFO
A CRITICAL EYE TOWARD THE CLASSIFIEDS

Be wary of blindly choosing the first several Classifieds search results. Like most search engines, the *Second Life* engine can be gamed, and sometimes the results are not terribly relevant to your particular query. For instance, the query *base* as in "underground secret lair" will return any ad that has the letter sequence *base* in it. So you will see ads for baseball and basements.

Don't be afraid to scroll to the bottom of the search results, either. Sometimes newer content developers buy inexpensive ads—but they might've just made exactly what you're looking for. A higher-placed listing in the Classifieds means just that the seller paid more money to the Classifieds system.

If the Classifieds are no help, then it's time to turn to your favorite Internet search engine. As *Second Life* and web technologies start to mesh, more and more in-world creations show up in queries provided to web search engines. This technique is especially useful if the thing you want to find has extensive blog coverage (like, for example, *Second Life* fashion).

Another technique that can help you find what you're looking for is to browse the online e-commerce OnRez and SL Exchange. Both of these sites have search engines that are bit more sophisticated than the one included in *Second Life*. Even if you don't have an account on these sites, you can find the name of a content creator and then go visit that avatar's store inside *Second Life*.

ADDITIONAL INFO
GROUPS FOR FASHION ADDICTS

If nothing else has worked, ask other *Second Life* residents for help. Some in-world groups may be able to point you in the right direction.

Have your avatar join the Fashion Emergency and Fashion Consolidated groups if you enjoy fashion or shopping in *Second Life*. Fashion Emergency can help you locate stores when you have a specific request in mind (for instance, you might ask the group to help you find a polka-dotted sundress in hot pink or a pair of to-die-for pumps to match a dress you've had your eye on). Fashion Consolidated is an outlet for hundreds of content creators to send members of the group new-release notices. You can join a group by clicking Search, selecting the Group tab, and then typing a group's name into the search box. Then select the group with your mouse and click Join.

MORE SHOPPING RESOURCES

Shopping is a big part of being in *Second Life*, and there's so much great content to explore that it would take an entire book to cover it all. This chapter is a good introduction, but you should take advantage of other shopping resources that can make your shopping in-world more productive, fun, and adventurous.

SECOND STYLE

Second Style is *Second Life*'s original style and fashion magazine (Figure 12.12). Published monthly, it can be downloaded as a high-resolution PDF from `http://www.secondstyle.com` or obtained from in-world kiosks as a wearable HUD (heads-up display).

CHAPTER 1
CHAPTER 2
CHAPTER 3
CHAPTER 4
CHAPTER 5
CHAPTER 6
CHAPTER 7
CHAPTER 8
CHAPTER 9
CHAPTER 10
CHAPTER 11
CHAPTER 12

CHAPTER 13
CHAPTER 14
CHAPTER 15
APPENDICES

Figure 12.12: A recent *Second Style* cover

Second Style publishes two blogs that are frequently updated with new content. Second Style Fashionista (`http://blog.secondstyle.com`) follows women's fashions in *Second Life*, and Men's Second Style (`http://mens.secondstyle.com`) tracks men's fashions and accessories.

There is also a 10-minute weekly fashion podcast called the Second Style Stylecast that highlights some of that week's new fashion releases and upcoming fashion events. Although the show is available through iTunes (or your favorite podcast directory), no special software is required to hear the show; simply browse to `http://stylecast.secondstyle.com` and use the built-in player.

LINDEN LIFESTYLES

The "unofficial shopping blog of *Second Life*" (`http://www.lindenlifestyles.com`) contains plenty of fashion reviews and the occasional review of other items of interest, including furniture, prefabs, and interior-design firms. The weekly fashion-release round-up is a handy way to keep tabs on new releases without obsessively reading the forums to find new items.

FASHION PLANET

Second Life resident Tao Takashi has created an aggregated feed of various fashion-review blogs and designer blogs called Fashion Planet. By tracking this one site, you can stay in touch with more than 100 independent fashion-themed commentary and new release outlets. Visit at `http://fashionplanet.worldofsl.com`.

⬇ Going Broke with Daphne and Tamara

Tamara Kirshner and Daphne Abernathy host this podcast (http://www.daphneandtamara.com), which helps you decide where to spend your Lindens in *Second Life*. The scope of the show is broad, but so far the duo has focused mostly on fashion designers and fashion content. Future shows may cover prefabs, furniture, and other style items in *Second Life*.

⬇ Virtual Suburbia

Virtual architecture critic Chip Poutine runs this blog (http://www.virtualsuburbia.com), which features in-depth commentary about his wanderings through the virtual landscapes of *Second Life*. You will frequently find discussions of urban planning, prefabs, and other topics as they relate to architecture and landscaping in-world.

⬇ SLShopper.com

This site (http://www.sluniverse.com/php/shop/) lets you quickly and easily search and shop for items from all sorts of content categories ranging from prefab houses to high-heeled shoes. You can build up a shopping cart of goods and then give the URL to your friends as a subtle hint for rezday presents.

CHAPTER 1

CHAPTER 2

CHAPTER 3

CHAPTER 4

CHAPTER 5

CHAPTER 6

CHAPTER 7

CHAPTER 8

CHAPTER 9

CHAPTER 10

CHAPTER 11

CHAPTER 12

CHAPTER 13

CHAPTER 14

CHAPTER 15

APPENDICES

CHAPTER 13

BUSINESS AND MONEY

In recent years, virtual riches that translate into real-life wealth have become a very hot topic. There are more and more stories about people earning a comfortable real-life income in virtual worlds—worlds where money literally grows on trees, and where starting up your own business is as easy as a couple of mouse clicks. And so, most people who sign up for *Second Life* expect to make some money, and many hope to make a lot of money. After all, some have succeeded, and their triumphs, trumpeted by the media, continue to motivate many would-be millionaires, along with a growing number of real-world corporations; there's money in them thar virtual hills!

So, can you get rich in *Second Life*? This chapter gives you a detailed answer to that question. Briefly, the answer is yes you can—but only if you put in the effort. Getting rich in *Second Life* requires as much effort, skill, and luck as getting rich in real life. Surprise, surprise! However, it is possible, and this chapter should give you a well-informed start.

CONTENTS

MONEY: THE COLD, HARD FACTS

There are two facts you must keep in mind. Here's fact number one: the Linden dollar isn't *money*. We'll call it money in this book—it sounds nice—but truly, it's like old-time scrip, paid to workers so that they could exchange it for goods at the company store. Like scrip, Linden dollars are units whose value is recognized by the payer and the payee: they are not currency per se. So, however much you have in Linden dollars, it's still not money—it's just scrip that can be used to buy stuff in the company store called *Second Life*. However, if you sell your Lindens for real-world money, what you end up with is real money. This real money constitutes real-world income, which means it could be taxable—don't say no one told you when the tax man cometh and starts asking questions. And no, the size of the *SL* economy doesn't permit it to become some sort of tax haven, in case you're having impure thoughts.

Here's fact number two: At the time of writing, there are 260–280 Linden dollars to one good old US dollar. This exchange rate has been stable for quite a while. That means it costs hundreds of L$ to buy bubble gum in the real world—chew on that. The exchange rate may surge or drop suddenly following an *SL* update that introduces a new money source/money sink such as a new stipend, or higher fees for sound and texture uploads. However, even then it is unlikely to break out of the 240–300 range.

Figure 13.1: Owning a virtual business can give you plenty of real-life thrills.

The conclusion? If you're an individual entering *Second Life* to make a living in real life, your starting position equals that of an unemployed 19th-century dockhand: you work all day for a single meal. Some *SL* residents have also wisely compared it to living in an impoverished country where the exchange rate is terrible. The awful truth is that if you want to make meaningful money in *Second Life*—money that will actually make a difference in your real life—you must be prepared to put in quite a lot of time and effort. Simply getting an *SL* job isn't likely to make you a lot of dough; most likely, you'll have to be a little more skilled and/or inventive, and at the very least start a profitable business of your own (Figure 13.1). Yes, it's possible to get rich eventually. But it's likely to be just as hard as in real life.

CHAPTER 1

CHAPTER 2

CHAPTER 3

CHAPTER 4

CHAPTER 5

CHAPTER 6

CHAPTER 7

CHAPTER 8

CHAPTER 9

CHAPTER 10

CHAPTER 11

CHAPTER 12

CHAPTER 13

CHAPTER 14

CHAPTER 15

APPENDICES

ADDITIONAL INFO
GETTING PAID

Many *SL* old-timers, when asked how they get L$, tend to shrug and state they simply buy 10 bucks' worth of Linden dollars from time to time. This is probably the best thing to do if you treat *Second Life* primarily as an opportunity to socialize and have adventures of all kinds and colors (see "Money Realities" sidebar).

RESIDENTS SPEAK
MONEY REALITIES

"I do make money here, but don't think for a second one has to just put up a vendor and wait for monies to fall down from the sky, because it really is like a second job. If you want to make a profit you have to work 24/7 for it."

—Marine Kelley

"There is no easy way to get money in *SL*. Attempting to go the easy route will get you mocked, banned, spoken down to, or thrown off the grid entirely. Learn a skill. Learn several skills."

—Coyote Momiji

"Less than 2% of the people who play *SL* make a net profit in any given month. Few of that 2% can make a net profit *every* month. Less than 500 people, out of the *millions* who have *Second Life* accounts, make anything close to a real-world working wage from what they do in *SL*. I certainly don't, nor do I think I could.

"Can you make money here? Yes, with hard work, and if you love what you're doing and are willing to spend hours and hours perfecting your skills and your products. Can you make a living just working in the virtual world? As in, pay for all of your rent and groceries in the real world? Very few do, but it is possible.

"Yet more than 98% will *not* make a net profit here. Think about that."

—Ceera Murakami

WAYS TO PROFIT

Fortunately, you can enrich yourself in more than one way in *Second Life*. To start with, you can make money in *Second Life*, and you can make money in the real world through or thanks to *Second Life*. One often leads to the other, and it's made very easy by *SL*'s integration into the World Wide Web: you can move between the Internet and the virtual world with a couple of mouse clicks.

Most *SL* members tend to think solely of making money *inside Second Life*. It's good but emotional logic: you enter a new world, so you make money in the new world—that's what appeals to most people, often just because it's much more fun that way. But if you want to make big money through your virtual existence, don't go there. Instead, copy the strategy of the *SL* magnates: all of them make money on their *SL* activities both inside *Second Life* and in real life, and it's the real-life activities that pay most. Similarly, most high-earning *SL* professionals cash in on their real-world skills. Remember that right now the price of labor—real-world labor, at a real-world computer!—in the virtual world is much lower than in the real world. *SL* wages and earnings have been climbing gently, and they'll continue to climb together with the number of *SL* residents. But it will be a very long while before pay in the virtual world begins to compare with real-world pay.

However, making your second life profitable isn't limited to making money. In fact, your big profit is likely to be non-monetary. The virtual world is a new dimension to the real world and as such, is part of the real world. It can enrich your real life, especially if you're not happy with what you're getting right now. Your needs define what you want. It may be more social interaction; it may be more education; it may be more money. It's up to you to decide how you want to profit from your virtual life.

Now that we've made this clear, let's see how some people got rich.

⬇ PROFIT PROFILES

The *SL* resident who best symbolizes success on the virtual path to riches is Anshe Chung, *Second Life*'s wealthiest denizen and a real-life millionaire. Anshe Chung got rich through a number of activities connected with *Second Life*: virtual real-estate sales and rentals, a real money/virtual money currency exchange, and real-world consulting on virtual worlds. At the time of writing, real-world Anshe Chung Studios employs 80 people busy creating stuff for virtual worlds. And yes, there is an Anshe Chung store selling some of that stuff in *Second Life*, but it's definitely not one of Anshe Chung's main moneymakers. Her success confirms a point made earlier: if you want to get really rich thanks to *Second Life*, look for the real-world/virtual-world link that will make you good money.

"Grab a niche that is underexploited. Lots of obvious stuff gets missed—I can name dozens of them. Early on, I got L$ being a proofreader and documentation writer, and there are still lots of opportunities to provide that as a useful service. Full-region terraforming/landscaping skills will become even more important in the times ahead.

"Look at it very simply: what are the needs that I can provide?

"I'm very personality-driven, so I think if I was going to, say, sell land, I'd do it with a twist only I could achieve … Watermelon Estates Yayzerama! You know how the maxim goes: to succeed in the market, either do what other people haven't thought of yet, or do what they aren't willing to sludge through.

"Provider of custom animations is another field that could use more experts. I see so many good chairs out there that have crap anims, and think, 'If this builder teamed up with a super animator, they'd have the market dominated.'

"And don't be a jackass! It wastes everyone's time. Good customer service is priceless."

—Torley Linden

"Honestly, I think all the media attention on 'people making money in *Second Life*' that happened in the end of 2006 led to a set of people who came in thinking that (a) it was easy to make a buck, and (b) that was the point of *Second Life*. Once I got over the idea of trying to earn back my tier by selling stuff and turned my gadget store into a freebie place where I'd give stuff away, I was able to relax and enjoy *Second Life* more. *Second Life* is huge. It's not all about making money for everybody. For some, that's what they do, and what they enjoy. For others— well, without spending a lot of your own money, you can do an awful lot. Find what you love, and don't feel like you *should* try to start or run a business. Running a business is real work, just like in first life!

"Then I got a job as a Linden, and that's how I really make money in *Second Life*!"

—Prospero Linden

277

CHAPTER 13

MONEY: THE COLD,
HARD FACTS

**WAYS TO
PROFIT**

PRIVATE
BUSINESS

VIRTUAL MONEY
MAKING

CORPORATE
MOVES

SECOND LIFE
PROFESSIONALISM

THE *SECOND LIFE*
SOLUTION
PROVIDER
DIRECTORY

SO … YOU SURE
YOU WANNA DO
THIS?

Figure 13.2: *Second Life* is a gamer's heaven.

Here's another example of this link in action: the astounding success of *SL* resident Kermitt Quirk. Having created Tringo as a game to be played inside *Second Life* only, Quirk went on to sell the game to a real-world game company, which developed it for the Nintendo Game Boy Advance—this on top of selling many copies inside *SL* at L$15,000 a pop. It's worth noting that games of all sorts are a big feature of the *SL* landscape; if you're a gamer, you're in for a lot of fun (Figure 13.2). First-person shooter fans especially can count on meeting plenty of like-minded friends.

⬇ PERSONAL CHOICES

Remember, *Second Life*'s virtual world is part of the real world. You don't have to be another Kermitt Quirk to profit from that connection, and you do not have to profit in a monetary sense. The virtual world is an excellent place to test and try out stuff—products, services, skills. That's how universities and corporations use it, and there's no reason why you shouldn't—you can make *Second Life* your personal training ground for the real world, too. For example, if you're harboring the popular delusion that it would be fun to be a writer, but real life isn't giving you a break because you have no experience, a job with one of the *SL* papers could be the first step to a literary career (see the "Help Wanted: Journalism" sidebar).

In addition to being a training ground, *Second Life* is a playground—and as we all know, playgrounds are helpful in unearthing hidden talents. If your everyday life doesn't give you the chance to develop your creativity, *Second Life* can be a very rewarding change of scenery. It's worth noting that *Second Life* offers a unique opportunity to artists who want to strut their stuff to a worldwide, *live* audience, and is quickly developing as a stage for new musical talent: setting up a *worldwide* "live" show with streamed music is incomparably easier and more pleasant than negotiating a gig at the local pub. Search the *SL* Classifieds, and you'll most likely find a show playing within the next few hours.

> 👁 ADDITIONAL INFO
> ## LIFE IMITATES *SECOND LIFE*
>
> You may also find a real-world job in or through *Second Life*. It does not have to be in network marketing or something similar, either. More and more organizations are looking for contractual employees for online programs being run in *Second Life*'s virtual world. These jobs pay real-world salaries in real money.

RESIDENTS SPEAK
HELP WANTED: JOURNALISM

CHAPTER 1

CHAPTER 2

CHAPTER 3

CHAPTER 4

CHAPTER 5

CHAPTER 6

CHAPTER 7

CHAPTER 8

CHAPTER 9

CHAPTER 10

CHAPTER 11

CHAPTER 12

CHAPTER 13

CHAPTER 14

CHAPTER 15

APPENDICES

"Hello everyone,

"I am the publisher for **SL Business** and we are currently looking for staff writers, columnists, and freelance writers. You can reach me in-world, of course, and also by email: `highlyfocused@gmail.com`.

"Here is a list of opportunities that are available:

Staff Writer: The staff writer works closely with the editorial team in the coverage of the monthly editorial outline. You will be given subjects from the outline to research and draft content for submission to the editors. This is a salaried position and requires regular attendance in *SL*. Salary is discussed in-world.

Columnist: The columnist covers one particular area and is usually a subject-matter expert. A columnist's submissions will appear in the monthly magazine and possibly in the weekly supplements. Columnists are paid per column at a rate of L$1,500/US$5.

Freelance Writer: The freelance writer picks up work that the editorial team may not be able to get to or lightens the load per se. Freelance writers that seek work from the magazine will receive subjects from the editorial team to research and draft for submission. Freelance writers are paid per article at a rate of L$1,500/US$5.

"I'm looking forward to your response and if interested I'm looking forward to introducing you to the **SL Business** team. Thanks!"

—Hunter Glass, Publisher, **SL Business Magazine**

The sections that follow describe what motivates people to work in the virtual world, and discuss some of the moneymaking and business options open to you inside *Second Life*. "Some," because the number of moneymaking and business options inside the virtual world doubles or triples every year. You'll see many interesting combinations, such as real-world companies doing business in the virtual world, and *Second Life* residents doing business in the real world. At the time of writing, a single job ad in the *SL* Classifieds neatly provides examples of both: Philips, a big real-world company, is looking for an *SL* designer/building expert to set up a virtual corporate headquarters in exchange for a good real-life salary.

ADDITIONAL INFO
THE RETURN ON VIRTUAL R&D

Second Life is a great testing ground for products, services, and ideas—a place where failure costs little and success is especially exciting. A growing number of real-world companies are using *SL* for research, design, and product prototyping. In the virtual world, creating and subsequently altering a design after receiving feedback costs a fraction of what it would if the whole process took place in the real world.

⬇ THE PLEASURES OF WORKING FOR PENNIES

Holding a virtual job or running a virtual business tends to pay peanuts, yet very many *SL* denizens do just that. This is because we're dealing with very special peanuts here.

Figure 13.3: A lot of the time, real fun in the virtual world is either free or inexpensive.

To begin with, inside *Second Life* the Linden dollar enjoys purchasing power that puts the US dollar to shame. To say that stuff is cheap in *Second Life* is to say very little. It is a world in which—right off the bat—you get stuff such as free houses and vehicles, to say nothing about all the clothes and various other items. On top of that, you can acquire tons of cool stuff for free, or at the symbolic price of L$1. And the "expensive" stuff isn't expensive: at the time of writing, a state-of-the-art *SL* weapon firing "smart" projectiles costs less than L$3,000 or US$10. A few US dollars won't buy you much in real life; but in *Second Life*, the same money buys you a whole lot of fun (Figure 13.3).

What's more, there is special magic in making money inside a virtual world. Earning the equivalent of a single real-life dollar feels more satisfying than making 50 dollars in real life. No matter how much effort you invest up front, money made in *Second Life* always feels free, and thus counts more. This special trait of virtual earnings is one of the most important reasons why almost everyone is willing to invest an hour to make the equivalent of US$1, including many people who would recoil in horror upon being asked to work for US$20 per hour in real life. It's not hard to imagine numerous real-world companies holding intense meetings, even as you read this, to determine how to profit from that phenomenon....

The bottom line is this: making money in a virtual world is much more fun than in the real world. To keep it that way, don't focus on making money in itself, but on making as much as you need inside the world, and doing something you like that just happens to be profitable.

 RESIDENTS SPEAK
THE JOY OF MAKING MONEY

"If you enjoy doing something, the money eventually follows."

—Kate Proudhon

"One of the best ways to make money is to sell stuff, of course. Find what you are good at and what you have a passion for and build it. With time and practice, residents will begin to show an interest and offer to buy whatever you have made. That's how I was eventually able to afford land, by designing and selling aircraft."

—Dustin Pomeray

"For most people, earning money is probably easier in the real world, so do enjoy *Second Life*, first and foremost. It is not a money-making tool; it is a game, a virtual community, a creative environment, and so much more."

—Elgyfu Wishbringer

PRIVATE BUSINESS

If you're out to make money in the virtual world, begin by determining how much you need:

- Enough money for the occasional small expense, such as buying a bunch of L$1 items, or an L$10 upload. You can get that kind of money for free, meaning you spend time and energy doing stuff that can't be called work: locating and participating in contests and raffles, finding money trees that actually have some money left, and taking the occasional "camping" job, which usually involves sitting in one spot for a number of minutes. For more details, turn to the "Real Virtual Jobs" section in this chapter.

- Enough money to buy the *SL* items you want and to engage in activities you want. This sets your Linden-dollar needs in the low thousands per month. You can make enough to cover needs like that even by taking relatively low-paid, unskilled *SL* jobs.

CHAPTER 1
CHAPTER 2
CHAPTER 3
CHAPTER 4
CHAPTER 5
CHAPTER 6
CHAPTER 7
CHAPTER 8
CHAPTER 9
CHAPTER 10
CHAPTER 11
CHAPTER 12
CHAPTER 13

CHAPTER 14
CHAPTER 15
APPENDICES

Enough money to cover the above, plus the real-life costs of a Premium membership, and possibly also low land-maintenance fees. To make that much money, you'll have to show some skill at an *SL* job, or run a modestly successful business of your own.

Figure 13.4: It isn't easy to make it big in *Second Life*.

Enough money to cover all *SL*-related costs, including low land-maintenance fees, plus put a meaningful amount of real-world currency in your pocket: Unless you're a genius scoring big with a brilliant business idea, a money goal like that means a commitment equivalent to a part-time job in real life. You have to be highly skilled, and/or run a successful, highly profitable business (Figure 13.4).

Enough money to live on in the real world, nevermind *SL*-related costs. Face it—if that's your goal, you're looking at the time commitment of a regular full-time job. Not only that, but you have to be a razor-sharp businessperson willing to make a big upfront investment of time and money. Top *SL* animators can also make this income bracket.

Enough money to be called a millionaire. If that's truly your dream, then your best bet is to follow in Anshe Chung's footsteps, and see how you can make money from *Second Life* in the real world. This involves becoming a *Second Life* expert—a highly specialized professional and supersharp businessperson by real-world standards.

That's it! The secret's out: becoming a real-life millionaire involves doing business with the real world, as much as you prefer *Second Life*. However, if your money ambitions are more modest, you may be able to fulfill them without leaving the virtual world. The next section tells you how.

VIRTUAL MONEYMAKING

In *Second Life*'s virtual world, money really does grow on trees. "Money trees" grow fruit that can be picked for money, and they can be hit for up to L$20 at a time; they're basically L$-distribution machines meant to help new *SL* residents. They can be loaded up with money through donations from the general public, as well as interested parties such as the owner of a store next to the tree. Money trees are meant to draw people to a certain spot (usually a commercial enterprise), and they succeed only too well: most often, they're tapped out. Unfortunately, this is partly due to *SL* resident abuse. If you've really set your heart on picking a fruit for L$10 or thereabouts, you may have to wait for quite a while.

CHAPTER 1
CHAPTER 2
CHAPTER 3
CHAPTER 4
CHAPTER 5
CHAPTER 6
CHAPTER 7
CHAPTER 8
CHAPTER 9
CHAPTER 10
CHAPTER 11
CHAPTER 12
CHAPTER 13
CHAPTER 14
CHAPTER 15
APPENDICES

ADDITIONAL INFO
FREE MONEY

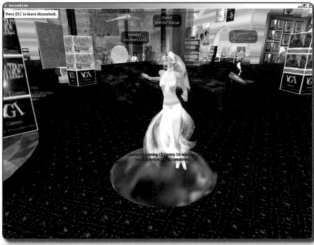

"Free money" is a heavily advertised commodity in the virtual world. However, obtaining "free money" often requires as much or more effort than simply earning it (Figure 13.5).

Figure 13.5: There really isn't such a thing as free money—not even in a virtual world.

You may also receive "free" money in the form of a signup bonus, or a regularly paid stipend. There have been many changes to the bonus and stipend systems. At one time, a stipend called "dwell" was paid out to residents with the highest popularity ratings, with popularity being determined by the amount of traffic to a resident-owned destination (such as a store, or even a private home). At another, both Premium and Basic account holders received a weekly stipend. At the time of writing, only Premium account holders receive a stipend, and since Premium accounts cost money, the Linden dollars you receive aren't exactly free. Whatever new changes come to the stipend system, it seems more than likely that *some* sort of stipend will always be a feature.

It's highly unlikely all your *SL* needs will always be covered by your "free" money. Appetite grows while eating, and sooner or later you're bound to hanker for a top-shelf item whose price runs into the many thousands of Linden dollars. Patiently saving up stipend payments is a pain, and you might have to buy a few real-world dollars' worth of Linden dollars.

If you're not willing to stoop to that level, or if you actually *want* to make money in-world because it's fun, you have plenty of options. You may start up a business, or take a virtual job. The following sections cover *Second Life* employment and money-making opportunities, with comments on their earning power.

ADDITIONAL INFO
THE TAX MAN

Keep in mind that upon converting Linden dollars into a currency, you may be required to report your virtual-world income to real-world tax authorities. The exact rules may differ depending on your place of residence in the real world; make sure you know what they are.

⬇ REAL VIRTUAL JOBS

The *Second Life* Knowledge Base contains a Guide to Jobs in *Second Life*. To access this guide, search the Knowledge Base for "job guide." It contains plenty of information, and though it isn't completely up-to-date or comprehensive at the time of writing, it's worth checking out.

The Knowledge Base's job guide classifies jobs as skilled or unskilled according to whether they require real-life skills. However, special virtual-world skills do exist: you'll find many *Second Life* skills are mandatory for certain jobs. Note that *SL* skills often assume a different *form* than real-life skills do: for example, being a good dancer involves having good dance animations and has little to do with your dancing abilities in real life. A *Second Life* skill may simply be a script that gives its owner a certain ability.

If you're new to the virtual world, it may be wise to begin your job research by visiting one of the many employment agencies that exist in-world: run a search and read the agency descriptions, then try to find one where someone will talk to you, answer your questions about the jobs on offer, and give you relevant advice. Another way to go around finding a job is to visit the forums at `http://forums.secondlife.com/` and check out Employment Ops & Help Wanted in the Classifieds subforum. If you're artistically inclined, you'll be pleasantly surprised to see many ads for artists of all kinds—writers, musicians, designers, and more.

ADDITIONAL INFO
SPEND MONEY TO MAKE MONEY

Many *SL* jobs require you to own certain items; others require an avatar with both outstanding looks and moves. Acquiring these could require a big investment. For example, to become a professional model, you'll need a great custom shape, skin, hair, and fairly expensive custom animations.

We'll now cover the most popular jobs in *Second Life*. Keep in mind that there are others, and that new job categories appear all the time. However, the professions listed here account for more than 90% of *SL* jobs. Note that some virtual hospitality-industry jobs don't pay salaries, but let workers keep all tips instead.

CAMPING

Figure 13.6: "Camping" acquires a new meaning in *Second Life*.

"Camping" is *SL* slang for a job that does not require anything more than your presence. It often consists of sitting in a chair in exchange for L$5–20 per hour, with money being paid out every 3–15 minutes. These very, um, virtual jobs were highly popular when dwell stipends were paid out, and it made a lot of sense to pay people to stick around. In spite of the death of the dwell stipend, camping jobs still appear because there's a real-life rule that applies in *Second Life*: people draw people. *Second Life* is not a densely populated world; most of the time, it resembles a city at five in the morning. When you look at the world map while you're in the world, you'll see that green "people" icons tend to form clusters. Therefore, it still makes sense for many business owners—especially retailers—to hire avatars to hang around for the equivalent of a few real-life cents per hour (Figure 13.6). Not surprisingly, camping jobs are most popular among freshly born residents.

GREETER

A greeter job is an upscale camping job. In addition to simply being there, you're required to speak (type) a simple greeting from time to time, possibly perform a simple gesture such as a bow. As you would expect, you won't make a fortune even when your avatar looks really sharp. At the time of writing, the standard salary is L$50–100 per hour; you may also get tips. Naturally, this requires an avatar of above-average appearance, social skills, and charm. You may work as a temp—a couple of hours at a specific event—or you can work the *SL* version of full time, which tends to hover around 10 hours a week. Don't expect to earn more than a few thousand Linden dollars a month—10 or 12 real-life bucks. To make a couple of thousand more, you'll have to develop outstanding social skills and invest in your avatar's appearance.

However, being a greeter can be lots of fun if you simply like meeting lots of new people and watching action happen. It certainly gives you the opportunity to make new friends and can be the right choice if socializing is what you want most out of *Second Life*. The temp or one-off greeter jobs can be handy if you have a Basic membership. They'll let you pay rent on a little *SL* space of your own to store your prims. They also let you have a little pocket money for all those L$1 bargains that abound in the virtual world.

CHAPTER 1
CHAPTER 2
CHAPTER 3
CHAPTER 4
CHAPTER 5
CHAPTER 6
CHAPTER 7
CHAPTER 8
CHAPTER 9
CHAPTER 10
CHAPTER 11
CHAPTER 12
CHAPTER 13

CHAPTER 14
CHAPTER 15
APPENDICES

CHAPTER 13

MONEY: THE COLD,
HARD FACTS

WAYS TO
PROFIT

PRIVATE
BUSINESS

VIRTUAL MONEY
MAKING

CORPORATE
MOVES

SECOND LIFE
PROFESSIONALISM

THE *SECOND LIFE*
SOLUTION
PROVIDER
DIRECTORY

SO . . . YOU SURE
YOU WANNA DO
THIS?

ADDITIONAL INFO
SOCIAL NETWORKING

Jobs that involve plenty of socializing and meeting new people, such as greeter or event host, can be very helpful if you're trying to get your newly formed business off the ground. You're likely to gain many customers from among *SL* residents you meet through your job. Just don't be too pushy! Some extra info in your profile and a custom calling card work just fine to draw attention to your other money-making activity.

SECURITY

Security jobs range from being a simple bouncer to an armed bodyguard; as you might expect, there are many more of the former than the latter. The simplest security jobs pay as little as L$50 per hour and usually do not require you to have any special equipment or to engage in any sort of combat. Bodyguard or special armed guard jobs are negotiable, but don't expect to get more than the high three figures. Very few security guards earn more than L$150 per hour.

Do *not* view a job in security as an open-ended opportunity to shoot people. As explained in Chapter 2, this makes you as much of a miscreant as any offenders you're dealing with. If shooting people is what you crave, go to a combat sim. That being said, the job does give you some virtual authority and can be great fun if you enjoy watching what people are up to in their second lives. These are basically the only reasons to take a security job; the pay is poor, and you don't get the same opportunities to socialize as a greeter does.

Most security-guard jobs require a steady time commitment of a few hours a week. There are not very many of them around, because a security guard is mostly for show; automated security systems do the job much better, and there are models available free of charge.

SHOP ATTENDANT/SALES REP

Most items you can buy in *Second Life* are sold directly by their owners—via ads in-world and in *SL* publications, through automated vendors, or in stores. Most stores employ automated sales, but at the time of writing there's a new trend toward sales staffing. There are two kinds of jobs within that category. Being a shop attendant requires your physical presence in the shop and usually pays a low (two-figure) hourly wage, plus a small commission on sales made. Being a sales rep doesn't require scheduled presence inside a shop—it's roughly the *SL* equivalent of real-life traveling sales reps. At the time of writing, neither job offers an opportunity for big income. However, this particular job sector is growing quickly along with *Second Life*.

CHAPTER 1

CHAPTER 2

CHAPTER 3

CHAPTER 4

CHAPTER 5

CHAPTER 6

CHAPTER 7

CHAPTER 8

CHAPTER 9

CHAPTER 10

CHAPTER 11

CHAPTER 12

CHAPTER 13

CHAPTER 14

CHAPTER 15

APPENDICES

ADDITIONAL INFO
JACK OF ALL TRADES

Figure 13.7: Developing a social network is crucial to business success in *Second Life*.

If you're a new *SL* citizen without a defined skill that would let you choose one of the *SL* professions without hesitation, consider trying out various jobs or working at two or more jobs in different professions at the same time. This makes it easier to find your true *SL* calling and also lets you develop a bigger social network—possibly the number-one prerequisite for success in money-making activities (Figure 13.7).

EVENT HOST/DJ

Event hosts organize and manage social events inside the virtual world: games, parties, fashion shows, etc. Of all the *SL* jobs discussed till now, this is the first that has true career potential. To begin with, good event hosts make decent money, and there's a big market for their services: business owners stage many events to attract new customers. Although the hourly rate isn't great, tip income is higher than a greeter's. In addition, event hosts often receive a cut of event profits. However, be warned that the job's money-making potential greatly depends on your skills and experience. Obviously, a good Tringo host who makes the game more fun attracts more players, and an experienced, well-known event host boosts event attendance simply by being there. However, being there is the catch. Attaining an income of more than L$10,000 a month is likely to require a serious time commitment.

ADDITIONAL INFO
HOSTING AS A STEPPING STONE

An event-hosting job is the ideal first step if you want to open an entertainment business of your own. Once you're an experienced event host, all you need is a copy of the game of your choice, and a space to hold game events. Game fans are likely to follow the host they like, so you'll have an audience right away. You may also rent both the game and the space, or possibly even negotiate a lease in exchange for a cut of the profits.

In return, you get a great opportunity to socialize in the virtual world. Event hosting makes it easy for you to build a large social network, which can pay off big time—your virtual friends are likely to show up at events you host and give you good tips. *SL* event hosts who also run businesses of their own are likely to profit even more: some of the people they meet at events become their customers.

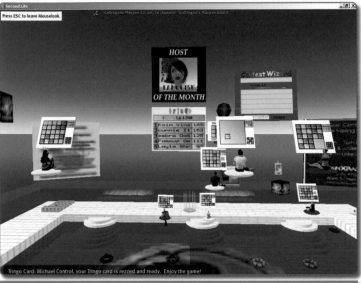

A successful event host must have strong social skills. A sense of humor, good writing skill, and the ability to type fast are essential. Attractive avatar appearance is another must—the more attractive, the better. Acquiring custom skin and clothing is a priority, and custom animations and gestures are very desirable too. Naturally, if you host specialized events such as games, you have to know how the games work (Figure 13.8).

Figure 13.8: Get basic event-host training by attending the kind of events you'd like to host.

A DJ is basically a highly specialized event host. You have to understand how audio streaming in MP3 format works—if you don't, consult the *SL* Knowledge Base. Naturally, you also have to have real-world DJ skills: you have to sense what your audience would like to hear next and react accordingly. Disc jockeys are both well-paid and in high demand. If you're good, you can expect to earn several thousand Linden dollars for a single session (two to four hours).This includes the hourly wage paid by the club/casino/establishment that hired you, plus tips from guests. Talented disc jockeys might well make the DJ job their *SL* career of choice: the high hourly earnings mean that working just a few hours a week can bring in a comfortable *SL* income (see also the "Working as a Musician" sidebar). The Knowledge Base contains a good selection of articles covering the practical aspects of making music in *Second Life*.

ADDITIONAL INFO
WORKING AS A MUSICIAN

Second Life is increasingly popular among musicians. Several real-life stars have already played "live" shows, and many new musicians are using the virtual world to find their audience. As a musician staging a "live" show, you're basically a DJ playing your own music, except that you need an instrument (an item attached to your avatar), plus at least a few custom avatar animations. Synchronizing those with the music is key—it's the "live" component of the show.

Event hosting and DJing are professions, not just jobs for unskilled workers. As you'll see, this also applies to many jobs listed as "unskilled" by the *SL Guide to Jobs*. Happily, it isn't hard to find entry-level positions that will let you gain experience (see the "Help Wanted: Various Fields" sidebar).

ADDITIONAL INFO
HELP WANTED: VARIOUS FIELDS

JOB FAIR FOR ENTRY-LEVEL AND EXPERIENCED POSITIONS THIS SUNDAY

Expansion and growth! Two Island Sims of virtual entertainment need more Part Time staff. Job Fair is in the front courtyard of the Black Dragon Pub on VooDooLive Island. Managers will be on hand to interview and hire on the spot.

THESE JOBS DO NOT REQUIRE ANY PRIOR EXPERIENCE—TRAINING PROVIDED:

- Dancer/Model—L$30 an hour to dance plus tips/FREE Designer clothes to participate in monthly designer showcase. Free Photoshopped portfolio and profile pictures.
- Event Host—Day and late-evening positions available—L$50 an hour plus tips
- Slingo/Bingo Host—After midnight *SL* time—L$50 a hour plus tips
- DJ (Drum N Bass, Hip Hop, Rave, Rock, Salsa, Top 40, '80s)—We give you the software and training you need to get started. 4 practice rooms available at all times. 4 radio streams available.

SOME EXPERIENCE NEEDED FOR THESE POSITIONS:

- Venue Manager & Assistant Manager—Six hours a week on-site. Knowledge of event posting and land tools a must.
- Magazine Associate Editor (Must have Photoshop)
- Writer for Magazine—L$500 per 400 word article
- Web Master—We have the domains and servers. We need simple websites developed and maintained to support our banner ad sales—flexibility and great income.

If you can't make it to the Job Fair, please send an e-mail to voodooisland@gmail.com.

CHAPTER 1
CHAPTER 2
CHAPTER 3
CHAPTER 4
CHAPTER 5
CHAPTER 6
CHAPTER 7
CHAPTER 8
CHAPTER 9
CHAPTER 10
CHAPTER 11
CHAPTER 12
CHAPTER 13

CHAPTER 14
CHAPTER 15
APPENDICES

DANCER/STRIPPER

The virtual world of *Second Life* features clubs galore (Figure 13.9). Practically all of them employ dancers to attract as many *SL* residents as possible. Most dancing jobs have set hours, but one-off gigs are a possibility and tend to pay more than regular jobs on a time-expended basis. The pay varies widely and depends on a dancer's skill and appearance. As you would expect, a successful dancer looks great

CHAPTER 13

MONEY: THE COLD,
HARD FACTS

WAYS TO
PROFIT

PRIVATE
BUSINESS

**VIRTUAL MONEY
MAKING**

CORPORATE
MOVES

SECOND LIFE
PROFESSIONALISM

THE *SECOND LIFE*
SOLUTION
PROVIDER
DIRECTORY

SO ... YOU SURE
YOU WANNA DO
THIS?

Extreme Turtle shouts: Finding a random Tip Winner!
Extreme Turtle shouts: Congratulations Fangorn Tiger!!! you have just been randomly tipped $10L!
Gino Portello shouts: thanks small
Fangorn Tiger shouts: OK we'll Minge!
Small Lake shouts: You are all welcome

Figure 13.9: There's no shortage of clubs in *Second Life*.

(meaning an investment in avatar appearance) and moves great (meaning an investment in custom animations).

In addition to an hourly wage, dancers receive tips. Truly good dancers derive most of their income from tips, even allowing for the 20% cut that usually goes to the event holder/club or casino owner. Top dancers can make good money, with hourly earnings in the high three figures.

In *Second Life*, the line between dancers and strippers is thin: many *SL* residents do both. If that's what you'd like, you should invest in suitable animations. Strippers make even more money than dancers do, and it's an investment that quickly pays for itself.

Given all the job flavors, it's not surprising that monthly earnings can vary widely. A beginner needs to try hard to make two or three thousand L$ per month, while a top dancer/good stripper will make that much in the course of a single working session (two to three hours). To stay at the top, you'll have to repeatedly invest in updating your avatar's appearance, and in new animations. It's the ideal job for anyone who yearns to be admired and likes to see practical proof of that admiration.

MODEL/PHOTOMODEL

This is another job that should appeal to anyone with an admiration deficit in real life. Modeling jobs are relatively scarce, however. If you want to embark on a modeling career, it might be wise to start out as a dancer and continue making money dancing while you invest in all the prerequisites to become a successful model. These involve great shape, skin, and animations (including special poses and catwalk animations). What's more, you'll need to work on your avatar's appearance constantly; modeling is a very competitive field. If you're interested in finding out more and possibly getting a lead on your first job, visit one of the modeling agencies that operate inside the virtual world (use the Search function).

There are two types of modeling jobs available: modeling in virtual flesh during fashion shows, and working as a photomodel. Pay varies wildly. Beginners make peanuts, but that's usually offset by free appearance enhancers (clothes, animations, attachments). Top models in either category are skilled professionals who may make thousands of L$ per hour and win prizes in competitions (see the "Help Wanted: Modeling" sidebar). Monthly earnings can reach five figures in Linden dollars.

CHAPTER 1

CHAPTER 2

CHAPTER 3

CHAPTER 4

CHAPTER 5

CHAPTER 6

CHAPTER 7

CHAPTER 8

CHAPTER 9

CHAPTER 10

CHAPTER 11

CHAPTER 12

CHAPTER 13

CHAPTER 14

CHAPTER 15

APPENDICES

RESIDENTS SPEAK

HELP WANTED: MODELING

PHOTOMODELS WANTED

"I am fixing to open up a studio of photos that I do. I want to post samples of work I do in the studio, so basically your picture would be put up on a wall with other pictures. I will pay you L$800 for your time. Should be like only 10 mins for me to find a pose for you and take the picture. You will get a free picture out of this.

"If you are interested in doing this, send me a notecard in-game with your picture.

"I'm only looking for about 6 people to do this, both males and females. I take all kind of avs. Look at my profile in game to find examples of my work. Thank you for your time."

—Sky Veloce

ALLURE TOP MODEL COMPETITION—ENTRIES DUE NLT SUNDAY AT MIDNIGHT

- *First Prize L$25K*
- *Please join us in this exciting competition which will determine the Allure Top Model.*
- *Allure Modeling Group is pleased to announce this competition to recognize the hard work and effort so many in SL put into professional modeling.*
- *It is simple to enter—send three photos to Bruno Buckenburger. One should be a head shot. The other two are completely up to you.*
- *On August 21, Allure will select the top 20 candidates.*
- *Those 20 will have the opportunity to practice runway modeling, receive a free portfolio from Allure, and will be judged by some of the most recognized and admired industry professionals:*

- Bruno Buckenburger—President, BBVision & AllureNET Media
- Jenn McTeague—Allure Modeling Group Vice-President
- Janie Marlow—Clothing Designer, Mischief
- Alyssa Bijoux—Jewelry/Accessory Designer
- Sophie Stravinsky—Photographer, Sophiesticated Photography

From this group of 20, five finalists will be selected to return and compete for the top prize and the honor of being named the Allure Top Model.

*****PLEASE pick up a notecard with complete rules at the Allure Model Group office on the fifth floor of The Offices at Bareum Beach Towers: Bareum (150,99,67) or at Socle—The Allure Model Showcase Center: Bareum (211,9,45). Good luck!

Virtual sex is a popular activity in *Second Life*; at the time of writing, it seems there are more sex clubs in *SL* than there are in real-world Amsterdam. Predictably, there are plenty of *SL* residents who make money from virtual sex—not only club owners and escorts, but also animators who create the necessary animations and gestures, builders who sculpt sexual organs, and texturers who endow all those joy-giving attachments with the blush of life. On the whole the scene compares favorably with what goes in the real world. No one ever gets really hurt, exiting any situation takes a couple of mouse clicks, everyone is healthy, and no one gets pregnant unless they script themselves that way.

Figure 13.10: Hmmm, wonder if I can get two moans for the price of one.

Making money on sexual favors is not easy in a virtual world where there's plenty of free sex on offer. A successful escort has to invest plenty of Linden dollars in avatar appearance, including the necessary sex-related attachments (your avatar comes *sans* sexual organs), and other special items (such as a Gensex bed). If you have the money, obtaining necessary gestures and animations isn't difficult (Figure 13.10). What's difficult is using everything to its best advantage in a situation where even the most passionate love scene smacks of a comedic cartoon.

Escort "jobs" in clubs and other entertainment centers are advertised frequently and are much less shameful than in the real world. Pay consists mostly of "tips" paid by appreciative guests, usually minus a 20% cut for the event host/owner; sometimes there's a low hourly wage as well to discourage absenteeism. Top escorts work the way top call girls do, receiving clients in lushly appointed private surroundings. Earnings go as high as L$5,000 per half hour, but on average they are in the low four figures. In either case, monthly earnings can be impressive, reaching six figures in Linden dollars.

ADDITIONAL INFO
THE FOUNTAIN OF YOUTH

If you're so inclined, being a virtual escort has real career potential. The money's good and tends to get better with time; escorts don't age in *Second Life*. Many *SL* dancers and strippers make money on the side as escorts.

A texturer uses an external application, such as Adobe Photoshop or Paint Shop Pro, to create original textures that are subsequently imported into and used in *Second Life*. Textures are what you apply to the surface of a prim to make it look a certain way (wood, metal, black, yellow, ridged, glossy, whatever). Texturing is a skill that is very much in demand, but there's also plenty of competition. Many builders are also texturers; however, if you're a texturer of outstanding skill, you can count on finding a well-paid job with a busy builder or clothing designer. You can also go into business for yourself—don't expect to earn megabucks on every original texture sale, though. Usually, custom textures are reasonably priced (under L$100), and you'll have to sell many to earn a meaningful amount of money. A good approach is to market a no-transfer eye-catching texture at an appealing price, and sell many copies. It's the sales volume that determines your profits, and they won't be easy to come by—the competition is quite fierce.

Creating textures pays best if you're also a builder, and your original textures are part of your new products. If you're definitely not into building, do your best to form a mutually profitable partnership with a talented builder. Your earnings may vary wildly and are determined solely by your creativity and marketing skills. If you're a mute genius, you'll most likely give away most of your stuff for free. If you're a marketing genius as well as a talented texturer, you can expect monthly earnings in the five figures (Linden dollars).

ADDITIONAL INFO
CREATIVE INSPIRATION

If you're interested in creating new textures, downloading the high-quality textures from `http://secondlife.com/community/textures.php` is a good start. You'll be able to see what's possible and gain a yardstick to measure your own creative efforts.

Figure 13.11: Everyone has a go at clothing design at least once in their second life.

CLOTHING DESIGNER

This is one of the most popular occupations in *Second Life* (Figure 13.11). Everyone tries their hand at it while editing their avatars' appearance, and very many *SL* residents take the next step and download the templates from `http://secondlife.com/community/templates.php`. The downloaded templates come with a tutorial that explains the basics of clothing design. However, if you're seriously thinking about making it a career, you should attend some of

CHAPTER 13

MONEY: THE COLD, HARD FACTS

WAYS TO PROFIT

PRIVATE BUSINESS

VIRTUAL MONEY MAKING

CORPORATE MOVES

SECOND LIFE PROFESSIONALISM

THE *SECOND LIFE* SOLUTION PROVIDER DIRECTORY

SO … YOU SURE YOU WANNA DO THIS?

the courses and tutorials offered inside the *SL* world. A few are listed in Chapter 2, including courses available free of charge. Look through *SL* Classifieds (both in the *SL* forums and in-world) to find more.

A clothing designer is a skilled professional who has mastered the art of creating something in 2D and making it look good in a 3D environment. It is not easy to design clothing so that seams, pockets, buttons, etc. stay where they should when an avatar changes poses. Every clothing designer needs to have a few posing stands, which "freeze" avatars in selected poses. This makes it possible to get a better idea of how a clothing item will look when worn by a moving, dancing, gesticulating avatar. In addition, some clothing items may require scripting: a good example is a sequin dress that sparkles.

A *Second Life* career in clothing design is not for the faint of heart. If you decide to go for it, be prepared for very strong competition. *SL* residents aren't likely to spend money on items that are inferior to clothing that's offered for free or at the symbolic price of L$1, and plenty of designer items can be obtained in this way. Earnings vary wildly: top designers make great money, and achieving a monthly income in six figures isn't impossible. However, most clothing designers make much less than that. Raking in enough to cover standard *SL* expenses plus business-related costs (store rental, texture uploads, advertising) is pretty tough going.

ADDITIONAL INFO
DESIGN SPECIALIZATION

Many clothing designers specialize in selected items: dresses, jackets, footwear, etc. Some specialize as tattoo artists—in *SL*, tattoos can be created as clothing that's fully transparent except for the tattoo part.

SCRIPTER

A scripter is someone who writes scripts in LSL—*Second Life*'s programming language. Many *SL* residents have real-life programming skills that they apply in *Second Life*, and there are many tutorials available inside the virtual world, as well as at `http://rpgstats.com/wiki/index. php?title=Main _ Page`. Predictably, there are quite a few scripters in *Second Life*.

It's not easy to make money selling free-standing scripts, and most top-earning scripters are also builders. The best way to maximize scripting income is to write scripts for objects you created yourself, as long as you have the needed building skills. The scripters who don't do this tend to work in tandem with builders who lack scripting skills.

Given all these considerations, income derived from scripting can vary greatly. Top scripters who aren't builders but are part of a well-known team can earn a monthly income in the five figures; however, income depends greatly on the partners' skills and marketing acumen. The hard truth is that adequate scripting skills plus good building skills are more likely to earn you good money than outstanding scripting skills on their own.

ADDITIONAL INFO
SCRIPTERS VS. ANIMATORS

Don't confuse scripters with animators. To put it very simply, scripters animate objects inside *Second Life* by using LSL; animators animate avatars by using an external application (most often Poser).

BUILDER/LANDSCAPER

The term "builder" covers a very wide variety of jobs, depending on the builder's specialization. A furniture maker is a builder; so is an architect; and so are jewelry makers, vehicle builders, and gunsmiths.

Every *SL* resident can have a shot at becoming a builder; it's easy to learn how to make basic, one-prim objects with *SL*'s prim-editing tools. However, thereafter the learning curve becomes much steeper. It takes experience to know up front what kind of prim is best for a task at hand. Chapter 8 is full of advice for everyone interested in creating objects inside *Second Life*.

A builder is someone who has conquered the steepening learning curve and reached the level of skill necessary to create attractive and useful items out of prims. A truly skilled builder can create attractive and useful items using the smallest number of prims possible. Prim density is always a concern because a simulator can handle a limited number of prims.

As mentioned earlier, many builders are also scripters, and quite a few are texturers. Skill requirements in each area can vary wildly. For example, a furniture maker has to be a good builder and texturer, but the scripting skill required is next to none (a simple "sit down" script may be copied from the chair in the Library). On the other hand, a gunsmith needs to be a good scripter to build weapons capable of dealing with increasingly sophisticated shields and security systems. Extra skills in other areas come in handy, too—for instance, an architect who builds prefab houses and includes streamed music and sound effects for opening/closing doors will enjoy an edge over a less-versatile competitor.

Most builders have their own businesses—sales outlets for what they build. Thus, the amount of money you can make as a builder in *Second Life* depends not only on your inventiveness and technical skills, but also on your marketing and sales acumen. Builders who are good in all of the mentioned areas can reach a monthly income in the six figures, and this is without considering the possibility of a real-world contract for *Second Life* building work. The steadily thickening trickle of real-world organizations into the virtual world has brought with it building contracts for serious, real-world sums.

CHAPTER 13

MONEY: THE COLD,
HARD FACTS

WAYS TO
PROFIT

PRIVATE
BUSINESS

**VIRTUAL MONEY
MAKING**

CORPORATE
MOVES

SECOND LIFE
PROFESSIONALISM

THE *SECOND LIFE*
SOLUTION
PROVIDER
DIRECTORY

SO ... YOU SURE
YOU WANNA DO
THIS?

ADDITIONAL INFO
THE IMPORTANCE OF BUILDERS

Becoming a builder is one of the most exciting career choices in *Second Life*. Talented builders are the creators of most of the virtual world's content; in that way, they're the creators of fun for everyone else, as well as for themselves.

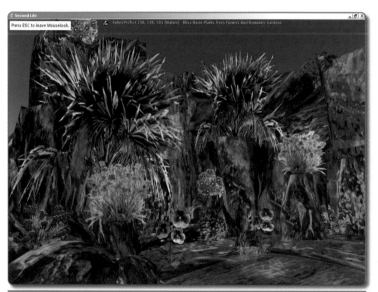

Landscapers are builders who are also accomplished at using *SL*'s slightly tricky land-editing tools, and at creating plants (Figure 13.12). A realistic-looking plant involves not only delicate prim manipulation, but also scripting (so that it moves in the wind, and so on) and frequently the creation of a new custom texture or two.

Figure 13.12: Creating realistic-looking plants is a highly specialized skill in *Second Life*.

ANIMATOR

Animators are the most highly paid among single-skill professionals. Creating complex animations for *SL* avatars is a difficult job requiring the mastery of an external application: the *SL* Guide to Jobs has the details. There are relatively few animators inside the virtual world of *Second Life*. At the same time, there is a big and constantly growing demand for new animations. Good animators can earn monthly incomes in the six figures more easily than specialists in any other profession.

Many *SL* residents are inspired to try creating animations. If you're interested, a good place to start is the Animation Guide in the Knowledge Base. Predictably, animation is not an easy career choice if you don't have the real-life skills required. It is a highly specialized job: with few exceptions, the rule is that either you're an animator before you even enter *Second Life*, or you aren't. However, don't let this discourage you if you've set your heart on animating!

In real life, real estate is regarded as a secure if long-term investment. In *Second Life*, real estate is a secure investment that pays off much more quickly. Real-estate speculation offers such attractive opportunities that almost everyone dabbles in it, and many *SL* people make it a permanent side occupation that delivers a steady stream of profits.

Becoming a big fish in the *SL* real-estate pool requires a substantial investment up front: the really big players order entire new islands from Linden Lab. Many real-estate barons are also skillful landscapers, while others order professional landscaping services from a specialist. Once land has been acquired, it is developed to increase its resale/rental value.

Figure 13.13: Rent your own little virtual paradise for just a few dollars a week.

Professional real-estate developers go to great lengths, often creating elaborate themed sims complete with custom-made, exotic vegetation; professionally scripted, sparkling waterfalls; and sandy beaches (Figure 13.13). Top developers also offer to customize land to client requests. Of course, all this carries a hefty price. Searching the Classifieds for land sales or clicking on the parcels offered for sale on the world map will quickly give you an idea of how things look.

✋ ADDITIONAL INFO
LOCATION, LOCATION, LOCATION

In *SL* real estate, location rules just like it does in the real world. All waterfront land is especially expensive, followed by parcels that adjoin a public road and thereby guarantee easy access and at least a little view.

Real-estate developers come in many shapes and sizes. Some offer land complete with rental buildings. Others specialize in developing shopping malls and commercial centers, and renting out or selling space within to business owners. There are roughly as many varieties of real-estate opportunities as there are in real life—some may be missing, but there are *SL*-specific opportunities instead: You may not make any money on garages and parking lots, because an *SL* resident can fit a brigade of tanks or a fleet of spaceships into a single Inventory folder or storage prim. However, you can make money on tiny 16-square-meter lots; renting out a lot like that for storage or advertising purposes can bring in nice income.

The real-estate business market in *Second Life* is very exciting, with players making virtual fortunes—or going bust. Those that fail are usually land syndicates formed by groups of *SL* denizens for the purpose of creating a special community or micronation. Political infighting in a virtual reality is just as common as in the real world, though in *SL* any sad consequences are less painful.

CURRENCY TRADER/FINANCIAL SPECULATOR

Currency traders are businesspeople making real-world money by exchanging Linden dollars for US dollars or euros. Some trading agencies, including Linden Lab's LindeX, make a profit by charging a small commission on transactions; others, like Anshe Chung's currency exchange, make money on the spread between buy and sell rates. Please note that this description does not constitute a recommendation for you to enter currency trading: although the profit potential is very healthy, a misfortune can get you in real trouble, just as in the real world. It's tricky career choice that's probably best left to those in the know.

Figure 13.14: *Second Life* lets you bank via virtual ATMs.

If you want to make money on your money in a passive way and don't mind taking a risk, you can open an account with one of *Second Life*'s financial institutions. *SL* banks admit to being high-risk institutions, but they pay excellent interest rates. Banking operations are usually conducted via automated tellers that dispense notecards with instructions (see Figure 13.14).

Always keep in mind that if you engage in any kind of financial speculation inside *Second Life*, you may lose your entire investment—people have lost sums running into hundreds of real-life dollars. Bank owners disclaim any responsibility for deposits and openly advise *SL* residents not to bet their life savings. What would you expect? They're virtual banks, after all, and the Linden dollar isn't a currency—it's just scrip, as explained at the beginning of this chapter. The story of Ginko's bank illustrates just how safe and secure virtual banks are: after a long, two-year period of stability, during which it achieved an enviable reputation for reliability, Ginko's went bust overnight when gambling was banned in *Second Life*. However, it had already established itself as an *SL* brand, and was subsequently resuscitated with the help of a bond issue from WSE, a virtual finance institution (see the "Wall Street It Ain't—Yet" sidebar) that actively promotes virtual business through share and bond issues.

If words such as "shares," "bonds," and "virtual finance" make your heart pound and your mouth go dry, by all means—go ahead and have a flutter. But be warned: buying shares and bonds of virtual companies is a very high-risk operation. Of course, it's the high-risk operations that are the most fun, and it's your money, your choice. Just keep in mind that it's a lot easier to lose your investment in the virtual world than it is in real life.

CHAPTER 1

CHAPTER 2

CHAPTER 3

CHAPTER 4

CHAPTER 5

CHAPTER 6

CHAPTER 7

CHAPTER 8

CHAPTER 9

CHAPTER 10

CHAPTER 11

CHAPTER 12

CHAPTER 13

CHAPTER 14

CHAPTER 15

APPENDICES

ADDITIONAL INFO

WALL STREET IT AIN'T—YET

At the time of writing, *Second Life* and other virtual worlds that utilize scrip have their own stock exchange: the WSE (World Stock Exchange), defined as a "fictional stock-market game that can be played by users without the need to have or use *Second Life* software." The WSE is in fact a cross between a stock exchange, a commercial bank, and a brokerage firm; for more information, visit `http://www.wselive.com/`.

BECOMING A BUSINESS OWNER

Without question, the most rewarding way to make money in *Second Life* is by running your own business. It is rewarding in more ways than one, too. You'll make more money working for yourself than working for someone else, and by the very act of creating a business you'll be adding to the virtual world's content.

Figure 13.15: Newly opened commercial centers often offer great rental deals to attract business.

Starting a business is truly easy. You do not need to go through any legalities; you don't even need a Premium account or any space of your own—you can advertise and promote your services through the Classifieds and in person. Remember that a well-developed social network is key!

If you do require space—for storage if nothing else—you can rent it. Special deals are often available as developers open up new malls and shopping centers (Figure 13.15). And many *SL* retailers are happy to carry products on commission, as long as they fit into their product range. That's the easy part. The hard part is making enough sales so that they add up to something. In a world where everyone has a godlike ability to create stuff, only really good stuff sells well!

ADDITIONAL INFO

FUN BEFORE PROFIT

Running a virtual business has a special magic all of its own; don't pressure yourself into thinking that you must make lots of money. Enjoy what you're doing, first and foremost.

CHAPTER 13

MONEY: THE COLD,
HARD FACTS

WAYS TO
PROFIT

PRIVATE
BUSINESS

**VIRTUAL MONEY
MAKING**

**CORPORATE
MOVES**

SECOND LIFE
PROFESSIONALISM

THE *SECOND LIFE*
SOLUTION
PROVIDER
DIRECTORY

SO … YOU SURE
YOU WANNA DO
THIS?

RESIDENTS SPEAK
RUNNING A BUSINESS IN *SECOND LIFE*

"The big income spinners are land [barons], although you won't make any friends doing that. Some DJs get paid quite well, but you have to have the huge amount of time and resources to do it. Designing a line of clothes/furniture, etc. takes time but can pay dividends if you're willing to invest in it."

—Samia Perun

"A lot of people get the impression from their first land sale … that moving land in *SL* is pretty simple. It's not. To effectively make money as a land baron in *SL* you have to be able to invest quite a lot of money in tier. Depending on [values] and buyer trends, you can end up sitting on plots of land for indeterminate amounts of time.

"The best thing you can do in *SL* is develop content that people enjoy. Back in November of last year when I started out, I did club/sim management and made a little cash for a couple of months while I learned the system and applied my inherent talents to it … but in January of this year, I developed my very first product, which turned out to be quite a hit. I haven't paid my tier out of my own pocket ever since … and I'm at the US$125.00-a-month tier level now.

"Business development in *SL* can be pretty simple. Many people simply rent mall space and sell their products there. There are thousands of malls in the world, so there's never really an end to mall space availability, and it's relatively cheap. The downside to mall space rental is you have no control over directing traffic to your products.

"However, the best thing you can do if you want to make and sell products is to go Premium, and buy a nice plot of first land. This won't cost you any more than 10 dollars a month (easily payable even on a dancer's in-world salary)."

—Suzanna Soyinka

The plan that works best for most *SL* residents is to try out a few different occupations before choosing the one that's most enjoyable and profitable and turning it into a business. Also, most residents like the role-playing aspect of making a living in *Second Life*. Although they could easily fund a business effort from the everyday spare change in their pockets, they prefer to act as if *SL* earnings were their only possible source of income. A fledgling business owner often spends several hours a week working as an event host or a dancer to cover business startup expenses that would not buy a cup of coffee in the real world.

CHAPTER 1

CHAPTER 2

CHAPTER 3

CHAPTER 4

CHAPTER 5

CHAPTER 6

CHAPTER 7

CHAPTER 8

CHAPTER 9

CHAPTER 10

CHAPTER 11

CHAPTER 12

CHAPTER 13

CHAPTER 14

CHAPTER 15

APPENDICES

ADDITIONAL INFO

PLAY THE FIELD

Do not limit yourself to any single occupation; try your hand at several to see what they're like. Many *SL* residents continue to earn income from multiple sources long after their primary moneymaker has taken off. Note also that most successful business owners tend to invest in real estate.

Starting a business is easy; what's not easy is making it a permanent and profitable concern, especially now that big real-world business has moved into *Second Life*. If running a virtual business is your ambition, be sure to read the final section of this chapter, which contains advice from a prominent *SL* businesswoman on how to achieve long-term success.

CORPORATE MOVES

For a while now, real-world organizations have been taking a growing interest in *Second Life*. Educational institutions were the first to recognize the potential of the virtual world to act as a new communications platform, but they were quickly followed by corporations doing what corporations do: looking for profit. Appendix C provides info about real-life brand presence and retail outlets in *Second Life*. Here we'll provide just a brief overview of what all those corporations are up to, and how they are conspiring to get at your real-world wallet via the virtual world.

At the time of writing, corporate activity in *Second Life* is still in its infancy. Although an impressive number of companies have made or are in the process of making a foray into the virtual world, many treat it as an experiment whose only sure payoff is the media publicity it generates in the real world. However, to others—perhaps more visionary—*Second Life* offers very tangible advantages: a visit to `http://secondlifegrid.net/how` will educate you in depth on how organizations utilize *SL*'s virtual environment. For readers interested in the corporate take on the virtual world, we feature here three voices from three countries, representing companies in different fields of business (see "The Corporate View" sidebars). For readers who just want to have an idea of the advantages the virtual world offers to a real-life company, here's a short list of potentially profitable areas for corporate involvement:

- **Marketing and advertising**. Media costs consume the lion's share of any advertising budget. The money spent on acquiring and developing a virtual island into a corporate showcase is a tiny fraction of what it costs to produce and broadcast a TV commercial. The virtual world is a hip medium, too, with the potential to deliver a captive young audience into the arms of the advertisers. Organizing well-publicized promotional events is a favored activity.

Design and prototyping. To a real-world company, the prim is building material that costs nothing in itself, and next to nothing to shape and manipulate. If you want to design the perfect hair dryer, you could do worse than to build a model in *Second Life* and ask avatars if they'd like to use it on their precious prim hair. Changes to design are easy and inexpensive, and once you see an avatar attempting to blow-dry prim hair, you've got a winner. That's the idea, anyway.

Market research. So, you're this wily car manufacturer that hopes to score big with a new body style, color scheme, or dashboard layout. No need to finish, is there? *Second Life* is a favorite with the automotive industry; you can test-drive and acquire (or be given) virtual Pontiacs, Toyotas, and more. You can be sure your preferences count, for once.

Sales. It's easier to sell a product when a customer can try out its virtual model, or even take a guided tour of its virtual insides. Retail companies that specialize in mail-order sales were quick to take an interest in *Second Life*. At the time of writing, real-world retailing is just taking its first baby steps into *Second Life*; it can do nothing but grow, though. Look out for your local grocer appearing in a sim modeled after your real-world neighborhood and delivering the goods after you've walked through his virtual store, admiring the fresh peaches and fat cucumbers.

Corporate communications. A number of companies use *SL* as an alternate platform for corporate networking. The employees like it, too: it's great to enter the office looking bronzed and fit while being pale and hung over in real life. Also, when they go on strike, the whole world gets to hear about it.

ADDITIONAL INFO
WORKDAY FUN

It's worth noting that the biggest spike in the number of active *SL* residents always occurs around 9 AM PST, when weary Californians begin work. It's hard to tell who is there to attend a corporate conference, and who is there to cyber a little and catch a show. But no doubt, you'll find out yourself.

Broadcasting and entertainment. Even the most bitter critic of *Second Life* has to admit that it's a communications platform that scores high on the entertainment scale. Several major real-world corporations have already cautiously dipped their toes into the pool, if only so that they could tell the world about it. It's already possible to indulge in the ritual of watching the evening TV news in both real and virtual life: watch for popular TV series turning interactive by being re-enacted with actual participation by the audience ("Hey, Zorro, your white underpants are showing").

Tourism. Companies with an interest in that field are bound to take a big interest in the virtual world. You get the idea: visit the hotel you'll stay in, walk around and see the sights even before you arrive there, and then decide whether that's the place to go for your real-world holiday.

In summary, *Second Life* seems to be headed into a sunny corporate future. A big chunk of the office time previously spent on viewing web pages is due to be taken over by a whole range of exciting virtual activities.

ADDITIONAL INFO

THE CORPORATE VIEW: MILLIONS OF US—CONSULTING, USA

"One of the most exciting things about *Second Life* is its sheer unpredictability, which mirrors that of the growth of the Web itself. People will come up with all kinds of applications that we can't even imagine yet. The virtual economy brings a level of abstraction and flexibility to three-dimensional goods that the Internet has brought to the two-dimensional presentation of printed information and flat images. It will change the world, to be sure, but we can't be sure how much or how fast. However, one area where the possibilities—and ROI—are most tangible is in the entertainment industry. For example, we helped Warner Bros. launch its *Gossip Girl* series on the CW network in the United States in late 2007 with a *Second Life* co-promotion. Both the series and the in-world content have enjoyed exceptionally high numbers (of viewers in the case of the TV show, and users in the case of the *SL* build).

"Virtual worlds are the richest and most immersive form of social media, and they're providing new venues where content viewers can weave themselves into the plots of their favorite TV shows or films. While this does create yet another form of competition for viewer time, smart content providers will use virtual worlds and other social media to cross-promote core content properties. The professionally produced content—the show or film—becomes the anchor for an ecosystem of user-generated content, where the professional and the amateur can blend, ultimately strengthening viewer loyalty to the core property.

"Not long after we launched our business, we helped Regina Spektor, a recording artist with Warner Bros. records, to launch her new album through *Second Life*. We created an environment that was perfectly matched to the aspirations of the artist's core demographic—urban hipsters. Visitors said it was like 'living in a music video' and 'MySpace on steroids.' Spektor's career has taken off, obviously not solely because of the *SL* promotion, but certainly in part—it was a strong component of the grassroots, community-oriented marketing used to introduce her to new audiences.

"*Second Life* takes the social media equation to the furthest point that technology allows today—and it will only get better. From a holistic entertainment brand perspective, virtual worlds and social media aren't a threat to content producers, but rather a complementary channel."

—Reuben Steiger, CEO, Millions of Us, Inc.

ADDITIONAL INFO
THE CORPORATE VIEW: HEINRICH HEINE, GMBH.—MAIL-ORDER SALES, GERMANY

"There are several reasons why we are investigating and investing in *Second Life*. We are a very successful international distance trade company in Germany, a company that belongs to the world's largest mail-order group in real life. We have re-created a part of our home town to make things more interesting for people. It has all the famous buildings and real-life infrastructure, and a tram one can drive with from one end of the city to the other. We have placed a mall in *Second Life* to represent our company, and to offer links to our webshop under www.heine.de where people can order one of our catalogs or place purchase orders right away.

"Some of our virtual merchandise was copied from real life to *Second Life*, to be used or worn by avatars. We are running fashion shows on a catwalk frequently, and many people attend. In order to run those events properly, we actually have founded a *Second Life* catwalk agency, and hired plenty of models. *Second Life* is a rapidly growing market. By one reasonable estimate, 80 percent of active Internet users will participate in an online world by 2011. Currently with millions of users, *SL* has grown rapidly and consistently. Therefore, *SL* is a dynamically collaborative content-creation platform, a medium that covers all the ideas of so-called Web 2.0. *SL* is an ideal touchpoint to interact with our real customers and ... to create new customers through promotional events such like catwalk fashion shows.

"Another idea which is just under development is to offer our customers virtual rooms where they can set up our furniture and hard goods by themselves, and then walk around the room to see how their arrangement works in practice. When they're done, they can fill out an order form to place an order for the real-life stuff. A lot of companies that started huge in *SL* are disappointed with the results and are leaving the virtual world. German companies—and ours as well—think differently. *SL* is an ideal place for consumers to 'play' with companies, and companies to 'play' with each other. For our company, *Second Life* is quite interesting because we are confident that virtual worlds are the future of the Internet. Currently, it's not our aim to generate turnover in *SL*, but to test-drive customer collaboration, communities, and such.

"In general, we are confident that we have the right strategy. Customers' reaction is quite positive. It's not our aim to make money in *SL* for the time being—we treat it as a cutting-edge communications and simulation platform. Just as the Web is already replacing and extending the capabilities of traditional print media (and our business relies on print catalogues), *Second Life* is likewise extending the capabilities of broadcast media and chat. We are happy that we got in on the ground floor. We have plans to create our own 3D world in the future as part of our website, and *SL* is an ideal platform to test that idea."

—Werner Lehl, vice president IT, Heinrich Heine GmbH

CHAPTER 1

CHAPTER 2

CHAPTER 3

CHAPTER 4

CHAPTER 5

CHAPTER 6

CHAPTER 7

CHAPTER 8

CHAPTER 9

CHAPTER 10

CHAPTER 11

CHAPTER 12

CHAPTER 13

CHAPTER 14

CHAPTER 15

APPENDICES

## THE CORPORATE VIEW: SUPREMUM GROUP—ADVERTISING, POLAND

"Supremum Group is full-service advertising agency for the city of Kraków, and an official developer in *SL*. One of our newest projects is Second Poland—a virtual representation of Poland. We are the first company in the world to commence building a precise representation of not just one city, but of a whole country.

"Second Poland will be spread over 63 islands, which will be home to eight of the most important cities in Poland: Kraków (which has been open to visitors since July 25, 2007), Warsaw, Poznań, Wrocław, Gdańsk, Łódź, Katowice, and Zakopane. These *SL* cities will be exact copies of their real-life prototypes. Around them, several commercial islands will be built: virtual real estate for companies that want to establish a presence in Second Poland.

"Second Poland will embrace the following areas:

- Education (learning through entertainment)
- Communication (interactive information banners)
- Promotion (e.g., promotion of institutions and companies in *SL* and real life)
- Commercial (sales of products and services)
- Entertainment (e.g., concerts, events—*SL* and streaming real life to *SL*)
- Cultural (e.g., museums, galleries, exhibitions in *SL*)
- Community creation (Internet forums, information services for Second Poland)

"A team of over a dozen graphic designers and programmers are committed to this project, whose completion is forecast for March 2008.

"*Second Life* is a pioneering enterprise that's also a wonderful marketing tool. Being an interactive advertising agency, we are enthusiastic about using this novel medium for promotion, marketing, and advertising, organizing conferences and events, and building communities."

—Zbigniew Woźnowski, CEO, Supremum Group

MAKING REAL-LIFE MONEY ON *SECOND LIFE*

At the time of writing, most mainstream real-world corporations with an in-world presence focus on marketing and research. However, integration of *SL* into the World Wide Web is bringing an increase in retail activity, too. It's no contest: the virtual world lets the seller demonstrate the product more effectively than a web ad.

SECOND LIFE PROFESSIONALISM

Aimee Weber is the founder of Aimee Weber Studio Inc. (www.aimeeweber.com) and is one of *Second Life*'s most well-known and respected developers. Recognized for her considerable achievements in virtual fashion, education, marketing, machinima, and writing, Aimee is considered one of the foremost experts in virtual entrepreneurship. What follows is her advice.

Ladies and gentlemen, welcome to Intro to Advanced Business in *Second Life*; my name is Aimee Weber and I will be your professor today. To attend this class, you should already have an impressive mastery of at least one prerequisite skill in *SL*, such as scripting, building, texturing, terraforming, or project management. I know many of you are quite the hotshots in one or more of these areas, but today we will address the time-honored question of, "How can my skillz pay the billz?"

Going professional in *Second Life* may seem like the start of a dream job. You get to tinker with the bleeding edge of 3D Internet technology while at home, in your pajamas, and possibly drunk. But before you quit your day job, you're going to have to make some changes in your perspective on *SL* and how you present yourself to the virtual world.

Now I know from talking to many of you that these changes don't sit well with the fiercely libertarian nature of the *Second Life* demographic. You guys don't want to dance for the man, and that's fine. But try to stick with me here and maybe we can strike up enough compromise between being a freewheeling beatnik and a corporate tool to get the bills paid.

When a client is considering you for a project, they're taking a great risk in terms of money, time, and even reputation. It's therefore upon you to make them feel as comfortable and safe as possible choosing you for the job. Nothing accomplishes this like a proven history of achievement with a sea of happy customers in your wake. While your status as *SL*-Foo Grand Master Ninja will aid you greatly, you should focus on demonstrating a few other professional traits:

Finish your projects—This stream of consciousness we call a virtual world is littered with half-finished experiments and muses. While many are technically brilliant, they will likely give the impression that you're not a "follow-through" kinda person. Go ahead and take the extra steps to finish a project, document it, package it, and maybe even market it. This tells employers that you're willing and able to stick with them from start to finish on a project.

Meet Your Deadlines—You would be shocked at how much a deadline can change your perspective on work in *Second Life*. *SL* can be fun when you have all the time in the world to tinker and experiment, but now people are adjusting their schedules around your promised delivery date. You'll need to learn to prioritize and if necessary, learn to let go of low-priority features. I know some of you want things to be just perfect, but a project that arrives a month late is far from perfect. You can still take breaks to play *World of Warcraft*, watch *Doctor Who*, or look for Butterflies Gone Wild websites, but now you must budget that time!

Get experience, no matter what—You ask the Zen Master how you can get a job without experience, and how you can get experience without a job? The Zen Master says, "work for free." While Midnight City was (and still is) a nonprofit project for me, it has been invaluable in proving that I'm capable of managing a large-scale project. Charitable organizations like Relay for Life can also provide high-profile opportunities to spotlight your work and to get gleaming recommendations. Just remember, even though you're working for free, don't act as if you are working for free. The objective here is to get a reputable organization to vouch for your talent and professionalism, so make sure that's what they see!

Market yourself—Doing all the right things won't help you if nobody knows you're doing all the right things. Increase your visibility. Prospective employers are not looking for modesty; they need to know what you've done in the past and what you can do for them in the future.

Build a portfolio—Prospective clients are prepared to pay you money to do work for them, so don't start your relationship by making them work to learn about you. You should have a nicely organized portfolio that includes descriptions, photos, testimonials, and client contacts from your past projects. If your work has appeared in the press, be sure to include links.

Get a website—I won't say that this is essential, but it's a tremendous help in creating the perception that you are a stable entity in the industry. Having the website could also increase your Google visibility associated with *Second Life* and may land you the occasional contract deal right off the street. If you can't afford a website, consider entering yourself and your accomplishments on the *Second Life* Wikia (`http://secondlife.wikia.com/index.php/Main _ Page`).

Network—I know many residents are self-proclaimed recluses and the idea of networking feels unnatural, insincere, or downright painful to them. The truth is, the more people you can stay in contact with on a regular basis, the more opportunities will likely come your way. This is a fact of life. If attending the occasional virtual mixer feels like torture, consider hiring somebody a bit more boisterous who can act as your agent while you continue your monastic pursuits.

Operate as a business—Now this part I hate with a capital 8. But if I can do it, you can do it … and by that I mean if I *have* to do it, you damn well had better do it! Seriously though, real-world organizations have a standard process by which they get things done. You will always be in a stronger position if you can integrate yourself into their process rather than being a confusing exception in their corporate flow control. That means yummy paperwork:

> **Write proposals**—These can vary widely depending on the task at hand, but most will include a statement describing your client's problem, your solution to the problem, a breakdown of cost, your needs/requirements, and some amount of self-promotion describing why you are the best person for the job.

> **Submit invoices**—Don't be caught off guard when a client requests an invoice! Microsoft Word and Excel provide templates for invoices, so take the time to familiarize yourself with them.

CHAPTER 1

CHAPTER 2

CHAPTER 3

CHAPTER 4

CHAPTER 5

CHAPTER 6

CHAPTER 7

CHAPTER 8

CHAPTER 9

CHAPTER 10

CHAPTER 11

CHAPTER 12

CHAPTER 13

CHAPTER 14

CHAPTER 15

APPENDICES

CHAPTER 13

MONEY: THE COLD,
HARD FACTS

WAYS TO
PROFIT

PRIVATE
BUSINESS

VIRTUAL MONEY
MAKING

CORPORATE
MOVES

SECOND LIFE
PROFESSIONALISM

THE *SECOND LIFE*
SOLUTION
PROVIDER
DIRECTORY

SO ... YOU SURE
YOU WANNA DO
THIS?

Make presentations—You may be asked to give a telephone or live presentation, and that means public speaking! Once again, if you're shy, consider teaming up with somebody who can do a good job wheeling and dealing in front of a crowd.

THE *SECOND LIFE* SOLUTION PROVIDER DIRECTORY

When real-world corporations approach Linden Lab about projects, they are normally directed to the *Second Life* Solution Provider Directory (`http://secondlifegrid.net/programs/ solprogram/directory`). This directory lists *Second Life* residents with a proven track record of professional success in *SL*.

But how does one get on this list? Linden Lab's senior vice president, Robin Harper, had this to say:

"I think the best way to get on the list is to send in your name and skill set, and a great portfolio— pics, happy clients, etc. It also really helps to be able to show that you are able to work on a 'professional' level. That is, you are ready to manage things like deadlines, invoicing, milestones, and progress reports."

When asked to elaborate on professionalism, Robin went on to say, "You might find that you need to do RL presentations, so public-speaking skills and salesmanship are also critical. I think setting expectations is part of being professional. People need to know what they're getting into, and you need to be realistic about what you can promise. In the long run that makes everyone a lot happier!"

SO ... YOU SURE YOU WANNA DO THIS?

Nobody knows what will become of this budding platform or if grooming a career in *Second Life* is a fruitful endeavor. If the phrase "get rich quick" finds its way into your thoughts about *Second Life*, I recommend you run away very fast. *Second Life* professionals work very long, hard hours and many have been doing this for years with only moderate payoffs. I'm not trying to discourage anybody. Instead, new residents looking for instant gratification in the world of *Second Life* business should try to maintain more-reasonable goals.

However, if you have talent, patience, passion, and just a touch of obsessive compulsive disorder, there may be some great opportunities waiting for you in *Second Life*. I leave you with this quote from Robin:

"Second Life is getting a lot of visibility lately, as you know. If someone is serious about building a developer business, this is a great time to get involved."

Class dismissed!

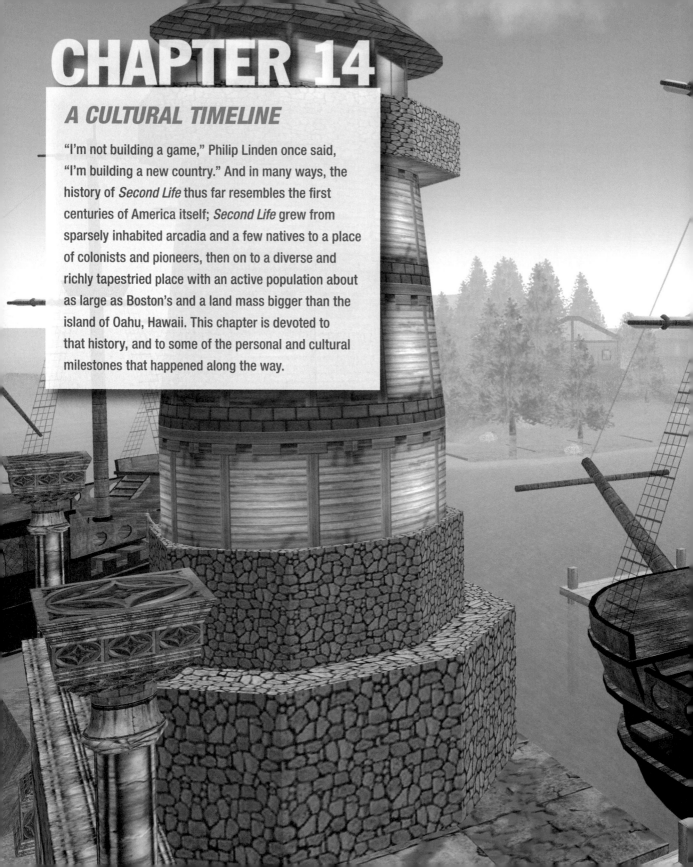

CHAPTER 14

A CULTURAL TIMELINE

"I'm not building a game," Philip Linden once said, "I'm building a new country." And in many ways, the history of *Second Life* thus far resembles the first centuries of America itself; *Second Life* grew from sparsely inhabited arcadia and a few natives to a place of colonists and pioneers, then on to a diverse and richly tapestried place with an active population about as large as Boston's and a land mass bigger than the island of Oahu, Hawaii. This chapter is devoted to that history, and to some of the personal and cultural milestones that happened along the way.

CONTENTS

FIRST ERA—2001 THROUGH EARLY 2003: PRE-HISTORIC, PRE-BETA

First created as a platform to test virtual reality and touch-interface technology, *LindenWorld* came into existence in 2001. In the beginning, avatars were known as Primitars, awkward robots composed of prims, which roamed the earth on stubby legs, occasionally terraforming it with ground-shaking grenades. They shared the world with snakelike creatures called Ators and rock-eating birds.

Re-dubbed *Second Life*, the world opened to non-Lindens in March 2002, welcoming small tribes of Alpha and closed Beta citizens by limited invitation. Land was shared in common, and tiny, close-knit tribes of tinkerers and utopians took root. (See the "Early-History Memories" sidebar.)

SECOND ERA—SUMMER 2003: NATIVES VERSUS COLONISTS

Public Beta of *Second Life* began in April 2003, and while most settlers intermingled with the original residents, cultural rifts appeared. Back then, the continent was tiny and three sims were called The Outlands, where combat was allowed, even encouraged. This often became the battleground to act out these conflicts.

RESIDENTS SPEAK
EARLY-HISTORY MEMORIES

"I had been searching for the Metaverse since I read *Snow Crash* … When I checked the link, I immediately knew I had found my Metaverse. That was in August 2002, and after a few excited e-mails to Linden Lab, I was allowed into *LindenWorld* in early September. *LindenWorld* was the pre-*Second Life* world, basically *SL* without water…

"In the early months the culture was definitely create-centric. At least I was. I love creating, and socializing is secondary for me. My most memorable event was one weekend (while the Lindens were away), BuhBuhCuh and I decided to build a bunch of Neo-Tokyo structures overshadowing the little downtown city the Lindens had built."

—bUTTONpUSHER Jones

"I've been living my second life for well over two years. Much as how Forrest Gump frequently found himself at the crossroads of historic events, it quickly became apparent to me, Torley Linden (née Torgeson), how many pioneering adventures I'd become caught up in. And not just as an observer, but a participant—something which continues for many resis (my shorthand for 'residents') to this day and beyond....

"As an avatar forever voyaging with my watermelon fetish, I'm still finding my way stumbling across fun times, many of them now recognized as monumentally important, some of them not, but ... it's all about the experience.

"If the journey's the reward, then *Second Life* has paid for itself many times over. Best US$10 I ever spent."

—Torley Linden

"I have been a resident of *Second Life* since July of 2003. It was a time when there was barely a landscape at all; bits of buildings dotting the world here and there and many days less than 50 people ever logged on at one time.

"There is no way to talk about my most cherished memories of *Second Life* without talking about the events. Somewhere during my early days, I began to stage events to publicize my early builds. It became apparent that my friends and indeed our residents at large were much more interested in the fun than the build, and so before long, I was back in the party business. (I had been an event planner for most of my professional life, but now retired. Sometimes we try to escape our past, but it often grabs us again.)

"After a score of early soirees, (fashion shows, store openings, and of course weddings) fashion designer Fey Brightwillow and I founded Spellbound Events, the first cohesive building, scripting, and animating team in *Second Life*. After deciding that storybook lore was our real love, we looked around for an idea that we thought would interest the entire community, male and female of all ages.

"So in Summer 2004, we gathered the Spellbound members together and staged Oz on one of the few private sims existing in *SL* at the time, Evie Fairchild's Island of Cayman. *SL* was barely a year past the beta stage, and yet Oz drew hundreds of visitors from our still-tiny world. Many came back repeatedly to put on the munchkin avatars provided, and dance the night away with their favorite characters, follow the yellow brick road, and watch the witch melt.

"Months passed, and the members of Spellbound quickly got restless to repeat the fun in an improved way. Therefore, I came to visit Linden Lab to ask for help to stage yet another

(Continued)

community event, one of a size that *Second Life* had never seen: a trip through early 20th-century London and a tribute to Peter Pan. The Lindens tried a pilot donation of three sims for a three-month period. We would have six weeks to construct our vision, and six weeks for the world at large to visit it.

"And visit it they did. They came in droves, by the thousands, logging an unprecedented number of visitor hours. People came repeatedly to role-play in Edwardian costume, [or as] raggedy boys, pirates, or Indian children. They chatted on the streets of London, foiled would-be bank robbers, flew out the Darlings' window across the water past the Jolly Roger in search of the Lost Boys, and had swordfights with Captain Hook himself.

"It was a window to the soul of what *Second Life* was and could really be as a community. Everything was provided free of charge. People came, played, and enjoyed in the spirit of good fellowship. It was a most special time. Even the *New York Times* covered the event in a story about *Second Life*, capturing its spirit forevermore.

"As I reflect on the early days, I remember how I marveled at the creativity of people. Every day some new way of making magic was happening. Today I see building groups formed whose sole purpose is constructing large projects but more of a commercial nature, which is just as wonderful. And no matter what the purpose, the idea of camaraderie to a single goal is an incredible benefit to *Second Life*. The work is more exacting and the standards are tougher but I still believe that our motives are the same. *Second Life* as a world wishes to be the best it can be.

"As our world has grown, events like Neverland are more difficult to arrange. Impossible no; nothing ever is. Each time I meet a wide-eyed new avatar I hear in them the amazement that is *Second Life*. They can immediately understand all that is possible. At any age, you are returned to an age of innocence. Your creativity is restored. In any life, it hardly gets any better than that."

—Baccara Rhodes

⬇ WAR OF THE JESSIE WALL

During public Beta, players of *World War II Online (WWIIOL)*, a massively multiplayer online, Allies vs. Axis military strategy game, discovered *Second Life* and arrived by the hundreds, using the building tools to meet and plan tactics for *WWIIOL*. They formed a group called WWIIOLers and unsurprisingly, they also built weapons and fortresses. This sudden influx of combat-minded residents was a culture shock to many. Before their arrival, many peaceful residents had put down roots and built homes in The Outlands, and they were upset by the arrival of armed avatars who opened fire on them in their own homes.

Open battle broke out between the WWIIOLers and indigenous resisters, and much of it centered around the Jessie Wall, an imposing barrier that separated the civilized districts of *Second Life* from

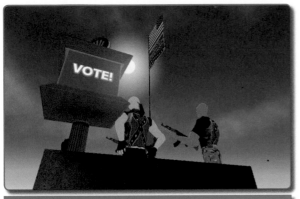

Figure 14.1: The WWIIOLers defend their territory in Jessie.

the war zone (Figure 14.1). The wall also became a billboard for pro- and antiwar sentiment over the war in Iraq, which was raging in the real world, and that spurred the antagonism even further. (Most of the WWIIOLers supported the war; many of the residents nearby did not.) Robot turrets, teleporting bullets, and other weapons were built and deployed in what was, in retrospect, a conflict to define the nature of *Second Life*: pacifist utopia, or gun-happy libertarian free-for-all. The battle was quelled eventually, and clashes like it are largely made moot by the continued growth of the world, with more than enough space for both pacifists and war gamers to be in *SL* without them even meeting each other, if they so choose.

SECOND ERA—SUMMER 2003: REVOLUTION!

As society forms, so does social upheaval. In *SL*, the most crucial conflict was the reaction to Linden Lab's "tax policy." In 2003, residents were being taxed (that is, Linden dollars were automatically deducted from their accounts) for objects they instantiated in-world. To the Lindens, this seemed like a simple way to prevent residents from overheating the servers with too many objects. But the Lindens got way more than they expected.

THE TEA CRATE REBELLION OF JULY '03

Figure 14.2: Fleabite Beach and other tax revolters pose in 2006 for a reunion portrait.

Objecting most strongly to Linden's tax policy was Americana, a group devoted to creating tributes to US landmarks. Feeling punished for their public-works project, Americana unleashed a protest suitable to their name, dropping giant tea crates across the world and setting their American landmarks on fire. A cat named Fleabite Beach sent out a Thoreau-style proclamation against "Mad King Linden," and led the revolutionaries into the streets with muskets and signs emblazoned with the words "Born Free: Taxed to Death!" (Figure 14.2) Much of the citizenry was drawn into the insurrection, either as rebels or redcoat "Linden loyalists."

But from conflict comes community, because it was one of the first times residents saw themselves together in a grid-wide struggle. And though the Lindens may not admit it, the protests helped encourage them to end the tax system.

THIRD ERA—WINTER 2003: A NEW NATION IS BORN

During this period, Linden Lab made three policy decisions considered radical at the time:

1. To end monthly subscriptions (the standard revenue model for almost all MMOs) and instead, begin charging monthly "land use" fees for virtual land

2. To announce a laissez-faire policy on buying and selling the official in-world currency on the open market for real money

3. To recognize residents' legally enforceable intellectual-property rights over the objects and scripts they created within the world

NOVEMBER 14, 2003: IP INDEPENDENCE DAY!

Figure 14.3. Lawrence Lessig

Advised by *Free Culture* author and Stanford law professor Lawrence Lessig (Figure 14.3)—basically the Thomas Jefferson of *Second Life*—Linden Lab established a new policy, dedicated to the proposition that residents should retain intellectual-property rights over works they created in-world. The impact was not felt immediately, but that coupled with the ability to trade L$ for US$ spurred the growth of a substantial mercantile class (artisans, entertainers, shopkeepers, weaponsmiths, etc.).

RESIDENTS SPEAK
THE HISTORY OF LUSKWOOD

"The beginnings of 'Furry in *SL*' certainly were not planned. The right people, at the right time, doing the right things, led to a sort of perfect environment for Luskwood to have its genesis.

"September 2003: Michi Lumin and Eltee Statosky had recently 'migrated' from a Furry-oriented text-based virtual world, and 3D seemed like the next natural progression. Michi had brought Liam along with her from anime-based mush/mud environments.

"While *SL* was promising, it seemed to confine you, at first glance, to a human avatar. Around this time, Eltee was running around with fox ears and a tail stuck to the normal human avatar, which was the closest thing *SL* had to Furries. This was around the time when Arito Cotton was experimenting with attachments to make an avatar which would be worn over the human avatar.

"Needless to say, Arito's first attempt went over well (even though he doesn't like to show that avatar to this day—it was certainly embryonic compared to what we have now). But word spread fast, and it wasn't long before Arito had made four or five custom prim avatars for other people…

"Over the next few weeks, the group ended up with well over 30 requests for custom Furry avatars. Thirty Furries in *SL* was considered quite a number then, and the Luskwood custom waiting list began to grow from one month to several months; each avatar took about a week to complete. Eventually, Arito figured that Luskwood could sell a 'basic' avatar, which would only have to be built once, and would be sold as modifiable so that the end user could easily change hair color or add customization to his or her own liking.

"The vendor—the first avatar vendor in *SL*, built in the same wooden style as Liam's owl lamp—inherited the name Luskwood Creatures. Arito figured that Luskwood would sell at most 100 of these avatars, declaring that if they sold more, he would 'eat a plywood prim. In real life.'

"To date [mid 2007], Luskwood has sold [30,000] avatars, and Arito has yet to eat a single block of wood."

—Michi Lumin

FOURTH ERA—LATE 2003 THROUGH EARLY 2004: EXPANDING THE FRONTIER

The great land rush began in December 2003, when Linden ended the tax system, eliminated monthly subscriptions, and adopted virtual-land usage fees as a revenue model. In the beginning, Linden held "land grabs" for new territory, similar to claim-staking events in the American frontier. *SL* residents by the dozens would hover around real estate controlled by "Governor Linden" and wait for the Lindens to release it to the open market at the top of the hour. Eventually the Lindens civilized this process with an auction system, in which plots of land and entire continents are put on the open market, both for Linden dollars and US dollars. The first island was put on the block on January 7th, 2004—and the rights to own it were sold for over US$1,200 to Fizik Baskerville. The day after news hit that Fizik owned a real-world commercial branding agency and was planning on using *SL* as a marketing platform, protestors were there to greet him, waving "Boycott the Island" signs.

From the moment the land-ownership policy began, real estate was rapidly claimed, bought, and sold, even as the company added new continents and private islands to keep up with demand. The "land barons" began to emerge, using their business acumen to acquire large swaths of territory, then charging a "rental" fee to other residents.

⬇ THE IMMIGRANT EXPERIENCE

Throughout the first three years, waves of Net-based cultures arrived: the technorati who read about *SL* on sites like Slashdot and Boing Boing, hard-core gamers who were looking for an online building-block set to play around with, the Furries, anime fans, and more. Impelled by policy changes or led en masse by pioneers, many were expatriates from other online worlds, seeking a place where they could make their own rules. After *Second Life* accounts were made free in mid 2006—previously there was a monthly subscriber fee, and later a US$10 sign-up charge for basic accounts—many apparent "immigrants" were in fact simply existing account holders who were starting secondary accounts.

FIFTH ERA—MID 2004 THROUGH MID 2005: INDUSTRIAL REVOLUTION

Significant integration of Web-based technology into *SL* began in June 2004 with the ability to stream audio onto land, and to incorporate custom animations with avatars. Later in the year came the ability to stream QuickTime video and the ability to export .xml data, and soon afterward, the means to create heads-up displays that let residents customize the interface with new functionality. Each of these innovations fostered whole industries: live music performance and DJs, machinima, in-world advertising, e-commerce websites, and more. On a cultural level, this is roughly when influential residents like SNOOPYbrown Zamboni (aka Jerry Paffendorf) began to speak of *Second Life* as a kind of 3D Web, a new medium that merged an online world with interfaces previously associated with the World Wide Web.

FROM LINDEN LAB
BREAKING THROUGH

"While *Second Life* has always received plenty of publicity and news coverage, I think the breakthrough happened in June 2004, with a Reuters wire story featured in *USA Today* and on MSNBC describing how residents owned virtual land. This culminated with Philip speaking live on CNN. A lot of us Lindens ran over to the bar across the street, watched his segment, then had a little celebratory drink before going back to work. That was the first time we understood that *Second Life* was going to make a difference."

—Catherine Linden

RESIDENTS SPEAK
MILESTONES IN THE LINDEN SCRIPTING LANGUAGE

CHAPTER 1

CHAPTER 2

CHAPTER 3

CHAPTER 4

CHAPTER 5

CHAPTER 6

CHAPTER 7

CHAPTER 8

CHAPTER 9

CHAPTER 10

CHAPTER 11

CHAPTER 12

CHAPTER 13

CHAPTER 14

CHAPTER 15

APPENDICES

"The history of scripting in *Second Life* can be divided into two categories—first, the points at which functions are placed into the eager hands of residents, and second, the points at which residents apply those functions in combination with existing ones to create working items, usually in an entirely unpredictable manner. For instance, objects which create other objects moving at high speed have been possible since at least January 2003; it has also been possible to have objects which give people money. Was the development of guns firing bullets which actually enrich the victim rather than harm them initially envisaged? I imagine not.

"Still, there have been certain points in the evolution of the Linden Scripting Language (Mark Two—Mark One was a very different beast, not to be mentioned in polite company) which one could call 'landmarks.' Perhaps the first is the development in release 0.6 (April 2003) of a function allowing the reading of notecards by scripts, which allows for considerable storage and retrieval of information.

"In 1.1 (October 2003) we find the introduction of llParticleSystem, the function allowing the generation of swirling patterns, firestorms, smoke clouds, rain, and immense torrents of teddy bears. Perhaps more significantly in terms of effects on the economy, in release 1.4 (June 2004) we see functions allowing for encryption and also for communication with *Second Life* via the protocol known as XML-RPC, which would make large-scale commercial enterprises such as SL Exchange far more practical.

"Returning to more cosmetic (and thus more central to the nature of *Second Life*) functions, in release 1.6 (March 2005) we see enhanced abilities to detect what an avatar is doing— allowing for the invention of the highly popular Animation Overrides. In 1.7 (October 2005) we have functions allowing the movement of attachments via llSetPos et al, which greatly enhanced the field of avatar creation—now tails could wag, wings flap, clockwork keys rotate.

"In 1.8 (December 2005) functions allowing the banning of people from land parcels by script were introduced, allowing security devices to take advantage of the protection functions of the world itself—and the later introduction of functions allowing scripts to gain detailed information on parcels (1.13, December 2006) allowed the gathering of many useful research data, and the automation of many tedious tasks.

"Perhaps one of the more important additions was in 1.10 (May 2006)—here we have llHTTPRequest expanding on the previous method of communication with Aethernet entities, allowing a script to further exploit the powers of machines far separated from the grid. Momentous changes in other areas of *Second Life* are also reflected, with residents now, say, being able to change the form of a sculpted prim via one simple command.

(Continued)   319

"Still, the ingenuity of residents when it comes to finding new uses for things continues to produce new results from old material. Only in May 2006 was it discovered that `llSetPrimitiveParams` could be used to move an object and any passenger an indefinite distance in a mere fraction of a second. The true effect of scripting on the world is defined less by the tools provided and the original intentions behind them, and more by the relentless efforts of residents to use every means at their disposal to affect the grid as they see fit."

—Ordinal Malaprop

Meeting the Lovemakers

Figure 14.4: Phil and Snow demonstrate an animation that helped grow their business—and their real-life relationship.

While many people are prone to giggle at the idea of residents using *SL*'s animation technology for making their avatars have close encounters of the most intimate kind, often it's just a kind of entertaining icebreaker that leads to genuine friendship. Some engage in a bout of passion like this as a kind of fun role-playing, as if their avatars were stars of a racy movie—then later on, they strike up a conversation and became close (but not romantic) friends. (One such couple became so close that when one of them was left homeless by the Katrina hurricane disaster, the other reached out, and without ever having met him, she purchased a bus ticket for him to her home and let him crash on her couch for several weeks.)

On another occasion, I interviewed Phil Murdock and Snow Hare of PM Adult, an animation and toy emporium they co-owned, and learned that their business partnership had made them a couple in real life. Their first kiss was an animation they were creating for their customers, and they tested it out on themselves. (Figure 14.4) It was, Phil told me, "awesome and special. Just as special as the first in real life."

CHAPTER 1
CHAPTER 2
CHAPTER 3
CHAPTER 4
CHAPTER 5
CHAPTER 6
CHAPTER 7
CHAPTER 8
CHAPTER 9
CHAPTER 10
CHAPTER 11
CHAPTER 12
CHAPTER 13
CHAPTER 14

SIXTH ERA—SUMMER 2005 THROUGH 2006: BOOM TIME

The world experienced a boom period. Kermitt Quirk's Tringo not only became an *SL* phenomenon during the sixth era, it became a Game Boy Advance title in April 2006 and started undergoing development as a television show.

During this time, Linden Lab launched the LindeX, an internal L$-for-US$ commodities market, effectively transforming virtual currency into a micropayment system. Constant stories in the media (the BBC, ABC, and the cover story for *BusinessWeek* in May 2006) described wonders and wealth beyond measure, spurring another wave of immigrants, many of them entrepreneurs—and carpetbaggers.

All this attention helped fuel the rise of metaverse development companies such as Rivers Run Red, The Electric Sheep Company, Millions of Us, and more, offering production services for real-world clients paying real cash. In tentative steps, studios like these brought the first real corporations into *Second Life*: Adidas, Reebok, Warner Bros., Major League Baseball, Starwood Hotels, Toyota, and other legacy institutions. The entrance of *Second Life* into the "Web 2.0" pantheon along with user-created content portals like Facebook and YouTube were well under way.

SEVENTH ERA—LATE 2006 THROUGH 2007: CONFLICT AND GLOBALIZATION

Through this period, conflict came in many forms: between real world laws and *Second Life* rules; between the community and the growing pains of the system itself; between outside detractors and the community's angry defenders; between the expectations of real-world companies and the results most of them got for their marketing efforts in *Second Life*.

Linden Lab issued a series of rulings throughout 2007 that were designed to protect the company legally, but provoked more than a little controversy and outcry: gambling was prohibited, as were the most extreme forms of sexual content; plans to conduct age verification through a third-party company were also announced. At the same time, the Lindens' struggles to handle such an explosive growth rate led to fairly frequent downtimes and frustrating performance issues, and this, in turn, led to in-world protests and petition campaigns.

If 2006 was the year of mainstream media hype over *Second Life*, 2007 was the year of backlash. Numerous stories noted that most real-world advertising sites in *SL* were empty, while respected academic Clay Shirky pointed out that *SL*'s active user base was much smaller than usually assumed. But hype and backlash are two sides of the same coin, one feeding off the other. It wasn't exactly true (as many 2006 articles implied) that *Second Life* was the next big thing in Internet marketing; it wasn't the case that the millions of people who'd created an *SL* account were active and regular users. The backlash was largely caused by these misunderstandings, but critics often added even more confusion to the mix by failing to note that several *SL*-based marketing efforts *were* showing positive results, and despite a high churn rate of new users, that the active user base *was* growing rapidly, both in absolute numbers and in amount of hours spent in-world.

Figure 14.5: Kowloon, made in Japan

As for globalization, that has varied meanings. First, it refers to the rapid internationalization of *Second Life*. By mid 2007, over 50 percent of active residents were from the European Union, while 26 percent were from the US. (Two years earlier, Europeans were the minority.) This cosmopolitan spread is being rapidly augmented by Asian and South American residents. By July '07, Brazilians and Japanese were among the second and third top active users by country, bringing amazing creativity with them (Figure 14.5), while South Korea ranked in the top 10 in terms of hours spent in-world by country.

Second, globalization refers to the open-sourcing of *Second Life*: in January 2007, the Lindens released the code that runs the *SL* viewing software under a GNU license so that programmers could create new versions of it. This inspired a variety of new ways to access *Second Life*, including several variations of the program, some offering totally new ways to go in-world. At least two companies, Comverse and Vodaphone, enable you to interact with *SL* from your cell phone, for example, while several more let you navigate it with the Nintendo Wii. (One enterprising team with Germany's I-D Media hooked *SL* up to the Wii *and* a treadmill.) Perhaps most interesting of all, an unassuming 15-year-old member of *Teen Second Life* named Katharine Berry created AjaxLife, a way of interacting with *SL* through the Web. In all, with this churn of innovation came the promise that *Second Life* would no longer be an activity or a community confined to computers.

> FROM LINDEN LAB
> ## DEVELOPMENTS OF LATE
>
> "There is never one development I can label as most significant for me, because all relevant developments are interconnected. To single out some is akin to removing basic food groups ... unhealthy.
>
> "For instance, sculpted prims have certainly improved the construction quality of certain objects, but they are even better with the advanced shiny, and lit in WindLight with glow atop— quite a synergistic combination.

"Similarly, it is not just 'Voice' alone that excites me, but how the tool is used. Text standup comedy really doesn't cut it. I look forward to budding Seinfelds being birthed, or at least discovered, on the fields of our humble metaverse.

"A lot of the behind-the-scenes, under-the-hood stuff which has improved performance and stability (an ongoing quest) is unquestionably essential. Give it up for the Lindens who contributed to those. But see, as I say that, it doesn't mean I deny/do not acknowledge anyone else's contributions—we each have a special role to play here."

—Torley Linden

"Voice is the biggest recent development, no question. It's a whole new platform with Voice. Voice was already in place by the time I joined Linden Lab, and it really is practical for us to have a substantial fraction of our company meetings in-world. They would have been harder to really do well without Voice."

—Prospero Linden

⬇ ADVENTURES IN MIXED REALITY

Second Life was originally designed to keep reality and the online world as separate as possible, but the real world has always found ways of sneaking through, from major personalities in arts, culture, and politics to very real businesses on the Fortune 500 list.

REAL-WORLD FIGURES

Figure 14.6: The avatar of Kurt Vonnegut

As I remember it, bringing real names into *Second Life* was first suggested by Web developer Jim Linden, in the days when I was still Linden Lab's "embedded reporter." I had just had my first "Hamlet Linden Book Club" with Cory Doctorow, though his avatar was called CoryDoctorow Electric—his surname taken from the default list. "Why not just make his name Cory Doctorow?," Jim asked casually. "We can do that on the server." And so the next time Cory entered the world to talk about his latest novel, he was called Cory Doctorow. So fellow novelist Ellen *The Bug* Ullman and game designer Harvey *Deus Ex* Smith entered the world with their

323

Figure 14.7: Governor Warner, the avatar

Figure 14.8: Judge Richard Posner and a Furry fan

own names, as did law professor Lawrence Lessig, technology guru and venture capitalist Joi Ito; and then in a series of summer-'06 appearances sponsored by public radio's *The Infinite Mind*, famed singer and "mother of the MP3" Suzanne Vega, Internet visionary Howard *Smart Mobs* Rheingold, and legendary novelist Kurt Vonnegut (Figure 14.6); politician Mark Warner (Figure 14.7; see the sidebar "Real-World Politics in *Second Life*") also got in on the action when he was debating a run for US president. In late 2006/2007, they were joined by short appearances from numerous politicians from Europe, the US, and Japan, Judge Richard Posner (Figure 14.8), actor Bruce Willis, columnist and blogger Arianna Huffington, *Wired* editor in chief Chris Anderson, cyberpunk legend William Gibson, graphic novelist Frank Miller, the lead team behind *300*, and many more.

In the near future, Linden Lab is expected to allow residents to designate avatar surnames of their choice, and many will surely come to the world with their real names. Perhaps many will choose their real surname while maintaining their avatar's first name. This is what I did when I left the company to write my own book on *Second Life*, in early 2006. Hamlet Au had already become more recognizable than my real-life name: Googling my actual name mostly turns up New World Notes and my avatar. As *Second Life* becomes even more important to the Internet, so will the names of *SL* residents—so choose yours wisely.

CHAPTER 1

CHAPTER 2

CHAPTER 3

CHAPTER 4

CHAPTER 5

CHAPTER 6

CHAPTER 7

CHAPTER 8

CHAPTER 9

CHAPTER 10

CHAPTER 11

CHAPTER 12

CHAPTER 13

CHAPTER 14

CHAPTER 15

APPENDICES

ADDITIONAL INFO
REAL-WORLD POLITICS IN *SECOND LIFE*

In August 2006 the former governor of Virginia took on avatar form, flew onto a stage, and met with a group of residents to discuss war in Iraq, terrorism, abortion, and his political action committee (which now has a branch in *SL*). It was a culmination of numerous visits to *SL* by real-world figures on the international political scene, including Lawrence Lessig (January '06), who pleaded a case before the Supreme Court; and Thomas P.M. Barnett (October 05), who worked for Donald Rumsfeld in the Pentagon and briefed Senator John Kerry during and after his bid for the US presidency in 2004. Many more were to follow. In early 2007, for example, two of France's leading political parties created official headquarters, while the top Democratic candidates for the 2008 US presidential race gained large (if unofficial) followings; sensing a new opportunity, the influential "net roots" YearlyKos convention of 2007 set up a presence in *SL*. At this rate, it's not implausible that the next election cycle will have a whistle stop in *Second Life*.

REAL-WORLD COMPANIES

IBM, Pontiac, Showtime, the Weather Channel, Nissan, and Microsoft are just a few of the real-world companies that have a permanent/ongoing presence in *SL*, engaging with residents through "branded experiences" that are meant to be promotion for them and fun for the community. Go on a scavenger hunt on Microsoft's island, take a Sentra or a customized Solstice for a spin around a race track, go surfing on the Weather Channel's beach, hang out with fans of Showtime's *The L Word* in a re-creation of the show's locations, then play around in IBM's Codestation developer sandbox. By the time you read this, of course, these companies and their experiences be joined by countless others, providing residents with a chance (if they're interested) to merge real-world consumerism with their second lives.

At the moment, it should be added, only a dozen or so handfuls of corporate sites are bringing in regular traffic (see Chapter 13 for detail in business in *Second Life*), while most are empty of visitors—a situation that encouraged the aforementioned media backlash against *Second Life*.

RESIDENTS SPEAK
FASHION MILESTONES

"Fashion in *Second Life* moves at Internet speed—and so does the underlying technology that gives *Second Life* such a dynamic and expressive way to customize an avatar.

"The first major innovation was the emergence of 'photorealistic' skins. The default system skins are not very realistic-looking, either in terms of musculature or skin tones. Innovative content developers decided they could 'hack' the *Second Life* default by—at first—creating files to replace the stock files which came with the *Second Life* viewer. Later, the idea of using a 'full-body tattoo' to store the skin texture made it easier, simpler, and safer for residents to find and buy a skin which not only looked incredible but permitted a diverse range of makeup, shading, and body-hair options, all things the default skins were not especially well suited to do in a believable way.

"The next major fashion innovation was the use of prims for hair and shoes. Using a collection of linked and specially textured prims as hair caused a fashion revolution, because many were dissatisfied with the options available in the default avatar-adjustment sliders. Prim hair changed all of that, and quickly. Soon after, people began to experiment with prim shoes which permitted developers to make realistic looking three-dimensional footwear—everything from athletic sneakers to boots any real-life dominatrix would be proud to stash in her closet.

"The final and most recent fashion revolution was the introduction of the flexible prim shapes in the 1.10 software release. Flexible prims allow three prim shapes (cylinders, prisms, and cubes) to react to the movement from in-world physics. From the day of 1.10's release, flexiprims took the fashion world completely by storm—from swaying minis to superhero capes and elegant wedding trains, the world of *Second Life* fashion just hasn't been the same since flexiprims arrived on the scene.

"Although *Second Life* definitely has its own fashion ebb and flow, the popular styles in-world often come from real-world inspiration. As just one example, this year's fashion trends have seen a revival of popular '80s couture such as leg warmers, plaid patterns, dresses and shorts with tights, and frilly embellished shirts.

"In general, most garments and shoes in *Second Life* tend more toward sassy (the uncharitable might even make that 'trashy') than classy, but in a virtual world where you can set the size of your avatar's butt using a slider and show off killer abs because of a developer's skill in Photoshop, why not dare to bare? That's the attitude of most residents and there is no shortage of revealing wild styles to tempt and tantalize.

"Fashion in *Second Life* continues to evolve as Linden Lab adds more features to the platform. One of the biggest redefinitions of fashion styles was with the introduction of sculpted prims in early 2007. This type of primitive begins as a sphere and uses a special map to decompose the sphere into a natural-looking organic shape. (Think of how a sphere could be transformed into a pear shape to get a mental image of how this works.) This new prim type led to the steady rise of sculpted sleeves and cuffs on blouses, sculpted shoes, sculpted hairstyles, sculpted handbags, and incredibly intricate bows and flower petals."

—Celebrity Trollop

BUILDING COMMUNITY: BURNING LIFE

Figure 14.9: Artemis Fate, Krysss Galatea, Torrid Midnight, Gonta Maltz, and Maxx Mackenzie re-create Burning Life.

Unsurprisingly, an annual tribute to the famed Burning Man festival is held during Labor Day weekend, and the Linden Lab–sponsored Burning Life is *SL* at its most free-form. What begins as an untouched flat island becomes, in the space of days, a kind of shared hallucination: the sculpture of a giant hand with a giant magnifying glass, frying the world; a human-sized, rideable Pac-Man tribute; a 3D re-creation of Edvard Munch's "The Scream" that lets *you* become the screamer on the boardwalk. The first Burning Life was in 2003, and it's grown twice as large each year, culminating in the ritual burning of the giant wooden man (Figure 14.9) then disappearing as quickly as it came.

BUILDING COMMUNITY: MAKING A DIFFERENCE

Figure 14.10: A Katrina donation site

Thanks to an army of volunteers, *SL*'s 2006 Relay for Life raised nearly $40,000 for the American Cancer Society, through a combination of telethon pledging and auctions held across the grid. (An anonymous donor bought a pink muscle car for the Linden-dollar equivalent of US$2,000.) As impressive as those numbers are, Relay for Life 2007 surpassed them grandly, raising well over $100,000. There have been numerous full-scale charitable efforts since then—and before. In the wake of the Katrina Hurricane disaster in 2005, thousands of residents quickly launched hundreds of impromptu events, parties, raffles, and other fund-raisers (Figure 14.10), a collective effort that eventually raised over $10,000 in donations, most of it going to the Red Cross.

CHAPTER 1

CHAPTER 2

CHAPTER 3

CHAPTER 4

CHAPTER 5

CHAPTER 6

CHAPTER 7

CHAPTER 8

CHAPTER 9

CHAPTER 10

CHAPTER 11

CHAPTER 12

CHAPTER 13

CHAPTER 14

CHAPTER 15

APPENDICES

The first known *SL* fundraiser began in April of 2004, launched by a casino magnate named Jason Foo. Before his second life, Jason was an active-duty Marine who saw fierce action in Iraq and elsewhere. Forced into retirement by an exploding mine, he turned to *Second Life* to supplement his VA benefits. As he became successful in-world, Jason reached out to fellow vets, creating donation boxes in his casinos to benefit a veterans-support group called New Directions; the group raised hundreds of US dollars.

In June 2004 a group fundraiser was coordinated by Bhodi Silverman and volunteers to benefit the online rights group the Electronic Frontier Foundation. Working with Gaming Open Market, a L$-to-US$ currency-exchange site popular at the time, Bhodi and her team held events and auctions that raised the L$ equivalent of US$1,768—extraordinary for an era in which the world was just several thousand active residents.

Both these efforts occurred very soon after Linden Lab enabled residents to buy and sell L$ for real currency. Among the very first uses of this L$-to-US$ feature, therefore, was to help real people outside of *SL*.

LINDEN-SPONSORED EVENTS

Once key attractions in life on the grid, official events put on by Linden Lab now compete with the dozens of other activities going on every hour. Besides Burning Life (see "Building Community" in this chapter), the company hosts at least two regular events. Check the Lindens' group blog (`http://blog.secondlife.com`) to find out more.

Town Halls. Usually held on a monthly basis, these are occasions to meet top Linden staff including Philip, Cory, and Community Development VP Robin Harper, to discuss issues affecting *SL*, and get word of system upgrades and planned changes. While these meetings often attract a capacity crowd, the Lindens take pains to make sure residents can participate, giving out "repeaters" (devices that transmit the Town Hall chat anywhere in the grid) or pointing residents to the Internet server where they can listen in. These events can get pretty wild, especially after a big announcement or a rash of technical trouble.

Campus *Second Life* Launch. Reaching out to the academic world, VP of Marketing and Community Development Robin Harper launched a new initiative for colleges and universities interested in using the grid as a pedagogical tool. Early adopters included Aaron Delwiche, an assistant professor at Trinity University, and University of Texas at Austin's Anne Beamish, who used it to teach principles of social design for her architecture students. Many educators and institutions followed, including Harvard's Berkman Center and USC's Annenberg Center on Public Diplomacy, both of which conducted lectures and events from their own *SL* islands.

Opening of Teen *Second Life*. Responding to countless requests from frustrated adolescents and their parents, Linden Lab opened up a separate realm of *Second Life* in August 2005, reserved for residents between ages 13 and 17. Growing slowly, *Teen Second Life* now has just less than 5,000 active residents, and it often acts as a training ground for teens preparing to enter "the adult grid." (Australian Liaison Nicole Linden even introduced a welcoming party for teen residents who turn 18 and are thus eligible for this graduation.)

ADDITIONAL INFO
THE *SECOND LIFE* COMMUNITY CONVENTION

Originally the brainchild of FlipperPA, Jennyfur Peregrine, Hiro Pendragon, Valadeza Anubis, and SNOOPYbrown Zamboni (with Jeska Linden serving as the liaison between Linden Lab and the organizers), the inaugural *SLCC* was in 2005 in New York and attracted 100-plus attendees. (While not an official Linden Lab event, the company and others help with sponsorship, and the Lindens appear there in force.) On a dare, Philip gave the first keynote dressed up to resemble his *SL* avatar, Rolling Stones T-shirt and sequined codpiece included. That was when the world had a scant 60,000 registered users, and those times are long gone; for *SLCC* 2006, held in August in San Francisco, the world was fast approaching about 200,000 active residents; nearly 500 of them attended the convention. By then, *SLCC* was no longer just an occasion for parties and exchanging *SL* tips, but also a business convention, with companies that do business in *Second Life* making announcements about deals they'd struck with major corporations. This became even more evident at *SLCC* 2007, held in Chicago, with four specialty tracks (business, education, machinima, and social), a reception sponsored by nearby Columbia College's Art Institute, dozens of *SL*-based musicians performing live, and a masquerade ball sponsored by two of the leading adult entertainment companies in *Second Life*. About 800 residents attended.

The official *SLCC* site is `http://slconvention.com/`. Keep an eye on it for news on dates and places for the next convention. And if you do go, remember that when meeting each other in person, *SL* residents—even Lindens—generally call each other by their avatar names. That's whether they look like a version of their alter egos or come without the fur, devil horns, alien skin, robot gear, and other enhancements you've come to identify them by in-world. What's amazing is how natural this feels, and how familiar you can quickly get with hundreds of people you've known only through 3D graphics.

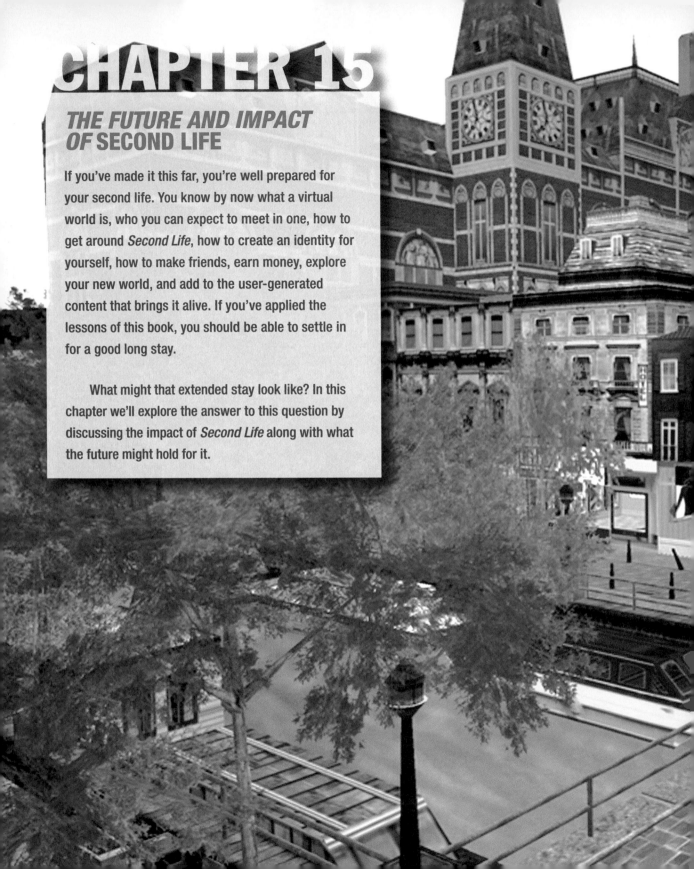

CHAPTER 15

THE FUTURE AND IMPACT OF SECOND LIFE

If you've made it this far, you're well prepared for your second life. You know by now what a virtual world is, who you can expect to meet in one, how to get around *Second Life*, how to create an identity for yourself, how to make friends, earn money, explore your new world, and add to the user-generated content that brings it alive. If you've applied the lessons of this book, you should be able to settle in for a good long stay.

What might that extended stay look like? In this chapter we'll explore the answer to this question by discussing the impact of *Second Life* along with what the future might hold for it.

CONTENTS

CHAPTER 15

IS THERE A
FUTURE FOR
VIRTUAL WORLDS?

THE NEXT
GENERATION OF
THE INTERNET?

AN EXTRA-
ORDINARILY
RADICAL IDEA

FROM TOYS
TO TOOLS

IS THERE A FUTURE FOR VIRTUAL WORLDS?

One of the most exciting characteristics of virtual worlds is that they do not stay the same for long. They are constantly patched up and altered, becoming larger or more detailed, with more things for users to do, and new places to explore. These online spaces evolve, often taking a germ of an idea and pushing it to its logical extreme. Consequently virtual worlds can last for years, and they can be quite different from one year to the next.

Most virtual worlds change and develop through the hard work put in by the people who created them. In *Second Life*, however, it's the *residents* of the virtual word who are the creators. It's our hard work that allows *Second Life*'s huge world to keep on changing. The tools are in *our* hands, rather than in the hands of a select group of developers, and that has enormous implications. Linden Lab's intention is, rather than to make a virtual world for themselves, to provide residents with the power to create whatever *they* choose. This means that the variety and, most likely, the longevity of *Second Life* far outstrips that of other online worlds, such as massively multiplayer online (MMO) games. As long as the residents themselves are creative and inventive, then there will be new things to see, new places to go, and new concepts to explore.

But will new residents continue to come? Will *Second Life* continue to grow as a community? And will the current interest in virtual worlds keep expanding? It looks that way to many people. Even if you ignore all the online projects and virtual-world concepts that *Second Life* has inspired, there is strong evidence to suggest that *SL* is just the beginning of something far more widespread.

Second Life's growth curve has been unusual among virtual worlds. For most MMOs—that is, games like *World of Warcraft* or *Ultima Online*—the population tends to spike soon after the game is released, and gradually fall back to some equilibrium point over time (or die off altogether, if the developers are unlucky). *Second Life*, on the other hand, never saw the early spike but has seen slow and steady growth ever since it appeared. It's the kind of growth curve that's characteristic of the way many important new technologies are adopted, according to Jerry Paffendorf, futurist in residence with the Electric Sheep Company, a development house doing work in *Second Life*. "The story of *Second Life* has been the story of this little virtual world that only had a thousand users," Paffendorf says. "Then it was the story of this little virtual world that only had 10,000 users. Then it only had 50,000 users. Then only 100,000. Now it only has 700,000 users, and soon it'll only have a million, and so on."

The implications of this kind of growth continuing could well be world-changing. Though it took *Second Life* nearly three years to reach 100,000 registered users, late 2006 saw the addition of around 100,000 new users every month! During the month of October 2007 just under 900,000 residents logged into *Second Life*. That's mighty impressive growth, and it suggests that virtual worlds have only just begun to reveal their potential audience. But perhaps what's most notable is not the number of users, but just how those people have begun to use their world.

Second Life is often held up as the perfect place to get your fantasy on—and yes, there's no other place like it for becoming something you aren't, or even for working out just what it is you want to be. In a sense, it's the epitome of the "walled garden," a place where reality dare not intrude and whatever fiction you want to create in the world is just as valid as anything your neighbor is constructing. Nowhere else can you be a bipedal fox decked out in sci-fi commando gear at the helm of your own spaceship with as much specificity and detail as in Second Life. Elves, witches, vampires, robots, yachtsmen, dominatrices, race car drivers, fashionistas, steampunks—the list goes on and on. If you can imagine it in Second Life, chances are you can become it. It's the perfect world for letting your flights of fancy run free.

But Second Life is fast becoming more than mere fantasy and escapism: It's becoming a toolkit that ties into our first, real lives. As you'll see later in this chapter, Second Life is becoming a way to launch artistic projects, to supplement business and marketing plans, and to engender scientific research. This is where the future for virtual worlds lies: not simply in fantasy and abstraction, but in real, practical applications for business, education, science, and culture at large. Virtual worlds are not toys, but complex evolving models that have application anywhere that visual, spatial, or audio communication has value. It's an entirely unmapped terrain, and one that all Second Life residents are exploring together.

At this point in the book, you've mastered much of what is required to make the most of Second Life, but to truly understand its potential and your future within in, it's worth considering the impact it could have on your everyday life. You must understand that virtual worlds are tools, and they have a future because we are constantly finding new uses for those tools. Let's look ahead to what some of those tools are being used for.

THE NEXT GENERATION OF THE INTERNET?

Here's a simple example of how Second Life affects your everyday life: Shopping, of course, is one of the most popular activities in Second Life. But did you know that you could search and shop for books and other items on Amazon.com from within the virtual world? The results are displayed in 3D, and when you find something you just can't resist, the Second Life client lets you launch the Amazon page in an external web browser to make your purchase.

What's remarkable about the Amazon site in Second Life is that it wasn't designed by Linden Lab but by a handful of Amazon developers who joined Second Life and are living out their fantasies as … Amazon developers. To them, Second Life is just another place to do what they spend most of the day doing anyway, and to be who they already are. Second Life isn't simply a way to spend some leisure time (though it can be if you'd like it to be); it's an application that allows people to pursue their goals more efficiently and more imaginatively. It is, first and foremost, a superb tool for communication. As the population expands, residents are increasingly using Second Life as simply another way to connect to each other. They also use it to access information on the Internet or the World Wide Web, albeit in a far richer and more colorful way than via traditional Web browsers. At the same time, as Second Life has become a more

CHAPTER 1
CHAPTER 2
CHAPTER 3
CHAPTER 4
CHAPTER 5
CHAPTER 6
CHAPTER 7
CHAPTER 8
CHAPTER 9
CHAPTER 10
CHAPTER 11
CHAPTER 12
CHAPTER 13
CHAPTER 14
CHAPTER 15
APPENDICES

IS THERE A
FUTURE FOR
VIRTUAL WORLDS?

**THE NEXT
GENERATION OF
THE INTERNET?**

AN EXTRA-
ORDINARILY
RADICAL IDEA

FROM TOYS
TO TOOLS

Figure 15.1: SLProfiles.com, the MySpace of *Second Life*

open technological platform, residents have begun to create ways to use the Web to enhance their second lives. A website called SLProfiles.com, for instance, created by *Second Life* resident Yo Brewster, acts as a kind of MySpace for *SL* residents (Figure 15.1). Residents can create pages devoted to their first- and second-life profiles (pages that are just as colorful—or as colorfully ugly—as MySpace pages), maintain friends lists and lists of favorite places in *SL*, publish a blog through the site, even communicate via the Web with users who are logged into *Second Life*. Within three months of the site's launch, almost 1,000 users had signed up.

As *Second Life* users reach out to the online world of the Web, both the Web and the offline world are reaching back into *Second Life*. Though *Second Life* may be known as a fantasy world, it's increasingly being used as a marketing platform for real products from among the real world's best-known companies. Over the last couple of years the real-world brands that made an entrance into *Second Life* included the following:

- Global business consultants McKinsey & Company, which demonstrated how the virtual world can be home to real-world business acumen as they launched a venture-capital competition in *Second Life*

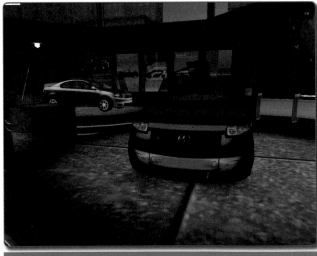

Figure 15.2: The Scion xB on display

- Toyota Motor Corp., which released a drivable model of its Scion xB (Figure 15.2) in the virtual world

- Mobile-phone and communications company Vodafone, which launched a portal with free toys for subscribers and the intention of delivering voice-chat through *Second Life* avatars

- Adidas, which now sells virtual versions of its a3 Microride shoes—complete with "bounce" functionality

- Hipster clothing retailer American Apparel, which opened an outlet in *Second Life* that sells virtual versions of its colorful clothing and offers discounts on purchases of the real thing

The entertainment industry has also found ways to take advantage of *Second Life*:

- Singer-songwriter Regina Spektor released an album in *Second Life* more than a week before it was available in stores.

- British rock band Oasis launched their presence in the virtual world with a preview of their documentary DVD *Lord Don't Slow Me Down*.

- 20th Century Fox screened portions of *X-Men: The Last Stand* in *Second Life* simultaneously with its premiere at the Cannes film festival.

- *The Infinite Mind*, a public radio show hosted by John Hockenberry, now does regular broadcasts from within *Second Life*.

- Hit '80s new-wave music group Duran Duran built a four-sim "futuristic utopia" where the band has played gigs, interacted with fans, and showcased the talent of some new acts.

At the same time that advertising and entertainment ventures are discovering *Second Life*, everyone from doctors to educators to the U.S. government is finding ways to use it:

- A doctor's re-creation of the hallucinatory experiences of schizophrenics seeks to raise awareness of the disease among the healthy; *Second Life* is also home to at least one psychologist who practices there.

- Reforestation charity Plant-It 2020 created an island on which residents could plant a virtual tree for a dollar, paying for the planting of a tree in the real world.

- Harvard Law School offers a course in "persuasive, empathic argument in the Internet space" that is taught partially within *Second Life*.

- Tourist agencies in Copenhagen, Denmark, (Figure 15.3) and Munich, Germany, created virtual city-centers within *Second Life* to encourage tourism and aid navigation.

Figure 15.3: The virtual city-center of Copenhagen

CHAPTER 1
CHAPTER 2
CHAPTER 3
CHAPTER 4
CHAPTER 5
CHAPTER 6
CHAPTER 7
CHAPTER 8
CHAPTER 9
CHAPTER 10
CHAPTER 11
CHAPTER 12
CHAPTER 13
CHAPTER 14
CHAPTER 15

APPENDICES

CHAPTER 15

IS THERE A
FUTURE FOR
VIRTUAL WORLDS?

THE NEXT
GENERATION OF
THE INTERNET?

AN EXTRA-
ORDINARILY
RADICAL IDEA

FROM TOYS
TO TOOLS

- The city of Hanover, New Hampshire, was re-created in *Second Life* by Dartmouth College for use in improving response measures in case of crisis.

- Both the State Department and the CIA are said to have established a presence in *Second Life*.

Discounts on T-shirts at your local American Apparel? A preview of a new album from a major label? A course at Harvard? And you thought this was supposed to be a fantasy world!

In fact, while *Second Life* continues to see just as much role-play, community-building, and fantasy-realization as ever, more and more of the projects that are being launched in the virtual world are designed more to be useful than simply entertaining. The companies that have come into *Second Life* over the last year are using it not as some wild way to give people new identities, but simply as they'd use a website: to get the word out, hear feedback, and conduct business. These kinds of uses for *Second Life* have only just begun, but the sense among those who are pursuing them is that they've been more successes than failures. And they're the kind of successes that have built on each other. Because the Web inherently supports user-created content and collaboration, *Second Life* is a kind of virtual world 2.0—a place where, like Web 2.0, the things that flourish are mashups, wikis, social software, and concepts organized around communities and customized content.

Not all of these things are good replacements for what we do today on the World Wide Web, of course. Reading a newspaper is far easier on a website than it is in a 3D online world. But imagine being able to click through a story and get launched into a 3D re-creation of the location where the story took place, where you could walk around and discuss the events with other readers who happened to be there at the same time. Instead of replacing the Web, *Second Life* holds vast potential to enhance it. Although the Web may never transform itself completely into something akin to *Second Life*, it's quite likely that 3D spaces will become an integral part of the online experience in the very near future, for a very large number of people.

So if you're wondering how useful your newfound skills at navigating the virtual world will be, the answer is probably that they'll be as useful as you want to make them. How long will your tenure in *Second Life* be? As long as you're connected to the Web, most likely. It's not just a virtual world you've entered. Welcome to the next generation of the Internet.

AN EXTRAORDINARILY RADICAL IDEA

To some people, of course, using *Second Life* as an extension of the World Wide Web seems utterly outlandish. According to the skeptics, three-dimensional online worlds are hard to get around (or else why would you need a guidebook?), they don't add much more functionality to the Web than a graphical chat room, and their text-based predecessors were just as powerful but never took off like the true believers expect worlds like *Second Life* to do. Don't drink the Kool-Aid, say the skeptics, it'll just leave a bad taste in your mouth.

These critics have numerous reasons to think as they do. It's true that the virtual worlds and 3D Web technologies that have come before have languished and fallen largely into disuse. The 1980s and early 1990s saw the rise of text-based MUDs (multi-user dungeons) and their variants (MUSHes, MUCKs, TinyMUDs and more), some of which featured almost as much user-created content as *Second Life*. But despite the fact that some people preferred the mental graphics system used in text-based worlds (commonly known as "the imagination"), MUDs and their cousins were never able to garner a wide audience. Though some of the earliest text-based worlds are still inhabited today, they exist largely as novelty backwaters, not as places that attract innovative new developments in online business and experiments in connectivity.

The words "3D Web" also bring to mind, for some people, a failed attempt to bring 3D environments to the World Wide Web itself in the mid 1990s. VRML, the Virtual Reality Modeling Language, can be used to describe 3D objects and environments for use in web pages and other applications. First defined in 1994, VRML enjoyed a few years of popularity, but then fell largely into disuse. Though some CAD and 3D modeling programs still support the format, it's hard to find people who still rely on it as a robust mode of communication. VRML has been superseded by X3D, which is being promoted as a standard format for 3D computer graphics. But although the X3D community is growing, it has yet to make a widespread impact on how people browse and use the Web.

So when the subject of 3D virtual worlds comes up, many people are understandably skeptical. Any disruptive new technology often engenders the same kind of skepticism, says Mitch Kapor. Besides being chairman of the board at Linden Lab, Kapor is also the creator of the Lotus 1-2-3 spreadsheet application and chairman of the Mozilla Foundation. He has seen many different technologies rise and fall. When he began his career in computing, the idea that there would one day be a desktop computer on every desktop was an outlandish proposition.

"It is very difficult to remember a time, even if you were alive then, when people did not have huge amounts of computing power at their fingertips," Kapor says. "But I can assure you that that was an extraordinarily radical idea." The same thing now goes for virtual worlds, Kapor says. "It's still a very radical idea that these are somehow going to be important and mainstream, and it's still only a very small fraction of the world's population that understands and appreciates that. We are very early; we are the early, early adopters."

FROM LINDEN LAB
THE FUTURE OF *SECOND LIFE*

"When Linden Lab chairman of the board Mitch Kapor addressed the *Second Life* Community Convention in the summer of 2006, he gave a convincing account of *Second Life* as a disruptive technology, one that would shake up the way most of the world goes about their daily business. But he also sounded a note of warning: to keep moving forward, the early adopters will have to remain open-minded and share their world with as broad a range of residents as possible.

CHAPTER 1

CHAPTER 2

CHAPTER 3

CHAPTER 4

CHAPTER 5

CHAPTER 6

CHAPTER 7

CHAPTER 8

CHAPTER 9

CHAPTER 10

CHAPTER 11

CHAPTER 12

CHAPTER 13

CHAPTER 14

CHAPTER 15

APPENDICES

CHAPTER 15

IS THERE A
FUTURE FOR
VIRTUAL WORLDS?

THE NEXT
GENERATION OF
THE INTERNET?

**AN EXTRA-
ORDINARILY
RADICAL IDEA**

FROM TOYS
TO TOOLS

"I think you are in a blessed position. You are the pioneers and the founders of this new world, and you have unbelievably great opportunities to put your stamp, to leave a legacy, to create things which will endure and have value. The opportunity to participate in the creation of a new world is really a rare one, and so I hope you cherish it. And you'll face challenges. In every disruptive technology I've seen, there has always been a dynamic in which the early adopters begin to be pushed aside as the whatever it is begins to become mainstream. There will be tensions as the frontier is civilized, on all sides, of people who like it the way it is, and people who want it to be what it might become.

"But the most important thing I want to say and leave you with is that with the privilege of creating a new world or new worlds, I believe, comes responsibility. And really the responsibility is to make that new world a better place. There is no one vision or value of what that better place will be, it will be slightly different or maybe very different to different people. But in a new world free of a lot of the constraints we're used to, which empowers individuals, my hope is that *Second Life* will continue to be a world that is more inclusive than the terrestrial world and will enable groups of people that are marginalized in the real world to be first-class citizens and residents.

"It's still very early. I'm hoping that inclusiveness and *Second Life* being a level playing field for everyone remains and increases as a core value. And finally I would just say to each of you, I hope you would think carefully about what a better world means to you, and as you go about *Second Life* you do things, build things, and interact in ways that further your own vision of that better world."

—Mitch Kapor

Even *Second Life* creator Philip Rosedale allows for the possibility that *SL* may not be the future of connectivity. But one doubts he really believes that. In any case, *Second Life* remains the only metaverse that matters at the moment: the most open, most inclusive, most technologically robust, and most rapidly growing virtual world there is. And indications are that it will continue to be that for a long time to come. (See the sidebar "How We Got Here; Where We're Going.")

 ADDITIONAL INFO
HOW WE GOT HERE; WHERE WE'RE GOING

To some, the very idea of a 3D graphical world that exists only on the Internet is a foreign concept. For most people above a certain age, a new technology like *Second Life* can be difficult to integrate into their lives. But by the same token, those who've grown up with similar technologies will have a far easier time incorporating new developments. Computer games are the technology that's probably done most to pave the way for *SL*'s adoption.

The first multiuser graphical worlds appeared in 1996, with the advent of an online game called *Meridian 59*. Since then, massively multiplayer online games like *Ultima Online*, *EverQuest*, *Lineage*, and *World of Warcraft*, to name only a few, have made 3D online worlds commonplace for a new generation of gamers. And though many gamers are unsure what to make of a world where there aren't any orcs to slay, they've mastered getting around the world itself—the biggest obstacle to adoption.

And just as MMOs are preparing people for an age of 3D online worlds, various other Internet-based applications and technologies are doing much the same thing. Though MySpace is not a virtual world, it is very much a Web-based social space in many of the same ways as *Second Life*: it is filled with user-created content, and with people forming new communities and trying on new personas. And with a staggering 100 million members, it will soon be funneling people into 3D worlds that go one step beyond the flat web pages of MySpace. Such a move is already happening: Korean social site CyWorld, a crudely 3D version of MySpace, launched a U.S. version in 2006, and 3D chat network IMVU recently added additional content-creation capabilities for its users. Applications like Google Maps and Google Earth have added powerful custom content capabilities in recent months and are becoming much more functional single-user virtual worlds.

CHAPTER 1
CHAPTER 2
CHAPTER 3
CHAPTER 4
CHAPTER 5
CHAPTER 6
CHAPTER 7
CHAPTER 8
CHAPTER 9
CHAPTER 10
CHAPTER 11
CHAPTER 12
CHAPTER 13
CHAPTER 14
CHAPTER 15

For people who've grown up in the embrace of such technologies, the migration to a place like *Second Life*—which offers most everything that other virtual worlds do, and more—will be second nature. If *Second Life* can continue to scale its capacity and continue to smooth the user experience with new features and releases, it should be around for a very long time to come.

Perhaps the most significant contributing factor to this continued growth will prove to be Linden Lab's 2007 announcement of their intention to open up *Second Life*'s client "viewer" software to development by third parties. Instances of alternative viewers have already seen use—such as in the CSI *Second Life* episode that came with its own complimentary CSI viewer. By the time you read this, third-party viewers will have appeared, like one being designed by The Electric Sheep Company.

Previously this doorway to the virtual world had been effectively centralized under Linden Lab and carefully managed by a small team. But this is changing. With the source code for the viewer made available to all, there's now scope for anyone with an interest in *Second Life* and the requisite programming know-how to create their own viewer. This means that individuals or companies can create their own doorway to the grid, potentially with its own applications and tools. They can even distribute this viewer themselves to give even more people a reason to participate.

This open-source approach also allows companies other than Linden Lab to provide new tools for use by the community. Some of these might even be included in the official Linden Lab-endorsed viewer software, so that the experience and utility of third-party *Second Life* tools and features can be developed by anyone and made available to everyone.

CHAPTER 15

IS THERE A
FUTURE FOR
VIRTUAL WORLDS?

THE NEXT
GENERATION OF
THE INTERNET?

AN EXTRA-
ORDINARILY
RADICAL IDEA

FROM TOYS
TO TOOLS

FROM LINDEN LAB

WHAT MOST EXCITES US ABOUT THE FUTURE OF *SECOND LIFE*

"What excites me about *Second Life*'s future is the notion that sometime in the next few years the server code will be open-sourced, and the platform architecture will support a wide variety of both agent domains and region domains. We really will be building the metaverse. At some point, it will be impossible for people to maintain the misconception that *Second Life* is the 'online game that Linden Lab runs.' I don't really like comparisons people make when they call it the '3D Web'—to me, that doesn't make sense—but the potential for *Second Life* is really far beyond anything that any company producing a game is doing. When people all around the world are running their own metaverse servers, and agents and avatars from a variety of providers can move between all of them, we really will have created something as huge and new, if not more so, than what the Web created when it was added on top of the Internet."

—Prospero Linden

"What excites me the most about the future of *Second Life* is its potential to fundamentally improve the human condition. By collapsing geography and helping people collaborate across the globe, *Second Life* is a crucible of creativity. Education and collaborative work will never be the same."

—Pathfinder Linden

"What excites me most is the potential collision between wearable computing (think LCD overlays in your eye glasses) and *Second Life*, allowing residents to literally be in two worlds at once. Imagine being able to access *SL* from literally anywhere, holding conversations across worlds, or overlaying your friend's *SL* avatar on them when you see them in your first life."

—Maurice Linden

This opening up of *Second Life* suggests exciting possibilities for the future, not least of which could be wider accessibility of the grid (the server software that hosts the world) to third-party hosting. If anyone could bring land into the *Second Life* grid, then this virtual world could end up being as diverse and as extensively distributed as the Internet itself. It's just a matter of time and a bit of technological problem-solving.

As I write this, more than 1,000,000 people have checked out *Second Life* at least once. By the time you read these words, that number will have grown to more than a couple of million if growth continues at the levels from the second half of 2007. Probably half of those people will be regular visitors to the world, dipping in at least once in any given 60-day period. Something like 100,000 different people will log on in a given day, and at the busiest times there will be around 30,000 different avatars occupying the world.

Figure 15.4: Check out new releases from major bands, like British rockers Oasis.

Already, the effects of having so many different people in the space are being felt. Besides the projects, builds, and initiatives listed toward the beginning of this chapter, a number of trends at work in *Second Life* could have broader ramifications in terms of shaping people's offline lives. But perhaps the most important of these is the way *Second Life* helps connect people. The listening station where Regina Spektor's album plays in *Second Life* is not just a place to hear good music; it's also a place to hang out with friends, meet new people, and expand the boundaries of your virtual life (Figure 15.4). In such an online environment, interactions that were formerly limited or went only in one direction—consuming media online, for instance—now take on much richer form. (See the sidebar "Take Me Out to the Ball Game.")

RESIDENTS SPEAK
TAKE ME OUT TO THE BALL GAME

When the Electric Sheep Company set out to re-create Major League Baseball's Home Run Derby in *Second Life*, their task was to do more than simply show off the league's heaviest hitters. By re-creating a real-world baseball stadium in *Second Life* and populating the field with bobble-headed sluggers, they not only brought the real game into the virtual world, but they provided a social focus around which people could gather and, most importantly, add their own entertainment to the experience of watching the game. Blogger Eric Rice was there, and he notes how much more a part of the experience he felt in *Second Life* than in any other online context:

"Tonight, a bunch of friends and I went to a baseball stadium, bought some hats and jerseys, some of us got some bling jewelry (Go RED SOX). Naturally, we had big foam fingers, hot dogs, beers. We talked smack, we cheered, we chatted it up. We watched the sun go down, we watched the boats in the drink, and we cheered for fireworks. And we watched home run after home run after home run.

"Now, if you stop reading here, there's nothing out of the ordinary going on. I participated in what millions participate in all the time. The only difference: my friends were scattered across the USA and the world. And I was a Boston-clad avatar.

CHAPTER 15

IS THERE A
FUTURE FOR
VIRTUAL WORLDS?

THE NEXT
GENERATION OF
THE INTERNET?

AN EXTRA-
ORDINARILY
RADICAL IDEA

FROM TOYS
TO TOOLS

"Do androids dream of home run kings? They do if those kings are the Electric Sheep Company, the metaverse design consultancy that knocked it out of the park by bringing Major League Baseball into *Second Life*.

"They built a stadium. They sold tickets. They created schwag—real schwag, not the frivolous nonsense we really don't care about—schwag of importance. And while we sat around with our foamie hands and hot dogs, we all watched the stream of the Derby piped into *Second Life* via ESPN HD (and commercial-free, I might add), we all did everything I mentioned above.

"Here's a secret: You can't really do this in real life. Well, not without plane tickets, season tickets, and a helluva lot of work. Sure, we can sit in IRC or other chat rooms and assume we are watching the same thing. But there's nothing quite like the shared experience of doing it together.

"Homeboy Makaio and others rezzed some kayaks way out in the water, and I followed suit. We got some boats out in the drink. It was close as we could come to brawlin' with oars for long drives out of the park. We took photos and shared 'em. The massive towers, the views of the oceans—all the stuff people love doing at PacBell/SBC/AT&T park here in the Bay Area. You just love being at the park. Because, things like that are baseball.

"MLB hit a home run, because they didn't do the stereotypical thing we expect big companies to do—they didn't talk *at* us, they played *with* us. They entertained us. They were there having fun too."

—Eric Rice

FROM TOYS TO TOOLS

As we pointed out in Chapter 13, several thousand people derive a significant boost to their incomes from their activities within *Second Life*. Most of these people are retailers—vendors of clothing, avatars, animations, scripted weapons and vehicles, even genitalia—who make the content they've created available to other users at a small price.

It's worth considering just what's being bought and sold here. Are these really skirts, haircuts, dances, guns, cars, and private parts? Well, yes *and* no. It goes without saying that these things don't have quite the same function as their real-life counterparts. A prim skirt will cover your *Second Life* self just fine, but you've still got to keep your first-life self dressed in the kind of clothing that would be acceptable in the physical world. In a sense, the outfit you buy your avatar is a small piece of media, like a video clip or MP3 music file, a "micro-entertainment" purchased for a few cents as one of a stream of such purchases that add up to a rich online experience (Figure 15.5).

Figure 15.5: Some of the micro-entertainments on sale in *Second Life*

That makes the person who created that piece of content a kind of game developer on a micro scale. In fact, there's no real term for what this kind of "micro-developer" actually is. It's almost like being a momentary movie producer, except that what you're creating isn't a narrative but a component of a story, one that the audience member (who's also a kind of movie director) can mash up with all the other components of the scene, which have been created by all the other micro-producers.

Perhaps most important when talking about *Second Life*'s impact on the Web and on the rest of the world is the fact that all of these micro-producers are getting a lot of micro-payments for their work. Some of them earn enough to support themselves without having a job in real life, but that's not really the point. The point is that there's a new kind of work going on here; a new kind of labor market is developing. By dint of the fact that anyone can produce and distribute practically anything in *Second Life*, a market has developed for purchasing content in chunks much smaller than a $50 video game.

And because the costs of production are so low, the market is open to a far broader range of participants. Yes, you too can become a developer in *Second Life*; that's the whole point. And if you live in a place like China or India, where average incomes are low in comparison to the rest of the world, your *Second Life* income may be a significant boost. (Note that the necessary broadband penetration is hardly universal, and some places have yet to accept payment systems like PayPal and other systems that help turn your Lindens into cold, hard cash, but those things are on their way.) It's interesting to think about: perhaps a place like *Second Life* could help level the playing field on a global basis. Its impact is exceedingly small at the moment, but if it grows the way Linden Lab thinks it will, it would help raise a significant number of fortunes.

Second Life, of course, isn't the first place this new kind of market has developed. What the phenomenon resembles is just what's happening on the Web, as the medium morphs into the collection of technologies and principles known as Web 2.0, in which more and more people are mashing up more and more sites and applications, creating a broader and broader development community, and charging on a piecemeal basis rather than for whole chunks of consolidated content at once. Just look at the market for music: with the rise of file-sharing sites and services like the iTunes Music Store, albums sales have dropped sharply in recent years, while sales of $0.99 downloads are way up. Online games, too, are increasingly powered by micropayments. They'll be free to play, charging you only for the objects your character might need: $0.50 for an engine upgrade in a racing game, $3 for that magic sword, and so on.

CHAPTER 15

IS THERE A
FUTURE FOR
VIRTUAL WORLDS?

THE NEXT
GENERATION OF
THE INTERNET?

AN EXTRA-
ORDINARILY
RADICAL IDEA

FROM TOYS
TO TOOLS

The micro-content that is traded in *Second Life* resembles the Web in another way as well. It's entertaining to dress your avatar up in virtual clothing and sit it in a virtual castle, mansion, office, or even a broken-down virtual shack, but it serves a more important purpose at the same time. The virtual accoutrements you adorn and surround yourself with are the things that help define your presence in the virtual world—much like the design of a MySpace page, a website, or a blog helps define your presence on the Web. That virtual outfit you've been admiring is more than just a decoration: it's a message, a way to transmit information to the people around you about just who you are in this context. And the people around you in *Second Life* may be friends, they may be strangers, they may be business contacts, or they may be Nick Rhodes from Duran Duran, who's quite a fan of the virtual world. As you go about your virtual life, ask yourself: do I want to invite these people to a castle, a mansion, an office, or a shack? For many people, at some point these things stop being toys, and instead become the tools of their online interactions, the fabric of a life online that serves many of the same functions as the offline portion of their lives.

ADDITIONAL INFO
DURAN DURAN MOVES INTO *SECOND LIFE*

When Duran Duran keyboardist and songwriter Nick Rhodes was first introduced to *Second Life* in mid 2006, he was instantly captivated by what he saw. "I just thought, this is what I've been waiting for," he recalls. "It's everything that I'd hoped for, and that people had been predicting for the Internet from virtually its inception—if you'll pardon the pun."

Soon, with the help of Rivers Run Red, a virtual-world branding and services company, the '80s new-wave music group was planning a "futuristic utopia" for *Second Life*, a four-sim wonderland where the band would play concerts, interact with fans, showcase new acts, and simply provide a place for residents to hang out and be entertained.

To Rhodes, *Second Life* has as much potential to revolutionize the music and entertainment industry as MTV did when it first came on the scene. Duran Duran, of course, has been at the forefront of entertainment technology throughout the band's nearly 30-year history. They've been on the leading edge of video and digital entertainment, so it only makes sense that they become the first major act to take up residence in *Second Life*.

For Rhodes, entering *Second Life* is a natural evolution for the band. "I love beautiful songs about the reality of our lives, but I also like sci-fi fantasy," he said. "I think *Second Life* is the beginning of it. There are inevitably going to be many, many, many other virtual sites that spring up that are equally as good and eventually will become the next level of it. But right now, this is the most exciting place for us to be."

So to prepare for the future of *Second Life*, the best advice is to assume that it's here to stay. Most likely, *Second Life* will come to resemble nothing so much as a 3D extension of the World Wide Web. Wild fantasies will be able to be realized there, even as more and more real-world functions will move into the world. It may be that we will one day do much of our business in virtual worlds like *Second Life*. Already it's not hard to imagine holding a full-time job there, attending a class there, developing a product there, doing your shopping there, and even falling in love there. As the population and possibilities grow, all these things will only come more easily.

CHAPTER 1

CHAPTER 2

CHAPTER 3

CHAPTER 4

CHAPTER 5

CHAPTER 6

CHAPTER 7

CHAPTER 8

CHAPTER 9

CHAPTER 10

CHAPTER 11

CHAPTER 12

CHAPTER 13

CHAPTER 14

CHAPTER 15

APPENDICES

ADDITIONAL INFO
IBM AND LINDEN LAB STRIKE A DEAL

If visionary companies like IBM are correct about the future of *Second Life*, then the virtual world that we're familiar with today could simply become a base for you to explore all kinds of other virtual worlds or 3D web applications. In October 2007 IBM and Linden Lab jointly announced their intention to enable people to use a single online persona in multiple online environments. There are some big technical hurdles for this kind of idea to become a reality, but there's every reason to expect that your avatar will eventually be able to step out of *Second Life* and into, say, the next *World of Warcraft* game.

The one thing that everyone agrees about for the future of virtual worlds is that they need to become slicker and more accessible. Eventually you'll have a kind of Internet passport connected to your character, allowing you to take your identity—and your money—with you wherever you go on the Net. Just as you move from one web page to another with little more than a click today, you'll move from one virtual world to another in the near future. This is just another facet of Linden Lab's open-source approach to developing *Second Life*. Open borders between virtual worlds are going to be an important aspect of their evolution—being able to craft a detailed avatar in one world and use it in another just makes things faster and easier.

And as we look a bit further out, places like *Second Life* could also become integral to how we interact with the real world. As virtual toolkits like Google Earth begin to more accurately mirror the real world, so 3D online spaces will simply become part of how we get the news and information we need every day. Imagine logging onto *Second Life* to find your way to a job interview before you get there. You might be able to get familiar with a district of a foreign city before you even arrive there. Or perhaps you'll visit a replica of your local hipster neighborhood. You can check out the bands that are playing, listen to some music, shop for clothes or music files, bump into your friends who are doing the same thing, and perhaps even encounter some interesting piece of art or a flyer for a party that takes you to some other part of the virtual world entirely—or that leads you to discover something new about the offline world. This commingling of the real and virtual worlds could become one of the most powerful uses for a platform like *Second Life* (as futurist Jerry Paffendorf explains in the sidebar "The Mario Brothers Would Be Blown Away").

CHAPTER 15

IS THERE A
FUTURE FOR
VIRTUAL WORLDS?

THE NEXT
GENERATION OF
THE INTERNET?

AN EXTRA-
ORDINARILY
RADICAL IDEA

**FROM TOYS
TO TOOLS**

In any case, the virtual world is not to be taken lightly. That might seem to be in sharp contrast with the idea that you can do anything, be anything, fly anywhere, and discover whole new forms of play in *Second Life*. That's all very true, but it's also true that the world holds far more potential than simple recreation does. It is a place of recreation and re-creation both; a way to explore new places and a way to harness the power of community in relation to the places we've already been. It's a world of imagination and play, but it's also a world of utility and hard work. It's your world; make of it what you will.

ADDITIONAL INFO
THE MARIO BROTHERS WOULD BE BLOWN AWAY

"*Second Life* and related metaverse technologies like multiverse promise the gradual addition of a social 3D layer on top of the Web," according to Jerry Paffendorf. Far from being a walled garden, *Second Life* is positioned to become an integral tool of browsing the Web, connecting via the Internet, and even of interacting with the real world around us. And *Second Life* is only the beginning.

"At a basic level we're experimenting with turning life and the planet into a Web-connected video game where we create and file-share experiences, some tracking-back to reality, some not," Paffendorf says. "Mirror-world technologies like Google Earth will further shrink the world and lead to surprising global insights by giving us the big-picture view that David Gelernter called 'topsight.' In the late '50s we marveled at the first photograph of the entire planet seen from space. Now we're building out the globe in 3D and lighting it up with location-specific information. People will use this interface to the planet to help manage and publish their lives, explore distant places, identify and support problem areas, re-create local landscapes in the real world, make informed political decisions, and better understand the movement of people, ideas, and money—as well as don giant fire-breathing monster avatars and slog through virtual cities. Christopher Columbus, Adam Smith, Thomas Jefferson, Godzilla, and the Mario Brothers would be equally blown away."

APPENDICES

The following section contains a variety of supplemental info to help you on your way in *Second Life*, including educational resources, a glossary of common terms, an overview of *SL*'s menu commands and functions, and quite a bit more.

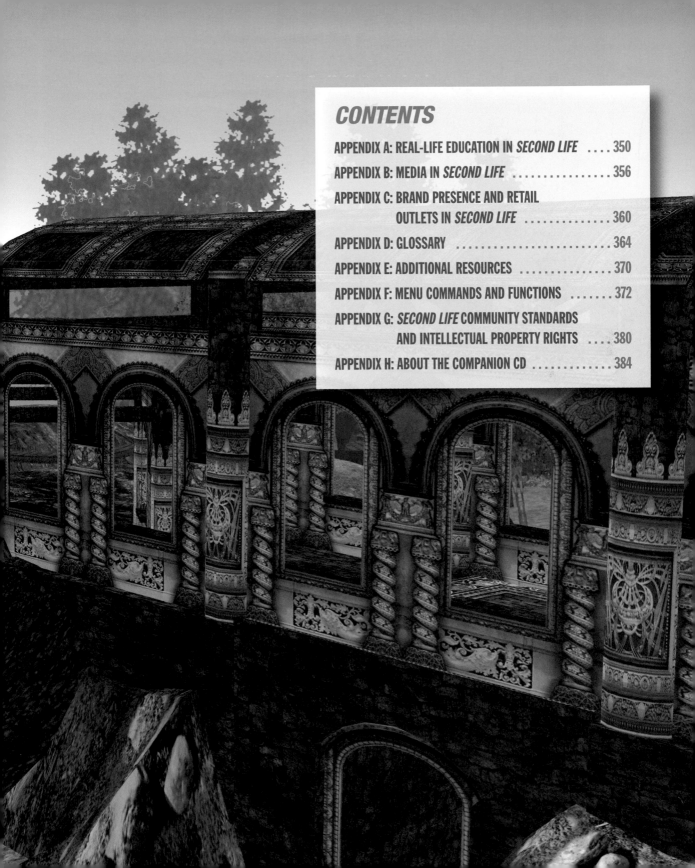

CONTENTS

APPENDICES

APPENDIX A:
REAL-LIFE
EDUCATION IN
SECOND LIFE

APPENDIX B:
MEDIA IN
SECOND LIFE

APPENDIX C:
BRAND PRESENCE
AND RETAIL
OUTLETS IN
SECOND LIFE

APPENDIX D:
GLOSSARY

APPENDIX E:
ADDITIONAL
RESOURCES

APPENDIX F:
MENU COMMANDS
AND FUNCTIONS

APPENDIX G:
SECOND LIFE
COMMUNITY
STANDARDS AND
INTELLECTUAL
PROPERTY
RIGHTS

APPENDIX H:
ABOUT THE
COMPANION CD

APPENDIX A: REAL-LIFE EDUCATION IN *SECOND LIFE*

In the last year, we've witnessed the growth of an international education community; the evolution of an extensive *Second Life* ecosystem that includes blogs, wikis, and mashups; and the development of model projects and practices that are shaping new policies for the integration of Web 2.0 and the 3D Web in education.

In August 2006, the *Second Life* Educators (SLED) listserv had 500 members; only a year later, membership is close to 3,900. Early adopters, now seasoned elders, pass along best practices, keynote conferences, and offer graduate courses about teaching and learning in *Second Life*. The Simteach.com SLED (*Second Life* Education) Wiki (`http://www.simteach.com/wiki/index.php?title=Second _ Life _ Education _ Wiki`) lists 161 colleges and universities active in *Second Life*.

The *Second Life* K12 community—SLEDT—has 475 members. Educators working with 13- to 17-year-olds have launched projects from the US, the UK, Australia, Tasmania, Singapore, Turkey, and Japan. Global Kids and the teen library project Eye4You Alliance provide creative contexts for teens to practice leadership. Communities for teen scripters, builders, and mentors have emerged—several teens serve as developers for new adult-owned K12 projects.

Figure A-1: Building interactive molecular models—dopamine

What's ahead? SLED members are influencing education policy, identifying how learning in *Second Life* develops knowledge and skills (SchomePark, Open University), bridging the gap between their *Second Life* projects and state standards (Ramapo Islands, Suffern Middle School, New York), and designing assessment models and tools.

As an educator, how do you get started? This appendix gives you some tips on how to get integrated into the educator community in *Second Life*, specific examples of what educators are currently doing (Figure A-1), and ideas on how to be successful in your exploration.

COLLEAGUES AND COLLABORATORS

Educators are most successful when they find colleagues and collaborators in real life to help them work through new teaching ideas and projects. Educators using *Second Life* face the same challenge, so the first thing to do is to get connected with the large community of real-life educators actively exploring *Second Life*. Share your ideas and project plans, listen to the experience of people who may be working along similar lines, and you'll be off to a great start!

The first place to go is the Educators Mailing List, which you can subscribe to at `https://lists.secondlife.com/cgi-bin/mailman/listinfo/educators`. This very active email list is a great place to interact with other real-life educators exploring how to effectively use *Second Life* for academic purposes. Your next stop should be the Education Wiki (`http://www.simteach.com/wiki/index.php?title=Second _ Life _ Education _ Wiki`), which serves as a clearinghouse for education-related information and links to useful resources. By leveraging the work of educators who have already used *Second Life* and engaging in discussions with other educators, you'll hit the ground running. Once your projects in *Second Life* are underway, be sure to share your own insights and knowledge on both the wiki and the mailing list. This will help grow the collective knowledge base for everyone!

There is also general page with more details on education in *Second Life* located at `http://secondlifegrid.net/programs/education`. And for a frequently updated list of interesting third-party websites and press articles, be sure to check out `http://del.icio.us/secondlife/education`.

Ready to dive into *Second Life* now? The first thing you should do when you log in is join a Real Life Education group. These groups are generally open for anyone to join, and are a great way to stay in touch with educators while you're in-world. Click the Find button and search under Groups for "Real Life Education;" you'll find a variety of groups, including ISTE and NMC Teacher's Buzz. Find one that looks interesting, click the Join button, and you'll be all set! Educators are encouraged to send instant messages to the group to coordinate in-world meetings and announce education-related events.

Figure A-2: Grad students meeting in-world to discuss research ethics

Congratulations! You're now connected with other educators around the world using *Second Life* for real-life education. Don't be afraid to ask questions, share your ideas and plans, attend some in-world meetings with other educators and students, and enjoy your newfound community of like-minded colleagues (Figure A-2)!

⬇ GETTING LAND IN *SECOND LIFE*

Having a place of permanence where you and your students can build and work requires owning land. One way educators accomplish this is to find colleagues who already own land in *Second Life*, and share some of their available space. There are other options for educators who wish to try out *Second Life* or own a large space of their own.

CHAPTER 1
CHAPTER 2
CHAPTER 3
CHAPTER 4
CHAPTER 5
CHAPTER 6
CHAPTER 7
CHAPTER 8
CHAPTER 9
CHAPTER 10
CHAPTER 11
CHAPTER 12
CHAPTER 13
CHAPTER 14
CHAPTER 15
APPENDICES

APPENDICES

**APPENDIX A:
REAL-LIFE
EDUCATION IN
*SECOND LIFE***

**APPENDIX B:
MEDIA IN
*SECOND LIFE***

**APPENDIX C:
BRAND PRESENCE
AND RETAIL
OUTLETS IN
*SECOND LIFE***

**APPENDIX D:
GLOSSARY**

**APPENDIX E:
ADDITIONAL
RESOURCES**

**APPENDIX F:
MENU COMMANDS
AND FUNCTIONS**

**APPENDIX G:
SECOND LIFE
COMMUNITY
STANDARDS AND
INTELLECTUAL
PROPERTY
RIGHTS**

**APPENDIX H:
ABOUT THE
COMPANION CD**

There are many organizations that will help educators get started with land, including the New Media Consortium (NMC), EduIsland and EduNation. See this blog post for more info: `http://blog.discoveryeducation.com/secondlife/2007/11/01/free-2-month-residency-available-on-eduisland-ii-in-second-life/`. In addition, many educators are interested in creative collaborations. Simply post to the SLED list and let others know what you're interested in.

If you wish to own a permanent plot of land, Linden Lab has special educational pricing for private islands. A private island will allow you to completely control access to your learning environment (e.g., optionally restrict access to just students and faculty), and gives you 16 acres of land to use however you like. This is an ideal setup if you want to create a true Intranet in *Second Life* and have a persistent virtual classroom. For verified real-world academic institutions and 501(c)(3) non-profit organizations using islands to support their organization's official work, the current fee for a 16-acre private island is a one-time US$980 setup charge and US$150 per month for maintenance. Visit `http://secondlife.com/community/land-islands.php` for details.

If you wish to buy a small plot of land on the mainland in *Second Life*, that's also possible. Linden Lab doesn't offer educational discounts for this type of land, and the land-management tools are not as comprehensive as the ones for private islands. For more information on how to purchase land on the mainland and the associated fees, please see `http://secondlife.com/community/land-getyours.php`.

Linden Lab provides educators with an acre of land for free for the duration of a specific class through the *Campus: Second Life* program. This is a one-time trial opportunity for educators wishing to explore *Second Life* for the first time, and you won't have to pay anything to use the land temporarily. This is a highly selective program and requires a syllabus for the planned class, as well as a general summary at the end of the class on how *Second Life* worked out for you as a platform. Full details on how you can sign up for *Campus: Second Life* can be found at `http://www.simteach.com/wiki/index.php?title=Campus:Second _ Life`.

Once you've got land and you're ready to start the actual development of your in-world space, you can either do all the building and scripting work yourself or work with one of the many resident-run development companies in *Second Life*. A comprehensive collection of developers is listed at `http://secondlifegrid.net/programs/solprogram/directory`. And be sure to ask other folks on the Educators Mailing List for recommendations. Linden Lab provides the building tools and land, while the development and creative work is entirely up to you!

⬇ EXAMPLES OF EDUCATION PLACES IN *SECOND LIFE*

There are hundreds of real-life educators using *Second Life* for academic purposes, dozens of different universities working on projects, and thousands of acres of virtual land across the world where they're doing it! Here are some tips on how to find these places and some examples of current educational projects.

Figure A-3: The New Media Consortium campus

Figure A-4: The Declaration of Independence exhibit at Info Island

Figure A-5: The International Spaceflight Museum

Figure A-6: Dreams

The New Media Consortium (Figure A-3) has created an experimental space called NMC Campus where they are exploring learning and collaboration in *Second Life*. This group is very active, and you can read more about their latest work on their NMC Campus Observe blog at `http://www.nmc.org/sl`.

A group of librarians with the Alliance Library System in Illinois has created Info Island, where they're exploring innovative exhibits of information, holding live in-world meetings with real-life authors, and providing space for other educators and non-profit organizations. They recently set up an immersive exhibit with information from the Library of Congress on the Declaration of Independence (Figure A-4), including dioramas, streamed audio, and even period furniture! Read more about their current work at `http://infoisland.org/`.

The International Spaceflight Museum (Figure A-5) is a great example of using *Second Life* to create something that would be almost impossible to build in real life. This private island includes built-to-scale rockets, interactive models of the solar system, detailed information about satellite designs, and planetary observation decks. Learn more here: `http://slcreativity.org/wiki/index.php?title=International _ Space _ Flight _ Museum`.

Second Life resident The Sojourner is a stroke survivor and has created a space called Dreams (Figure A-6) that offers self-help support groups and education for other stroke survivors. Dreams is a supportive and creative environment where people dealing with stroke recovery can keep their minds sharp by engaging in collaborative community events and round-table discussions. Many stroke survivors must cope with physical mobility limitations and paralysis in real life—issues they are free from while exploring the world of *Second Life*.

Figure A-7: Ancient Egypt and immersive archaeology

Second Life resident Aura Lily has a passion for ancient Egypt and has been using *Second Life* to re-create the artifacts and architecture of ancient Egypt using maps drawn by Napoleon's engineers. She's currently working on an accurate re-creation of temples and buildings from the real-life island of Philae. Aura's work (Figure A-7) is a great example of how *Second Life* can be used as an immersive way to explore ancient architecture and culture.

As you can see, there is a wide range of educational activities in *Second Life*, and these are just a few examples. For more, please see the list of Top 20 Educational Locations in *Second Life* at `http://www.simteach.com/wiki/index. php?title=Top _ 20 _ Educational _ Locations _ in _ Second _ Life`).

SUCCESSFUL STRATEGIES

As the saying goes, "Pioneers are the people who catch arrows in their backs." Being a pioneering educator in *Second Life* is definitely a challenge, and academia in general sometimes discourages educators from exploring new teaching methodologies that appear a bit "out there." Here are seven tips to help you be as successful as possible in using *Second Life* for real-life education.

1) Spend as much time as possible exploring *Second Life*.

This sounds obvious, but it's most critical. To fully understand the potential of *Second Life* as a platform, you'll need to dedicate some time getting to know how *Second Life* works, how people interact, and what the overall community is like. Reading this book is a great start! Keep it next to your computer while you explore in-world. Talk to every resident you meet, and don't be afraid to ask questions.

2) Talk to other educators who are currently using *Second Life* for real-life education purposes.

Get plugged into the existing educator community as soon as possible. They will help you better frame your ideas, as well as give you new ones!

3) Come up with clear and measurable goals for your academic use of *Second Life*.

Every course curriculum has clear goals, and your work in *Second Life* should have clear goals as well. Keep them in focus, and do your best to measure your accomplishments. (Check out the proceedings from the 2007 *Second Life* Community Convention Education Workshop at `http:// facstaff.buffalostate.edu/polvinem/SL/slccedu2007final.pdf`.) This will be good ammunition for you when trying to convince other faculty that your projects in *Second Life* have merit.

4) Publish or perish!

Write a paper about your experiences in *Second Life*. Get it published in a peer-reviewed journal. Keep a public blog about your work, and encourage other colleagues to visit it. Get your students to blog about their work in *Second Life*. Contribute to the Education Wiki. As a pioneer, what you learn in using *Second Life* for real-life education is a priceless resource for others who will follow. Share the knowledge!

5) Remember that *Second Life* is a platform for a wide range of activities.

While you explore *Second Life*, you'll meet an incredible range of residents, all using *Second Life* in different ways and for different purposes. In many ways *Second Life* is like the Web, representing the broadest possible range of interests and people you can imagine. Embrace this diversity! Don't forget: you can create any experience you want. If you wish to have a very private area where you can completely control your environment, look into the private-island option.

6) Work at unlearning.

Second Life is a new medium that is unlike anything else you've experienced. As human beings, when we are faced with a completely new medium for creativity and interaction, we instinctively compare it to preexisting mediums and then apply our old ways of thinking to re-create old models.

When the motion-picture camera was invented, it was initially stuck on a fixed pole and used to film plays on a single stage. Only after many years did directors think "Maybe I can film with multiple cameras and cut between them. Or maybe I can move the camera around while filming!" That insight was the birth of film montage. In a similar example, when educators first explored the Web, they simply scanned books and put them online. Both of these are examples of how we typically embrace new mediums.

Unlearn your old ways of thinking. Don't re-create pre-existing models of education. If you want to teach biology, instead of re-creating a virtual classroom with desks and a blackboard in *Second Life*, imagine building a whole interactive human cell. It's possible in *Second Life*.

7) Learn from your students.

Your students have most likely grown up with the Internet. They have always lived in a world where computers, instant messaging, email, and multiplayer games exist and are used daily. If they've never experienced *Second Life* before, they'll probably take to it like a fish to water and use it in ways you could never imagine. Learn as much as you can from them and their experiences, as the future of virtual worlds like *Second Life* and all new technologies truly belongs to the digital natives!

—John Lester and Claudia L'Amoreaux
(aka Pathfinder Linden and Claudia Linden)

CHAPTER 1

CHAPTER 2

CHAPTER 3

CHAPTER 4

CHAPTER 5

CHAPTER 6

CHAPTER 7

CHAPTER 8

CHAPTER 9

CHAPTER 10

CHAPTER 11

CHAPTER 12

CHAPTER 13

CHAPTER 14

CHAPTER 15

APPENDICES

APPENDICES

APPENDIX A:
REAL-LIFE
EDUCATION IN
SECOND LIFE

APPENDIX B:
MEDIA IN
SECOND LIFE

APPENDIX C:
BRAND PRESENCE
AND RETAIL
OUTLETS IN
SECOND LIFE

APPENDIX D:
GLOSSARY

APPENDIX E:
ADDITIONAL
RESOURCES

APPENDIX F:
MENU COMMANDS
AND FUNCTIONS

APPENDIX G:
SECOND LIFE
COMMUNITY
STANDARDS AND
INTELLECTUAL
PROPERTY
RIGHTS

APPENDIX H:
ABOUT THE
COMPANION CD

APPENDIX B: MEDIA IN *SECOND LIFE*

Second Life is a virtual world—and a new communications platform. So perhaps it's not surprising that the virtual world is turning out to be a fertile breeding ground for media organizations of all sizes and shapes. Many of these are *SL*-only enterprises that exist and function solely in *Second Life*. But just as real-life media giants are invading the virtual world, the biggest and best virtual-world media empires are bound to expand, at some point, into the real world. Yes, you may yet see an *SL* avatar reading the news on your real-life TV. There are already enough media professionals inside *SL* that they've formed a professional association: the *SL* Closed Press Club ("Closed" as in, non-professionals need not apply).

Second Life has also spawned many media consultancies, some run by professionals, some by amateurs. These offer a variety of services related to the dissemination of information in the virtual world. Proceed carefully before entering a deal with one of these companies; vet them thoroughly first. (And note that many of the organizations that list themselves as virtual TV stations are in-world video production companies.)

The sections that follow list some of the main players in *Second Life* media. By the time this book goes to print, this list is likely to have grown significantly.

⬇ REAL-LIFE MEDIA ORGANIZATIONS IN *SECOND LIFE*

A virtual world is a newsworthy phenomenon, and each year sees more articles, shows, radio talks etc. about *Second Life*. Real-world media interest has grown to the point where major media organizations such as Reuters have established a permanent presence in *SL*. Many others, such as the BBC and MTV, have already visited the virtual world to organize special events, and some are (at the time of writing) in the process of establishing a permanent presence. Here's a list of real-world media organizations that have taken up residence in *Second Life*:

Axel Springer AG: Europe's premier publishing giant. Publishes *The AvaStar,* a professionally edited tabloid paper, in partnership with *Bild* (a real-life popular German tabloid).

CNET Networks: A fan club/discussion group for followers of real-life CNET.

ITV: Producers of an "Independent TV" arts show broadcast in the real world through Fox network affiliates in the Pacific Northwest US—and now also in *Second Life*.

Reuters: The renowned international press agency has opened a virtual newsroom in *Second Life*.

Sky News: The 24-hour British domestic and international television channel maintains a virtual showroom in *SL*. Gives out free virtual TV sets that let you watch Sky News in-world—but only if you own/rent land so that you can rez the free set.

⬇ SL-Exclusive Media

CHAPTER 1

CHAPTER 2

CHAPTER 3

CHAPTER 4

CHAPTER 5

CHAPTER 6

CHAPTER 7

CHAPTER 8

CHAPTER 9

CHAPTER 10

CHAPTER 11

CHAPTER 12

CHAPTER 13

CHAPTER 14

CHAPTER 15

APPENDICES

Second Life is the perfect venue in which to start your own media empire: startup and distribution costs are next to nothing, and the potential audience numbers in the millions. "Print" (newspapers, magazines), radio, TV—they're all there, busy with real news from the virtual world. Radio and TV stations are accessed via streamed audio and video in-world or via the web; some "print" publications are distributed in-world via vendor boxes, while others are accessed through external websites.

A handful of "print" publications have existed almost as long as the virtual world itself (most notably The *Second Life Herald* and *The Metaverse Messenger*). However, every month sees the appearance of many new publications, as well as radio and TV stations—and the disappearance of at least a few existing ones. For this reason, the lists here are intended simply to give you an idea of what's on offer; some of the organizations listed might not be around by the time this book hits the shelves. Others might have changed names or distribution channels; for up-to-date info on what's what, use Search in-world, and a search engine on the web.

NEWSPAPERS AND MAGAZINES

Austrian Times: A newspaper created by Austrian *SL* citizens. Covers world news, lifestyle, and business.

The Darkside Sun-Times: A local community newspaper serving the town of Darkside.

La Tribuna SL: A Spanish-language magazine that publishes both real-world and virtual-world news and articles.

Remeta News: A newsletter specializing in virtual real-estate news. Covers *SL* residential, commercial, appraising, mortgage, auctions, and various real-estate-related areas.

Semajno: A weekly published in many languages—at the time of writing, it is published in Danish, English, and Esperanto, with plans for German, French, Portuguese, and Spanish editions.

SHout! Magazine: A virtual take on girlie mags of the real world, featuring nude virtual women, highbrow social gossip, and product, event, and location reviews.

SL-GERMAN-NEWS: A German-language virtual publication that claims to have the inside track on *SL* events, shops, clubs, etc.

SL News Reporter: A boulevard newspaper featuring news, location reviews, and business news for the *SL* community.

SLibero.net: An Italian-language newspaper with virtual-world news.

APPENDICES

APPENDIX A:
REAL-LIFE
EDUCATION IN
SECOND LIFE

**APPENDIX B:
MEDIA IN
*SECOND LIFE***

APPENDIX C:
BRAND PRESENCE
AND RETAIL
OUTLETS IN
SECOND LIFE

APPENDIX D:
GLOSSARY

APPENDIX E:
ADDITIONAL
RESOURCES

APPENDIX F:
MENU COMMANDS
AND FUNCTIONS

APPENDIX G:
SECOND LIFE
COMMUNITY
STANDARDS AND
INTELLECTUAL
PROPERTY
RIGHTS

APPENDIX H:
ABOUT THE
COMPANION CD

The Metaverse Messenger: An online newspaper covering events within *Second Life* as well as real-world news that concerns *SL*. The paper was founded in August 2005 by Kristan Hall (known in *Second Life* as Katt Kongo) and Alan Seeger (known in *Second Life* as Phoenix Psaltery).

The Second Life Herald: This is the nestor of *SL* publications—the equivalent of *The Times* in the real world. Its mission: "to observe, record and study the legal, social, and economic implications of life in the virtual world." Established in 2004.

The Second Life Newspaper: This publication claims to be one of the most read newspapers in *SL*—Over 10,000 daily hits on `www.sl-newspaper.com`. Reports real-world as well as *SL* news.

ZWEISEITENonline: A German-language monthly about the virtual world.

RADIO

African Radio: The best of African tunes, daily.

FUZE FM: A 24/7 no-commercials station broadcasting classic rock, hard rock, R&B, country, and hip-hop.

IDIOT Radio: Self-described as "the first radio in *SL* with all the entertainment and music you want to hear."

KONA Radio: Plays music from the '60s, '70s and '80s.

Old Time Radio: A radio station specializing in radio plays and music (24/7, commercial-free) from the golden age of radio—the 1920s to the early 1960s.

Radio Riel: Provides music to listeners interested in the Victorian era: classical, baroque, Celtic, folk, English Renaissance, and late-19th-century popular music.

Radio Sparta: Plays high-tech music for high tech listeners—techno, electronic, house, and dance.

Radio V-Day: Italian-language, Italy-oriented talk radio.

Sexy Radio: Claims that its name says it all, but the jury's still out on this one. Plays a range of pop music—don't expect to hear "Je t'aime" over and over again.

SL Rock Radio: Plays rock music from the '60s, '70s, and '80s.

The Radio Theatre: Listen to old-time radio plays here.

VirtuaL SouL Radio: An *SL*-only station playing hip-hop, R&B, soul, jazz, and reggae music.

WHRT Radio: *SL*'s country-music station.

! DBC Radio Tv: A radio/tv station specializing in live music and talk shows that broadcasts from virtual Switzerland in *SL*. Free virtual TV/radio sets!

Nothing Shockings Brutal Television: Rock music videos, with emphasis on metal, plus porn.

SLCN TV: *SL*'s cable television, modeled on its real-life Australian equivalent. As of September 2007, SLCN has 10 regularly scheduled weekly shows that include a talk show inside *Second Life* (*Tonight Live*), live music shows (*Music on the Isle*), and meet-a- real-world-author events (*Authors in Your Pocket*). Also covers selected in-world events such as promotions, conferences, etc.

SLUUB NEWS TELEVISION: An Italian-language news station.

TVSL: Television *Second Life*, broadcasting in-world news and videos.

APPENDIX C: BRAND PRESENCE AND RETAIL OUTLETS IN *SECOND LIFE*

What do you do when you're the marketing veep of a big company, and you hear of this new world numbering—gasp—several million consumers? Why, you go there right away to see if they'll buy your stuff! Real-world companies—big-name giants such as Coca-Cola and Dell—did just that, and many others are sure to follow.

This appendix contains two lists. The first is a short list meant to give you an idea of what real-life companies are up to in *Second Life*, and includes companies that are still in the process of establishing a virtual presence. The second is a location list of real-world companies present in *SL* at the time of writing. They're there for a variety of purposes: to build their brand name, test products, sell merchandise, or simply work. Yep, that's "work," as in "work at the office." *Second Life* is a great networking platform that offers many advantages over traditional teleconferencing; for example, you can shoot whoever's talking nonsense, and get away with it. Or more practically, leave a boring conference and lay blame on a bad Internet connection (it's not a secret any more, is it?).

Finally, please remember that things change fast in the virtual world. In any given week, a number of companies enter or leave *SL*, while others relocate in-world. So, to find out whether your favorite brand is strutting its stuff in *SL*, use the in-world search engine and select the All tab while conducting your search. A company that does not own virtual real estate can still do business in-world!

⬇ WHAT THEY'RE UP TO

Adidas: The world-famous sportswear company chose *Second Life* to promote a new real-world shoe. Called the a3 Microride, the shoe has a sole that gives the wearer a feeling of bouncy lightness. The virtual model in *SL* imitated the effect through a script inserted into the shoe; avatars wearing it could bounce and jump like nobody's business, which was good business for Adidas.

Amazon.com: At the time of writing, the world's best-known online bookseller is replicating its real-world list of titles in the virtual world.

Circuit City: Circuit City, an electronics retailing company, opened a store with virtual copies of their real-life products. Visiting *SL* denizens can try them out and order the real things for delivery in the real world.

Coca-Cola: The soft-drink giant entered the virtual world with a splash, hosting an event that featured an award-winning Coke ad, a guest appearance by Avril Lavigne, and of course the mandatory red carpet and limos. Coca-Cola also asked *SL* residents to design and prototype a virtual soft-drinks machine, forming a special *SL* group—Virtual Thirst—to handle the contest.

Dell: The computer-hardware retailing giant has a big presence in the virtual world: Dell City on Dell Island. Visitors can examine and buy virtual or real-life computers, visit a virtual Dell factory, and take a tour of the insides of a gigantic model of a Dell XPS 710 PC ("Wow! You just gotta take my picture right next to that cool pink condensator."). Dell worshippers may also visit the virtual replica of Michael Dell's University of Texas dorm room, where the company was founded.

Herman Miller, Inc.: The high-end furniture maker from Michigan in the US got interested in *Second Life* upon learning that virtual knock-offs of its products were sold in-world. *SL* denizens who purchased one of these can visit the virtual Hermann Miller store on Avalon Island to exchange it for the virtual real thing, so to speak. Of course, the store also sells virtual furniture to all comers

IBM: The Big Blue maintains a big virtual presence, using the virtual world for marketing, business-to-business networking, and corporate communications: it owns around 50 virtual islands containing virtual facilities for research, induction of new employees, and meetings, including the IBM Business Center. Open around the clock five days a week, the Business Center functions as a virtual meeting place for IBM staff, ongoing and prospective clients, and partners. IBM's *SL* venture had an unexpected side effect when Italian IBM workers staged a strike in the virtual world over a very real-world issue—low pay.

ING Group: The Dutch bank runs an island called OurVirtualHolland: in the bank's own words, "a place where people have the opportunity to create their own 'Holland.' You can set up a small business, build a new house or design new products either on your own or together." Designed as a ministate that showcases the best of everything Dutch, OurVirtualHolland is bound to work out great as a listening post for bankers trying to figure out how to make real-world money from virtual properties and currency.

Leo Burnett: The international ad agency uses *SL* for networking and creative collaboration—and maybe, just possibly, snaring new corporate clients who want to advertise in *Second Life*.

Mazda: Mazda Motor Europe used Nagare Island in *Second Life* to launch a new concept car—the Mazda Hakaze. Residents that take one for a test drive and show driving skill get the car *and* a virtual kite-surfing board. Everyone is looking forward to Mazda's transplanting this concept into the real world.

Philips: Philips has chosen *Second Life* as the right place to experiment with new product design. Good move: in a virtual world where people single-handedly build spaceships complete with cannon inside a couple of hours, changing the look of, say, a hair dryer is bound to be simple and inexpensive. At the time of writing, Philips is advertising for an *SL* project manager and designer. It involves relocating to Europe, and a real-world salary in euros. Remember: it always pays to read the Classifieds, in first or second life.

Playboy: Playboy Enterprises has set up shop on Playboy Island, which is shaped like a ... go on, take a guess ... you got it: a bunny's head. Avatars longing for a taste of the famous Playboy lifestyle can obtain virtual Playboy merchandise and, um, socialize at events.

CHAPTER 1

CHAPTER 2

CHAPTER 3

CHAPTER 4

CHAPTER 5

CHAPTER 6

CHAPTER 7

CHAPTER 8

CHAPTER 9

CHAPTER 10

CHAPTER 11

CHAPTER 12

CHAPTER 13

CHAPTER 14

CHAPTER 15

APPENDICES

Pontiac: General Motors has created a paradise for car enthusiasts on Motorati Island, offering free land lots to *SL* residents committed to creating a virtual automotive business (predictably, repair shops aren't an option). Visitors can purchase virtual cars in a Pontiac showroom, and view or participate in races at the Motorati Island racetrack. It's worth noting that *Second Life* is particularly popular with car manufacturers (see the full company list below).

Sears: One of the best-known retailers in the world has set up a virtual home—literally. Visitors walking through the Sears Virtual Home can explore interior-design options, choose the virtual items they like best, then order the real-life equivalents on the Internet.

Sony: Sony Music Media Island is home to both Sony BMG Music Entertainment (music) and Sony Ericsson (mobile phones). The first lets *SL* residents watch music videos, listen and dance to music, and purchase tunes to play inside the virtual world. Sony Ericsson focuses on product sales and promotion—meaning virtual models of Sony Ericsson mobiles, free T-shirts, and a chance to win a new W880 mobile phone every day.

Starwood Hotels: The owner of the real-world Sheraton, Westin, and W hotel chains has tested the concept for its new hotel brand—Aloft—inside *Second Life*. As their name indicates, the new hotels will feature loft-style rooms; getting this right was deemed to be easier with feedback from the virtual world. The opening party featured a virtual appearance by singer Ben Folds.

Sun Microsystems: Sun is heavily involved in *SL*, so it's no surprise that it was the first Fortune 500 company to host a press conference in the virtual world. Sun technology plays an important part in powering *Second Life*'s simulators; *Second Life* plays an important part in powering Sun's drive to develop better server-side technology for developers of online games. In the company's own words, Sun also uses the virtual world for "experimentation with new forms of communication, collaboration, and economic activity;" lately this has included the promotion of Sun's environmentally friendly Blackbox portable data center.

⬇ Who and Where They Are

Accenture (virtual meeting center): SecondWeb Island 190, 24, 22 (PG)

ABN AMRO: ABN AMBR 238, 15, 22 (PG)

Adidas: Adidas 104, 183, 55 (PG)

AMD: AMD Dev Central 124, 151, 31 (PG)

AOL Pointe: AOL Pointe 128, 128, 0 (PG)

Autodesk: Autodesk 128, 125, 54 (Mature)

BMW: BMW New World 195, 66, 23 (PG)

Calvin Klein, IN2U fragrance promotion: Avalon 21, 146, 25 (PG)

Circuit City: IBM 10 136, 38, 22 (PG)

Cisco Systems: Cisco Systems 128, 127, 30 (Mature)

Coca-Cola (Vending Machine Competition): Crayonville 172, 83, 532 (PG)

Coldwell Banker (Headquarters): Ranchero 210, 229, 32 (Mature)

Comcast: Comcast 17, 231, 23

Dell Computer, Main Island: Dell Island 43, 162, 24 (Mature)

H&R Block: HR Block 113, 48, 37 (PG)

IBM Business Center: IBM Business Center 128, 128, 0 (Mature)

IBM Sandbox: IBM 121, 154, 33 (PG)

ING, Our Virtual Holland: Virtual Holland 119, 133, 22 (PG)

Intel Conference Center: Intel Software Network 153, 122, 90 (PG)

Intel Ignites OCC: Intel Ignites OCC 128, 128, 0 (Mature)

iVillage: Sheep Island 42, 150, 25 (Mature)

Jean Paul Gaultier: Caricavatars 147, 170, 27 (Mature)

Kelly Services: Kelly Services 128, 128, 0

Kraft Foods: Phil's Supermarket 108, 96, 28 (PG)

Leo Burnett: Leo Burnett 162, 93, 34 (Mature)

Major League Baseball: Baseball 214, 129, 27 (Mature)

Mazda Motor Europe: Nagare Island 185, 114, 38 (Mature)

Mercedes-Benz: Mercedes Island 128, 128,0 (PG)

Microsoft Visual Studio Island: Microsoft Visual Studio Island 128, 128, 0 (PG)

MovieTickets: MovieTickets 128, 80, 23 (PG)

NBA: NBA Jam Session 128, 128, 0 (PG)

Nissan 19, 129, 26 (PG)

Nissan Altima Island 122, 180, 28 (PG)

PA Consulting: PA Consulting 116, 119, 27 (PG)

Packaging & Converting Essentials: Sede di Marte 217, 50, 38 (Mature)

Philips Design: OurVirtualHolland 99, 49, 28 (PG)

Playboy: Playboy 140, 137, 28 (Mature)

Pontiac Main Island: Pontiac 179, 96, 24 (PG)

Reebok: Reebok 111, 100, 97 (PG)

Reuters: Reuters 127, 98, 25 (Mature)

Samsung: Softbank Slim Japan 128, 8, 25 (PG)

SAP Network: Silicon Island 208, 45, 28 (PG)

Saxo: Saxo Bank 99, 164, 85 (Mature)

Sears: IBM 10 75, 29, 23 (PG)

Semper International: Human Resource Island 196, 112, 27 (PG)

Sony BMG: Media Island 108, 111, 21 (Mature)

Sony Ericsson: Sony Ericsson 94, 151, 27 (Mature)

Sprint: Sprint Center 175, 141, 41 (PG)

STA Travel: STA Travel 11, 126, 30 (Mature)

Starwood Hotels: Aloft Island 68, 69, 27 (Mature)

Sun Microsystems: Sun Pavilion 182, 144, 55 (Mature)

Sundance Channel: Sundance Channel 49, 177, 38

Telstra Big Pond: The Pond 127, 135, 41 (PG)

TELUS: Shinda 187, 72, 22 (PG)

Thompson NetG: Thompson 182, 123, 35 (PG)

Toyota: Scion City 44, 40, 23 (PG)

UGS: UGS Innovation Connection 168, 157, 22

Unitrin Direct Auto Insurance: Burns 145, 71, 67 (PG)

Vodafone: Vodafone Island 128, 128, 0 (Mature)

Wirecard Bank AG (Germany): Wirecard, 128, 128, 0 (PG)

APPENDIX D: GLOSSARY

This appendix contains definitions of popular *SL* terms and abbreviations. Some are transplanted from the Internet, but most are specific to *Second Life*. If you cannot find a term here, try `http://wiki.secondlife.com/wiki/Glossary` (mostly technical terms) or `http://www.slhistory.org/index.php/Category:Glossary` (mostly everyday in-world terms); both online glossaries are updated regularly.

ad space: A tiny land parcel (most frequently, 16 square meters) used for advertising purposes: signs, billboards, etc. Can also be used as storage space (see "storage").

AFAIK: Short for "as far as I know."

AFK: Away from keyboard. AFK means a resident may appear to be online, but there's no one at the keyboard typing. This tells people you are online, but not responding. Typing "AFK" in chat causes your avatar to display "(AWAY)" after its name. After 30 minutes of inactivity, you will be logged off automatically.

allocation: 1) The total amount of land a resident/account can own or otherwise hold. Premium subscribers receive an allocation for 512m² at no additional Land Use Cost; 2) The total amount of land a group can own. A group cannot own land unless it has an allocation equal or greater than the land size. Group allocation is donated by group members, who pay for the amount they donate (in addition to any land they themselves own), regardless of whether the group is currently using the allocation.

alpha channel: The transparency channel in image files such as textures.

alt: Short for "alternate account/avatar." Do not confuse with Alt, as in the Alt keyboard key.

animation: Avatar animation, or a sequence of avatar moves scripted in an external application (most commonly, Poser) and imported into *Second Life*.

AO: Animation override; generally a scripted object that plays specific animations in response to your character's actions. These animations take over (or override) default animations (walking, etc.).

AR: Short for Abuse Report, accessed from the Help pull-down menu and sent in when being griefed by someone (see "to grief; griefer").

attachment: A virtual object that can be attached to an avatar (for example, a hat, a gun, or a ring).

autoreturn: automatic return of lost/abandoned objects into their owner's Inventory.

av, avi, avie: Short for "avatar."

ban: 1) The act of explicitly forbidding entry. Landowners have ban tools to prevent specified residents from entering their land; 2) To add someone to your ban list and thus eject them from your land; 3) The permanent removal of someone from *Second Life*. This can be done only by Linden Lab. Thankfully, most people who break the rules learn to behave well before this happens. Not to be confused with a suspension, which is a time-out of sorts.

bling: Flash and glitter, *SL* jewelry, or any object containing a script that makes it sparkle.

boxhead: A newbie that hasn't figured out yet that wearing an attachment involves opening the box it's in first.

to bork, borked: To spoil; something is "borked" when it doesn't work properly.

build: 1) To make something out of primitives; 2) An object composed of one or more primitives; 3) An engineering term for a specific version of the *Second Life* (or other) software.

bump: 1) The act of pushing another resident, either by running into them, hitting them with a physical object, or using a scripted object to apply a force to them; 2) A projectile designed to push residents. These projectiles are usually named "bump." Improperly scripted bump objects occasionally litter no-script areas, as their scripts are disabled (thus preventing them from deleting themselves); 3) Adding a comment to a forum post to place it at the top of the topic's list. Forum topics are sorted with most-recent postings at the top. Bumping an old post can get it back to where people will notice it—often done when the post has fallen off the first page.

camping job: A virtual job that involves staying in one place—sitting in a chair, dancing on a dance pad—in exchange for a few Linden dollars paid out every 10 or 15 minutes.

charter member: An *SL* resident who has lived in-world almost since it began.

Classifieds: Advertisement listings in the *SL* Search window.

CopyBot: A debugging tool, originally created to assist with *SL*'s AI (artificial intelligence) and NPC (non-player character) development. Enables backup and import/export functions independently of *SL* servers. Recompiled into the controversial application used to replicate objects and avatar appearances without permission (see below).

copybot: A self-replicating object designed to irritate and annoy, popular among *SL* griefers (see "to grief").

covenant: A set of rules and regulations governing a particular estate (see "estate").

cu, cya: Short for "see you" ("see ya").

damage: Describes any region marked "Not Safe," where *Second Life*'s rules of damage and death are in effect. Any scripted object can be set to damage avatars (usually by firing damage-enabled projectiles). An avatar that takes lethal damage is instantly teleported to its home location. The overwhelming majority of *Second Life* is not damage-enabled.

dance ball, dance pad: Objects scripted to animate avatars, making them dance.

debug menu: A menu that is hidden by default but includes some useful advanced commands. It can be toggled on and off by hitting Control-Alt-Shift-D.

deep-think: Related to sim performance. A deep-think happens when a physical interaction within a sim is taking a very long time to compute. A deep-think can be caused by a large number of colliding physical objects, when a physical object is stuck in an awkward position, or when advanced shapes are interacting in some weird way. Symptoms of a deep-think are slow avatar movement, your avatar continuing to move after it should have stopped, or logging-off issues. You may still be able to chat normally while moving and other physical movement are impaired.

estate: An administrative unit of private or group-owned virtual land (usually a region or a collection of regions) with special tools for large-scale real-estate management.

CHAPTER 1
CHAPTER 2
CHAPTER 3
CHAPTER 4
CHAPTER 5
CHAPTER 6
CHAPTER 7
CHAPTER 8
CHAPTER 9
CHAPTER 10
CHAPTER 11
CHAPTER 12
CHAPTER 13
CHAPTER 14
CHAPTER 15
APPENDICES

APPENDICES

APPENDIX A:
REAL-LIFE
EDUCATION IN
SECOND LIFE

APPENDIX B:
MEDIA IN
SECOND LIFE

APPENDIX C:
BRAND PRESENCE
AND RETAIL
OUTLETS IN
SECOND LIFE

APPENDIX D:
GLOSSARY

APPENDIX E:
ADDITIONAL
RESOURCES

APPENDIX F:
MENU COMMANDS
AND FUNCTIONS

APPENDIX G:
SECOND LIFE
COMMUNITY
STANDARDS AND
INTELLECTUAL
PROPERTY
RIGHTS

APPENDIX H:
ABOUT THE
COMPANION CD

First Land: The historical *SL* equivalent of the land grant given to early pioneers and colonizers—a specially priced, 512-square-meter land parcel offered to Premium *SL* account holders. Discontinued at the time of writing.

first life: Real life or "RL."

flexiprim: A flexible prim used as a building block in *SL* (see "prim").

FPS: 1) frames per second; 2) first person shooter (as in, "a first-person shooter sim").

Furry: An anthropomorphic animal avatar, usually bipedal. Furries comprise one of *SL*'s prominent resident groups.

gesture: A mix of avatar animation, sound, and sometimes special effects activated by a typed command or keyboard shortcut.

ghost: An avatar or an object that has been moved/removed in-world, but remains in its former location on a user's screen because of connection problems.

Gorean: A member of the Gor community based on the real-world novels of John Norman, in which master/slave relationships are the norm.

grid: Slang for the *SL* virtual world and its server network, as in "the grid is down" or "the grid is up again."

to grief; griefer: To bother or harass another *SL* resident through offensive actions; an *SL* resident who bothers other residents. Griefing violates *Second Life* community standards.

Help Island, HI: The place most new residents reach having passed through OI (Orientation Island). Mentors often help out new residents here.

home: The in-world location your avatar considers the center of its *Second Life* existence. You can teleport directly home at any time by opening the World menu and choosing Teleport Home. You can change your login location so you always start *Second Life* at home. If you wander (or march) into a damage-enabled area and are killed, your avatar will teleport home immediately (none the worse for the experience).

IM: Instant message

Inventory: The collection of clothing, objects, textures, etc. that your avatar possesses in-world. Your Inventory travels with you and you can use any of it at any time.

in-world: Anything that takes place within the virtual environment of *Second Life*. Also, the state of being logged into *Second Life*.

island: A simulator/region that is detached from the main continent and accessible only by directly teleporting to it (e.g., "Cayman is an island sim."). Sometimes also used in the more general definition of the word, to refer to a small land mass surrounded by water.

L$: A Linden dollar (L$ or "Lindens") is the in-world currency. Most transactions in-world take place in L$.

lag: 1) The delay inherent to a connection between two computers on the Internet, especially an unusually long delay between a client and a server; 2) A delay or interruption in a network or Internet connection caused by slow response times and/or lost or missing data. 3) Slow or jerky performance in a 3D application caused by an overworked processor, memory bandwidth, video card, or hard drive. 4) Any situation in which part of the *Second Life* experience is not performing as desired.

land baron: A resident who owns a significant quantity of land, especially with the intent to sell it at a profit.

land owner: A resident who owns land—anything from a parcel to multiple estates.

landmark: A beacon marking a specific location in-world, *and* the teleport shortcut to that location stored in the Landmarks folder in your avatar's Inventory.

liaison: A Linden Lab employee who serves as an in-world representative and contact for all residents, especially newcomers. They're the people you see with names like Liaison Ralph Linden.

landmark: A beacon marking a specific location in the *SL* world, *and* the teleport shortcut to that location stored in the Landmarks folder in your avatar's Inventory.

LindeX Currency Exchange: The online currency exchange where you can change real-world money into Linden dollars, and vice versa.

LL: Linden Lab—the creators of *Second Life*.

LSL: Linden Scripting Language, used to animate objects in the *SL* world.

machinima: A computer movie made using a real-time, 3D game/virtual-world engine instead of a special application dedicated to making computer movies. The term has its origins in "machine animation" and "machine cinema."

Mature: A region rating permitting adult-only activities such as explicit sexuality.

mouselook: The first-person camera view. The mouse is used to move the camera around. Often used for weapons, vehicles, and grabbing objects.

newbie, noob: A newcomer to *Second Life*; a resident who has been in-world for a relatively short period of time and/or is not familiar or comfortable with *Second Life*'s nuances. Also spelled "noob" or "n00b."

no-copy: An object permission that forbids the object's current owner to make additional copies of it. These objects have "(no-copy)" in their name in the Inventory.

no-fly: Any land parcel that does not permit flying. You can fly through no-fly parcels, but as soon as you touch down and stop flying, you'll be unable to fly again until you exit the no-fly parcel. If you get really stuck, teleport somewhere else.

no-modify: An object permission that forbids the object's current owner to modify it. These objects have "(no-modify)" in their name in the Inventory.

no-transfer: An object permission that forbids the object's current owner to transfer it to another *SL* resident. These objects have "(no-transfer)" in their name in the Inventory.

notecard: An in-world text document, such as the instructions attached to an object.

object: Anything that exists in the virtual world and is built of one or more prims.

OI, Orientation Island: the first place most new residents see when they enter *Second Life*. Teaches the basics of getting around, customizing your avatar, and communicating.

parcel: A piece of virtual land that can be bought or sold.

CHAPTER 1
CHAPTER 2
CHAPTER 3
CHAPTER 4
CHAPTER 5
CHAPTER 6
CHAPTER 7
CHAPTER 8
CHAPTER 9
CHAPTER 10
CHAPTER 11
CHAPTER 12
CHAPTER 13
CHAPTER 14
CHAPTER 15
APPENDICES

APPENDICES

APPENDIX A:
REAL-LIFE
EDUCATION IN
SECOND LIFE

APPENDIX B:
MEDIA IN
SECOND LIFE

APPENDIX C:
BRAND PRESENCE
AND RETAIL
OUTLETS IN
SECOND LIFE

**APPENDIX D:
GLOSSARY**

APPENDIX E:
ADDITIONAL
RESOURCES

APPENDIX F:
MENU COMMANDS
AND FUNCTIONS

APPENDIX G:
SECOND LIFE
COMMUNITY
STANDARDS AND
INTELLECTUAL
PROPERTY
RIGHTS

APPENDIX H:
ABOUT THE
COMPANION CD

partner: An *SL* spouse, friend, or business partner shown in an avatar's profile.

permissions: Rules and regulations that define what an object's owner can do with it (for example, copy or modify).

PG: Region rating banning "mature" activities.

pie menu: The round, context-sensitive menu opened by right-clicking inside the virtual world.

pose stand: A pedestal-like object containing a script that animates and freezes an avatar in a chosen pose.

prim: Short for "primitive"—a virtual solid of any shape, used as a building block in the *SL* world. Also used as an adjective, as in "prim hair" to denote hair made out of prims instead of texture. "High-prim" and "low-prim" describe virtual objects containing a high/low number of prims. Note that high prim numbers may cause lag.

push script: A script, usually for a virtual weapon, that results in the targeted avatar being moved to another location—for example, many thousands of feet up in the sky.

region: A named area within *Second Life*, also commonly called a *simulator* or a *sim* (see "simulator"). *Second Life* is divided into square regions, each 256m on a side and assigned a name. The regions are aligned and assembled so that the borders between them are, for all intents and purposes, seamless. You can stand a one side of a region border with your friend on the other. Despite the fact that the two of you are in different regions, you can chat freely, throw a baseball across, even drive a car back and forth without interruption.

relog: To log out of *Second Life* then log back in again. Usage: "I've got to relog, be right back."

reputation: Your in-world prestige, as rated by other players. (See "rate.")

resident: A person who uses *Second Life*. Can refer to the user of the account as well as their in-world avatar.

to rez: This term is commonly attributed to the movie *Tron*. To bring an object into 3D space within *Second Life*, usually by dragging it from Inventory into the world; 2) To create a new primitive in *Second Life* through the building tools.

rezday: The day you joined *Second Life*, or "rezzed" in-world. Many residents treat their rezday as a *Second Life* birthday.

RL: Real life.

sandbox: A public area where *SL* residents are allowed to create new objects. There are many sandboxes scattered around the world; most are "safe" areas that don't allow selling, gambling, or combat.

security system: An elaborate script, usually contained within an object, used to protect privately owned land from griefers and virtual weapons.

shield: An attachment that protects an avatar from virtual weapons. There is no perfect shield; as soon as it's invented, new weapons appear.

simulator, sim: A square, named region that makes up part of the *Second Life* world (not an avatar or character).

skybox: A "box" in the sky that can be used for many different functions—a continuation of what's on the ground, a private area, a workshop, etc.

SLURL: A URL that links directly to a location inside *SL*. Clicking on a SLURL starts *Second Life*, and takes the user in-world to the specified location.

skin: What you see when you strip your avatar naked. May include body shape and features such as eyes and tattoos in addition to the avatar's actual skin. Often used to denote a custom-made avatar skin of superior appearance.

snap, snapshot: A screenshot or photograph taken in-world using *SL* software. You can take snapshots using *SL*'s Snapshot button.

stipend: A weekly allowance paid in L$ to qualifying residents. Stipend rules change frequently; at the time of writing, they're limited to Premium-account holders.

storage: Space where virtual objects built out of prims may be stored. Each region can support a limited number of prims.

suspension: The temporary removal of someone from *Second Life*. A suspended resident will be unable to log into *Second Life*. The resident will receive an email stating the reason for suspension. A suspension is not to be confused with an administrative kick, which includes a short time-out from *Second Life* that's usually not accompanied by an email.

Teen *Second Life*; Teen Grid: A special *SL* area for 13- to 17-year-old members only; more info at `http://teen.secondlife.com`.

Telehub: Originally a teleporting "port" or location in the *SL* world. At the time of writing, Telehubs are used to direct teleporting traffic on private estates.

texture: An image or graphic applied to an object or avatar. You can create your own textures in any third-party graphics program and upload them to *Second Life* for L$10 per image.

themed community: An area, frequently an entire region or more, built to represent a specific entity—for instance, a medieval Japanese village or a Polynesian island. Many themed communities are also historical communities—the Victorian-inspired community of Caledon is a famous example.

tier; tier up: 1) One of *Second Life*'s levels of land ownership and land-use fees. Each tier has a monthly price and a maximum amount of land that can be held. 2) To make a land purchase that increases your monthly Land Use Cost.

Town Hall: Events at which the *SL* governing staff (the Lindens) meets with *SL* residents to introduce and discuss virtual-world issues.

tp: Short for "teleport," often used in teleport requests by residents (as in "Can you tp me to your location?").

ty, tya, tyvm: Short for "thank you," "thank ya," and "thank you very much"

vendor: A *Second Life* resident or a scripted object that sells objects, clothing, or other items.

sim, simulator: Originally the term for an *SL* region, created back in the ancient times when one LL server or simulator supported one region. Still used to denote a region, although servers now support two or more regions each.

welcome area, InfoHub: A location serving new residents, featuring numerous notecard dispensers, freebies, and *SL* mentors providing guidance and answering newbies' questions.

APPENDIX E: ADDITIONAL RESOURCES

This appendix presents selected URLs that will come in handy when you want to find out more about an aspect of *Second Life*. Most of the sites included here have been around for a long while and are likely to be there for long while more, and all contain links to other sites of *SL* interest—several hundred of them. For more resources, please check out the enclosed CD.

http://secondlife.com/

This, as you might have guessed, will take you to the home page of the official *SL* site. Generally speaking, this is the site you should visit first when seeking clarification about any *SL* issue: it contains late-breaking information plus a series of links to other very useful sites.

http://secondlife.com/
knowledgebase/

This takes you to a treasure trove of information on just about every aspect of *Second Life*. Be sure to visit the site and glance through the topics even if you do not need info on a specific problem; new residents particularly may discover—just by looking at the topics covered!—new issues and possibilities they've been unaware of.

http://forums.secondlife.com/
index.php

This is the main page of the Linden Lab–sponsored *SL* forums. You'll find a wealth of info there, and it's a great place to go to when you need help with a specific issue.

http://blog.secondlife.com/

The site of the official Linden blog contains the most up-to-date info about changes that affect *Second Life*. This is the link to use when you're looking for news about the latest *SL* updates, as well as fresh info on miscellaneous developments.

http://lslwiki.net/

The LSL Wiki is a great source for tutorials and plenty of general info on writing scripts in the Linden Scripting Language. Chapter 8 provides additional LSL-specific URLs.

http://secondlife.com/community/

This page links to hundreds of useful sites. A table of contents lets you choose websites by topic.

http://secondlife.com/
community/fansites.php

This is a particularly important section of the community website. It lists a multitude of *SL*-related sites run by residents, including resident-run *SL* forums, blogs, etc. A sidebar contains links that will let you view even more *SL* websites—they're listed by topic, from architecture to videos.

http://secondlifegrid.net/
resources

This page features a comprehensive directory of resources: general, business, solution providers, education and non-profit, plus a selection of articles and overviews with plenty of useful info. A visit here is mandatory if you're serious about achieving great things in the virtual world, be it in business or other fields.

http://secondlife.com/community/resident_resource.php

This page has links to third-party tools and services, by category—from animations to textures and prim tools. It is the doorway to plenty of attractive freebies, such as free animation kits. Predictably, there's a lot of free clothing, too. But don't limit your focus to what can be had for free: services include virtual hairstyling, and creating custom avatar skins based on real-life photographs.

http://www.second-life.com/links.html

This page on the official *SL* site is a good place to start if you're looking for external websites with *SL* resources.

http://www.sltutorials.net/

A great resource for new *SL* citizens, this website features a collection of tutorials on all *SL* subjects of interest, from animation to snapshooting. It welcomes submissions of new tutorials created by *SL* members.

http://shop.onrez.com/

At the time of writing, this is probably the number-one online store for *SL* items, with a wide range of offerings in every product category. Easy to navigate, it also features special-offer freebies, so it's worth a visit whewn you're going shopping for *SL* stuff.

http://www.sluniverse.com/php/vb/

This is a fairly technical forum for dedicated *SL* fans. If you're a techie with a techie problem, it's the place to go for help.

http://primperfectblog.wordpress.com/

This blog is home to a monthly e-magazine that styles itself as *Second Life*'s version of *Home and Garden*. A good place to check out when you're looking for something extraspecial for your virtual home.

http://www.slba.info/

This is the website of the *Second Life* Bar Association, "an informal professional organization that helps members navigate the *Second Life* legal landscape." Members consist of real-life legal professionals interested in the application of law in the virtual world.

http://www.secondlife-online.com/

The place to go if your dream is to be an Orc in *Second Life*. This site is run by *SL* citizens interested in MMORPGs—massively multiplayer online role-playing games. However, it also features general news from *SL* as well as links to *SL*-related info sites.

APPENDICES

APPENDIX A:
REAL-LIFE
EDUCATION IN
SECOND LIFE

APPENDIX B:
MEDIA IN
SECOND LIFE

APPENDIX C:
BRAND PRESENCE
AND RETAIL
OUTLETS IN
SECOND LIFE

APPENDIX D:
GLOSSARY

APPENDIX E:
ADDITIONAL
RESOURCES

**APPENDIX F:
MENU COMMANDS
AND FUNCTIONS**

APPENDIX G:
SECOND LIFE
COMMUNITY
STANDARDS AND
INTELLECTUAL
PROPERTY
RIGHTS

APPENDIX H:
ABOUT THE
COMPANION CD

APPENDIX F: MENU COMMANDS AND FUNCTIONS

This appendix reviews the commands in the *SL* top-bar pull-down menus. All information is accurate at the time of writing, but things may change slightly as *SL* continues to evolve. At the very end of the appendix, you'll find a section discussing selected mouse functions and commands. It's intended mainly for newcomers to *Second Life*, but more experienced *SL* denizens may discover a useful tip in there, too.

In many cases the commands in the pull-down menus duplicate commands available elsewhere; for example, a number of commands are also available through the pie menu that pops up when you right-click on your avatar. If you choose to hide the bottom bar and its button menu, you can still issue the button commands through the pull-down menus. The *Second Life* Knowledge Base contains more info on this and other *SL* interface issues.

The first four pull-down menus (File, Edit, View, World) contain a mix of commands that may be a little confusing to new *Second Life* residents. By contrast, the Tools menu contains only commands for managing, building, and editing objects, including object scripts—in this context, all the commands are self-explanatory. The Help menu includes shortcuts to internal and external *SL* info sources as well as a variety of other options, such as reporting bugs and abuse of *SL* regulations, and *Second Life*'s Message of the Day.

⬇ FILE

Upload Image lets you import a graphics file into *SL*. Selecting it takes you to your operating system's Browse Files window, where you can find the image you want to upload. Select the file

you want to upload to see a preview. At the time of writing, upload costs L$10 per file. The uploaded file is saved in your Inventory in the Textures folder.

Upload Sound lets you import a sound file into *SL*. Procedure and price are similar to the ones described above. However, you can import only .wav files with a 44.1k sample rate, and the file will be saved in the Sounds folder in your Inventory.

Upload Animation lets you upload animation files created in an external application such as Poser. Procedure and price are the same as above, except that the file gets saved in your Animations Inventory folder.

Bulk Upload lets you import all files contained in the selected folder. You are charged L$10 per file contained in the folder. Note that only files meeting *SL* criteria will be uploaded, and that each type of file will be saved in a corresponding folder—for example, images will be saved in the Textures folder.

Close Window closes the topmost window you have open in your *SL* client (an Inventory window, for instance).

Close All Windows closes—you got it!—all currently open windows.

Save Texture As saves the currently active texture file to your hard drive.

Take Snapshot opens the snapshot Preview panel.

Snapshot to Disk takes a snapshot and saves it on your hard drive after letting you choose the folder and name the file. Selecting this command again retains the original name, followed by 002, 003, etc.

Start/Stop Movie to Disk gets the camera rolling! What you see onscreen is saved as a Windows Media Player file on your hard drive. Manipulate views using *SL* camera controls—mouselook works best. Select this command again when you're ready to yell "Cut!"

Set Window Size lets you select screen resolution/monitor type to optimize *SL* performance on your system.

Quit exits *Second Life*.

⬇ EDIT

Undo becomes active only when you're in the building mode, letting you undo your last action. It won't let you undo other *SL* actions, so consider yourself warned.

Redo (aka "I've changed my mind again") is another command that applies to building mode only. It lets you redo the last action you undid.

Cut, **Copy**, and **Paste** become active when you're working with text within *SL*. You can also use them to import/export text. For instance, you'll use Paste to insert text you've cut or copied from an external application such as Microsoft Word, and Cut or Copy when you want to export text to an external application.

Delete works for both text and objects that you're permitted to delete.

Search doubles for the Search button in the bottom bar and opens the Search panel. Use tabs within the panel to refine your search after typing or pasting keywords into the text box.

Select All, **Deselect**, and **Duplicate** become active when you're in the building mode.

Attach Object and **Detach Object** open a submenu that lists attachment points: spots where objects can be attached to your avatar, such as on the right hand or the nose. The submenu choices become active only when you have an object selected *in the world*—it doesn't work for objects that are still in your Inventory; you have to take 'em out first!

Take Off Clothing—poof, and you're naked.

Gestures opens the Active Gestures panel, which lists gestures you have activated. If you haven't activated any (by checking the Active box in the Gesture panel), the list will be empty.

Profile opens your *SL* Profile panel.

Appearance switches to avatar-appearance-editing mode, just like the same command in the pie menu that pops up when you right-click on your avatar.

Friends opens a panel that lists the friends you've made in *SL* by offering them friendship and having them accept. You can add new friends by clicking Add Friend on the Friends panel.

Groups opens a panel listing all the groups to which you belong.

Preferences opens the Preferences panel that's also available through the Preferences button on the *SL* login screen.

⬇ VIEW

Mouselook switches to first-person view. Note that the quickest and easiest way of switching to mouselook is simply to use the mouse wheel to zoom in on your avatar until your view actually enters its head.

CHAPTER 1
CHAPTER 2
CHAPTER 3
CHAPTER 4
CHAPTER 5
CHAPTER 6
CHAPTER 7
CHAPTER 8
CHAPTER 9
CHAPTER 10
CHAPTER 11
CHAPTER 12
CHAPTER 13
CHAPTER 14
CHAPTER 15
APPENDICES

APPENDICES

APPENDIX A:
REAL-LIFE
EDUCATION IN
SECOND LIFE

APPENDIX B:
MEDIA IN
SECOND LIFE

APPENDIX C:
BRAND PRESENCE
AND RETAIL
OUTLETS IN
SECOND LIFE

APPENDIX D:
GLOSSARY

APPENDIX E:
ADDITIONAL
RESOURCES

**APPENDIX F:
MENU COMMANDS
AND FUNCTIONS**

APPENDIX G:
SECOND LIFE
COMMUNITY
STANDARDS AND
INTELLECTUAL
PROPERTY
RIGHTS

APPENDIX H:
ABOUT THE
COMPANION CD

Build activates the building mode.

Reset View sets the camera to its default position in your current view mode.

Look at Last Chatter turns your avatar's head so that it is looking at the avatar that most recently spoke in an open (i.e., not private) conversation within hearing distance.

Toolbar can be toggled to hide/show the bottom-bar button menu.

Chat History opens a panel listing all dialogue and messages, spoken or otherwise, that took place within hearing distance or were received during your current *SL* session.

Instant Message opens the Instant Message panel.

Inventory opens the Inventory panel.

Active Speakers works only when you have speech enabled. It opens a panel that lists, by default, all active speakers within hearing distance (i.e., near you), and lets you adjust volume and mute selected speakers.

Mute List opens a panel that lists, by name, muted residents and objects. You can mute anyone who is nearby or whose calling card is in your Inventory; you can also mute object chat and instant messaging, but not object sounds.

Camera Controls opens a panel that lets you move the camera or your point of view. Mastering camera controls is worth the trouble: you'll be able to see what goes on behind walls and closed doors.

Movement Controls opens a small panel with an assortment of clickable arrows, and its very own Fly button. Useful if you dislike mouselook and using the arrow keys, which most people find the easiest way to move exactly where you want to.

World Map opens the World Map panel, just like when you click on the Map button on the button menu.

Mini Map activates a small map in the upper-right corner of the screen—you can move the map around by clicking on the top bar and dragging it to your preferred spot. The map shows your nearby environment; clicking on it opens the World Map panel.

Statistics Bar opens a transparent panel that displays hard *SL* data—among others, current connection speed and quality (packet loss), and (importantly) the number of current active objects and running scripts.

Property Lines toggles on nifty colored lines showing land-parcel boundaries.

Land Owners paints land parcels by putting a color overlay on land. Your own land is green, land owned by someone else is a rusty red. Land for sale is yellow.

Hover Tips opens a little submenu where you can switch on hover tips for land parcels and objects that you point out with your cursor; this can be very useful. Note that hover tips do not appear in mouselook view.

Beacons Always On turns on all the beacons selected in the Beacons submenu (see "Beacons" below).

Highlight Transparent highlights all transparent surfaces within your view with a rusty red.

Beacons opens a small submenu that lets you set up beacons (thin red lines) for scripted objects, physical objects, plus sound and particle sources. Can be very useful when you're managing an environment in which too many things are happening and causing lag. You can also turn off particles here to improve performance, but watch out—that waterfall you've been admiring may suddenly disappear!

Show HUD Attachments controls whether HUDs will show on your screen; even when this option is unchecked, HUDs will respond to commands.

Zoom In, **Zoom Default**, and **Zoom Out** reposition the camera slightly; useful if you don't have a mouse wheel.

Toggle Fullscreen toggles between *SL* in full-screen or windowed mode.

Set UI Size to Default is useful if you've moved the UI size slider a bit too far on the Preferences panel (Graphics tab).

⬇ WORLD

Chat opens the Chat window; usually it's easier just to hit the Enter key.

Start Gesture opens the Chat window and inserts a slash, so all you need to do is type in a gesture name (/bow, /clap, and so on). Remember that you need to precede the gesture name with a forward slash to mark it as a gesture command as opposed to a chat line.

Always Run makes your avatar run instead of walking when you press the forward-arrow key.

Fly toggles between flying and falling down to earth with a bump.

Create Landmark Here sets a landmark for your current location on the world map and adds it to the contents of your Landmark Inventory folder.

Set Home to Here is where you enter into *Second Life* when you log in, if you so choose (not necessarily your home). Could be a money tree,

could be a swingers' club—it's your choice, as long as it's land you own or has been deeded to a group you belong to. Home is the landmark marked with a little blue house on the world map.

Teleport Home teleports you to the place you call home (see "Set Home to Here").

Set Away instructs your avatar to instantly adopt the pose it assumes when you haven't been active for a while: head forward, shoulders slumped as if it were sleeping on its feet.

Set Busy is the *SL* equivalent of a Do Not Disturb sign. All messages are hidden and all offers are automatically declined. A Set Not Busy button appears onscreen to remind you that you're incommunicado.

Account History takes you, via login screen, to the *SL* website pages that deal with your *SL* account and *SL* finances. At the time of writing, the first page you see is your Linden-dollar transactions history; click on the link to My Account to view the main account page, with numerous links to website pages with more account info.

Manage My Account takes you directly to the My Account page on the *SL* website.

Buy has the same effect as clicking on the little round L$ icon on the top menu bar—it opens a LindeX currency exchange panel that lets you buy *SL* currency for real dollars.

My Land opens a panel with your personal real-estate info. The panel lists your current land holdings, their locations, and land contributions you've made (if any) to groups. It also tells you how much more land you can acquire within your land-fee tier; if you get more, you'll pay higher Land Use Costs.

CHAPTER 1
CHAPTER 2
CHAPTER 3
CHAPTER 4
CHAPTER 5
CHAPTER 6
CHAPTER 7
CHAPTER 8
CHAPTER 9
CHAPTER 10
CHAPTER 11
CHAPTER 12
CHAPTER 13
CHAPTER 14
CHAPTER 15
APPENDICES

APPENDICES

APPENDIX A:
REAL-LIFE
EDUCATION IN
SECOND LIFE

APPENDIX B:
MEDIA IN
SECOND LIFE

APPENDIX C:
BRAND PRESENCE
AND RETAIL
OUTLETS IN
SECOND LIFE

APPENDIX D:
GLOSSARY

APPENDIX E:
ADDITIONAL
RESOURCES

APPENDIX F:
MENU COMMANDS
AND FUNCTIONS

APPENDIX G:
SECOND LIFE
COMMUNITY
STANDARDS AND
INTELLECTUAL
PROPERTY
RIGHTS

APPENDIX H:
ABOUT THE
COMPANION CD

About Land opens the About Land panel with info about the land parcel your avatar's currently in. Note that you can bring up the About Land panel for any parcel within view by right-clicking on the parcel's land—this opens a pie menu that contains an About Land option.

Buy Land is active only when you're on a land parcel that's being offered for sale. Selecting it marks the parcel boundary in yellow and opens the Buy Land panel.

Region/Estate opens a Region/Estate management and info panel that lets the estate manager (owner or designated person) exercise ownership rights and options. The tabs open submenus that deal with specific aspects of land ownership and management, including the land covenant.

Force Sun lets you issue orders to the sun; how's that? Selecting this command opens a submenu that lets you experience continuous sunrise, noon, sunset, or midnight (that last option is particularly useful for vampires). You can also reset the sun to the region default.

⬇ Tools

Select Tool contains the following options: Focus, Move, Edit, Create, Land. When you select one of them you'll open the Build window and enter the appropriate mode.

Select Only My Objects allows you to toggle your ability to select other users' or groups' objects when building. This ensures easy cleanup of your objects, as well as easy object linking when surrounded by others' objects.

Select Only Movable Objects allows you to toggle whether you select locked objects when building.

Select by Surrounding lets you select multiple objects by dragging a selection box around them. Using this in conjunction with Select Only My Objects or Select Only Movable Objects allows for quick and easy object selection for builders.

Show Hidden Selection allows you to see objects that are ordinarily invisible when building.

Show Light Radius for Selection toggles your ability to see the extent of the light emitted by that object (when you're editing a light-emissive object).

Show Selection Beam toggles whether your avatar extends its hand and shoots a beam of particles toward the object you're editing (thereby indicating to everyone else that you're editing that object).

Snap to Grid toggles "snap to grid" when building. When it's on, you can quickly position an object to exact grid coordinates. When it's off, you can position an object anywhere you like.

Snap Object XY to Grid moves an object to the nearest grid intersection, as if you manipulated it with Snap to Grid manually. It doesn't matter if Snap to Grid is active or not.

Use Selection for Grid allows you to use the selected object as the origin for the grid rather than using the region's default.

Grid Options opens the Grid Options window, allowing you to set the building grid frequency, extents, and opacity.

Link allows you to combine two or more open objects into a single object.

Unlink breaks a selected linked object apart into its component prims.

Stop All Animations terminates all the animations currently running on your avatar. This can be useful if you get "stuck" running or dancing.

Focus on Selection repositions the camera to focus on the object currently being edited.

Zoom to Selection repositions the camera to zoom in on the object currently being edited.

Take moves the selected object(s) into your inventory, removing them from the world. (You must have the proper permissions, however.)

Take Copy copies the selected object(s) into your inventory, leaving the original copy in the world. (You must have the proper permissions, however.)

Save Object Back to My Inventory is handy when rezzing a copy of an object from your Inventory. This option allows you to save any changes you've made to the version of an object you have in the world to the version that exists within your Inventory. This is useful because it avoids cluttering up your Inventory with old versions of an object.

Save Object Back to Object Contents is useful when working with an object that normally resides within another. This option allows you to update the copy that exists within the other object without having to copy it manually.

Show Script Warning/Error Window opens the Script Errors/Warning window, where you can see errors and debug messages from all scripts running in the region.

Recompile Scripts in Selection lets you recompile all the scripts in all the primitives you currently have selected. This puts them back to their initial state.

Reset Scripts in Selection resets all the scripts in all the primitives you currently have selected. This puts them back to their initial state.

Set Scripts to Running in Selection sets all the scripts in all the primitives you currently have selected to "Running," turning them on.

Set Scripts to Not Running in Selection sets all the scripts in all the primitives you currently have selected to "Not Running," turning them off.

⬇ HELP

Second Life **Help** takes you to the *SL* website's Support page, which contains links to the Knowledge Base and Solution Finder and, most importantly, the *Second Life* forums. Searching both the Knowledge Base and the forums is almost guaranteed to yield a solution to your problem; if it doesn't, try posting a question on the forums. Most of the time, you'll get several informed answers within 24 hours.

In-World Help opens a panel with three choices. Pressing the F1 key has the same effect as selecting *Second Life* Help (see above). Orientation Island Public and Help Island Public are copies of the islands you visited as a newly born *SL* citizen. Located on the *SL* mainland, they provide you with an opportunity to refresh your early education about the virtual world.

Additional Help opens a panel that contains links from the two aforementioned Help options. You can visit the Support page on the *SL* website and revisit Help Island to talk to the mentors there. This panel also contains links for easy filing of abuse and bug reports.

CHAPTER 1
CHAPTER 2
CHAPTER 3
CHAPTER 4
CHAPTER 5
CHAPTER 6
CHAPTER 7
CHAPTER 8
CHAPTER 9
CHAPTER 10
CHAPTER 11
CHAPTER 12
CHAPTER 13
CHAPTER 14
CHAPTER 15
APPENDICES

APPENDICES

APPENDIX A:
REAL-LIFE
EDUCATION IN
SECOND LIFE

APPENDIX B:
MEDIA IN
SECOND LIFE

APPENDIX C:
BRAND PRESENCE
AND RETAIL
OUTLETS IN
SECOND LIFE

APPENDIX D:
GLOSSARY

APPENDIX E:
ADDITIONAL
RESOURCES

**APPENDIX F:
MENU COMMANDS
AND FUNCTIONS**

APPENDIX G:
SECOND LIFE
COMMUNITY
STANDARDS AND
INTELLECTUAL
PROPERTY
RIGHTS

APPENDIX H:
ABOUT THE
COMPANION CD

Official Linden Blog links to the blog's website. Checking it out on a regular basis is mandatory if you're serious about your virtual existence: it contains the latest news on issues that affect *Second Life*, including upcoming application and membership plan changes.

Scripting Guide and **Scripting Portal** link to the LSL Scripting Guide and the LSL Wikipedia. These are the way to go if you've run into a problem while writing a script in LSL (Linden Scripting Language).

Message of the Day displays the message that's shown as you log in. Messages of the Day often contain very helpful tips for newbies to the virtual world.

Report Abuse opens a panel that's the *SL* equivalent of a complaint form. If someone's making you suffer, fill in the details and file your grievance.

Bumps, Pushes, and Hits lists the abuse you've suffered during your current online session so that you can include it in your report.

Release Notes opens the ReadMe file that came with your latest *SL* update, notifying you about bug fixes and new software features.

About *Second Life* shows you more than just *SL* info such as version number and a credits list; you'll also see you own system info—processor, operating system, graphics card, etc.

⬇ The Power of the Mouse

Your mouse is a lion in *Second Life*, but many new users aren't fully aware of its power. This section highlights important mouse functions, introducing a couple of tricks that are useful yet frequently overlooked by newborn *SL* denizens. (Note that as with most things *SL*, some details may change after this book is published.)

MOUSE TIPS AND TRICKS

Been to Help Island twice, yet still asking yourself questions about the mouse functions? Relax. Here are the main mouse facts:

- Left-clicking selects whatever you clicked on, as long as it's selectable. Left-clicking on an object may also activate a script inside that object—that's how vendor boxes work, for example.

- Right-clicking on anything but the sky and the sea brings up a pie menu. The pie-menu choices are context-sensitive, which means they vary depending on what you clicked on. For example, right-clicking on virgin ground lets you set a navigation point ("Go There"); right-clicking on pavement will offer an option to sit down instead. A couple of things to remember: choosing More always opens a pie submenu, while selecting Delete moves the deleted object to the Trash in your Inventory. It will stay there, contributing to your Inventory count, until you empty your trash can.

- You can click on an item and move it by holding down the left button and dragging the mouse. You can drag objects in-world (as long as you're permitted to move them), or folders in your Inventory. However, by clicking on *any* part of your avatar and dragging, you can move the world. The camera will move with your mouse, and once you've discovered this, you'll never use the Camera Controls panel again. Moving the mouse forward and back zooms in and out.

- Holding down the Alt key changes the cursor into a magnifying glass. Alt-left-click centers the view on the cursor.

Zooming in and out is accomplished with the mouse scroll wheel. Scroll forward to zoom in, and back to zoom out. If you zoom in on your avatar until the view enters its head, you'll suddenly find yourself looking at the virtual world through your avatar's virtual eyes. This phenomenon is known as *mouselook*.

ADDITIONAL INFO
CAMERA CONTROLS

Learn how to control the camera with ALT-mouse, ALT-Control-mouse, and ALT-Control-SHIFT-mouse. Try it out on your next visit to the world, and you'll never open the Camera Controls panel again: using a keyboard/mouse combo is much easier, faster, and more precise.

USING MOUSELOOK

Mouselook lets you view everything from a first-person perspective. Moving the mouse moves your (avatar's) head and eyes. Walking is much easier in mouselook, and so is flying. When flying, keep the up arrow or W key pressed, and move the mouse to turn, climb, dive, and perform even the most complicated aerobatic maneuvers with the greatest ease.

ADDITIONAL INFO
MOUSELOOK MOVES

Use keyboard shortcuts for menu commands, and hold down the Alt key for mouse functions while staying in mouselook. Mouselook is the most natural way of looking at the virtual world, and it also lets you avoid the aggravation (read: lag) caused by your very own, high-prim hair.

When you enter mouselook, the cursor changes into a white point and always remains in the center of the screen—moving it moves the view. However, you can still use the mouse the way it's used in the default third-person view if you press and hold the Alt key. This lets you access all the previously described mouse functions: right-clicking on an object opens a pie menu, etc. It also lets you manage your Inventory without leaving mouselook—very useful, since an *SL* citizen averages about one Inventory visit for every five minutes spent in-world.

CHAPTER 1
CHAPTER 2
CHAPTER 3
CHAPTER 4
CHAPTER 5
CHAPTER 6
CHAPTER 7
CHAPTER 8
CHAPTER 9
CHAPTER 10
CHAPTER 11
CHAPTER 12
CHAPTER 13
CHAPTER 14
CHAPTER 15
APPENDICES

APPENDICES

APPENDIX A:
REAL-LIFE
EDUCATION IN
SECOND LIFE

APPENDIX B:
MEDIA IN
SECOND LIFE

APPENDIX C:
BRAND PRESENCE
AND RETAIL
OUTLETS IN
SECOND LIFE

APPENDIX D:
GLOSSARY

APPENDIX E:
ADDITIONAL
RESOURCES

APPENDIX F:
MENU COMMANDS
AND FUNCTIONS

APPENDIX G:
SECOND LIFE
COMMUNITY
STANDARDS AND
INTELLECTUAL
PROPERTY
RIGHTS

APPENDIX H:
ABOUT THE
COMPANION CD

APPENDIX G: *SECOND LIFE* COMMUNITY STANDARDS AND INTELLECTUAL PROPERTY RIGHTS

It's important to know *Second Life*'s community standards and excellent intellectual property policies. Here they are, and you can visit `http://secondlife.com/corporate/cs.php` to get the latest community standards and see Section 3.2 of the Terms of Service (`http://secondlife.com/corporate/tos.php`) for up-to-date intellectual property information.

COMMUNITY STANDARDS

Welcome to *Second Life*.

We hope you'll have a richly rewarding experience, filled with creativity, self expression, and fun.

The goals of the Community Standards are simple: treat each other with respect and without harassment, adhere to local standards as indicated by simulator ratings, and refrain from any hate activity which slurs a real-world individual or real-world community.

Within *Second Life*, we want to support Residents in shaping their specific experiences and making their own choices.

The Community Standards sets out six behaviors, the "**Big Six**," that will result in suspension or, with repeated violations, expulsion from the *Second Life* Community.

All *Second Life* Community Standards apply to all areas of *Second Life*, the *Second Life* Forums, and the *Second Life* Website.

1. Intolerance: Combating intolerance is a cornerstone of *Second Life*'s Community Standards. Actions that marginalize, belittle, or defame individuals or groups inhibit the satisfying exchange of ideas and diminish the *Second Life* community as whole. The use of derogatory or demeaning language or images in reference to another Resident's race, ethnicity, gender, religion, or sexual orientation is never allowed in *Second Life*.

2. Harassment: Given the myriad capabilities of *Second Life*, harassment can take many forms. Communicating or behaving in a manner which is offensively coarse, intimidating or threatening, constitutes unwelcome sexual advances or requests for sexual favors, or is otherwise likely to cause annoyance or alarm is Harassment.

3. Assault: Most areas in *Second Life* are identified as Safe. Assault in *Second Life* means: shooting, pushing, or shoving another Resident in a Safe Area (see Global Standards below); creating or using scripted objects which singularly or persistently target another Resident in a manner which prevents their enjoyment of *Second Life*.

CHAPTER 1

CHAPTER 2

CHAPTER 3

CHAPTER 4

CHAPTER 5

CHAPTER 6

CHAPTER 7

CHAPTER 8

CHAPTER 9

CHAPTER 10

CHAPTER 11

CHAPTER 12

CHAPTER 13

CHAPTER 14

CHAPTER 15

APPENDICES

4. Disclosure: Residents are entitled to a reasonable level of privacy with regard to their Second Lives. Sharing personal information about a fellow Resident—including gender, religion, age, marital status, race, sexual preference, and real-world location beyond what is provided by the Resident in the First Life page of their Resident profile is a violation of that Resident's privacy. Remotely monitoring conversations, posting conversation logs, or sharing conversation logs without consent are all prohibited in *Second Life* and on the *Second Life* Forums.

5. Indecency: *Second Life* is an adult community, but Mature material is not necessarily appropriate in all areas (see Global Standards below). Content, communication, or behavior which involves intense language or expletives, nudity or sexual content, the depiction of sex or violence, or anything else broadly offensive must be contained within private land in areas rated Mature (M). Names of Residents, objects, places and groups are broadly viewable in *Second Life* directories and on the *Second Life* website, and must adhere to PG guidelines.

6. Disturbing the Peace: Every Resident has a right to live their Second Life. Disrupting scheduled events, repeated transmission of undesired advertising content, the use of repetitive sounds, following or self-spawning items, or other objects that intentionally slow server performance or inhibit another Resident's ability to enjoy Second Life are examples of Disturbing the Peace.

⬇ POLICIES AND POLICING

Global Standards, Local Ratings

All areas of *Second Life*, including the `www.secondlife.com` website and the *Second Life* Forums, adhere to the same Community Standards. Locations within *Second Life* are noted as Safe or Unsafe and rated Mature (M) or non-Mature (PG), and behavior must conform to the local ratings. Any unrated area of *Second Life* or the *Second Life* website should be considered non-Mature (PG).

Warning, Suspension, Banishment

Second Life is a complex society, and it can take some time for new Residents to gain a full understanding of local customs and mores. Generally, violations of the Community Standards will first result in a Warning, followed by Suspension and eventual Banishment from *Second Life*. In-World Representatives, called Liaisons, may occasionally address disciplinary problems with a temporary removal from *Second Life*.

Global Attacks

Objects, scripts, or actions which broadly interfere with or disrupt the *Second Life* community, the *Second Life* servers or other systems related to *Second Life* will not be tolerated in any form. We will hold you responsible for any actions you take, or that are taken by objects or scripts that belong to you. Sandboxes are available for testing objects and scripts that have components that may be unmanageable or whose behavior you may not be able to predict. If you chose to use a script that substantially disrupts the operation of *Second Life*, disciplinary actions will result in a minimum two-week suspension, the possible loss of in-world inventory, and a review of your account for probable expulsion from *Second Life*.

Alternate Accounts

While Residents may choose to play *Second Life* with more than one account, specifically or consistently using an alternate account to harass other Residents or violate the Community Standards is not acceptable. Alternate accounts are generally treated as separate from a Resident's principal account, but misuse of alternate accounts can and will result in disciplinary action on the principal account.

Buyer Beware

Linden Lab does not exercise editorial control over the content of *Second Life*, and will make no specific efforts to review the textures, objects, sounds or other content created within *Second Life*. Additionally, Linden Lab does not certify or endorse the operation of in-world games, vending machines, or retail locations; refunds must be requested from the owners of these objects.

Reporting Abuse

Residents should report violations of the Community Standards using the Abuse Reporter tool located under the Help menu in the in-world tool bar. Every Abuse Report is individually investigated, and the identity of the reporter is kept strictly confidential. If you need immediate assistance, in-world Liaisons may be available to help. Look for Residents with the last name Linden.

 INTELLECTUAL PROPERTY

You retain copyright and other intellectual property rights with respect to Content you create in *Second Life*, to the extent that you have such rights under applicable law. However, you must make certain representations and warranties, and provide certain license rights, forbearances and indemnification, to Linden Lab and to other users of *Second Life*.

Users of the Service can create Content on Linden Lab's servers in various forms. Linden Lab acknowledges and agrees that, subject to the terms and conditions of this Agreement, you will retain any and all applicable copyright and other intellectual property rights with respect to any Content you create using the Service, to the extent you have such rights under applicable law.

> ADDITIONAL INFO
> ## WHAT ARE IP RIGHTS?
>
> A thumbnail version of the *Second Life* intellectual property is (quoting from `http://secondlife.com/whatis/ip_rights.php`): Linden Lab's Terms of Service agreement recognizes Residents' right to retain full intellectual property protection for the digital content they create in *Second Life*, including avatar characters, clothing, scripts, textures, objects, and designs. This right is enforceable and applicable both in-world and offline, both for non-profit and commercial ventures. You create it, you own it—and it's yours to do with as you please.

Notwithstanding the foregoing, you understand and agree that by submitting your Content to any area of the service, you automatically grant (and you represent and warrant that you have the right to grant) to Linden Lab: (a) a royalty-free, worldwide, fully paid-up, perpetual, irrevocable, non-exclusive right and license to (i) use, reproduce and distribute your Content within the Service as permitted by you through your interactions on the Service, and (ii) use and reproduce (and to authorize third parties to use and reproduce) any of your Content in any or all media for marketing and/or promotional purposes in connection with the Service, provided that in the event that your Content appears publicly in material under the control of Linden Lab, and you provide written notice to Linden Lab of your desire to discontinue the distribution of such Content in such material (with sufficient specificity to allow Linden Lab, in its sole discretion, to identify the relevant Content and materials), Linden Lab will make commercially reasonable efforts to cease its distribution of such Content following the receipt of such notice, although Linden Lab cannot provide any assurances regarding materials produced or distributed prior to the receipt of such notice; (b) the perpetual and irrevocable right to delete any or all of your Content from Linden Lab's servers and from the Service, whether intentionally or unintentionally, and for any reason or no reason, without any liability of any kind to you or any other party; and (c) a royalty-free, fully paid-up, perpetual, irrevocable, non-exclusive right and license to copy, analyze and use any of your Content as Linden Lab may deem necessary or desirable for purposes of debugging, testing and/or providing support services in connection with the Service. Further, you agree to grant to Linden Lab a royalty-free, worldwide, fully paid-up, perpetual, irrevocable, non-exclusive, sublicensable right and license to exercise the copyright, publicity, and database rights you have in your account information, including any data or other information generated by your account activity, in any media now known or not currently known, in accordance with our privacy policy as set forth below, including the incorporation by reference of terms posted at http://secondlife.com/corporate/privacy.php.

You also understand and agree that by submitting your Content to any area of the Service, you automatically grant (or you warrant that the owner of such Content has expressly granted) to Linden Lab and to all other users of the Service a non-exclusive, worldwide, fully paid-up, transferable, irrevocable, royalty-free and perpetual License, under any and all patent rights you may have or obtain with respect to your Content, to use your Content for all purposes within the Service. You further agree that you will not make any claims against Linden Lab or against other users of the Service based on any allegations that any activities by either of the foregoing within the Service infringe your (or anyone else's) patent rights.

You further understand and agree that: (i) you are solely responsible for understanding all copyright, patent, trademark, trade secret and other intellectual property or other laws that may apply to your Content hereunder; (ii) you are solely responsible for, and Linden Lab will have no liability in connection with, the legal consequences of any actions or failures to act on your part while using the Service, including without limitation any legal consequences relating to your intellectual property rights; and (iii) Linden Lab's acknowledgement hereunder of your intellectual property rights in your Content does not constitute a legal opinion or legal advice, but is intended solely as an expression of Linden Lab's intention not to require users of the Service to forego certain intellectual property rights with respect to Content they create using the Service, subject to the terms of this Agreement.

APPENDIX H: ABOUT THE COMPANION CD

In this appendix:

What you'll find on the CD

System requirements

Using the CD

Troubleshooting

⬇ WHAT YOU'LL FIND ON THE CD

The following sections are arranged by category and provide a summary of the software and other goodies you'll find on the CD. If you need help with installing the items provided on the CD, refer to the installation instructions in the "Using the CD" section of this appendix.

Some programs on the CD might fall into one of these categories:

Shareware programs are fully functional, free, trial versions of copyrighted programs. If you like particular programs, register with their authors for a nominal fee and receive licenses, enhanced versions, and technical support.

Freeware programs are free, copyrighted games, applications, and utilities. You can copy them to as many computers as you like—for free—but they offer no technical support.

GNU software is governed by its own license, which is included inside the folder of the GNU software. There are no restrictions on distribution of GNU software. See the GNU license at the root of the CD for more details.

Trial, demo, or **evaluation** versions of software are usually limited either by time or functionality (such as not letting you save a project after you create it).

TEMPLATES AND TOOLS

Here you'll find a collection of templates and software to get you started with *Second Life* content creation.

The avatar texturing templates by Chip Midnight and another set by Linden Lab will help you create beautiful clothing and skins. Use them with the avatar mannequin in the disc's "Animation Resources" section. You can get more info on Chip's templates at `http://goodies.onrez.com/shop/chipmidnight/`.

Backhoe (http://www.notabene-sl.com/Backhoe/), by Zarf Vantongerloo, is a region terrain editor for Apple computers. Even if you don't own an island yet, you can experiment with the RAW terrain files Linden Lab has provided.

ANIMATION RESOURCES

Get an avatar mannequin and more than 100 great sample animations. You'll also find Vince Invisible's Avimator (http://avimator.com/) and the follow-up port QAvimator (www.qavimator.org), excellent open source tools for easily creating avatar animations. Use them with the templates in the "Animation Resources" section of the disc.

SCRIPTS

Check out all the scripts from Chapter 9, "Using the Linden Scripting Language." We've also included a pair from Jopsy Pendragon: his very well commented basic particle script as well as his Scrubber, which is a great tool for cleaning many of the persistent and annoying attributes that only scripts can set or reset. Visit Jopsy's Particle Lab at http://slurl.com/secondlife/Teal/200/50/21/. Hop in the balloon when you get there, and you'll be on your way.

TEXTURES

Give those prims some texture! Here you'll find tons of textures created by Linden Lab—everything from floors and walls to clothing and cloth.

MACHINIMA

We've included a sampling of great resident-created video. Check out the following:

Lip Flap, by David Laundra (a.k.a. Kronos Kirkorian), http://kronostv.com

Watch the Worlds and *Better Life*, by Robbie Dingo: http://digitaldouble.blogspot.com/

Battle for Truth: The Birth of Stephen Eagleman (a.k.a. *Stephen Colbert's Dream*) by Silver and Goldie: http://silverandgoldie.com

Tale from Midnight City by Tracey Sanderson (a.k.a. Lainy Voom and Tracechops). Drop her a line at tracesanderson@hotmail.com.

Silver Bells and Golden Spurs, by Eric Call: http://ericcallmedia.com

Reflexive Architecture, by Jon Bouchard (a.k.a., Keystone Brouchard). He also has a fascinating blog at http://archsl.wordpress.com/

CHAPTER 1
CHAPTER 2
CHAPTER 3
CHAPTER 4
CHAPTER 5
CHAPTER 6
CHAPTER 7
CHAPTER 8
CHAPTER 9
CHAPTER 10
CHAPTER 11
CHAPTER 12
CHAPTER 13
CHAPTER 14
CHAPTER 15
APPENDICES

Gregory Ain: Mar Vista Residence (1948) by Octal Khan: `http://archsl.wordpress.com/2007/09/07/mar-vista-residence-by-gregory-ain-built-by-sl-resident-octal-khan/`

GUIDES

Here you'll find some additional resources, including a great building demonstration video as well as Robbie Dingo's *Suzanne's Guitar* video so you can see how fast the pros operate. There is also more information on the Linden Scripting Language and making machinima.

SYSTEM REQUIREMENTS

Make sure that your computer meets the minimum system requirements shown in the following list. If your computer doesn't match up to most of these requirements, you may have problems using the software and files on the companion CD. For the latest and greatest information, please refer to the ReadMe file located at the root of the CD-ROM.

- A PC running Microsoft Windows 2000 (service pack 4) or Windows XP (service pack 2).

- A Macintosh running Apple OS X 10.3.9 or better.

- A CD-ROM drive

USING THE CD

To install the items from the CD to your hard drive, follow these steps.

1. Insert the CD into your computer's CD-ROM drive. The license agreement appears.

ADDITIONAL INFO
WHEN YOU INSERT THE CD...

Windows users: The interface won't launch if you have autorun disabled. In that case, click Start > Run (for Windows Vista, Start > All Programs > Accessories > Run). In the dialog box that appears, type `D:\Start.exe`. (Replace `D` with the proper letter if your CD drive uses a different letter. If you don't know the letter, see how your CD drive is listed under My Computer.) Click OK.

Mac users: The CD icon will appear on your desktop, double-click the icon to open the CD and double-click the Start icon.

2. Read through the license agreement, and then click the Accept button if you want to use the CD.

The CD interface appears. The interface allows you to access the content with just one or two clicks.

⬇ TROUBLESHOOTING

Wiley has attempted to provide programs that work on most computers with the minimum system requirements. Alas, your computer may differ, and some programs may not work properly for some reason.

The two likeliest problems are that you don't have enough memory (RAM) for the programs you want to use, or you have other programs running that are affecting installation or running of a program. If you get an error message such as "Not enough memory" or "Setup cannot continue," try one or more of the following suggestions and then try using the software again:

Turn off any antivirus software running on your computer. Installation programs sometimes mimic virus activity and may make your computer incorrectly believe that it's being infected by a virus.

Close all running programs. The more programs you have running, the less memory is available to other programs. Installation programs typically update files and programs; so if you keep other programs running, installation may not work properly.

Have your local computer store add more RAM to your computer. This is, admittedly, a drastic and somewhat expensive step. However, adding more memory can really help the speed of your computer and allow more programs to run at the same time.

CUSTOMER CARE

If you have trouble with the book's companion CD-ROM, please call the Wiley Product Technical Support phone number at (800) 762-2974. Outside the United States, call +1(317) 572-3994. You can also contact Wiley Product Technical Support at `http://sybex.custhelp.com`. John Wiley & Sons will provide technical support only for installation and other general quality-control items. For technical support on the applications themselves, consult the program's vendor or author.

To place additional orders or to request information about other Wiley products, please call (877) 762-2974.

CHAPTER 1

CHAPTER 2

CHAPTER 3

CHAPTER 4

CHAPTER 5

CHAPTER 6

CHAPTER 7

CHAPTER 8

CHAPTER 9

CHAPTER 10

CHAPTER 11

CHAPTER 12

CHAPTER 13

CHAPTER 14

CHAPTER 15

APPENDICES

Note to the Reader: Throughout this index **boldfaced** page numbers indicate primary discussions of a topic. *Italicized* page numbers indicate illustrations.